England and Wales under the Tudors

Sinclair Atkins

Edward Arnold

© Sinclair Atkins 1975

First published 1975
by Edward Arnold (Publishers) Ltd
41 Bedford Square, London WC1B 3DQ

Edward Arnold Australia (Pty) Ltd
80 Waverley Road, Caulfield East,
Victoria 3145, Australia

Reprinted 1978, 1980, 1982, 1983, 1986, 1988

ISBN: 0 7131 1982 9

By the same author:
From Utrecht to Waterloo, Methuen, 1965

Set in 10 on 11pt Baskerville and printed in Great Britain by
Butler & Tanner Ltd, Frome and London and bound by W. H. Ware & Sons Ltd,
Clevedon, Avon.

Foreword

We already have more than a few good books on Tudor England. But it is right that we should always be wanting more. History has to be continually re-written because each generation has its own insights and understanding to contribute to the advance of historical knowledge, and each generation needs scholars to synthesize the fruit of recent research.

The amount of learned research is now so considerable and the volume of learned articles and monographs so formidable, however, that it is a brave man who will undertake a general history of even a century of English history. My first duty, therefore, is to commend Mr Atkins for his courage.

I commend him for his rare skill in fitting together the thousand bits of his story into a balanced and well-shaped whole. (It seems simple enough when it is done, but the doing of it in fact requires true craftsmanship.) I commend him for his awareness of the complexity of his story and his lucidity. I commend him for making abundantly clear that the sixteenth century was a profoundly important one in England's evolution.

University of Warwick J. J. SCARISBRICK

Preface

This is intended to be an 'A' level text book. Long experience of teaching sixth-formers has taught me that they find the usual university text-books, written by dons, difficult. Yet the few school-masters' books which have been on the market have almost all now gone out of date (especially on the reigns of Henry VII and Henry VIII and the economic history of the period). There seems therefore to be a need for a new book which takes account of the great explosion of research on this period which has taken place in the last ten or fifteen years.

I began writing this book several years ago. After I had completed its first draft, I submitted it to Professor Scarisbrick of Warwick University (whom I had never previously met). I requested only his comments on the chapters on Henry VIII. To my surprise and delight he read the whole manuscript right through and gave me a list of suggested alterations and a recommended course of reading which he assured me would take six months. In fact it took me two years and necessitated the complete rewriting of several chapters. I am most grateful to Professor Scarisbrick for this generous help and for his encouragement that I persevere with the task.

I am well aware that text-books for sixth-form work are out of fashion and that 'topic books' are all the rage. But topic books, valuable as they are, are needed in such great quantity to cover the whole period that few school budgets can provide the necessary number, and all sixth-form teachers of my acquaintance still lean heavily on three or four text-books which cover the whole or most of the period. Besides, topic books are now escalating in price.

I make no apology for having relied entirely upon secondary sources. No schoolmaster has time to study the original documents. He must attach himself to the coat-tails of the experts, men who specialize in a very narrow field. If the experts differ, as they very often do, he must attempt a synthesis. This is what makes writing a book like this exceedingly difficult. Time alone will tell whether the work has been well done.

I would like to thank my wife for her long-suffering patience in watching this book come to birth, and my daughter, Sarah, for invaluable help with the typing.

S.R.A.

Brynmawr, 1974.

v

Contents

Preface   v

Introduction. The Fifteenth Century

The Lancastrians   1
The Yorkists   3
The second period of Edward's reign   5
The reign of Richard III   6
Henry Tudor   8
The Battle of Bosworth Field   9
The state of England   9
Growth of a middle class   11
Law   13
Parliament   13
The Church   14
Universities   16
Wales   17
The North and the Fens   18

1. The Reign of Henry VII. The King Establishes His Position

The traditional picture of Henry   19
Henry establishes his position   20
Henry's personality   20
Rebellion   21
Interference abroad   23
Perkin Warbeck's rebellion   24
Ireland   26

2. Henry VII. His Policies and Methods of Government

Trade   30
Henry's finance   31
The King's Council   33
Conciliar jurisdiction   34
Foreign policy   35
Parliament   39
The Church   40
Law and order   40

3. The Renaissance and the Influence of Erasmus

The Renaissance in Italy	43
Machiavelli	47
The Northern Renaissance	48
Erasmus	50

4. The Early Years of Henry VIII's Reign. Wolsey

A Renaissance prince	55
War with France	55
Thomas Wolsey	57
Wolsey and the law	58
Wolsey and finance	59
Wolsey and the Church	60
Wolsey's foreign policy	62
The 'Divorce'	72
The fall of Wolsey	73

5. Luther, Anti-Clericalism and the Years of Crisis (1529–31)

Martin Luther	74
Henry VIII's character	76
Anti-clericalism	77
Henry summons Parliament	79

6. Thomas Cromwell and the Breach with Rome

Thomas Cromwell	82
The breach with Rome	82
The end of Anne Boleyn	86
The dissolution of the lesser monasteries	87
The Pilgrimage of Grace	89
Moves towards an Erasmian position	91
The dissolution of the greater monasteries	93
The results of the dissolution	93

7. Cromwell's Other Policies. His Fall and Achievement. Henry's Last Years

The union with Wales	95
Ireland	96
The danger from the Catholic powers	97
The Act of Proclamations	99
The Cleves marriage	99
The fall of Cromwell	100

Cromwell's achievement   101
Administrative reforms   102
Henry's last years, 1540–1547   104
Henry's death   106

8. The Swiss Reformers and the Reign of Edward VI

Zwingli and Calvin   109
The Duke of Somerset and Scotland   114
The growth of Protestantism   115
The fall of Somerset   116
The mid-century crisis   119
The rule of Warwick   120
Warwick's religious policy   121
Warwick maintains his power   122
Commerce and exploration   123
The death of Edward VI   124

9. The Reign of Mary

A cautious beginning   126
The Queen's marriage   127
Reconciliation with Rome   129
The persecutions   130
Mary's tragic end   131
The case in favour of Mary   133

10. The Counter-Reformation

The reforming popes   134
The Council of Trent   136
The Society of Jesus   137
The political Counter-Reformation   139

11. The Reign of Elizabeth. The First Ten Years

The young Queen   140
The danger to the realm   141
The Church Settlement   142
Foreign affairs: Scotland   145
The marriage question   146
The expedition to Le Havre   147
Mary Stuart   148
The murder of Darnley   150
Elizabeth's dilemma   151

12. Strained Relations with Spain

The drift from the Spanish alliance	152
The Duke of Alva	154
Elizabeth's attitude to the Netherlands revolt	155
Decline of the Netherlands trade	155
Further friction with Spain	156
The Rising of the Northern Earls	157
Elizabeth excommunicated	159
The Ridolfi plot, 1571	160
The Treaty of Blois	160
The descent on Brill	161
The massacre of St Bartholomew	162
The renewal of the Netherlands trade	163

13. Religious Opposition to the Church Settlement. The Approach of War

The Puritan movement	164
The Catholic influx	170
Events in the Netherlands, 1575–1584	173
Scotland	174
War draws near	175

14. Elizabethan Seamen. The Tudor Navy

Exploration	176
The Caribbean—Hawkins and Drake	179
Colonization	182
Later voyages	184
The Navy	185

15. The War with Spain

The scope of the war	189
The first three years of war	190
The end of Mary Stuart	191
The Armada	192
The war at sea continues	196
Expeditions to the Continent	198
The war at sea revived	199
The conquest of Ireland	201

16. Elizabeth and her Parliaments. The Church of England. The Essex Conspiracy

Elizabeth's Parliaments 203
The Church in the 1590s 209
The Essex conspiracy 211
The death of the Queen 214

17. Economic and Social History

The rise in prices 214
The land and social status 216
Enclosure 221
Farming methods 224
Woollen manufacture 225
Industry other than woollens 228
The Statute of Artificers 229
Guilds 230
London and its Livery Companies 232
Overseas trade 234
Elizabeth's revenue 236
Poor relief 236

18. Music, Art, Literature and Science

Music 238
Poetry 242
Drama 244
Prose 245
History 246
Architecture 247
Furniture 250
Painting 250
Education 251
Science 252

Appendix A. Were the Tudors Despots? 255
Appendix B. The Fall of Empson and Dudley 260
Select Bibliography 261
Time Chart 263
Index 269

Maps and Family Trees

The Houses of York and Lancaster   2
The Descendants of Richard, Duke of York   4
Ireland   27
The Anglo-Habsburg Connection   37
Southern Scotland and the Border   64
Europe in 1519   66
The Caribbean   179
North America   183

Photographs

opposite page

1   Henry VII by Pietro Torrigiano   20
2   Erasmus at 55 by Holbein   21
3   Henry VIII by Holbein   60
4   Thomas Wolsey by an unknown artist   61
5   Thomas Cromwell by Holbein   104
6   Embarkation of Henry VIII from Dover   105
7   Queen Mary by Antonio Moro   128
8   Elizabeth I by Nicholas Hilliard   140
9   Mary, Queen of Scots, as a girl   190
10   Robert Dudley, Earl of Leicester   191

Acknowledgments

The Publisher's thanks are due to the following for permission to reprint copyright material:

Penguin Books Ltd for extracts from Owen Chadwick's *The Reformation*; New American Library Inc. for extracts from *The Essential Erasmus* by John P. Dolan. © 1964 by John P. Dolan; Methuen & Co. Ltd for extracts from G. R. Elton's *England under the Tudors*; Victor Gollancz Ltd for extracts from Peter Ramsay's *Tudor Economic Problems*; Eyre & Spottiswoode (Publishers) Ltd for extracts from J. J. Scarisbrick's *Henry VIII*; Blandford Press Ltd for extracts from R. L. Storey's *The Reign of Henry VII* and Longman Group Ltd for extracts from J. A. Williamson's *The Tudor Age*.

Acknowledgment is also due to the following for permission to use copyright photographs:

Victoria and Albert Museum (Photograph *1* and cover)—Crown Copyright;
Musée du Louvre (Photograph *2*);
Galleria Thyssen, Lugano (Photograph *3* and cover);
National Portrait Gallery (Photographs *4* and *5* and cover);
Museo del Prado, Madrid (Photograph *7* and cover);
Bibliothèque Nationale, Paris (Photograph *9*);
Trustees of the Wallace Collection (Photograph *10*).
Photograph *6* is reproduced by gracious permission of Her Majesty the Queen.

Introduction. The Fifteenth Century

The Lancastrians

To understand the Tudors we must of course look back to the England of the fifteenth century. Most students of this period will know that the Lancastrian king, Henry IV, usurped the throne from Richard II, only son of the Black Prince, in 1399 and that Richard left no descendants. Henry Bolingbroke (who became Henry IV) was eldest son of John of Gaunt, Duke of Lancaster and third son of Edward III (*see family tree next page*). Henry IV and his son Henry V were strong kings, but the early death of the latter while campaigning in France (1422) left the throne in the hands of his baby son, Henry VI, who grew up to be a very weak king, rather a simpleton, quite incapable of discharging the responsibilities of office, and in later years, subject to attacks of insanity.

The constitution of England at this time demanded a strong king. Henry VI left his councillors a free hand and it was the abuse of this power by his favourites, such as Edmund Beaufort, Duke of Somerset, which led in the end to the outbreak of the civil wars known as the Wars of the Roses. The old view of historians was that these wars were a struggle for the crown between York and Lancaster, which almost destroyed the aristocracy and caused untold havoc and misery. Recent research, however, has caused historians to believe that these 'wars' have been much overrated; that, far from devastating the country, they only caused disturbance in a few counties; that in the whole of their thirty-two years (1455–1487) there was only active campaigning for three months, (and a lull at one time of fourteen years); that 'the period saw little intermission in the piling up of great fortunes by wool merchants or in the building of expensive churches';* that, despite executions, murders and deaths in battle a surprising number of aristocratic families survived; and lastly that only in the later stages of the war was the crown the prize aimed at.

The Paston Letters, letters left by a wealthy Norfolk merchant family, have given historians a false idea of the disorderliness of the Wars of the Roses, owing to the fact that Norfolk was 'an unusually stormy county' in those years. Other counties were far more peaceful and life went on much as before.

'The extent to which the Wars of the Roses actually wiped out the old families has been exaggerated.' The baronage numbered in the fifteenth century between fifty and sixty families. About twenty-nine

---

* See *The Tudors* by Christopher Morris, Batsford, 1955.

1

THE HOUSES OF YORK AND LANCASTER

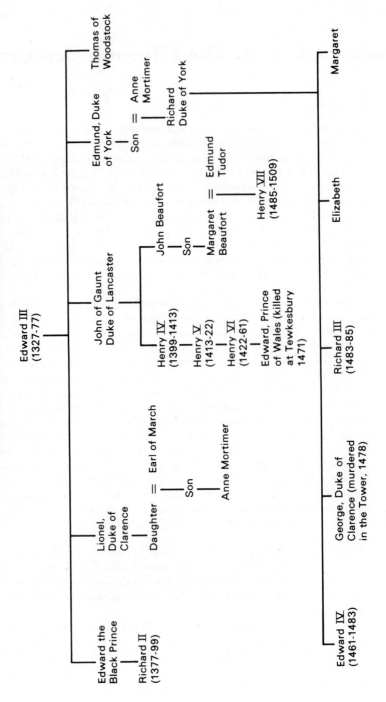

remained at the beginning of Henry VII's reign, death and attainder having thinned their ranks.* But many of the attainders were reversed by Henry and by the end of his reign the number had risen to forty (five of them new creations). The term 'Wars of the Roses' was first used by Sir Walter Scott. Doubtless he took his idea from Shakespeare's *King Henry VI, Part I*, in which the dukes of York and Somerset pluck white and red roses and adopt them as their badges. There is no historical evidence whatever for Shakespeare's scene. Certainly in these wars the crown changed hands five times, but in the early stages the issue was not who should reign. The wars started when the Earl of Warwick and Richard Duke of York tried to oust the King's favourite, the Duke of Somerset, from power. Various lords lined up on one side or the other for motives of self interest. The objective was control of the King's Council (the king Henry VI being disinclined or unable to control it himself). The majority of the population and even some of the lords took no active part in the civil war, which only gradually became a struggle for the crown when the followers of Richard Duke of York and his son, Edward, became aware that they could only hold power in the Council if their leader was king. The family tree on p. 2 will show that in fact Richard and his son had quite a good claim, being descended from both Lionel, Duke of Clarence, and Edmund, Duke of York, the second and fourth sons respectively of Edward III.

The Yorkists

Thus by 1460 the 'Yorkists' had decided to go for the throne, and in 1461, after victories at Mortimer's Cross and Towton, they got it, Edward, Earl of March, being crowned king as Edward IV (his father the Duke of York having been killed the previous year).

Thus began the dynasty of York. The King, Edward IV, was young, good-looking, pleasure-loving and popular. He was only nineteen when he gained the throne and had already shown himself to be a first-class soldier. But naturally, as a very young man, he was not, as yet, skilled in politics, and he fell in love with a lady far below his station and married her. The lady was Elizabeth Woodville, widow of a Lancastrian knight and daughter of a nobleman's steward. Now if there is one rule kings must never break it is not to marry for love. To marry badly is, for a king, to throw away half the trump cards in his hand. Edward made this terrible mistake and his dynasty never recovered from it.

The date of the Woodville marriage was 1464. It was a secret marriage. Members of the Council were not told until five months afterwards. As if this was not sufficient slight, Edward proceeded to elevate all his wife's numerous relations (she had five brothers, seven sisters and two sons)

---

* An Act of Attainder declared a man to be a traitor. It thus led to his execution (if he could be captured) and confiscation of his estates.

THE DESCENDANTS OF RICHARD, DUKE OF YORK

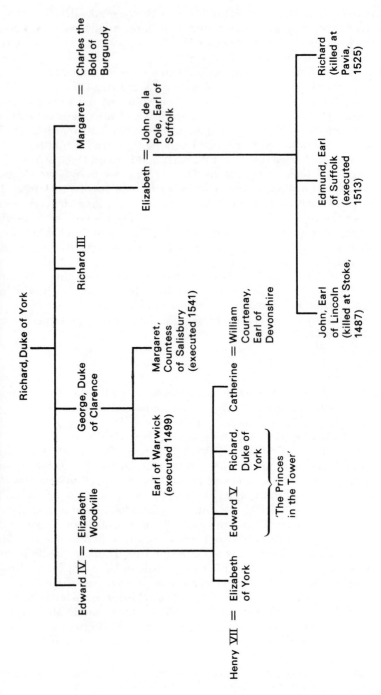

to the peerage. 'Eight new peerages came into existence in the Queen's family.... This was generally thought excessive.'*

The Woodville marriage and other disagreements led to the rebellion of Edward's most powerful subject, the Earl of Warwick (the King-maker). In 1470 he made common cause with Henry VI's Queen, the redoubtable 'she-wolf of France', Margaret of Anjou, staged an invasion with the help of the King of France and, having rescued the half-mad King Henry VI from the Tower, replaced him on the throne. But the second period of rule of Henry VI lasted only six months. Edward turned for help to France's enemy, Burgundy, landed with a small army in Yorkshire and soon routed the Lancastrian forces at Barnet (where Warwick was killed) and Tewkesbury (where Margaret was captured and her only son, the seventeen-year-old Edward, killed—some say in cold blood after the battle).

Edward IV thus regained the throne. Henry VI was kept in the Tower for the rest of his natural life, which was probably not long, as he is thought to have been murdered quite soon after Tewkesbury.

The second period of Edward's reign

Edward was now a mature statesman and his reign contains no further domestic strife. He ruled well and was master in his own Council. Soon the Treasury became full. 'Confiscations of the lands of attainted nobles and the efficient management of these and his own estates increased the crown's wealth.' Public order and respect for the law were restored. Trade was encouraged and began to thrive and this most popular king became a favourite with the citizens of London.

Edward had two brothers and two sisters. The elder brother, George, Duke of Clarence, had betrayed him and sided with Warwick back in 1469. He had been pardoned and had returned to Edward's favour, but Edward never forgot his desertion and in 1478, exasperated by his haughty ways, he called a Parliament, had him attainted a traitor and placed him in the Tower, where he died soon afterwards (according to Shakespeare he was drowned in a butt of Malmsey wine). Clarence left a young son, the Earl of Warwick, of whom we shall hear more later.

On the other hand, the younger brother, Richard, Duke of Gloucester, served Edward well, and, once Clarence was dead, was the hope of the old nobility, who had never really become reconciled to the upstart relations of the Queen.

Of Edward's two sisters the elder, Elizabeth, married John de la Pole, Earl of Suffolk, while the younger, Margaret, became the third wife of Charles the Bold, Duke of Burgundy.

All would have been well for the House of York had Edward lived to a ripe old age and died leaving a grown-up son. But he had lived

* This quotation is from Winston Churchill's *A History of the English-Speaking Peoples*, Vol. I, Cassell, 1956, a book which, though inclined to be too sweeping in its judgments, makes plain the outlines of the story, and is very readable.

a life of debauchery and his health suddenly gave way. He died in 1483 at the age of forty, leaving two sons, Edward and Richard, aged twelve and nine respectively, and two daughters.

The reign of Richard III

Richard of Gloucester had been named as Protector of the young prince by Edward before he died. Around him in the north gathered the old nobility, notably the Duke of Buckingham. The young King, having until now been Prince of Wales, was at Ludlow on the Welsh border under the care of his uncle, Lord Rivers (one of the numerous Woodville clan). Gloucester could not afford to allow Edward V to rule, for he would be under the thumb of his mother and her relatives who would inevitably influence him against his uncle, whom they hated. He and Buckingham therefore marched down from Yorkshire with their private armies of retainers, arrested Rivers and his nephew, Earl Grey, and themselves took charge of the King. Elizabeth Woodville, realizing what was intended, took sanctuary in Westminster Abbey.

Gloucester and Buckingham then conducted the young Edward to London, where he and his brother were lodged in the Tower of London, a royal palace from which they were never again to emerge. At the same time Rivers and Grey and one or two other of the Queen's supporters were summarily executed without any sort of a trial. The next problem was how to get rid of the young Edward V's claim to the throne. Gloucester and Buckingham accomplished this by spreading around the story that the Woodville marriage had been no true one because Edward was already betrothed to someone else (in those days this invalidated a marriage). Probably very few people believed this story. A better argument was the strength and number of Richard's troops marching down from the north and threatening London.

A Parliament was then called by the Protector and, having been presented with a roll showing that the Woodville marriage was invalid and the children of the late King bastards, it petitioned Richard, as rightful king, to accept the crown. Buckingham himself, as a member of the House of Lords, led the deputation which awaited Richard's answer. 'Modestly and reluctantly' he accepted!

Soon afterwards Richard was crowned as King Richard III. But his way to the throne had been bloody. He had gained the crown, but he had lost the goodwill of his people and on all sides he was recognized as what he was, a usurper.

Within a few months of his coronation his main supporter, Buckingham, had turned against him. Brooding in his Welsh castle at Brecknock, he suddenly rose in rebellion, but was captured and executed. The rebellion had been intended to restore the young King Edward V to the throne, but probably before it took place he and his brother were dead. They were last seen at play in the Tower garden in July 1483. Who murdered the Princes in the Tower? No one knows for certain

6

the answer to this question. Recently there has been a tendency among historians to whitewash Richard and put the blame on his successor, Henry VII. Richard's portrait 'by an unknown artist' which hangs in the National Portrait Gallery shows a refined, sensitive face. Certainly he was not the fiend incarnate portrayed by Shakespeare in his play *Richard III*. Shakespeare got his ideas from a series of histories written by chroniclers in the reign of Henry VII and enlarged on by Sir Thomas More who wrote his *History of Richard III* in 1513. More and the chroniclers who preceded him all wrote to please their royal masters, who were, of course, Tudors. Their accounts are hopelessly biased against Richard. Most contemporary writers do not even mention the alleged deformity of his spine which More asserted earned him the nickname of 'Crookback' (nor does it appear in his portrait).

Richard may be absolved from the guilt of three of the murders imputed to him by Shakespeare. He almost certainly did not strike down the youthful Prince Edward, Lancastrian heir, on the field of Tewkesbury. Nor is there any evidence that he killed either Henry VI or his own brother, George Duke of Clarence, when imprisoned in the Tower.*

But it is hard to absolve him from the murder of the Princes. The fact is that most of his contemporaries believed him guilty of it, and two hundred years later the skeletons of two boys were found bricked up under a staircase in the White Tower. Recently (1933) these bones have been carefully examined by medical experts and they appear to be those of boys of about the ages the princes would have been in 1483 (twelve and nine). Anyway, if the princes were still alive in 1484, why did not Richard bring them out and parade them around London to scotch the ugly rumours about their deaths?

In many respects Richard's government was as good as his brother's or as those of his Tudor successors. He enforced the law, fostered trade, built up the financial resources of the Crown. He was a busy administrator. That fine historian, Keith Feiling, calls him 'this businesslike ruler whom Yorkshire and the north followed to the end, who set to work vigorously in conciliating Scotland and the Kildares in Ireland, besides making commercial treaties and a survey of Crown lands'† But these good qualities were to avail him little. The country believed he was a child-murderer and this was something that even the men of those cruel times could not stomach. Also he alienated many great lords who had served his brother well by giving land and authority to such men as William Catesby, Richard Ratcliffe and Lord Lovel—'the Cat, the Rat and Lovel the Dog'—men whom he had raised up from nothing. He even took great magnates' children as hostages to guarantee their loyalty. These were not the actions of a lawful king, but of a nervous usurper.‡

* For a clear discussion of the guilt or innocence of Richard III read *The Character of Richard III* by A. R. Myers in *History Today*, August 1954.
† *A History of England* by Keith Feiling, Macmillan, 1950, p. 313.
‡ I am indebted to R. L. Storey's *The Reign of Henry VII*, Blandford, 1968, for much of the material in this and the next chapter.

7

Many of the nobles therefore turned against Richard and some of them, including the Earl of Oxford, fled to Brittany where a number of Lancastrians and discontented Yorkists were already gathering round a young man in his middle twenties called Henry Tudor.

Henry Tudor

Henry Tudor came of a Welsh family which, in two generations, had risen in the world by successful marriage. Owen Tudor, Henry's grandfather, had been a plain gentleman of Anglesey, too poor, they say, even to take out patents of knighthood. He had gone to court to seek his fortune, had become Clerk to the Wardrobe in the household of Catherine, widow of Henry V, and had married his royal mistress secretly. Of this marriage there had been two sons, Edmund and Jasper, who, through the kindness of their half-brother, Henry VI, had been created earls of Richmond and Pembroke respectively. Edmund had also married well— Margaret Beaufort, a descendant of John of Gaunt, the great ancestor of the House of Lancaster. The Beauforts had some sort of claim to the throne, but not a very good one. They had been born, not of John's wife, Blanche of Lancaster, but of his mistress, Catherine Swynford (whom he did eventually marry, but only after their children had been born). The Beauforts in fact were illegitimate, though in the reign of Richard II they had been legitimized by act of Parliament and by the Pope.

In 1457 Margaret Beaufort, who was not quite fourteen at the time, bore a son, Henry. He was born in his uncle Jasper's castle of Pembroke (and you may see today the remains of the tower in which he is believed to have been born), because his father, Edmund, was already dead. He was brought up in Wales and probably spoke Welsh better than English. At the age of fourteen he became an important person, for young Edward of Lancaster, heir of the Lancaster inheritance, was murdered on the field of Tewkesbury. Henry was now Lancaster heir (by his Beaufort descent), and his uncle, Jasper, prudently took him over to Brittany to keep him out of the clutches of Edward IV. His mother, Margaret Beaufort, had by this time married again and was soon to marry a third time, a certain Lord Stanley, of whom more anon.

On Christmas day 1483 a solemn ceremony took place in the cathedral of Rennes in Brittany. A number of British nobles swore allegiance to Henry Tudor, Earl of Richmond, as though he were already king, and he himself gave his oath he would marry the Princess Elizabeth (daughter of Edward IV and elder sister of the Princes in the Tower) as soon as he obtained the crown.

Richard knew that danger was brewing. He strengthened the coastal defences and posted himself at Nottingham to be in a central position when Henry should strike. He also demanded from the Duke of Brittany (which was as yet separate from France) the surrender of Henry, and the latter was forced to flee across the border into France disguised as a page-boy.

The Battle of Bosworth Field

In 1485 Henry's plans were ready. He equipped half a dozen ships at Rouen, the French King lent him 60,000 francs and 1800 mercenary soldiers, and he set sail in August for Milford Haven in South Wales, arriving there six days later. His hopes lay with the Welsh and with the Stanley family, who held great lands in Lancashire and Cheshire. At first, as he marched north and then east, few Welshmen joined him; but by the time he reached Shrewsbury about 3000 had come in and his army had swelled to 5000 men.

Richard marched out of Leicester to meet him with 10,000 disciplined men, but Lord Stanley and his brother, Sir William Stanley, (the former was Henry's step-father) had joined him with the Cheshire and Lancashire levies and no one knew how they would fight.

Battle was joined near the village of Market Bosworth. Henry unfurled, beside his own banner (that of St George), the red dragon on a green field, that of Cadwaladr, a semi-mythical Welsh prince of the seventh century (for this was to be something of a Welsh crusade). In the battle the Stanleys changed sides, and Richard, shouting, 'Treason! Treason!', hurled himself into the thickest of the fray and was killed. Tradition has it that Henry of Richmond found the crown, which Richard had worn in the battle, under a thorn bush and Lord Stanley placed it upon his head.

So ended what in a way was the last battle of the Wars of the Roses. Lancaster had won after all, and the decision has been permanent. Of the great families which fought on the right side at Bosworth many still sit in the House of Lords today. The Stanleys, now Earls of Derby, still hold big possessions in Lancashire. The present royal family obtained the throne by direct descent from Henry Tudor—so great has been the issue of the battle fought that day.

The state of England

What sort of a country was it that this landless adventurer had conquered? The population of England and Wales at this time was probably about two and a half million, and was almost certainly less than it had been 140 years before, when the terrible Black Death had struck the country. Most of them were engaged in agriculture, though the manufacture of woollens was a swiftly growing industry, bringing new wealth to its main areas, East Anglia, the West Country, Lincolnshire and Yorkshire. In the Middle Ages Britain had been the Australia of Europe, the great producer of raw wool. She still exported huge quantities of wool to the great wool-weaving towns of the Netherlands—Bruges, Ghent, Ypres, Antwerp—as well as to other parts of Europe. But she had come now to export less than half her production. The rest was spun and woven in the cottages of the poor up and down the country. Hardly a cottage in some areas did not now have its spinning-wheel, where the unmarried

9

women of the family (the 'spinsters') occupied their time and spun the woollen thread which paid for their keep.

In one respect England was ahead of most other parts of Europe: she had emancipated her serfs. In the heyday of the feudal system the poorer people had been villeins or serfs, tied to the soil, unable to sell the land on which they laboured and for which they owed about two days' labour a week without pay to their manorial lords, as well as other services. Since the Black Death the villeins had become free, able to sell their land and move elsewhere, taking wages for the work they did for others, and able to plead as free men in the King's courts. Nowhere else in Europe had this change become so complete.

Feudal military service had also practically disappeared in England. No longer did men have to fight forty days a year without pay for their overlords (as had all the higher ranks of the feudal system at one time). Instead they paid a rent for their land or sometimes even possessed it freehold.

The private armies which fought in the Wars of the Roses had been armies of 'retainers'. A retainer was usually a country gentleman, living on his own estate, but engaged by contract 'to ride and go with the same lord—upon reasonable warning'. This practice has been called by historians of the late nineteenth century and since 'bastard feudalism'. By the form of indentures drawn up, both parties undertook to fulfil certain conditions. 'The retainer promised to attend the lord under arms if necessary and with such a following as he could muster whenever the lord ordered him to do so.'* This might be in the king's service. 'In return the lord undertook to reimburse his retainers' expenses for this service and to pay an annual pension.' The latter was quite small, at the most about £20 a year. Indentures contained clauses which stated that the retainer's overriding loyalty was to the king. They also usually contained a clause by which the lord undertook to protect the private interests of his retainer. Until recently historians believed that retaining was an evil from which the country was rescued by Henry VII (who forbade it). But now historians have come to believe that 'bastard feudalism' was not necessarily an evil, but rather that it was useful, providing a new form of cohesion to society as the feudal structure decayed. Nor was it illegal (though an act of 1390 had forbidden men under the rank of baronet to give liveries, which were the equivalent of uniforms). In fact the king seems to have welcomed the practice. It provided him with a ready army in an emergency. Also the lord and his retainers could be expected to act as a police force and keep order in their locality. But to make the system work the king had to be on good personal relations with his nobles, and to be strong enough to restrain those who used their power for selfish ends.

When a weak king like Henry VI ruled, the great lords of the Council abused their privileges and used their influence to suborn sheriffs, pack

* *Ibid.*, p. 37.

juries to favour their clients (a few good retainers on a jury could do wonders) and even to intimidate juries to enforce dubious claims to property. The packing of juries to maintain a suit was known as 'maintenance', while intimidating juries by perhaps posting a squad of archers outside the court house, all dressed in the lord's livery and wearing his badge, was called 'embracery'. The fact that Henry VII forbade these practices has led historians to believe that they were widespread in the period of the Wars of the Roses. So they were, when Henry VI ruled, but not, we now believe, under the stronger Yorkist kings, at least after 1471. Again, the Paston letters give us a false view. 'Go, get you a lord, for thereby hang the law and the prophets' John Paston was told. This was wise advice at the time it was given. When the king was weak, the law provided no remedy for losses incurred, and a country gentleman needed to attach himself to a powerful lord in order to survive. Indentures were supposed to be for life, but many country gentlemen changed their lords when the one they had been attached to became too weak to protect them. There was no necessity for a retainer's lord to be also his landlord. Very often of course a lord's retainers were also his tenants, but it did not necessarily follow.

Growth of a middle class

One of the distinctive features of English society at this time was the growth of a middle class. This was composed of the merchants of the towns and the knights and gentlemen of the country. A gentleman was, roughly speaking, one who owned rather more land than he could farm himself and therefore rented some out to other people. He was distinguished socially by the carrying of a sword and could fight a duel if offended by anyone else of rank. He also sported a coat of arms. About this time the gentry were increasing in wealth and numbers. One reason for this was that rich merchants had bought land, becoming themselves country gentry and bringing new strength to the class.*

The merchants were growing rapidly in wealth and importance. They owed this to the growth of trade, particularly overseas trade. Trade had been growing all over Europe since the time of the Crusades. Even in the thirteenth century great manor houses had been built in England by merchants who had made money out of the export of wool.

London had grown to great size (about fifty thousand people) by 1485. It was close to the mighty international trading centre of Antwerp. Money was its god. Back in the fourteenth century it had made the fortune of a certain poor boy, Richard Whittington, who became 'thrice Lord Mayor', as the child's story tells. Here dwelt men who were powerful and wealthy, yet never donned a suit of armour nor fought a battle; men who lived in beautiful town houses guarded by town walls, instead of in castles; who dressed in beautiful velvets and furs while their wives

* For a fuller definition of a gentleman see Chapter 17, section entitled 'The Land and Social Status'.

and daughters wore silks and brocades; men who mixed socially not only with barons (and indeed with a king or two, like Edward IV), but with bankers from North Italy and Germany, merchants and money-lenders from the Netherlands and ship-owners from the Hanse cities of the Baltic or from Bristol or Southampton. The London merchants were organized in their great Livery Companies, such as the Grocers, who had grown rich on importing spices, the Mercers who dealt in silks, the Drapers who handled other cloths, and so on. A company known as the Merchant Adventurers exported woollen cloth to Antwerp and North Germany. Older than them were the Merchant Staplers who exported raw wool, woolfells and hides. They exported these almost entirely through Calais (which had been captured by Edward III in the Hundred Years' War and was still an English town). Only Italian buyers were allowed to buy raw wool other than through the Staple, and then only on condition that they did not sell it north of the Alps.

Like London, most of the other big towns were ports. One was Hull, outlet for the cloth and raw wool of Yorkshire, the town where the de la Pole family had originally made its fortune. Still greater was Bristol, which handled the West Country's wool exports, also imports of wine from the once-English port of Bordeaux, besides importing a variety of other goods from Spain, Portugal, Ireland and even Iceland. Then there was Southampton, which, besides exporting wool, imported, via Venetian and Genoese shippers, spices from the Far East, mohair and carpets from the Middle East, currants and malmsey wines from the Greek islands and 'superfine cloth, glass, armour and other luxury goods' from the cities of northern Italy. Nor should we forget Plymouth, nursery of so many great seafaring men in the sixteenth century. Other great cities were Norwich, York, Lincoln and Gloucester; but none was anything like London in size. Not even Bristol could compare with London, which was not only a great port, but had the king's court nearby at Westminster and the law courts with all their hangers-on, situated between the city and the palace. By 1485 it was evident that he who held London held England (as Charles I was one day to find to his cost).

The growing power of the middle classes at this time meant more power for the king, for the bigger towns were independent of baronial control. Most of them had obtained charters, giving them powers of self-government and freedom from feudal interference, back in the days of the Crusades, when needy kings like Richard I would grant such charters for sums of money. Thus, while the king could tax the towns, the barons could get nothing out of them. Moreover, merchants can only trade and grow rich when law and order is enforced; so the middle classes were inclined to support a strong monarchy.

In almost every country in Europe we find these phenomena evident at this time—a weakening of the barons, a growth of the middle class and the emergence of a strong monarchy. England was not unique. And with it all there was a mighty abundance of that commodity so lacking in feudal times, money.

Law

By 1485 the rule of law had become, in theory at least, the basis of English life. Back in the thirteenth century Henry Bracton, one of the King's judges, had written his *Treatise on the Laws of England*, in which he taught that the English Common Law bowed to no other law, that it was to be found in the previous decisions of the courts, 'whose solemn ruling no royal writ might supersede, and by which even the King himself was bound'. Then in the fifteenth century we have Sir John Fortescue, Chief Justice to Henry VI and Councillor to Prince Edward his son, teaching, in his *Governance of England*, that the King could not change the law, or impose taxes, without consent of Parliament. He was only stating what most educated people already believed.

Fortescue gloried in a system of law which included trial by jury, which forbade torture, and 'gave us a stout middle class, archers ready to defend their country'.

Already by 1485 the four great Inns of Court were established, as a legal university, 'where the best counsel of the day expounded the practice of the courts'. The Year Books had been circulating since Edward I's time, first of course in manuscript, but latterly in printed form.

Thus, despite the Wars of the Roses, despite disputes and quarrels for the throne and the weakness of government which thus arose, the England of 1485 was a great deal more civilized and law-abiding, a great deal more developed, than are most African and Asian countries today.

Parliament

Parliament had been growing now for two hundred years. It was not quite the clearly defined body we have today, for sometimes the Lords might meet without the Commons, but the 'lords spiritual and temporal' (the former were bishops and abbots) already did not dare raise a general tax when the Commons were not there, and the Commons had already defined what boroughs were to elect members (each county, except those in Wales, elected two) and who was to vote in the counties, to wit, solid freeholders with property worth not less than 40s a year.

There were only seventy-four county members of the Commons, but there were 224 representatives of the boroughs. The latter were elected by various franchises, but usually members of wealthy families who had lived a long time in the borough got the vote. The franchise was thus in the hands of 'an oligarchy of traders and wealthy craftsmen', usually the same people who formed the town council. This meant that, in any one borough, perhaps less than a score of voters elected the two members. The only way to gain a vote was to marry the daughter of one of the wealthy burgesses, or to be apprenticed to him.

The large towns often returned wealthy burgesses as their members, but the smaller towns usually elected local landowners, because none of their burgesses would be rich enough to stand the expenses involved and because the patronage of a local landowner was valuable. Since the forty-shilling freeholders in the counties (a much broader franchise, be it noted) also elected landowners, the squires of England formed the vast majority of the Commons.

Voting took place in public, but very often there was no election at all, the seat going, as if by hereditary right, to the greatest landowner in the district or his son. After all a man with £4000 a year in land was almost certain to get more votes than one with only £1200 a year, for he could distribute more favours in return; therefore it was not worth the while of the smaller landowner to stand.

The Lords was a much smaller house than the Commons. In it sat 'the two archbishops, the nineteen bishops and twenty-eight mitred abbots', though few of the abbots actually attended. As already stated the temporal lords, at the beginning of Henry VII's reign, numbered only twenty-nine, but, by the end of the reign, their numbers had increased to forty.

The Lords was the more important house. It was an integral part of the High Court of Parliament and possessed the right of impeachment, a process wherein it sat as the 'grand jury of all England' and could condemn even one of the King's ministers to death. Yet, as the middle classes grew in wealth, the Commons was becoming more powerful. Already it possessed the right of initiating money bills and of electing its own Speaker.

The Parliament of England was far better developed than any other parliament in the world at this time and certainly the Scottish Parliament was but a shadow of it. It is true that the King could make minor laws by proclamation, but he could not make laws on really important matters, for it was already recognized that 'only statute could add felonies and treasons to the body of the law'. Thus only by statute could a man be deprived of life, limb or liberty.

The Church

No account of England at this time would be complete without some mention of the Church. This was of course the Roman Catholic Church—no other Christian church existed at this time in western Europe.

Things were not well at this time with the Church. In the fourteenth century the pope had lost much respect when the kings of France had removed him to Avignon. Then there had for a time been two popes, one in Rome and one in Avignon. This had naturally shaken people's faith. Also the medieval Church had grown immensely wealthy and, latterly, very corrupt. Prelates lived in palaces, and thought more of the style of their living, their feasts and entertainments, than of their spiritual cares. They were inclined to the abuses of simony and nepotism (simony, so-called after Simon the Sorcerer in *Acts*, ch. 8, means the buying of promotion in the Church; nepotism is the promotion of nephews, who

14

were sometimes really illegitimate sons), of pluralism (holding more than one benefice) and of non-residence.

The Church at this time included, not only bishops and parish priests, but also monks, nuns and friars. In the fourteenth century the face of England, particularly the rich eastern Midlands, was covered by monasteries and nunneries; comprising nearly twelve hundred separate foundations. But here also there was decline and corruption. By 1485 many of the great monasteries were more than half empty. Mighty Cistercian houses like Fountains in Yorkshire (which had such great lands that it was said that its abbot could ride thirty miles in a straight line on his own sheep pasture) had only a score of monks in their cells. This was because people no longer respected the monastic life. The monks had become worldly. They kept numerous servants. They followed wordly pursuits such as hunting and hawking. They lived on the fat of the land, the abbots particularly being prone to a lavish style of life. They spent little on charity, and with the invention of printing, they were no longer absolutely necessary for the making of books. The subject of monastic decline is a vexed one among historians, as Catholics and Protestants disagree about it. It is further discussed in Chapter 6. Writers of the later Middle Ages, such as Chaucer, certainly have very little good to say about monks and friars, the latter being usually described by them as frequenting inns and chasing after women.

Most good men thought the Church needed reforming. The popes, however, were quite unfitted to do this, being almost invariably Italian princelings, bent on increasing their powers and lands in Italy in the hope of providing for their 'nephews'. Usually they stopped short of murder, but there was not much else they would not stoop to in order to get rid of their rival Italian princes.

Two men had made attempts to reform the Church. The first was John Wycliffe, an Oxford don who preached and worked about 1380. He attacked the Church for its wealth and the priests for their evil lives. Among other things he called the pope 'a limb of Lucifer', the friars 'ravening wolves' and the monks 'fat cows'. His main themes were (like those of later reformers) that no priest could stand between a man and his God, that pope and priest were nothing if they were not good men and did not possess 'grace', and that the Bible was the only true authority (not pope nor Church Council). Wycliffe and his followers translated the Bible into English for the first time since the Norman Conquest (the Catholic Church used a Latin version), and his followers set out on preaching tours which earned them the nickname of 'Lollards' (or Flemish heretics). The Pope issued a bull for Wycliffe's arrest, but it was never carried out, and, protected by his patron, John of Gaunt, he died peacefully in bed in 1384 at his rectory at Lutterworth.

Not so lucky was John Hus of Bohemia, the next reformer. He was burned by order of a Church Council in 1415, the year of Agincourt.

Helped by the terrible statute of 1401, *De Heretico Comburendo*, the Lancastrian kings, Henry IV and Henry V, carried out a thorough

15

persecution of the Lollards. Many were burned, many recanted; but, although the movement was driven underground, it was never extinguished. It lingered on in the houses of the poor, particularly in East Anglia and the Home Counties and in towns like London and Bristol, to flare forth again at the end of the fifteenth century.

But I have painted too black a picture of the Church in 1485. As one historian has said, 'the good outweighed the bad. The regular clergy formed a social bond, their services inculcating beliefs and conduct without which chaos would have prevailed'.* In fact most of the good points about the people of fifteenth-century England could be traced to the influence of Christianity, and Christianity, in effect, was the product of the teachings of the Church. So we must not be too hard on a body which, like all human institutions, was naturally prone to imperfection.

Universities

Before leaving the Church we should look at two of its offshoots, those strange medieval corporations, the universities of Oxford and Cambridge.

Medieval universities were 'not formed by buildings and examinations, but by the attraction of great teachers'. The teaching was done in Latin. The teachers were all men in holy orders (many of them friars), and had the right of electing their chancellor. Four out of every five students became secular priests; the others became lawyers, doctors, monks or friars. But after the Black Death (1348–1350) monasticism declined, and rich men began to leave their money to endow Oxford and Cambridge colleges instead of monasteries. Many colleges were then built, and Oxford and Cambridge flourished more than ever as the centres (perhaps Cambridge more of the mind, Oxford more of the spirit?) of English mental and spiritual life.

In the fifteenth century new influences began to be felt at these two centres of learning. 'They began to go to the fountain-head in the Mediterranean.' Scholars travelled to Italy which had recently become the centre of a new approach to teaching and education. This New Learning, as it was called, meant largely a study of the Greek classics and particularly of that great philosopher, Plato. At the University of Padua medicine was making great strides; at Bologna Roman law was much studied. At Florence and Venice the study of Greek was opening new doors into the human mind.

These ideas flowed into England through her two universities. The process was greatly helped by the invention of printing (which came from China via Germany). In 1476 Caxton set up his printing press at Westminster, soon to be followed by others at Oxford and St Albans. There was a great hunger for learning. Many schools were founded, some not attached to any cathedral, monastery or chantry, but founded by

* J. A. Williamson, *The Tudor Age*, p. 5

merchants and under the control of city companies (quite a new thing this). Already Winchester and Eton were in existence, as were many little schools up and down the country, attached to a monastery, cathedral, gild or chantry. There was in fact a vigorous intellectual life in the England of 1485, and it was soon to blossom forth in many new and unforeseen ways.

Wales

I have written of 'England'. I mean of course really 'England and Wales'.

Wales at this time was split into two parts. In the north-west was the Principality of Wales, the area which had been independent until the time of Llewelyn, and had been conquered by Edward I and turned into shires on the English model. But the rest of Wales consisted of marcher lordships, lands conquered by the lords to whom William the Conqueror had given land on the Welsh border so that they might hold back the wild Welsh. Over the centuries these marcher lords had advanced along the river valleys (Severn, Wye and Usk) or along the coastal plains (north and south), driving back the Welsh and setting up new lordships for themselves, in which they acted like Welsh princes, holding their own law-courts and raising their private armies. The time came when these border lords were more dangerous to the Crown than were the Welsh. It was the marcher lords who had taken the lead on both sides in the Wars of the Roses. The important names in these wars are mainly border names—Gloucester, Shrewsbury, Pembroke, Worcester, Hereford and the Earl of March. There were some 140 lordships by 1485, some great ones like Glamorgan and Monmouth, which were destined to become counties, others consisting of little else but a castle with a few square miles of land around it. The king had some control over them, but not a great deal, except when, as in some cases, he happened to own them.

The Welsh people in those days were much more distinct from the English than they are today. For one thing they were all Welsh-speaking. For another they had strong tribal loyalties (particularly in the north), whereas feudalism had long broken these down in England. Thirdly, of course, they had the Celtic character—imaginative, poetic, illogical. The Welsh had rebelled under Owen Glendower (or *Glyndwr*) in the reign of Henry IV, and had been punished for it by being made second-class citizens. They had lost the full rights of Englishmen at Common Law. It was thus a dissatisfied Wales, as he well knew, that Henry Tudor chose for his landing-place in 1485. Moreover, it was a martial Wales. The hardy hill-folk, with their pastoral farming and their general shortage of money, had enlisted in great numbers in the armies of the Hundred Years' War. It was Welsh archers who had been largely responsible for the victory of Agincourt, and it was upon Welsh infantry that

17

Henry VII was mainly to rely, not only at Bosworth, but also in crushing the two great rebellions of his reign.

But we should not overestimate the influence of Wales, for its population at this time was very small (perhaps 250,000) and it was very poor indeed beside England, and in some ways very backward. What is more, the Welsh were not likely to give much trouble, because they greatly feared their western neighbours, the Irish, who at this time (unlike today) outnumbered them considerably.

The North and the Fens

North of the Humber and the lower Trent was an England more barren, less civilized and more feudal than the wealthy Midlands and South. Here, in remote valleys, lay most of the big sheep-farming abbeys. Here were the hardy folk who took the brunt of the Scottish border raids, which, century after century, had broken in upon them. The North was conservative. We shall find it clinging to the old religion when the Reformation gets into its stride; its people tended to believe that the local feudal lord, be he Percy, Neville or Dacre, was more fit for their allegiance than a king in far-off London. The wealthiest part was the wide Vale of York and the East Riding, areas which were to take the lead in the great rebellion of Henry VIII's reign, the Pilgrimage of Grace.

And should we not mention the Fens, that large area of low-lying land round the Wash which included much of South Lincolnshire, Huntingdonshire and Cambridgeshire? As yet the Fens had not been drained. They were the haunts of fishermen and wild-fowlers, and contained very little land fit for agriculture. Through them flowed such sluggish rivers as the Witham, the Welland and the Great Ouse. At the mouths of the first and third of these respectively were the great Wash ports of Boston and Lynn. The former had once (in the late thirteenth century) been the greatest wool-exporting port in England (greater even than London), for the wolds of Lindsey produced very high quality wool, much in demand in Flanders. Boston and Lynn exported salt as well as wool and imported wine from Gascony, timber and herrings from the Baltic and woad from Picardy. But the great days of the Wash ports were coming to an end. The increase of woollen cloth manufacture meant less raw wool was exported. London was taking the trade of the Wash ports, though the Hanseatic League still had its steelyards at Boston and Lynn as well as at London. Lincoln and Stamford were great cloth-manufacturing towns as they had been since the days of Henry III, while Ely was a powerful bishopric whose bishop (later the famous Archbishop Morton) was the first man to attempt fen drainage on a large scale with any success.

1 The Reign of Henry VII. The King Establishes his Position

The traditional picture of Henry

No Tudor monarch (not even Henry VIII) has received more attention in recent years from historians than has Henry VII. As a result our concept of him has greatly altered. Books recently published* have torn up the old concept of a sort of genius of kingship, who, from the moment of his triumph at Bosworth, set about building up the power of the Crown, admitting mainly middle-class men into his Council, weakening the barons (by forcing them to abandon the keeping of retainers and punishing them with enormous fines in Star Chamber if they disobeyed), modernizing the Crown's finances so that money flowed into his private coffers, restoring law and order where none had existed before, and wisely pursuing a trade policy which favoured the merchants, members of that middle class on which he had decided to rely.

This false concept of Henry VII has been handed down to us from Francis Bacon, who published *The Life of Henry VII* in 1622. So striking and vivid is Bacon's prose that it has influenced generations of historians, just as Macaulay's magnificent prose has influenced our views on Clive or William of Orange. It is partly examination of the years that immediately preceded Henry's reign, that has led modern historians to put forward new interpretations. It is now believed that the Yorkist kings, Edward IV and Richard III, had already adopted most of the policies we so admire in Henry. Moreover, since he came to the throne at the early age of twenty-eight and was then quite inexperienced in any sort of administration, Henry's early years show little mastery of the art of kingship. He was forced to feel his way cautiously, had a good many strokes of luck and only developed many of his wise policies in the latter half of his reign—the act against liveries and maintenance, for instance, came in the nineteenth year of his reign. This 'wonder for wise men', as Bacon called him, was in fact less far-seeing than Bacon would have us think. Only gradually did he fumble his way to a successful system of finance (adopting Yorkist methods which derived from private estate management). Moreover, he relied as much on the barons as on the middle classes in the task of government, the former as great landowners having 'a strong vested interest in the preservation of public order and competent government'.

Bearing these things in mind (and there are several other errors in

* R. L. Storey, *op. cit.*; *The Crown Lands 1461–1536* by B. P. Wolffe, Allen & Unwin, 1970; and *Henry VII* by S. B. Chrimes, Eyre Methuen, 1972.

the traditional view in addition to those I have mentioned in this brief survey) let us turn our attention to the course of events.

Henry establishes his position

Bosworth was fought in August 1485. In October Henry was crowned and in November Parliament was summoned. Henry did not owe his crown to Parliament. Nevertheless on a petition from the Commons an act was passed declaring that 'the inheritance of the crown and all its appurtenances are and remain in the person of Henry VII and the heirs of his body'. The act merely registered Henry's accession. It did not make him king. Henry owed his throne to conquest. He could not even claim strict hereditary right, for his mother, Margaret Beaufort (through whom he claimed royal descent), was still alive and long remained a powerful influence behind the throne. If the throne descended by hereditary right, she should have ruled.

Many of Edward's old councillors remained, the first two lord chancellors being bishops who had served Edward; but men who had been in exile with Henry also received office. Thus Richard Fox (soon to be a bishop) received the confidential post of King's Secretary. Likewise, Henry's uncle, Jasper Tudor, Morton, Bishop of Ely, the Earl of Oxford and Sir Edward Poynings, who were all companions of Henry's exile, remained near the King. A new man added was Reginald Bray, Margaret Beaufort's steward, who had helped Margaret plan an abortive rising against Richard in 1483.

There were no swift executions after the battle of Bosworth, as there had so often been after other battles of the Wars of the Roses, but certain supporters of Richard were attainted by Parliament and had their estates confiscated by the legal fiction that Henry's reign had begun the day before the battle and that therefore all who fought against him were guilty of treason. In this way Henry was able to confiscate the Yorkist estates of Richard III.

This first Parliament of Henry did little except grant the king the revenues of the customs for life and the royal estates including the duchies of Lancaster and Cornwall.

In exile, as we saw in the last chapter, Henry had declared his intention of marrying Elizabeth of York, Edward IV's elder daughter. This he did in January 1486. It was a wise marriage and did something to heal the wounds of Yorkist and Lancaster rivalry. Richard III's allegations against Edward's marriage which had made out Elizabeth to be a bastard, were conveniently ignored. Soon a son was born to Elizabeth and was given the name of Arthur, after the Welsh legendary hero.

Henry's personality

We have few eye-witness reports of Henry and most of those we have come from the latter part of his reign. The historian Polydore Vergil
20

1 Henry VII by Pietro Torrigiano

2 Erasmus at 55 by Holbein

describes him as above average height and slender, although well-built and strong, with golden hair which went thin in his later years. Polydore also wrote, 'his face was cheerful, especially when speaking'. Others speak of his cheerful aspect. Thus Bacon's picture of a grave, suspicious figure, who had few pleasures and preferred book-keeping, is probably false. Nor is there any evidence to confirm Bacon's assertion that his marriage was poisoned by his hatred of the house of York. Henry seems to have been a faithful and affectionate husband. There is a moving account of how they consoled each other when the news came of the death of Prince Arthur in 1502. When Elizabeth died in childbirth two years later, Henry 'privily departed to a solitary place and would no man should resort unto him'.

Henry was a very pious son of the Church. He went to mass two or three times daily, gave alms frequently, visited famous shrines like Canterbury and Walsingham, founded two convents and in his will bequeathed money for 10,000 masses to be said for his soul within a month of his death. No English monarch since Henry III had made such provision for his after-life. On the other hand, unlike his mother and many of his contemporaries, he did nothing for education.

Henry was fond of hunting, hawking and coursing, played tennis, gambled for high stakes (he once lost £47 at cards—we know because his losses are recorded in the Chamber accounts) and enjoyed the antics of professional fools and tumblers.

He kept a sumptuous court, dressed richly and entertained lavishly. He appears to have been fond of music and kept a company of minstrels.

All in all then he was a much more human person than Bacon made him out to have been. Yet he was never popular. He had none of that bluff, masculine charm which had endeared Edward IV to the people of London and was to endear Henry VIII likewise. A Spaniard noted in 1498 that the king was 'little loved', whereas his Queen and elder son, Arthur, were.

Rebellion

Henry was lucky in that when he got his throne he had few powerful European neighbours. Scotland was in disorder and its king, James III, was soon to be murdered by a faction of nobles (1488). Louis XI, the great king of France, had died in 1483 and was succeeded by Charles VIII, a boy of thirteen, whose sister became Regent (and helped Henry VII to gain his throne). The ruler of Burgundy was a minor and his father, the Emperor Maximilian, governed so badly that there were revolts in the great towns.

Henry was also lucky in that there were no great nobles in England to rival him in power. 'The English aristocracy had certainly not killed itself off in the Wars of the Roses, but it was a less formidable body than it had been in 1460 or even in 1484. There was no Duke of York in 1485;

21

the great estates of his duchy, including the earldom of March, had become royal property when Edward seized the crown and Henry was now their owner. The earldom of Warwick had disappeared, for the "Kingmaker" had fathered only two daughters who added their inheritance to the lands of York. The heir of the Duke of Buckingham executed by Richard III had been restored the title in 1485, but, as he was a child, his estate remained in Henry's keeping. Another powerful magnate, the Duke of Norfolk, had been killed at Bosworth; his heir, the Earl of Surrey, was kept in prison for four years, and his lands were confiscated.'*

This state of affairs, and not merely the support of the middle classes, was the secret of Henry's power. 'The balance of power had swung markedly in favour of the crown.'

But Henry was to need all his luck. His right to the crown has been shown to be very slender. Several Yorkist claimants had better claims. One was the Earl of Warwick, ten-year-old son of the murdered Duke of Clarence and nephew of Edward IV. He was speedily arrested and placed in the Tower. Then there were the de la Pole brothers, sons of Edward IV's sister, Elizabeth (*see the family tree*, p. 4). They had made their peace with Henry and had been admitted to his councils, but both were dangerous and both were to rebel. Finally, there was a Yorkist in high position on the Continent—Margaret, younger sister of Edward IV. She had married Charles the Bold of Burgundy and now, her husband being dead, held court in that opulent and powerful trading nation, and controlled some of its lands. Margaret was Henry's most implacable enemy, and from her court emanated the chief rebellions against him.

The first of these came in 1486. A certain Oxford priest called Symonds had a pupil called Lambert Simnel. Simnel was twelve years old, and was taught to impersonate the Earl of Warwick, whom the Yorkists imagined now to be dead, murdered, like his father, Clarence, in the Tower. The plot was hatched in the Netherlands and in Ireland, the latter being pro-Yorkist because the Yorkist kings had always treated it well. Symonds took the boy over to Dublin in 1486, and the Irish chiefs really believed in him and proclaimed him king as Edward VI. Meanwhile discontented Yorkists were flocking to the court of Margaret, dowager duchess of Burgundy. John de la Pole, Earl of Lincoln and a real claimant to the throne, fled here from England in 1487. Margaret was the mainstay of the rebellion. She had already collected 2000 German mercenaries and a fleet of ships. This expedition now sailed to Dublin.

An army was concentrated at Nottingham. The real Earl of Warwick was taken from the Tower and paraded through the streets of London.

In 1487 the expedition landed in Lancashire (making for Yorkshire). Few people joined it. Henry met it at Stoke (near Newark). The Irish fought with knives and spears and without armour, the Germans with their long pikes. The battle was bloodier than Bosworth, but the rebels

* R. L. Storey, *op. cit.*, p. 124.

were routed. The Earl of Lincoln was killed. Lambert Simnel was captured and was treated kindly by Henry (he was a gentle enough child). He was put to work as a kitchen boy in the royal household and later made a falconer in the King's service.

Interference abroad

Although France had helped him to his throne, Henry saw this powerful neighbour as his chief enemy. France was no longer the weak country which English armies had been able to invade in the Hundred Years' War. Under her great ruler, Louis XI, the 'Spider King', she had grown very strong and various semi-independent vassal states like Anjou and Provence had been absorbed into the kingdom. But after Louis' death (1483) one remained independent. This was Brittany, a maritime province with excellent harbours and a hardy, sea-faring population. It was Brittany which had protected Henry in the early days of his exile. But now the Duke of Brittany was an old man; and since he had no sons, the duchy would descend to his elder daughter, Anne. This was a golden opportunity for France to absorb Brittany in the same way as so many vassal states had been absorbed—by marriage. The French government planned to marry Anne to the young French King Charles VIII. The Breton nobles disliked the match and Henry saw it as a serious threat to England since France would now control the valuable Breton ports.

But Henry could not take on France alone. He looked for allies. The two obvious ones were Spain and Burgundy. Spain, newly created by the marriage of Isabella of Castile to Ferdinand of Aragon, was fast becoming powerful, and the kingdom of Aragon was an old enemy of France.

Burgundy was a collection of duchies and counties on the north-east borders of France, which had been obtained by marriage, conquest or legal artifice by the dukes of Burgundy. Duke Charles the Bold, a life-long enemy of Louis XI, had died in 1477, leaving a daughter, Mary, who had married Maximilian, the King of the Romans or Emperor-elect of the Holy Roman Empire. But Mary had been killed quite young in a hunting accident (1482) leaving two children, Philip and Margaret. As Philip was too young to rule, it was his father, Maximilian, now Emperor, who was ruling Burgundy at this time.

In 1488 the French attacked Brittany and won a crushing victory. The old duke was forced to sign a treaty promising he would not marry his daughter without permission from the French king. Two weeks later he died.

Early in 1489 Henry was active in diplomacy. First he made a treaty with Maximilian, 'restoring the Anglo-Burgundian accord of Edward IV's time', then he made a treaty with Brittany promising to lend her 6000 men if she would pay their wages. Finally he signed the treaty of Medina Del Campo with Spain. Under the terms of this treaty his little son, Arthur, was to marry Ferdinand and Isabella's third daughter,

Catherine. Medina Del Campo was also a treaty of mutual defence and contained commercial clauses, allowing freedom of commerce and residence for the subjects of each in the dominions of the other. Finally, both countries agreed to make war on France—though it is doubtful if this clause was ratified. Recognition by Spain undoubtedly strengthened Henry's position. The treaty is the beginning of a period of association between the two countries which was to last over half a century.

Henry sent the promised 6000 men to Brittany but they had little success there. French power was too great and in 1491 a French army marched into Brittany, defeated the British and Spanish and compelled the submission of the duchy. Anne was married to Charles VIII, and the Breton contest was over. Ever since Brittany has been part of France, though the memory of the last duchess, *Anne de Bretagne*, is still very much alive among Bretons today.

'English blood had been shed and there was nought to show for it.'* Henry could not afford the loss of face. To stop Yorkist murmurings (Perkin Warbeck had made his appearance) Henry prepared a great expedition against France in 1492. An army, which included no less than 25,000 foot and 1600 horse, was assembled and crossed to Calais late in the year. Henry himself went with it, and laid siege to Boulogne.

However, the young King of France, Charles VIII, was already planning his great attack on the wealthy peninsula of Italy, and he did not want war in the north. Nor did Henry really. He only wanted to make a grand gesture, and, when Charles offered him 745,000 gold crowns to go home (a crown was about four shillings), he speedily made peace at Etaples. Beside the money payment, which was to be made at the rate of 50,000 crowns a year, the treaty arranged that neither king should help the enemies of the other and that their subjects might trade on equal terms.

Henry was careful to pay off his army, which had been disappointed of plunder and glory. Though it was undoubtedly a wise piece of diplomacy, the treaty of Etaples was not likely to make Henry popular. Many must have remembered the triumphs of Agincourt and drawn adverse comparisons between the seventh Henry and the fifth. Henry was going to need all his popularity, for already a new Yorkist plot was brewing.

Perkin Warbeck's rebellion

Perkin Warbeck was a handsome Flemish lad of seventeen in the employ of a Breton clothes merchant. In 1491 he visited Cork and walked its streets in fine clothes, advertising his master's wares. Some Irish malcontents saw at once that 'here was their Earl of Warwick'. Warbeck at first would have none of their plans, but eventually agreed to impersonate Richard, the younger of the two Princes in the Tower. He soon proved himself a daring adventurer 'of high intelligence, ability and

---

* The quotation is from *The Earlier Tudors* by J. D. Mackie, Oxford, 1952, p. 106, who gives a very interesting but detailed account of these wars.

charm of personality'. After establishing relations with some Anglo-Irish lords and with James IV, King of Scotland, Warbeck went to France. But the King of France had just made peace with Henry in 1492 and would give him no support; so Warbeck moved on to the Netherlands. Here Margaret of Burgundy received him with open arms as 'another nephew delivered from the Tower'. Whether she really believed that he was the young Richard of York is doubtful.

Yorkist supporters flocked to the Netherlands, where Warbeck held court as Richard IV of England. Henry was alarmed. He put pressure on the rulers of the Netherlands by prohibiting his subjects to trade there and moving the Merchant Adventurers' cloth mart from Antwerp to Calais (a terrible blow for the wool merchants of the Flemish cities). Then he dismissed the Earl of Kildare from his post of Lord Deputy in Ireland, to show the Irish he meant business.

By 1494 the plot was at its height. The air in England was full of expectancy. Maximilian, the genial Emperor of the Holy Roman Empire, had given the cause his blessing (and also some soldiers and ships). Surely with such supporters the cause could not fail! Even Sir William Stanley, one of the victors of Bosworth and a chamberlain of Henry's household, believed in it enough to become involved. He was arrested, attainted by Parliament and executed.

But fail it did. In 1495 Warbeck appeared off Deal and landed some troops, but prudently stayed on board himself. His troops were easily mopped up. Then he sailed to Ireland and tried to capture the loyal town of Waterford without success. Thence to Scotland, where James IV received him with full honours and gave him a high-born Scottish lady for a wife. After a year's delay James marched with a small army across the border in support of Warbeck, but was easily driven back.

Warbeck then moved back to Ireland and managed to raise a few men. With these he decided to land in Cornwall, where a formidable rebellion had broken out because of Henry's taxes for the Scottish war. (In those days the Cornish spoke a language much like Welsh and did not think of themselves as Englishmen.)

What was making things particularly difficult for Henry's enemies was his small but efficient fleet. A squadron sailed up the east coast to supply Surrey's army, attacking James IV. Another squadron watched the route from Southern Ireland to Cornwall. Thus the ship which was carrying Warbeck across was actually boarded by an English ship and searched. But its master hid Warbeck in a cask and he was not found. So he got through to Cornwall.

Within ten days of landing, Warbeck had an army of 8000 men, so great was the discontent of the Cornish; but, when the King's army approached in overwhelming strength, the Pretender lost heart, deserted his army and fled to the coast; but all the ports were guarded and he had to give himself up (1497). Henry treated him reasonably kindly, and kept him in not-too-rigorous confinement. But two years later he tried to escape and he was hanged by the King's order. The young Duke of Warwick, now grown to manhood, whose life, Henry believed, was a threat to himself, was likewise executed, after having been trapped into plotting with Warbeck in the Tower. Henry was not the man to make Richard III's mistake and gain the reputation of child-murder. The execution of this innocent young earl, even after a public trial in Westminster Hall, is a blot on Henry's record. Perhaps it was necessary. At any rate it seems to have caused a struggle in Henry's mind, for someone who saw him in the spring of 1499 wrote that he had aged twenty years in a fortnight.

The Cornish rebellion ended in failure. Led by a blacksmith and a lawyer, the rebels marched to the outskirts of London, but they were there defeated by a royal army.

Throughout the Warbeck troubles Ferdinand of Spain had been a good friend to Henry. The reason for this was that Charles VIII's invasion of Italy in 1494 had greatly alarmed Ferdinand. He had been one of the main members of the Holy League (formed in 1495) to drive the French out of Italy. (Its others members were the Pope, the Emperor, Venice and Milan.) Ferdinand feared that Henry would be enticed into an alliance with France. He therefore concluded a new and strong agreement with Henry, confirming the marriage alliance between Arthur and Catherine originally arranged at Medina del Campo. He also persuaded Maximilian to abandon Warbeck, with the result that trade between Flanders and England was resumed early in 1496. (Bacon calls the treaty the *Intercursus Magnus*.) Thirdly, he brought pressure to bear on James IV of Scotland to persuade him to give up supporting Warbeck. Truly, the English-French accord at Etaples had alarmed France's enemies.

The capture of Warbeck in 1497 marked the end of any serious Yorkist threat. But Henry had not achieved this result only by the use of force. It was part of his policy to try to conciliate the Yorkists by kindness. We have already seen that he pardoned the Earl of Surrey, restored his lands and gave him high office. In 1495, after the failure of Warbeck's landing at Deal, many other Yorkists had their attainders reversed by Parliament. Few of the Cornish rebels were executed—Henry preferred to fine them. Thus, he won over many hitherto discontented men. Few will rebel when life under their king is reasonably comfortable.

The Parliament of 1495 also passed the De Facto Act. This stated that 'service to an overthrown king was not treasonable, even if he had not rightly been king. Its object was to reassure former servants of Richard III that Henry did not harbour designs against them.'*

Ireland

In theory Ireland belonged to the English crown. But, with the exception of the Pale (a coastal strip round Dublin about fifty miles long and twenty miles wide) and a few coastal towns which traded with England, Ireland in fact followed its own feudal lords and chieftains. In the north and

* See R. L. Storey, *op. cit.*, p. 83.

west these were wild Celtic tribal leaders, but in the south and east they
were the 'Anglo-Irish lords', descendants of Norman barons who had
conquered Irish lands back in the twelfth and thirteenth centuries. The
greatest of the Anglo-Irish lords were the earls of Kildare, Desmond and
Ormond, who between them owned almost the whole of Leinster and
Munster.

By the latter part of Edward IV's reign Kildare had become easily
the most powerful of these three, and, aided by the Irish Parliament (a

body which represented only the county of Leinster and a few towns), the Anglo-Irish lords had been able to defy the English government and establish what was virtually Home Rule.

Henry's legacy in Ireland then was a difficult one. Gerald, eighth Earl of Kildare (known to the Irish as Garret More) was 'the real King of Ireland' with the title of Justiciar accorded him by the Irish Council, though John de la Pole, Earl of Lincoln, had been Richard III's last legal Lieutenant of Ireland.*

The Battle of Bosworth of course presented Kildare with new problems. Yorkist rule had suited him well and Henry Tudor was an unknown quantity. He therefore supported Lambert Simnel's rebellion, had Simnel crowned in Dublin as King Edward VI of England and Ireland (using a golden circlet taken from a statue of the Blessed Virgin), and supplied troops for the Earl of Lincoln's ill-fated invasion of England which came to an end at the Battle of Stoke.

Henry, as usual, moved cautiously. He pardoned Kildare and left him in power in Ireland with the title of Lord Deputy. Consequently in 1491, when Warbeck appeared in Ireland, Kildare was not one of the several Anglo-Irish lords who supported him. Nevertheless Henry felt it was time to take firm action. In 1492 he removed Kildare from his post as Lord Deputy, substituting first an Irish archbishop and then, when he was unable to cope, Lord Gormanston. The latter persuaded Kildare to visit England, which he had hitherto refused to do.

By 1494 then Henry had taken his measure of Kildare and formulated a new policy. This was to appoint his baby son Henry as Lieutenant and to send over one of his most trusted ministers, Sir Edward Poynings, as Deputy. About seven hundred men, equipped with muskets and artillery, were to back him.

Poynings arrived in Ireland in October 1494, accompanied by Kildare. His orders were to re-establish English rule there. He summoned a Parliament at Drogheda and, while awaiting its meeting, set off to punish a rebellion in Ulster in which Kildare was, in some obscure way, involved. Then he returned to Drogheda to meet the Parliament.

By a mixture of threats and bribes Poynings persuaded this Irish Parliament to pass a number of laws known to historians as Poynings' Laws. The importance of these has been much exaggerated by eighteenth-century politicians and historians. The first of them simply stated that 'all statutes lately made in England for the public good of the same should be deemed good and effective in law and be ... executed in Ireland.' Since this was already accepted law (however badly enforced), the act did no more than emphasize the *status quo*. The second of Poynings' Laws said that no Parliament was to be held in Ireland until the King and his Council had been informed why it was being summoned and what acts it intended to pass. This was an attempt to end the Wars of the

---

* I am indebted for much of this material to the Methuen paperback *A History of Ireland* by Edmund Curtis, Methuen, 1950.

Roses in Ireland by making sure that no Irish Parliament gave support to an illegitimate king. Only much later was it interpreted as an attempt to subordinate the Irish Parliament completely to the English Crown.*

One of the last acts of the Drogheda Parliament was to attaint Kildare, who was already under arrest for helping the Ulster rebellion. He was shipped off to the Tower of London. This no doubt 'mightily impressed the Irish'.

While Kildare was in England (1495–1496) Henry established friendly relations with him, provided him with a wife in the person of his second cousin, Elizabeth St John, and finally had his attainder reversed by the English Parliament of 1496.

Early in 1496 Poynings was withdrawn from Ireland. His rule had been expensive and difficult to maintain. Whether or not the story is true that Henry said of Kildare, 'Since all Ireland cannot rule this man, this man must rule all Ireland,' the fact remains that the Earl was now appointed Deputy and returned to Ireland to rule it for the rest of his life. The move was probably a wise one on Henry's part. It ended the Wars of the Roses in Ireland, for when Warbeck reappeared at Cork in 1497, he got no support. Kildare carefully followed the procedure of Poynings' Law when calling his first Parliament in 1498. Henceforth he ruled, not, as he had before, as a rebel or semi-rebel, but with Henry VII's full approval and support. It is true that the 'wild Irish' in the north and west still owned one third of the land, but they had never threatened the English Pale and could be disregarded. The three great Anglo-Irish families, the Kildares, Desmonds and Ormonds, had ceased to be threatening. It was about as much as Henry could hope to achieve under the circumstances.

As for 'Garret More', 'he marched over more of Ireland than any viceroy had done for generations, bringing local chiefs into vassalage, securing the succession of the O'Neill or the O'Kelly he favoured, and blowing down with the royal artillery the castles of private opponents.'†
Henry VIII kept him on as Deputy and in 1513 he died in a petty skirmish, while he was trying one of his new guns on a chief who had dared to defy him.

* See S. B. Chrimes, *op. cit.*, pp. 267–268.
† Edmund Curtis, *op. cit.*, p. 154.

2 Henry VII. His Policies and Methods of Government

Trade

Henry VII has been credited with being a 'mercantilist' in his economic policy, that is to say with having built up English trade with the specific object of making the country strong. In fact, in this as in everything else, he was an opportunist and had no far-reaching policy. Thus his famous Navigation Acts of 1486 and 1489, stating that the Gascon wine trade must be carried in 'English, Irish or Welsh ships, with mariners of the same complexion or men of Calais' originated as a petition from the House of Commons. It was probably a petition from Bristol in 1486 which influenced Henry to make a treaty with Denmark in 1490, allowing English merchants to trade in Iceland. It was a petition from the Commons which caused him to put pressure on Venice in 1491 to try and break her virtual monopoly of the carrying trade with the Eastern Mediterranean; Venetian galleys came to Southampton annually, loaded with spices, wines and dried fruits and returned with wool and woollen cloth for northern Italy. There is nothing new in all this. The House of Commons with over 200 burgesses had a long record of promoting statutes to safeguard English economic interests. The point is the King moved as opportunity prompted him.

Undoubtedly overseas trade did increase in Henry's reign, but how far this can be attributed to actions taken by the government is a matter for doubt. Cloth exports are known to have increased by about sixty per cent (while wool exports declined by thirty per cent 'gradually killed by heavy taxation and the demands of the home cloth industry'). Imports likewise grew by about fifty per cent or more. But there is evidence that the expansion of trade began ten years before Henry began to rule, and Edward IV's government had also been responsive to the demands of merchants.

Henry's paramount aims were peace and security, and he sacrificed trade to dynastic or strategic interests on several occasions. One example is his breaking off of the valuable Netherlands trade in 1493 to bring pressure to bear against Perkin Warbeck's supporters. Another is his treatment of the powerful Hanseatic League of German cities in the Baltic. The Hansards had helped to restore Edward IV in 1471 and had received valuable trading privileges from him, privileges which gave them advantages over native English merchants. Henry knew their power and treated them with kid gloves. He did at first, however, make some attempt to whittle away their privileges, but in 1504 he reversed this policy and got Parliament to pass an act restoring to them all their

30

old privileges. The probable reason was his fear that they might again favour the cause of the White Rose and help the Earl of Suffolk to invade as once they had helped his grandfather.

It was to the King's interest that overseas trade should increase, for he derived revenue from the customs. With this in mind no doubt he backed John Cabot, a Genoese of Venetian citizenship, when he came to England in 1495 to enlist support for the project of reaching Asia by sailing westward (already some Bristol merchants are thought to have discovered Newfoundland and opened up fishing grounds there). Henry issued letters patent allowing Cabot to take five ships on a voyage of discovery. In the end one ship went in 1497 and Cabot found land (where precisely we do not know) and became famous. A year later he set out again, but was lost without trace. Henry was interested enough to back Cabot's son, Sebastian, who set off westward in 1508 and may have discovered Hudson Strait and part of Hudson Bay, returning after Henry's death.*

Henry's finance

Finance was a subject which 'next to his life, throne and dynasty, lay nearest to Henry VII's heart'. We have no need to modify Bacon's statement that 'of nature assuredly he coveted to accumulate treasure'.

Customs duties have already been mentioned. They consisted of a duty on the export of wool, and 'tunnage and poundage' (duties on wine, cloth, corn, wax, spices etc. both when exported or imported). Both these were granted to Henry for life by his first Parliament, following the usual precedent. Henry could not do much to increase them, apart from encouraging trade. Customs brought him in annually about £33,000 at the beginning of his reign and £40,000 towards the end of it.

Henry did not rely much on Parliamentary grants (known as 'fifteenths and tenths'). He got two in 1487 after the Battle of Stoke, two in 1491–1492, when war with France was impending, and three more in 1497 when war with Scotland was impending (these last caused the Cornish revolt). Each fifteenth and tenth brought him in about £31,000 and the method of collection was so stereotyped that it did not increase as the country's wealth increased. As the reign went on and his finances improved, Henry came to ask Parliament less and less for grants and relied instead on other methods of taxation.

Henry's foreign policy was sometimes remunerative. The Treaty of Etaples for instance brought him in the handsome sum of £159,000.

A 'benevolence' (a sort of forced gift from rich individuals) in 1491 brought him in £48,000, but was difficult to collect and was never used by him again.

Profits of justice (fines) undoubtedly brought him a fairly large annual sum, but we do not know how much.

Crown lands were a good source of revenue, as Henry inherited lands

* See S. B. Chrimes, *op. cit.*, pp. 228–230.

from all sides. The earldoms of March and Warwick, which had belonged to the Yorkist kings, fell to him after the battle of Bosworth. The inheritance of Lancaster was his as was the duchy of Richmond, while as king he automatically held the revenues of the royal duchy of Cornwall and the earldom of Chester.

For the first year or two of his reign he reverted to Lancastrian methods of collecting land rents through the Exchequer. But these were cumbersome and inefficient and from 1487 onwards he managed his lands well, using Yorkist methods of collection and getting the rents paid to the Treasurer of the King's Chamber. As a result land revenues, which had been about £24,000 a year under Richard III, rose to £42,000 at the end of Henry's reign (though this sum includes the revenue of the Prince of Wales, who was still a minor).

The revenue from none of these sources could easily be increased. It was in the sphere of prerogative feudal rights that Henry found most opportunity to exploit his subjects to his own advantage since so many rights and privileges and so many powers of the monarchy were undefined. Feudal dues were owed to the king on certain occasions by tenants-in-chief (men or women holding land direct from the king under the feudal system). For instance, on taking over land from his father, an heir paid 'relief' to the king. If an heir was a minor, he owed 'wardship', and the land came into the king's hands until the owner came of age. If the heir was a woman, her hand in marriage could be disposed of by the king.

Such dues had long been accepted as lawful, but Henry found ways of increasing them. Early in his reign commissions of enquiry were set up to go into the matter. Lawyers and officials were to set to work to get every penny obtainable. For one thing the number of people rated as tenants-in-chief could be (and was) increased. The Council Learned in the Law, a sort of committee of the Council, became responsible for collecting debts in this field. Its members, of whom Empson and Dudley were the most prominent, kept within the framework of the law, but, where there was any doubt what the law was, they became adept at resolving it in the king's favour. Thus, as the reign proceeded, larger and larger sums were collected from this source—rising from about £11,000 a year in 1492 to £40,000 a year in the last three years of the reign. The King took a great interest in the Chamber accounts, and audited them himself. His signature or sign manual appears on every page, sometimes five or six times.

Empson and Dudley were also concerned in enforcing bonds and recognizances. These were bargains struck with wealthy law-breakers in which they pledged large sums as a guarantee of future good behaviour. Bonds were not only a rich source of income for Henry, but also an instrument for enforcing the law. Through them he made powerful, aristocratic families 'toe the line' and obey his laws. Bonds were secret things, signed in private, and their use was probably an easy way of supplementing the creaking machinery of the common law and conciliar courts. They were extensively used. Recent research has shown that 'out of sixty-two peerage families in existence between 1485 and 1509 a total of forty-six ... were for some part of Henry's reign at the king's mercy. ... The system was so extensive that it must have created an atmosphere of chronic watchfulness and fear.' * Moreover, it was by no means only members of the peerage who were put on good behaviour by this method.

Henry's rapacity seems to have increased after 1502, and many historians believe that there would have been rebellion if he had ruled five or six years longer. Certainly he left the royal coffers full of jewels and plate. Foreign ambassadors remark upon his wealth from 1497 onwards. We can reckon his gross annual revenue at the last period of his reign at about £113,000, and probably something like double this amount was left in jewels and plate to his son and heir.

The King's Council

Here again so many misconceptions have arisen about Henry VII's Council that we need to say first what was *not* true about it. 'It has often been said about Henry VII that he broke the lords' domination of royal councils and preferred the services of men of humbler origin, whom he could more easily curb.'† In fact about a quarter of Henry's Council was composed of peers, a proportion about the same as that in Edward IV's council. Another quarter consisted of bishops and abbots.

There were about 140 councillors at any one time and as many as forty might meet at once. Usually, however, a small inner ring of about seven met, forming a sort of working council which included the Lord Chancellor, the Treasurer and (if he was not following the king around elsewhere) the Keeper of the Privy Seal. The king presided over Council meetings if they were important ones. If he was in progress away from Westminster, he took a number of councillors with him.

Usually the Chancellor presided if the king was not present, but Archbishop Morton, who had been Chancellor since 1486, was an old man approaching eighty in 1497 and from that date onwards we hear of a President of the Council, a man appointed to preside when Morton was not available.

Much has been written by historians of the reign about offshoots of the Council in the North and in Wales. But the later Tudor Council of the North did not exist in Henry VII's reign. Henry had a Warden of the March in the north—until his murder in 1489 the office was held by the Earl of Northumberland; after that it was held by Thomas Howard, Earl of Surrey. The Warden appointed his own councillors and his own president of his council.

Likewise a council was set up to govern the Principality of Wales soon

* Professor J. R. Lander's article, *Bonds, Coercion and Fear: Henry VII and the Peerage*, University of Toronto Press, 1971.
† R. L. Storey, *op. cit.*, p. 94.

after a Prince of Wales (Arthur) had been created in 1489. As the prince was a child of three, his great-uncle Jasper Tudor presided over it. This council sat at Ludlow and had a precedent in Edward IV's council which had been set up to 'advise' his baby son Edward in 1473. Just as Prince Edward's council had extended its jurisdiction beyond the principality to the English Marches and the Crown Lordships, so did Prince Arthur's council extend its jurisdiction to the same areas, and the time would come (but not in Henry VII's reign) when there would be a Council in the Marches of Wales which would be an offshoot of the King's Council. But as yet it was the Prince of Wales' council, although it continued to exist under a president in the years between Arthur's death in 1502 and the creation of Henry as Prince of Wales in 1504.

Conciliar jurisdiction

'The King's Council was not only an advisory and executive body; it was also a court of law.' In fact it was the oldest law court in the realm, for originally the Anglo-Norman kings had dispensed justice with their advisers in attendance (only later did they delegate their judicial powers to judges). As a court it might sit in a chamber in Westminster Palace which had a blue ceiling decorated with stars, or it might sit elsewhere. There was then no Star Chamber Court as such at this time. There was only a place called Star Chamber where the Council often sat.

The Council's jurisdiction was not primarily criminal. It dealt just as often with civil disputes (disputes between two or more private persons). When it did deal with criminal matters, they did not extend to felony and treason.

Cases which came before the Council originated as petitions from private persons. The Council could proceed by methods not available to the common law courts. It could proceed without a jury and in secret (at least until judgment was given). It could examine defendants on oath. But the picture we have from Bacon of a ruthless chamber, dragging magnates before it and fining them huge sums, is quite false. The Council in Star Chamber or elsewhere was not used as an instrument of government coercion. It was used for the benefit of aggrieved suitors. As far as we know its fines were quite moderate and it only imprisoned until the fine was paid.

A group of councillors, 'including among themselves a high proportion of persons "learned in the law", attracted to themselves the occasional label of "the Council Learned"'.* They were not a committee of the Council; they were just 'a part of the King's Council who habitually gave their attention to particular tasks'. We know a little about the Council Learned because some of its records have survived 'among the archives of the Duchy of Lancaster, of which Sir Reginald Bray, a leading member of the Council Learned was Chancellor. Nothing is known

* See S. B. Chrimes, *op. cit.*, p. 99.

about its activities before 1500, and it disappeared in 1509', probably because of the odium in which it came to be held. For the Council Learned acted as a royal debt-collecting agency as well as a court. That notorious pair, Empson and Dudley, were both members of it. Unlike the Council in Star Chamber, most of the cases heard by the Council Learned were initiated by the government.

Henry VII's Council often dealt with poor men's cases or 'requests'. It was the councillors attendant on the king who did this. As yet the group of councillors who specialized in this sort of business was not called the Court of Requests, a title which only appears after Wolsey's time. The Yorkist kings had a similar arrangement. In fact Richard III appointed a clerk to take charge of poor men's requests.

In 1487, at the time of Lambert Simnel's rebellion, an act was passed to set up a special tribunal composed of the Chancellor, the Treasurer, the Lord Privy Seal (or any two of them), a bishop, a councillor and two judges, which would have powers to proceed against 'maintenance, retaining, embracery, corrupt practices in the conduct of juries and rioting'. We do not know what this special tribunal achieved, though we do know it functioned for quite a number of years. In the later sixteenth century some clerk scrawled in the margin of the statute setting it up the words, 'pro camera stellata', which has confused generations of historians, causing them to think that the court thus set up was Star Chamber. In fact it was a special tribunal quite separate from the King's Council.

Foreign policy

Henry's foreign policy can be divided into three distinct periods.* The first, 1485–1492, comes to an end at the Treaty of Etaples, and has already been dealt with under the heading 'Interference abroad' in the last chapter. The second and most successful period is from 1493 to 1503, when he was free of all threat from France since she was engaged upon her invasions of Italy. This phase has been partially dealt with in the section of the last chapter headed, 'Perkin Warbeck', but it needs further consideration here.

Scotland is vital to the story. By tradition she was the friend of France and the enemy of England. We have seen that James IV gave help to Warbeck. A Scottish army crossed the border in his support in the autumn of 1496, but retreated hastily when an English army drew near. Henry wanted peace not war with Scotland and as early as 1495 he was proposing the marriage of his elder daughter, Margaret, to the King of Scotland. In 1497 the Treaty of Ayton was made between the two countries and peace was established. (It was the first treaty of peace made between England and Scotland since 1328.)

But Henry wanted something more lasting and in 1502 a marriage

* See S. B. Chrimes, *op. cit.*, Chapter 15, to which I am much indebted.

treaty between Margaret and James IV was eventually signed. A year later the marriage took place.

This treaty brought peace at last to the restless border. For the rest of his reign Henry had no more trouble from Scotland. No one could have foreseen at the time that the marriage of Margaret and James would eventually lead to the union of the two countries (for Margaret was not heir to the English throne), but so it came about. Thus the 'marriage of the thistle and the rose' turned out to be not the least of Henry's achievements.

To this second period also belongs the commercial treaty with the Netherlands in 1496, known as the Intercursus Magnus (see the section of the last chapter headed 'Perkin Warbeck') and the treaty with Spain in 1499 which confirmed the betrothal of Arthur and Catherine first made at Medina del Campo back in 1492. Catherine arrived in England in October 1501 and was married to Arthur amidst great jubilation and pageantry a month later. Alas, rejoicing soon turned into sorrow, for within five months of his marriage Arthur was dead. Ferdinand and Isabella then proposed that the sixteen-year-old widow should be betrothed to Arthur's younger brother, Henry, now heir to the throne and only eleven years old. The treaty arranging this was formally signed in 1503, but a dispensation had to be obtained from the Pope, for by canon law it was illegal for a man to marry his brother's widow. This dispensation was granted, and the marriage eventually took place after the death of Henry VII, when the boy had become king as Henry VIII.

Throughout this second period there was constant pressure on Henry from his ally Ferdinand to join the Holy League, formed to drive the French out of Italy. He did join it, in 1496, but only as an associate and managed to remain friendly with France at the same time and even make a commercial treaty with her the following year. Moreover, when Charles VIII died in 1498, Henry established friendly relations with the new king, Louis XII. Henry's steadfast refusal to go to war with France after 1492 was one of the wisest parts of his foreign policy, and one which his son Henry VIII would have done well to emulate. It was of course a necessary corollary of his Scottish alliance.

The third phase of Henry's foreign policy begins in 1503 and extends to the end of the reign. In this period two deaths greatly altered the European situation. The first was that of his beloved wife, Elizabeth of York, who died in childbirth in 1503. This left Henry free to marry again (he was only forty-six) and the sovereigns of Europe were eager enough to secure his friendship by this means. Ferdinand suggested his niece, the widowed Queen Joan of Naples, and Henry investigated the proposition very thoroughly before he rejected it. Louis of France suggested his niece, Margaret of Angoulême. But it was Maximilian's offer of his daughter, Margaret, widow of the Duke of Savoy and effective governor of the Netherlands, which really attracted Henry. Unfortunately, the lady rejected him, and in fact Henry never married a second time.

The second death which altered Henry's policies was that of Isabella

THE ANGLO-HABSBURG CONNECTION

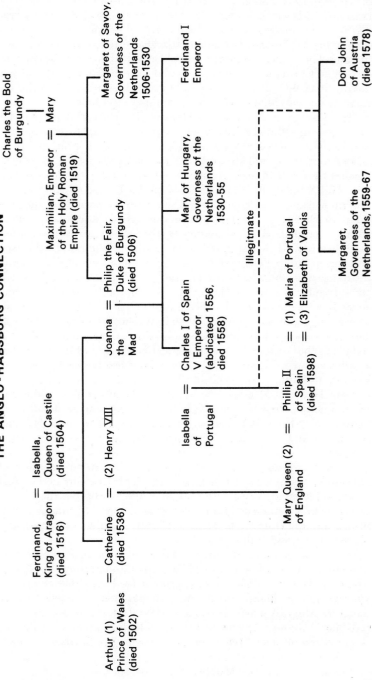

37

of Castile in 1504. She left as heir her daughter, Joanna, who was already married to Maximilian's son, the Archduke Philip of the Netherlands. The question now was whether Joanna would become Queen of Castile or whether Ferdinand, her father, would control all Spain during his lifetime. The matter was further complicated by Ferdinand's remarriage in 1506 to Germaine de Foix, Louis XII's niece (Ferdinand and Louis having first concluded a treaty of alliance at Blois in 1505). If this marriage produced children all sorts of results would follow.

Here was a difficult choice for Henry. Hitherto Ferdinand had been his closest ally. But the Netherlands were important to English trade, and Henry at once decided to back Joanna against her father. He proceeded to make several large monetary loans to Philip and Maximilian. Then early in 1506 he had an opportunity to establish still closer relations with Philip, for Philip and Joanna set out for Castile to claim Joanna's inheritance and their small fleet was forced by storms to put into Weymouth harbour and was unable to proceed. Henry at once invited them to Windsor and fêted them lavishly. By the time Philip left three months later the two rulers had signed the secret treaty of Windsor. By this Henry recognized Philip as King of Castile and both princes promised mutual assistance and not to countenance the rebels of the other. This led to the surrender of Edmund de la Pole, Earl of Suffolk, Yorkist claimant to the English throne, who had fled from England in 1501 and attempted to get support first from Maximilian and then from Philip. Philip had hitherto refused to give him up. Now he was despatched to England and lodged in the Tower where he remained for the rest of the reign, being finally executed by Henri VIII, who did not feel bound by his father's promise to Philip to spare his life.

'The Treaty of Windsor countered the Treaty of Blois (which Ferdinand had made with Louis XII) and the realignment of Europe was completed.'* Henry VII had now aligned himself with the Habsburgs in Spain (i.e. Joanna and Philip) against the schemes of Ferdinand of Aragon.

Before Philip embarked from Falmouth to continue his journey he authorized his agents to conclude with Henry a commercial treaty, which so favoured the English that, according to Bacon, the Flemings called it the Intercursus Malus. This treaty, however, was never confirmed and the Intercursus Magnus of 1496 continued to regulate the Netherlands trade with England.

Within six months of signing the Treaty of Windsor Philip had died. Once more Maximilian controlled the Netherlands through his daughter Margaret. In 1506 Maximilian had proposed to Henry that his grandson Charles, son of Philip and Joanna, should marry Henry's younger daughter Mary. A marriage treaty to this effect was drawn up in 1508, but Mary was only eleven when Henry VII died, and in fact this marriage never took place. Henry also had a scheme (scotched by Ferdinand)

* See *Catherine of Aragon* by G. Mattingly, Cape, 1942, pp. 67–8.

that he himself should marry Philip's widow, the supposedly mad Joanna.

The last phase of Henry's diplomacy then was one of mounting hostility to Ferdinand (with his new French alliance) and increased friendship with the Habsburg family ruling the Netherlands. One may ask under these circumstances why he continued to keep in being the betrothal of his son Henry to Catherine of Aragon. The answer is that he very nearly broke it off. From 1506 onwards the young widow, who was still living in England, was badly treated. Her allowance was stopped and she was forced to live in inferior accommodation. There were plans to marry Prince Henry to Eleanor, the Archduke Charles's sister. Only right at the end of his life did Henry VII relent and begin to treat Catherine better, and there may be truth in the story which Henry VIII told to Margaret of Savoy that it was his father's death-bed wish that the long-arranged marriage should take place.

Perhaps the most notable feature of Henry VII's foreign policy was his refusal, as his financial and domestic situation improved, to squander everything upon glorious enterprises. Peace with France and peace with Scotland (the two old enemies), these were no mean achievements. Henry became respected in Europe. He worked his ambassadors hard and was thorough in investigating the probable consequences of every step he took. He made himself an expert on European affairs. He kept friendly with three successive popes, yet did nothing to help the two later ones drive the French out of Italy. His close friendship with the rulers of the Netherlands fostered the wool trade. He gave as good as he got when dealing with the foxy Ferdinand. When he died in 1509 England's position in Europe was solid and secure.

Parliament

Henry summoned seven parliaments during his reign. He could not do without parliaments, because he needed them for money grants (and every one of his parliaments made some sort of financial contribution), and because he needed them to pass acts of attainder and acts of restitution for those previously attainted, the judges having decided that an attainder without consent of the Commons was invalid. But none of his parliaments passed any statutes of major importance. In fact his parliaments were not notable for their legislative activity. When he dismissed the last one in 1504, he stated that 'he was not minded for the ease of his subjects to summon another for a long time without great and necessary and urgent causes'.

But quite often (five or six times in fact) the Lords (what we would call the House of Lords) were summoned without the Commons. This was done usually in an emergency, such as a time of rebellion, when there was not time to call a full parliament. These Great Councils, as they were called, attended by the Lords spiritual and temporal, often authorized the imposition of financial aid in advance of a parliamentary

39

grant. It was a Great Council of 1491 which authorized the war with France and the exaction of a benevolence to pay for it. Another Great Council in 1496 considered the threat of an invasion by Scotland and granted a loan to deal with it.

As far as we know no changes occurred during Henry's reign in the constitution of the Commons. 'Electoral arrangements continued ... as they had been during the preceding generation. The constituencies remained the same; no new parliamentary boroughs were created.'* This most conservative of kings was content to leave things unaltered, except when change was desperately needed.

Nor did the constitution of the Lords change. The twenty-one archbishops and bishops continued to be summoned. So did the twenty-seven abbots and priors. The temporal lords were hardly increased at all in number. Thirty-four were summoned to the first Parliament and forty-three to the last, but this increase of nine was made up, in all but two cases, of old baronies and viscounties revived. Henry did not think of rewarding his most distinguished and faithful servants with 'peerages' as later kings did. Instead he gave them the Garter, besides, of course, the tangible rewards of lands and offices.

The Church

Henry's relations with the Church and the papacy were uneventful. He kept on good terms with the three popes with whom he had to deal, was at least outwardly very pious, and appointed bishops, as previous kings had done, for political reasons. Several of his bishops served on his council and Archbishop Morton was made a Cardinal at his request. Nothing in his reign foreshadowed the great clash with the papacy which was to come in Henry VIII's reign.

Law and order

Here again we have to deal with a myth—the idea propagated by Bacon and his followers that Henry VII in some magical way brought law and order to a country hitherto riotous and unruly. Certainly Henry VII's government paid great attention to law and order, and certainly it had some success. But the Yorkist kings had also given the matter much attention and achieved success. The point is that Henry VII's achievements in this sphere were not as spectacular as has been thought hitherto.

By 1485 the feudal courts, the courts of the great lords, had become of minor importance. Sheriff's courts had likewise declined. The task of maintaining law and order rested mainly with the Justices of the Peace. There were about two thousand of these in the country. The office had been started back in 1361 and a statute of 1439 decreed that all JPs should hold land worth £20 a year. They were unpaid and were appointed each

* See S. B. Chrimes, *op. cit.*, p. 144.

40

year by the Lord Chancellor (as they are today). The fact that they were unpaid made them somewhat less prompt in obedience to the government than, say, the paid officials of Spain. They were inclined not to enforce laws, such as the enclosure acts, of which they disapproved. But it was an honour to be a JP, and a country gentleman would lose his status in county society if his name were removed from the list at the annual review. This gave the government a good deal of control.

The Yorkist kings had both passed statutes increasing the powers of JPs. Henry likewise realized their importance. No less than twenty-one of his total of 192 statutes made some reference to them. Here they were instructed in their manifold duties, which were to include 'enquiring into damnable bargains grounded in usury ...; of hearing and determining faults in weights and measures; of hearing complaints against collectors of fifteenths and tenths; of punishing keepers of houses for dicing and other unlawful games and regulating ale-houses ...; of assessing subsidies ...; of enquiring into the destruction of deer and herons', and so on.

Five acts of the reign 'referred to the duties of JPs in regard to riots, unlawful retainers and the extortions of sheriffs', and one act made it quite clear that the government was aware of the shortcomings of JPs, and attempted to lay down remedies.

JPs in Tudor times had administrative duties as well as judicial ones. They were responsible for the upkeep of roads and bridges and for keeping the watch. In fact they did many of the things now done by county councils.

How successful then was Henry's government in enforcing the law? Professor Chrimes thinks it 'difficult to find' that it attained 'any marked success'.* This, he thinks was because people in high positions (including the King) were not very interested in law enforcement except where it gave them some financial advantage. Often corruption and the abuse of the law worked to the advantage of such people. So they allowed it. Abuses, such as maintenance, the corruption of juries, embracery, the giving of liveries and keeping of retainers, continued to be legislated against right up to the last parliament of the reign. Obviously then they had not been cured, despite the setting up of a special tribunal to deal with them in 1487 (see p. 35).

Four statutes of the reign attempted to deal with the abuse of retaining. But the Crown did not often prosecute, and 'it can hardly be said that Henry VII sought to abolish the practice of retaining. On the contrary he clearly wished to preserve it, but so far as possible only so that he himself got the benefit of it for his own purposes.'

As already explained in the Introduction, retainers were useful in repelling invaders and putting down rebellion. It was considered 'proper that a noble should be attended by a company of men of respectable social status and sartorial appearance.'† In fact royal policy was a

* See S. B. Chrimes, *op. cit.*, Chapter 10. Other quotations in this section are also from it.
† See R. L. Storey, *op. cit.*, p. 152.

mixture of 'connivance and restraint'. Lords were allowed to keep retainers but were expected to keep them in order.

In 1468 Edward IV had passed a statute forbidding retaining, but he appears to have made no attempt to enforce it, and in any case the definition of retaining in it was so vague that the courts were unable to convict under it.

Henry VII passed four statutes against retaining, culminating in the famous statute of 1504 forbidding the giving of livery or the retaining of persons 'other than menial servants, officers or men of law'. But there were few prosecutions under any of these acts. Discounting Bacon's story about the Earl of Oxford, which is almost certainly false, the only peer prosecuted was George Neville, Lord Bergavenny, who had been implicated in the Cornish rebellion. In 1507 he was prosecuted before King's Bench for having retained 471 men, mostly yeomen 'from four score towns and villages in mid-Kent'. Bergavenny pleaded guilty and was fined £70,000. But this was just a way of 'drawing his teeth'. In other parts of the country retaining seems to have continued. The King could not do without it. Later Tudors also allowed it.

Recent research, as yet unpublished,* shows that after 1500 law enforcement was improved but mainly in the sphere of foreign trade and customs duties where it was of obvious financial advantage to the King to prosecute. Otherwise Henry's record of law enforcement was 'relatively unimpressive'. So much for the legend of the king who restored order after the chaos of previous reigns!

Nevertheless, taken over all, one is bound to feel that Henry VII's record of kingship is impressive. The fact that Bacon and other historians have exaggerated it, should not blind us to its real worth. Henry was a king who tried to do the job—honestly and patiently. He did not underrate the difficulty of the task. Certainly many things helped him—the temporary weakness of the baronage, France's preoccupation with Italy, the stability of the currency in an age of growing prosperity— but great men are entitled to their share of luck. What is impressive is that Henry VII never neglected his opportunities. Instead he improved them. He was never afraid of hard work and there is a notable absence in his reign of the follies of his son. No war was fought simply for glory. No minister who had served him well was ever cast headlong to ruin. No woman ever made him her tool. Bacon's verdict must, I think, stand. He was 'a wonder for wise men'.

* By Professor Guth of Michigan University, quoted by S. B. Chrimes, *op. cit.*, p. 192.

3 The Renaissance and the Influence of Erasmus

The Renaissance in Italy

It is impossible to understand the reign of Henry VIII without knowing something of the great upheaval in thought which scholars have come to call the Renaissance. This great awakening began in Italy, where a rich, urban society, sophisticated and leisured, had time and energy to question the teachings of medieval theologians and philosophers whose ideas had for centuries moulded the thoughts of men.

Medieval theology, like all theology, had been an attempt to reconcile faith and reason. It had reached its height in the writings of the Dominican friar, Thomas Aquinas, in the thirteenth century. Using new and accurate translations from the Greek, Aquinas managed to reconcile the philosophy of Aristotle (then newly discovered) with the teachings of the Church.

Aquinas' universe was God-centred. He began with God and His plan, and fitted everything neatly in. The discovery of Aristotle's writings did not shake his (or anyone else's) faith in the teachings of the Church. 'In that age it was not expected of a philosopher that he should approach the accepted doctrines of the Church with an open mind.'*

The Middle Ages, though steeped in Latin, had neglected Greek, 'the key to the most original and valuable portion of the ancient culture'. Even their Latin had become barbaric and stereotyped. The Bible was only read in an edition known as the Vulgate, which was not of the highest quality. Monks and clerics discoursed in Latin, laws and treaties were made in Latin, scholars used Latin,—but not Latin which would have been acceptable to the finest classical writers, in fact a Latin which was crude and oversimplified.

In the fourteenth century, however, many Italian scholars became interested in the study of the great Latin classics. Manuscripts which had long been lying on monastery shelves, gathering dust, were taken down and read. People got excited about the new ideas they found in Virgil, Horace and Cicero. They began to write in an elegant style themselves, not only in Latin, but often in the vernacular as well. In Italy we have Petrarch, the author of charming sonnets, and Boccaccio, the inventor of the short story. Both wrote in Italian as well as Latin. Both were humanists, that is to say their universe was man-centred. They did not write about heaven and hell and the human soul, as had the poet, Dante, in the late thirteenth century. They wrote about human beings, people with failings and hopes and fears—frail but loveable and real.

* This quotation is from H. A. L. Fisher's *A History of Europe*, Eyre & Spottiswoode, 1935; Chapter 37.

Medieval popular literature was chiefly about knights rescuing fair maidens from dragons and following impossible ideals. The Arthurian legend, originating in Wales and Brittany, and the Song of Roland, celebrating the death of one of Charlemagne's knights, slain fighting the Saracens in Spain, were typical. Boccaccio on the other hand told saucy little stories about priests who seduced other men's wives, and he filled them with all the colour and movement of contemporary Italy.

Humanism also prevailed among the painters and sculptors of Italy. The typical painting of the thirteenth century would show a virgin and child, both with halos round their heads, angels with wings, a golden glow at the top, indicating heaven, and marble steps at the bottom for the figures to stand upon. The faces of the Virgin and any other characters would be very cold and ethereal and unlike those of any human beings ever known.

Contrast this with pictures of Botticelli (died 1510). His Virgins were warm-blooded Italian girls whom he had actually known (and indeed he used them as models). The sky would be blue, with clouds and a bird or two flying across it, while the grassy foreground would, as like as not, include a rabbit or some flowers.

Humanism emphasized the dignity of man. The ancients had done this in a way the Middle Ages had not. The humanists then were men who studied classical authors and ideas. To the classical world the individual had been important. To the Middle Ages he did not count. Now he was to count again.

A book by L. W. H. Hull entitled *History and Philosophy of Science** contains an illuminating passage on humanism. Hull points out that the early Christian fathers distrusted human knowledge, as indeed the allegory of Adam and Eve taught them to. He writes (p. 106), 'Knowledge obtained by human enterprise and daring had long been recognized as dangerous. Christianity spread the view, never widely held before, that such knowledge was valueless or positively harmful. The attack was conducted with force and ability by St Paul. He says (*I Corinthians* 3 : 21): "Therefore let no man glory in men". This superficially innocent remark is aimed at the vital point. It condemns the underlying humanism—the self-confidence of man—essential to progress in science and the arts.'

The Renaissance taught the Italians once more to 'glory in men'.

The study of ancient literature taught men a new respect for the human body. The medieval attitude to the body was that it was something to be ashamed of, something that was best forgotten or else tortured and starved until it was brought into subjection to the spirit. Man was 'altogether conceived in iniquity', and the 'flesh and the devil' were one and the same thing, to be struggled with and overcome. To glory in the flesh was a sin.

But the study of classical literature and art gave men a new attitude

* Longmans, 1965.

44

to the body. They came to regard it as something beautiful, to be gloried in. Sculptors and painters began to portray the beauty of the human body and to search for perfection in it.

Shakespeare, who was a child of the Italian Renaissance, reflects this new glorification of man, this humanism, in his play *The Tempest*, where he makes Miranda say:

> How many goodly creatures are there here!
> How beauteous mankind is! O brave new world,
> That has such people in it!*

The great century of the Italian Renaissance, however, was not the fourteenth but the fifteenth. It is now that the works of Plato were discovered. Plato had been known to Petrarch, but it was not until the early fifteenth century that the study of this great philosopher and of his master, Socrates, gained momentum. Platonic manuscripts were brought back from Byzantium to Italy (for trade and the pressure of the Turks against the ancient Byzantine Empire had led to much coming and going between Italy and Byzantium or Constantinople). Platonic academies were founded at Florence, Naples and Rome.

The thought of Socrates is, above that of all other philosophers, challenging and awakening. It worked like a ferment on the minds of the Italians. Here were ideas which challenged the old set ways of the medievalists. Here was a philosopher who questioned everything, indeed who taught men never to accept authority but to think for themselves. Now the whole basis of education in Italy (and thence in Europe) began to change. Boys were no longer taught, 'This is the truth; just you remember it'; instead they were taught, 'This is what I think, but I would not want to suggest you think likewise. Please make up your own mind'. What an advance! Instead of being the accumulating of knowledge, education was to become learning to think. Despite an ominous emphasis on examinations, it remains so on the whole today throughout what we call the western world. Yes, education is still Platonic in Britain and many other countries. Long may it remain so!

So great was the influence of Plato upon European thought that the humanists acquired quite a new concept of the objects of education. In the twelfth and thirteenth centuries men studied Latin for utilitarian reasons. It was the vehicle of learning. At universities men studied law to become lawyers, medicine to become doctors, theology and philosophy to become priests, and the necessary books for all these subjects (and the necessary lectures) would all be in Latin. But the humanist view was that the classics were worth studying for their own sakes, because the philosophy of the ancient world would make you a better citizen, a better person. You absorbed from it nobility of soul. This was the educational theory of the classical world. The Italians now grasped

* Quoted in *Renaissance and Reformation*, by V. H. H. Green, Edward Arnold, 1952, which has a good chapter on the Renaissance.

it with both hands, and education became, as it had been in ancient Greece, largely non-vocational. This is how it has remained in the best schools of Europe and her offshoots, right up to this day. We are, you and I, dear reader, whether we like it or not, children of the Renaissance.

Alexander Pope wrote, 'The proper study of mankind is man.' The humanities (Latin, Greek, French, English, History, etc.) are the subjects in which we study the thought of the great men of the past. The study of the humanities encourages style, because only when it is well expressed can a great thought survive. Nay rather, only when it is well expressed is it a great thought (for style and matter cannot really be distinguished). To be well expressed a thought must first be passionately believed and clearly cognized. No one's thinking was ever clearer and more beautifully expressed than that of Socrates, whose sayings Plato wrote down.

So great was the influence of Plato upon European thought that it is almost possible to say that Modern Europe equals Medieval Europe plus Plato. The Age of Faith began to fade when those old manuscripts were dug out and translated, and the Age of Doubt began to dawn.

As the classical age revealed itself in all its grandeur to the Italian intelligentsia, the basic standards of their lives altered. Plato did not displace Christ any more than Aristotle had displaced him. In fact, like Aristotle, he fitted in surprisingly well with Christian doctrine. But now that humanism was taught and practised, it was more fun to be alive. The Church had taught too much about the beauties of death. The Greeks had believed in life and loved it. The Italians too fell in love with the beauty of life, and because Jesus and the Christian Fathers and St Francis had lived, they found even more beauty than perhaps the Greeks had, or rather they found beauty of a different sort.

One thing that the Renaissance brought was a new emphasis on gracious living. Princes and their courts (which invariably now included scholars and artists) began to take a new delight in their surroundings. Palaces and houses were not only rebuilt in the revived classical style, but they were filled with beautiful things. Dress became more decorative and elaborate. Table manners, and indeed manners in general, were vastly improved. White napery appeared on dinner tables, spotless and fresh. Forks came into general use among the upper classes. Carpets appeared on floors (instead of rushes), curtains on windows. The art of conversation was developed.

Classical ideals combined with Christian ones to mould men's views on life. It is now that a clear idea emerges of what a well educated man should be like. Castiglione's book, *Cortegiano* (the Courtier), written in 1516, enjoyed great popularity and was translated into several languages. H. A. L. Fisher says of it 'The Courtier must be trained in the school, not only of the court, but of the camp. He must be a man-at-arms and a sportsman, an athlete and an intellectual, a virtuoso in the arts and a citizen in the world, well read in Greek, Latin and Italian, with some practical knowledge of drawing and music, and a superficial and apparently effortless mastery of all the fashionable graces and accomplishments of his time.' Is not this the ideal behind the education given in all the best public and grammar schools in Britain today? Here we see the origin of Milton's view of education as that which 'fits a man to perform justly, skilfully and magnanimously all the offices both private and public of peace and war'. When we talk of Henry VIII or Francis I of France as 'Renaissance kings', it is partly because, like Castiglione's Courtier, they were all-rounders, able to perform on one or two musical instruments, run a course in the lists, shoot and wrestle, discourse learnedly on theology, speak Latin and Italian, appreciate fine art, lead armies and perform well whatever task lay to their hands.

Machiavelli

No account of the Italian Renaissance, however brief and sketchy, should be without mention of one of its greatest figures, Niccolo Machiavelli. The Greeks had studied political science or the science of politics, but in the Middle Ages it was neglected, and treatises on the moral duties of governments replaced its study. Machiavelli in his *Principe* (*The Prince*) showed that politics was a science quite apart from morality. He regarded it as a pure science, having no more connection with morality than had the science of navigation. Himself a practical politician, having long served the Republic of Florence, his book was a superb manual of statecraft, showing how a ruler should act if his government was to succeed. The criterion he consistently applied to political actions was not 'Are they good?', but 'Will they work?'. He saw the justification of any political act in its results.

The Prince was published in 1513, a year after the Medici had returned to power in Florence and banished Machiavelli to his country estate. An Italian patriot, Machiavelli hoped to teach his countrymen how they might yet create a strong, united Italy. His book shocked the world; yet he only pointed out what is in fact true, that governments are invarably actuated by self-interest, and that it pays other governments to recognize the fact. His definition of good was shocking, at least to the Church. 'I believe good', he wrote, 'to be that which conduces to the interests of the majority, and with which the majority are contented.' Appealing to history and to reason, he investigated and recorded the laws which seemed to govern men's actions. In fact he only wrote down what was already taking place. But men, then as today, preferred to live in a dream world and assume themselves the possessors of high motives, which in fact they did not have.

Medieval treatises on Government dealt with what kings should do in order to be good. Machiavelli dealt with what kings should do in order to be effective. 'The notion that efficient government was as worthy of investigation as the moral principles of Christian dominion was a new one.' *

* This quotation is from Vol. I of the *New Cambridge Modern History*, p. 5.

Machiavelli has been branded as a cynic. He wrote, 'When the entire safety of our country is at stake, no consideration of what is just or unjust, merciful or cruel, praiseworthy or shameful must intervene.' And again 'A prince, especially a new one, cannot observe all those things for which men are esteemed, being often forced in order to maintain the state, to act contrary to fidelity, friendship, humanity and religion.' Notice the word 'forced'. Machiavelli was not pointing a moral, but mentioning a fact.

He taught that 'Although it may suit the Prince to keep his word and be just, he need not do so unless it serves his interests.' This seems, on the face of it, to be a cynical attitude. Yet, is it not in fact what every government, modern or medieval or ancient, always has done and always will do? The history of every country is strewn with its government's broken promises. Were it not so, no country would survive, and the world would be a great deal more plagued with wars than in fact it is. Politics is the art of expediency, or as someone has said, 'the art of the possible'. Machiavelli was the first to see this clearly and write it down. He has been reviled ever since. Yet what people criticize is not the teachings of Machiavelli, but 'an ill-defined body of doctrine loosely called Machiavellism'.*

The Northern Renaissance

Italy was the cradle of the Renaissance, but by the middle of the fifteenth century the New Learning was beginning to spread north of the Alps, and particularly in the thriving trading cities of Burgundy, and in German cities like Nuremberg, Basle and Augsburg, which lay athwart the old river routes down which trade had flowed for centuries. The time was shortly to arrive when these old trade routes would decay, as Portuguese discoveries (such as that of the Cape of Good Hope route to India, pioneered by Vasco da Gama in 1497) opened up new oceanic routes, improvements in the science of navigation having made it possible to use the oceans more freely. But until this Maritime Revolution took place, German cities were immensely prosperous. Here wealthy merchants supplied the patronage without which art and literature cannot flourish.

Burgundy likewise had its wealthy merchants to patronize the arts, but there the Dukes of Burgundy, holding court at Brussels, provided another great source of patronage, for the Burgundian court was famous for its lavish display. The result was the appearance of a thriving school of painters including the Van Eyck brothers, Rogier Van der Weyden, Hans Memlinc and many others. In many ways these painters were ahead of the Italians— in their mastery of detail for instance; and the Van Eycks pioneered the use of oils in painting. But, like the Italians,

---

* This quotation is from the old *Cambridge Modern History*, Vol. I. Its chapter on Machiavelli is most helpful.

they were humanists, delighting in portraiture and the study of human types. Their source of inspiration appears to have been two-fold, the primitive Gothic art of Germany and the Latin element from France.

In Germany we have the great painter and engraver Albrecht Dürer (1471–1528) who came from Nuremberg, and numerous lesser carvers, sculptors, engravers, painters and metal workers whose craftsmanship was the wonder of all Europe. But the greatest contribution made by Germany was the invention of printing by moveable type. This was largely the achievement of John Gutenberg of Mainz who set up his first press in that city in 1450. In the next fifty years German printers moved into all the main areas of Europe (to Italy in 1465, Paris in 1470, London in 1477 and Madrid in 1499).

The craftsmanship of these early printers and book-binders was superb, and of course printing did much to spread the new humanist ideas. Although these stemmed from Italy they 'crossed the Alps slowly, leading to a revival of classical learning and to the transformation of the curricula of schools and universities'. Humanist scholars arose in both Germany and France. One was Cardinal Nicholas of Cusa (in the Moselle valley). His dates are 1401–1464. As a young man he studied mathematics and canon law in the University of Padua. He returned to Germany, obtained a Tyrolean bishopric and spent a busy scholastic life delving into monastic libraries, translating Latin texts and writing a book of philosophy. Eight new universities were founded in Germany in the second half of the fifteenth century.

What of England? Here it was not until the end of the century that the humanist ideas began to be noticed. About 1478 Oxford imported an Italian scholar 'to inaugurate the study of Greek'. Among his pupils was William Grocyn, who in turn inspired a number of young men, including Thomas Linacre, Thomas More and John Colet. Grocyn, Linacre and Colet all visited Italy. All three were in holy orders and lectured on Greek at Oxford. Linacre was mainly interested in medicine and became tutor to Prince Arthur and later physician to Henry VIII. In 1518 he founded the College of Physicians.

Colet's main interest was in the Bible and there was a sensation at Oxford when, on his return from Italy in 1496, he began a course of lectures on St Paul's Epistle to the Romans, using the original Greek text as the basis of his study, instead of the old Latin Vulgate and the commentaries of medieval schoolmen. When, in 1505, he became Dean of St Paul's, he preached the new ideas 'from his pulpit and in his life'. About 1509 he founded St Paul's School, the first school 'in which Greek was publicly taught in England after the revival of letters'.

Thomas More was the only one of these four great English humanists who was not in the Church. He became a lawyer and eventually Lord Chancellor of England, but like his friends, Colet and Erasmus, he longed to reform the Church and 'to foster true piety based upon careful study of the word of God'.

It is time we turned our attention to Erasmus, the greatest figure of all in the Northern Renaissance, and the one with the deepest influence on British and indeed European history. Born in 1466 in Rotterdam, the illegitimate son of a priest, he was educated from the age of nine at a well-known school at Deventer run by the Brethren of the Common Life, a very go-ahead body who used humanist teachers. The young boy took to scholarship as a duck takes to water, but he was less happy when in 1487, having no parents or influential friends, he was persuaded to enter an Augustinian monastery. The monastic life irked him. He could see little point in it, and he acquired a dislike of monasticism, which was to remain with him all his life. When, therefore, in 1493 he was offered the post of Latin Secretary to the Bishop of Cambrai, he jumped at the chance. In this post he met some of the finest society in Europe, for the Bishop was Chancellor of the Order of the Golden Fleece, the leading chivalric order of Burgundy.

As a reward for his services the Bishop sent Erasmus to the University of Paris, but here he found to his disgust the teaching was still based on out-of-date medieval schoolmen such as Duns Scotus and William of Ockham. 'You would not know me', he wrote to a friend, 'if you could see me sitting under old Dunderhead, my brows knit and looking thoroughly puzzled.'

At Paris Erasmus tutored a group of young English students, and one of these, Lord Mountjoy, invited him to England in 1499. He was charmed with England, and although he stayed there only a year, he made friends with John Colet and Thomas More. This friendship 'helped to direct his interests away from the classics and a career of tutoring towards a study of the ancient Fathers of the Church' (particularly St Jerome and St Augustine, who both lived about A.D. 400) 'and the Scriptures. . . . A restoration of theology, not the conventional, hair-splitting dialectics of the schoolmen, so devoid of life and inspiration, but rather a study of the very fonts of faith as interpreted by the wisdom of the early Fathers, now became his persistent ambition.' *

In 1500 he returned to Paris and soon published his first great work *Enchiridion Militis Christiani* (*The Handbook of the Militant Christian*). This was a most tremendous sermon, earnestly commending the true Christian life to the reader. To read it even today is to be uplifted, so lively is the style, so sincere and urgent the exhortations. Erasmus has been compared to Voltaire, the apostle of European enlightenment in the eighteenth century, but in the *Enchiridion* there is little satire and sarcasm. He appears more as a John Wesley, urging his readers to leave the outward show of Christianity and to make religion of the heart.

Here are a few quotations from Professor Dolan's translation:

'Christ alone grants that peace that the world cannot give. There is but one way to attain it; we must wage war with ourselves.'

* Quoted from *The Essential Erasmus* by John P. Dolan, New English Library, 1964.

'As you advance on the path to perfection, you must determine not to turn back. Neither the affection of your loved ones, the allurements of the world, nor the cares of domestic life should stand in your way'.

'You must dare to believe in Him with your whole heart, and to distrust yourself entirely.'

'Make Christ the goal of your life. Dedicate to him all your enthusiasm, all your effort, your leisure as well as your business.'

Erasmus despises the veneration of saints, and compares people who burn a candle in honour of St Jerome 'so that lost goods might be recovered' or mumble prayers to St Barbara or St George 'so that they will not fall into the hands of the enemy' to the ancients sacrificing a cock to Aesculapius 'to regain their health' or a bull to Neptune 'to avoid mishap at sea'.

He speaks of Jesus' words 'God is a spirit and they who worship him must worship him in spirit and in truth', and comments: 'To whom do you suppose he directed those words? It was certainly to none other than those who think their salvation consists of wearing a blessed medal or carrying an indulgenced relic.'

He deprecates ceremonial on its own. 'Perhaps you celebrate Mass daily. Yet if you live as if this were only for your own welfare and have no concern for the difficulties and needs of your neighbour, you are still in the flesh of the sacrament.... I think there are far too many who count how many times they attend Mass and rely almost entirely upon this for their salvation.... If you are filled with ambition and envy, even though you offer the sacrifice yourself, you are far from the real significance of the Mass.'

Of baptism he writes, 'You have been sprinkled with holy water, but this accomplishes nothing unless you cleanse the inner filth of your mind.'

On the fashionable worship of relics he is severe. 'Perhaps you are wont to venerate the relics of the Saints, yet at the same time you condemn their greatest legacy, the example of their lives. No veneration of Mary is more beautiful than the imitation of her humility. So you have a great devotion to St Peter and St Paul. Then by all means imitate the faith of the former and the charity of the latter. This will certainly be more rewarding than a dozen trips to Rome.... You worship his bones, hidden away and preserved in nooks and niches, but you fail to worship the great mind of Paul, hidden in the Scriptures.... You may gaze in silent amazement at the tunic that reputedly belonged to Christ, yet you read the wonderful sayings of that same Christ half asleep.'

Again of ceremonial he writes, 'Charity does not consist in many visits to churches, in many prostrations before the statues of saints, in the lighting of candles, or in the repetition of a number of designated prayers.'

For the monastic life he had a great contempt, 'Of what advantage to you is a body covered by a religious habit, if that same body possesses a mind that is worldly? If your habit is white should not your mind be white too?'

Of the granting of indulgences, one day to be the centre of Luther's controversy, he writes, 'Perhaps you believe that by wax seals, by sums of money or by pilgrimages your sins are washed away immediately. If you are confident that these are the ways of forgiveness, you are sadly mistaken. If you wish to be forgiven, you, who have loved what you should have hated and who have hated what you should have loved, must attack the enemy within.'

The *Enchiridion* was published in 1503 and became a best seller. Between 1514 and 1518 eight Latin editions of it appeared. Between 1518 and 1526 it was translated into English, Czeck, German, Dutch and Spanish. In Spain especially the enthusiasm for it was unbounded. Throughout Europe Erasmus's name became renowned.

Yet the author of this best seller remained poor. His illegitimate birth, and the fact that he was technically still a monk, made it impossible for him to get a living in the Church, the usual reward for great scholars.

In 1502 he moved from Paris to Louvain. In 1504 he made his second visit to England, and two years later had the opportunity, which he longed for, to visit Italy (as tutor to the children of Henry VII's court physician). While in Rome, in 1509, he heard of the death of Henry VII and immediately returned to England, for the young King Henry VIII, whom he had often met, was his admirer. It was while staying at Thomas More's house at Bucklesbury in 1509 that he wrote the book for which he is most famous, *Moriae Encomium (Praise of Folly)*.

This begins as 'a piece of good-humoured banter'. Folly praises herself and shows how large a part she plays in life. Is she not present at the begetting of man, at marriage, in extreme youth and extreme age? Is she not the companion of Bacchus, of Cupid, of Venus? Is not woman the patron of Folly? Is Folly not the chief guest at any party? Is not friendship incomplete without her? Then Folly describes how important she is to the life of various persons, nobles, professors, merchants, scientists, those who are keen on hunting, those who have a craze for building and so on. But, when Folly reaches theologians and monks, the work becomes a 'bitter attack on the schoolmen with their sterile and hair-splitting logic and on the wasteful fussiness of monastic life'.*

Medieval learning was an easy target for Erasmus. The schoolmen (that is to say teachers in schools of theology at the universities) had come to have an exaggerated faith in the value of logic. The syllogism (logical step in reasoning) was believed to be capable of arriving at true knowledge. Today we reason by common sense (or intuition, if you prefer it). Medieval scholars reasoned by strict logic, putting an undue reliance on words. As a result, though they did not (as later stated), have debates on how many angels could stand on the point of a needle, they did discuss 'whether, if angels have local motion, they pass through intermediate

* See V. H. H. Green, *op. cit.*

52

space, or whether an angel can be in more than one place at one and the same time'.* Also they pondered 'the possible fate of the fish in the Lake of Geneva were they excommunicated by the bishop'. Erasmus makes Folly say of them, 'They explain the most mysterious matters to suit themselves, for instance ... through what channels original sin has come down to us through generations, by what means, in what measure, and how long the omnipotent Christ was in the Virgin's womb.' He points out that even the apostles, though they knew Jesus and Mary personally, could not have defined the finer points of theology like the pupils of Duns Scotus.

When she comes to monks Folly is even more biting. She points out that 'when Christ will demand a reckoning of that which he has prescribed, namely charity ... one monk will then exhibit his belly full of every kind of fish, another will profess a knowledge of over a hundred hymns. Still another will reveal a countless number of fasts that he has made.... Another will show a list of church ceremonies over which he has officiated so large that it would fill seven ships, while still another will brag that he hasn't touched any money in over sixty years unless he wore two pairs of gloves.... Another will take pride in the fact that he has lived a beggarly life as exampled by the filthiness and dirtiness of his hood, which even a sailor would not see fit to wear. Another will take glory in the fact that he has parasitically lived in the same spot for over fifty-five years. Another will exhibit his hoarse voice, which is a result of his diligent chanting.'

But Folly does not stop at chastising theologians and monks. She goes on to attack bishops, cardinals and even popes. Thus 'the priestly caste, once so formidable and dominant, was held up by this light and engaging satirist as an object of amusement and contempt'. *Praise of Folly* was another best seller.

In 1511 Erasmus was made lecturer in Greek at Cambridge. But he did not enjoy his stay there. So he went to live at Basle, a great centre of Renaissance scholarship. He had long been working on a translation of the New Testament from the original Greek into Latin. In 1516 this was published and made an immediate impression on the scholarly world.

By 1517 Erasmus 'had become the unquestioned idol of Europe's literati.... The agents of half a dozen printing houses clamoured for his works; his letters were purloined and published. Wolsey coaxed him to England with promises of ecclesiastical preferment. Cardinal Ximénez invited him to the University of Alcala in Spain. The previous year he had been appointed Chancellor to the Prince of Burgundy, the future Emperor Charles V, and the King of France was urging him to take up residence at the royal court. The cities in the Rhineland welcomed him as a national hero wherever he travelled.'†

The reason why I have given Erasmus's ideas in some detail is that

* See *The Reformation* by Owen Chadwick, Pelican, 1964
† John P. Dolan, *op. cit.*

these ideas were a powerful force in the England of Henry VIII. The King himself and most of his courtiers were Erasmians. Indeed by the time of Wolsey's fall (1529) enlightened opinion in England (or opinion which prided itself on being enlightened) had embraced the ideas of the great scholar. Many acts of the reign become understandable when this is realized. Thus Erasmus despised monks; Henry VIII dissolved the monasteries. Erasmus believed that the scriptures should be made available in every language ('I long', he wrote, 'that the husbandman should say them to himself as he follows the plough, that the weaver should hum them to the tune of his shuttle, that the traveller should beguile with them the weariness of his journey' *); Henry had an English translation of the Bible placed in every parish church. Erasmus condemned the purchase of pardons; Henry did likewise in his Ten Articles of 1536. Erasmus ridiculed shrines, relics and pilgrimages; Henry instructed the clergy in 1536 to preach against 'the veneration of images and relics, and the making of pilgrimages'. In 1538 Henry (or Cromwell) went further and ordered the removal of all shrines to which pilgrimages and offerings were made. Finally, Erasmus had urged a knowledge of scripture, and Cromwell's Injunctions of 1538 ordered 'the public reading in English every Sunday of the Lord's Prayer, Creed and Commandments'.

Thus an understanding of Erasmus is the key to a great part of the reign of Henry VIII, that 'Renaissance prince' who was so well-read in the learning of his day. Of course many of Henry's actions were anti-Erasmian—for instance his execution of Sir Thomas More, Erasmus's friend, or the passing of the Statute of Six Articles of 1539, which included the prohibition of the marriage of priests (Erasmus had little respect for clerical celibacy, which he knew had been no part of the Early Church's practice). But these actions were taken for political reasons under considerable pressure of circumstances, and were not in line with Henry's personal inclinations. So strong an admirer of Erasmus was Henry, that Gardiner, Bishop of Winchester, did not dare to denounce Erasmus during the King's life, but only did so after his death.†

It gives us a kinder view of Henry's court when we remember how the gentle Dutch scholar was revered in it. For Erasmus, though the admired of princes and, strangely enough, of popes, remained to the end a simple man with a mission, and, when in his last years he saw the church he had loved and striven to reform, split into two by the Lutherans, he wrote his final work, *On Mending the Peace of the Church*, and dedicated it not to any great prince or potentate, but to an unknown customs officer in a little Rhenish town 'who had befriended him fifteen years before, and to whom he had promised a work on the psalms'.

* Quoted in H. A. L. Fisher, *op. cit.*, which contains a fine summary of Erasmus's life and work.
† See J. D. Mackie, *op. cit.*, p. 511.

4 The Early Years of Henry VIII's Reign. Wolsey.

A Renaissance prince

Henry VIII was eighteen when his father died. 'Plantagenet as well as Tudor, for his mother was Elizabeth of York ... he had her personal beauty and his father's vigorous brain.' Here was the very pattern of a prince. He excelled in everything. Exuberant in mind and body, he was a musician, scholar and athlete. At sixteen he was an accomplished bowman (in an age when fathers gave their sons little bows when they were seven years of age, and increased the size of the bows as the boys grew). He was a fine horseman, tennis player, and wrestler, an expert performer on the organ and the harpsichord, and a good linguist, speaking French, Latin and some Italian. He revelled in jousts (his jousting armour may still be seen in the Tower of London), and was cheerful and generous as his father had been dour and close.

The English court became a centre of sport and gaiety. It seemed that the golden age had come, though a Spaniard did remark, as he watched the revels, that the King seemed interested 'only in girls and hunting'.

One of Henry's first actions was to obey his father's dying wish by marrying Catherine of Aragon, who was six years his senior. He also put to death his father's old councillors, Sir Richard Empson and Edmund Dudley, against whose tax-collecting zeal many complaints had been lodged.

Many historians think these two faithful servants of the Crown were sacrificed to appease the great lords of the realm, whom the young King could not control. A further account of the matter will be found in Appendix B, p. 260.

Henry was interested in the sea, and from the start of his reign began to build up the British navy. His father had made a good start and bequeathed him two first-class ships, *Sovereign* and *Regent*, and three smaller ones. Henry quickly doubled the size of his fleet, and appointed Thomas and Edward Howard, sons of the Earl of Surrey, as young fighting admirals (the previous Lord Admiral had never been to sea!).

War with France

Henry VII, as we have seen, had maintained a policy of peace with the old enemy, France. His son was not so wise. Being young, he was ambitious to excel in war, as he already had excelled in so much else.

The opportunity came in 1511, when the warlike Pope, Julius II, formed the Holy League to drive the French out of northern Italy. Spain (still ruled by Ferdinand, though his wife Isabella had died) and Venice had joined the League. Henry decided to do so also.

But warlike ambition was not his only motive. Since France had obtained Brittany with its great port of Brest, she had been building a navy whose power and position threatened the valuable British Mediterranean trade, which must of course pass by the shores of Brittany. Henry hoped to reconquer the port of Bordeaux which had belonged to English kings until the latter part of the Hundred Years' War, and still had a thriving wine trade with Britain (though Englishmen were just beginning to drink a concoction from the Netherlands, called beer). Bordeaux would be a counterpoise to Brest in balancing sea power in the Bay of Biscay.

An English Army was duly despatched to Spain, where Ferdinand was going to help it advance and conquer Bordeaux. But Ferdinand played false and did nothing to help the English, but only busied himself with the conquering of Navarre, a kingdom on the Spanish–French border, which he had long coveted. Henry's expedition, therefore, was a fiasco, and had to return to Britain without accomplishing anything.

Henry could not afford the consequent loss of face, and so, in 1513, he determined on an invasion across the Straits of Dover. At mid-summer he himself crossed the Channel to Calais with an army of no less than 35,000 men. With these and a force of 14,000 German mercenaries he laid siege to Thérouanne. Louis XII, the King of France, sent forward a force of horsemen to relieve the town, but they were easily routed in a skirmish which, because of the speed of the French retreat, has been named the Battle of the Spurs. Henry went on to capture Thérouanne, and a larger town, Tournai. Then he returned home.

But 1513 'had seen a much greater battle than any in France'. James IV of Scotland, despite the fact he was Henry VIII's brother-in-law, was tempted to renew the 'auld alliance' of the Hundred Years' War and come to the help of France. He crossed the Tweed with a great army and soon captured Norham Castle. The Council, which had been expecting this, sent the Earl of Surrey north to meet him, and the two armies fought it out with terrible slaughter at Flodden. The English prevailed. James IV himself, many Scottish nobles, and 10,000 Scotsmen were killed. Surrey was created Duke of Norfolk as a reward for his victory.

Henry had now gained what he wanted, military glory, and he decided it was time to make peace, especially as he was the only one of the members of the Holy League who was doing any fighting. By 1514 he had built up his navy to a strength of twenty-seven sail, large and small, including the prestige ship the *Great Harry*, of 1500 tons. This naval strength gave him a good bargaining power, and he and his young minister, Thomas Wolsey, (who had organized the French expedition) were able to make a good peace with France.

France ceded Tournai and promised greater money payments than those fixed by the Treaty of Etaples, while the King of France, Louis XII, newly widowed, was married to Henry's seventeen-year-old sister,

56

Mary. She detested the idea of being married to the old widower, and was no doubt relieved when he died in 1515, and she was able to marry (for love) Charles Brandon, Duke of Suffolk.*

Charles Brandon was the son of William Brandon, a simple squire who had been Henry of Richmond's standard-bearer on Bosworth Field and as such had been 'singled out and killed in personal encounter by Richard III'. Charles was created a duke in 1513 for his part in the French campaign, as was Norfolk for his part in the Scottish. There were then only three dukes in the kingdom, Buckingham being the third. Suffolk was a bold and handsome man, a great jouster, and his secret marriage to Mary at the French court was a rash move. But Mary was Henry's favourite sister and the King soon forgave the couple and gave them his blessing. It is from this marriage that Lady Jane Grey was descended.

By his first venture into European politics Henry had really gained very little. Tournai was sold back to the new King of France four years later, and the main result of the war was that most of Henry VII's carefully accumulated treasure had been dissipated.

Thomas Wolsey

The rising star at court was the 'ambitious priest', Thomas Wolsey. Son of a butcher and innkeeper of Ipswich, Thomas went to Oxford and entered the Church. He became a Fellow of Magdalen College, and in 1507 entered Henry VII's service. On the old king's death, Henry VIII made Wolsey Royal Almoner, and in 1511, when he was still under forty, a member of the Council. He was entrusted with equipping and organizing the great expedition to France in 1513. In this he was so successful that he was made Bishop of Tournai, and then, in 1514, Archbishop of York. In 1515 he was made Lord Chancellor and Leo X made him a Cardinal. By now he had ousted all other men from Henry's confidence. In fact from 1515 to 1529 he was virtually Henry's only minister. All other offices but his own, the Chancellorship, were filled with his friends and followers. Such a concentration of power in the hands of one of the king's subjects had not been seen since the days of Thomas à Becket. It is true Wolsey never became Archbishop of Canterbury, for Warham, though an older man, outlived him; but in 1518 the Pope made him legate *a latere* (*see later*, p. 60) which gave him higher authority than the Archbishop of Canterbury, and he certainly 'lorded it' over poor old Warham on every possible occasion.

Wolsey had a great appetite for grandeur (common I suppose among rich men of poor origins). His wealth was extraordinary—perhaps £35,000 a year, while the whole revenue of the Crown was only £150,000. The money came from his numerous offices in Church and

* Mary was a great beauty. A. F. Pollard in his magnificent biography, *Henry VIII*, Longman, 1905, describes her as 'one of the most fascinating women of the Tudor epoch'. Her marriage to the fifty-two-year-old Louis shocked public opinion.

State (he was Abbot of St Albans, the richest abbey in England, though of course he had never been a monk) and from bribes. With his vast revenues he built himself two palaces (Whitehall and Hampton Court), dressed, ate and drank lavishly, entertained on a princely scale, and surrounded himself with a huge household. Needless to say he was hated as an upstart by the old nobility, but as long as he kept the King's favour he was secure. Henry was no idler in these years, but he was young and he did not see why Wolsey, who was a tremendous worker, should not run the country while he enjoyed himself. So while the King danced and flirted late into the night or ran thirty courses in the lists in one day (taking hard knocks in the process), the Cardinal spun his webs of diplomacy and power and ruled the roost, before all men's eyes.

Wolsey and the Law

As Lord Chancellor Wolsey was head of the legal system of England. He seems to have been interested in the work and to have taken it seriously. Being of poor origin himself he was concerned that the poor should get justice.

As society became more complicated, the Common Law was no longer able to attend to all cases involving trade, contract and property. The Court of Chancery existed to deal with cases for which the Common Law was inadequate. It administered what was called 'equity', in other words justice where the Common Law would have been (because out of date) unjust. Wolsey presided over this court well. He seems to have enjoyed acting as a judge. Under him Chancery increased its amount of business, decisions were speeded up, and a great many people got justice, who would not otherwise have had it.

Star Chamber also flourished under Wolsey. Unlike Chancery this was partly a criminal court. Two years after becoming Lord Chancellor, Wolsey boasted to the King that 'the realm was in such good peace and order as has not been known before'. There had certainly been a big improvement.

Wolsey made an attempt to rectify the great social injustice of enclosure. Because of the high price of wool rich men had begun (in the fifteenth century) to enclose common land (and sometimes arable-strip land) for private pasture. Henry VII had made an attempt to stop the practice, without avail. The JPs who had to enforce the law were the very people who benefited from enclosures. Wolsey got an Enclosure Act passed in 1515, and two years later sent out seventeen commissions to discover if the law was being enforced. Where it was not, cases were brought against offenders in the Chancery and Exchequer Courts, but all to no avail. Enclosure went on, and was to be a headache to English governments for some time to come. But at least Wolsey had tried to do something about it.*

* For a fuller discussion of enclosure, see Chapter 17.

Finance was Wolsey's weakest point. He was very extravagant in his personal life, and his foreign policy, with its frequent wars and subsidies, made the government continually short of money. The treasure left by Henry VII was soon spent. Its dispersal aggravated the rise in prices which was already taking place in Britain. The causes of this inflation, which had begun about 1500, are discussed in Chapter 17. It meant that the value of money in 1525 was only about four-fifths of what it had been at the beginning of the century. The King's income being more or less fixed, he was one of the worst hit.

Under such circumstances even Henry VII would have been hard put to it to make ends meet. Wolsey failed completely. He dismissed the Parliament of 1515 before it had made a grant, because the Commons had attacked the immunity of the clergy from the King's law (they were tried in special Church courts). For several years he called no Parliament. When war broke out in 1522, the coffers were empty, and he tried to fill them with a Forced Loan, levied without Parliament's consent; but he did not get enough, and, in 1523, he was forced at last to call another Parliament. The amount he asked for was £800,000, four shillings in the pound on land and goods 'on the new and more realistic assessment which he had used for the 1522 forced loans'. This was a staggering demand and led to heated debates. 'There is not so much coin in the whole country', said one member. The Commons began to discuss matters of foreign policy usually accounted as too high for any but the King and his expert councillors to understand. One member, probably Thomas Cromwell, prepared (if he did not deliver) an able speech in which he denounced the whole policy of intervention on the continent. On one occasion Wolsey came in person to the Commons to demand his grant. He was met with 'a marvellous obstinate silence', and Sir Thomas More, the Speaker, explained to him humbly that the Commons, although they would accept messages, must debate among themselves. In other words his presence was not wanted.

In the end the Commons voted barely three-quarters of what Wolsey had demanded. Its collection was to be spread over two years. It was found hard to collect and eventually only about £150,000 was collected.

In 1525, the King being intent on an invasion of France, Wolsey wanted more money. Without calling Parliament he again tried to levy a forced loan, which he called an 'Amicable Grant'. He was met with unexpected hostility. In East Anglia 20,000 men gathered to resist. All south-east England was soon in an uproar and Henry was forced to abandon the idea and pardon all those men who had opposed paying.

If we compare Wolsey's period of office with that of Thomas Cromwell two things stand out. The first is that in the latter period Henry had profited by his earlier experience and become less keen on aggressive war. Thomas Cromwell therefore never had to find the enormous sums which Wolsey was expected to produce. Secondly, the fact that Parliament (or at least the Commons) was strongly anti-clerical made it willing to work with the anti-clerical Cromwell but antagonistic to the proud prelate, Wolsey. The two parliamentary sessions of 1515 provoked, as the Clerk of Parliaments put it, 'most dangerous discords between the clergy and the secular power over the liberties of the Church'. It was rather hard on Wolsey that in these clashes with Parliament the King appeared very ready to listen to the other side.

All in all Wolsey's path was a difficult one, but one must conclude that his arrogant manner and lack of tact in dealing with the House of Commons made it harder.

Wolsey and the Church

The Church at this time was ripe for reform. It was full of abuses. Popes and bishops were usually worldly men. They preferred power and wealth to holiness. The immense riches of the Church had corrupted it. Pluralism (the holding of more than one benefice) and simony (the buying of position in the Church) were rife. Nepotism (the promotion of nephews or illegitimate sons to benefices) and non-residence were common. Everyone knew that reform was needed. Erasmus, the great European scholar, had come to Cambridge in 1509 attracted by stories of the intellectual vigour of Henry's court, and had written books which made fun of the superstitious side of the Roman Catholic Church—the pilgrimages, the relics, the futile observances of the monastic life.

Wolsey received his powers as legate *a latere* for the specific purpose of carrying out reforms. The great concentration of power in his hands gave him the opportunity to do it. Yet, though he talked a lot about reform, he did nothing. In fact his own career was the most glaring example of abuses. He always held at least one bishopric beside that of York (in the end it was Winchester, the wealthiest of all). As we have seen, though not a monk, he was Abbot of St Albans. His private life was far from strict. 'He had probably several daughters and certainly one son whom he promoted rapidly to some valuable benefices in his extreme youth.' The Pope had given him special power over monasteries and nunneries, which normally did not come under the archbishops. Instead of reforming them he merely interfered, and on one occasion 'appointed a woman of distinctly low morality to a nunnery'.

In fact Wolsey cared very little about reform and much about power. He had a great scheme for the dissolution of a number of great abbeys and the formation of thirteen new bishoprics with the proceeds, but this came to nothing. The only reform he did effect along these lines was the suppression of a score of small monasteries. With the money he obtained from these he founded Cardinal College, Oxford, and another college in Ipswich. Cardinal College is today Christ Church College, and Wolsey's portrait (*see* opposite p. 61) may still be seen frowning down from the wall at the head of its hall.

3 Henry VIII by Holbein

CARDINAL WOOLS

4 Thomas Wolsey by an unknown artist

In the end, instead of strengthening or reforming the Church in England, Wolsey weakened it. He appointed Italians to bishoprics, paid them fixed stipends, and collected the incomes of their sees himself. When he fell from power five English bishoprics were in foreign hands. In this way he weakened the bench of bishops (for the foreign bishops never even came to England) and made it less able to resist Henry's attacks later on. Moreover, Wolsey interfered in every detail of church administration, making appointments to minor offices, which should have been made by bishops, taking cases away from the bishops' courts to his own legatine court, and forbidding the two convocations of Canterbury and York to meet except when he himself presided over them to extract taxes from the clergy. Thus he became well hated by the clergy, and this hatred spilled over, as it were, onto the Pope, whose representative he was. The fact that the Church's powers had become so concentrated in one pair of hands was to make it easier for Henry to seize these powers. The reins of power were already gathered for his grasping. Also, the Church's will to resist the King had been reduced, for the clergy had begun to think that any sort of rule would be better than this. Thus the effect of Wolsey's rule was to weaken the Church and to decrease its allegiance to Rome.*

Wolsey was certainly unique in the power he held over the English Church. He received his title of *legatus a latere* (literally 'legate from the side') from Pope Leo X in 1518. Usually a *legatus a latere* was a special ambassador from Rome (Wolsey of course had never been to Rome). It was a temporary title assumed for a special commission. Wolsey received it for three years, but he badgered various popes to extend the period from three to five and then from five to ten years, until he finally got Clement VII to grant him the title for life. In the words of Pollard,† 'thus the special envoy from Rome became a contradiction in terms and a papal fixture in England'. The title really meant that the whole authority of the Archbishop of Canterbury was suspended and taken over by Wolsey for the term of his life. Indeed it meant that the Pope delegated most of his control over the English Church to Wolsey during the latter's life-time. It was Wolsey's position as chief minister to Henry, of course, that gave him the power to extract such privileges from successive popes. The popes hoped thus to buy Henry's support in the Italian wars.

The result of Wolsey's legateship was to stifle all reform, for when Warham summoned a Convocation of Canterbury to consider how the province should be reformed, Wolsey threatened him with legal action under the Statute of Praemunire. Wolsey's own Legatine Council, which was summoned instead, achieved nothing. Pollard remarks that 'the annals of convocation were seldom, if ever, so scanty and barren as they were under Wolsey's oppression'.

But it is wrong to state, as did Pollard, that Wolsey's tyrannical rule

* See *England under the Tudors*, by G. R. Elton, second edition, Methuen, 1974, p. 87.
† A. F. Pollard, *op. cit.*, p. 170.

over the Church made Henry VIII's breach with Rome inevitable.* This view, which has been followed by numerous text-book writers since, is clearly rejected by Professor Scarisbrick. He writes,† 'It is not just to accuse Wolsey (as he has been accused) of having left the Church brow-beaten and dispirited—easy prey in other words to the king—and, to compound his guilt, of having clearly pointed the way to the Royal Supremacy by his own union of high spiritual and temporal authority.' As we shall see in Chapter 5, there were plenty of other reasons, apart from Wolsey's behaviour, why the Church at this time was unpopular. Nor (as we shall also see) was the bench of bishops so weakened by Wolsey's placing Italians on it, as to be unable to display vigorous opposition to Henry's moves against the Church. What can be said is that, at a time when clerical privilege and power were much resented by laymen, Wolsey brought both into sharp focus.

Wolsey's foreign policy

Wolsey's foreign policy has puzzled historians over the years. At one time he was considered to have been extremely skilful, holding the balance of power in Europe between Spain and France, insuring that neither grew too strong. Then Professor Pollard, writing at the beginning of this century, produced the theory that Wolsey was chiefly guided by his self-ish ambition to become pope, that he 'hitched England to the Holy See', if the pope changed sides in the endless wars between Spain and France, so too did Wolsey, hoping thus to gain favour with the cardinals or whoever else might have influence in Rome. But this idea, though still held by some leading historians, is rejected by two very great authorities, Professors Wernham and Scarisbrick.‡

Both of these take the view that Wolsey's power and influence over Henry have been exaggerated, that historians have been perhaps misled by the statement of the Venetian ambassador that 'this Cardinal is the person who rules both the King and the entire Kingdom'.

Certainly Henry, as a young man, was inclined to take his pleasures more seriously than his work, but a wet summer, when there was no hunting, could cause him to interfere in Wolsey's schemes (sometimes with furious energy) until a fine spell took him once more after hound and hart in Windsor Forest. Therefore, it is probably impossible to decide what Wolsey aimed at in his foreign policy, because it is impossible to be sure which moves were made at his instigation and which at the King's. With this caution in mind let us proceed to examine the course of events.

Wolsey was not ruling England when the French war of 1512–1514 was entered upon by Henry (the war we considered earlier in this chapter), but he was ruling by the time peace was made in 1514, and

* See A. F. Pollard's *Wolsey*, Fontana, 1970, p. 216.
† *Henry VIII* by J. J. Scarisbrick, Eyre Methuen, 1968, p. 240.
‡ *Before the Armada* by R. B. Wernham, Cape, 1966, and J. J. Scarisbrick, *op. cit.*

must be held largely responsible for that peace, which came originally from the initiative of the new Pope, Leo X. Henry afterwards told the Pope, 'no one laboured and sweated for that peace as did the Bishop of Lincoln' (i.e. Wolsey).

The King of France, Louis XII, who, by the peace treaty, had been espoused to the Princess Mary, died in 1515, soon after marrying his young bride. The new king, Francis I, a cousin of Louis', was only twenty-one-years-old, good-looking (though some said he 'looked like the devil'), ambitious and eager for knightly adventure. Henry was intensely jealous of him, especially when he proceeded to lay claim to Milan, renew the war in Italy and defeat the Swiss in the great battle of Marignano (1515). Here was a prince far eclipsing Henry in renown.

Now let us turn to Scotland, which is, I believe, vital to our story. At the Battle of Flodden (1513) the King of Scotland, James IV, husband of Henry's elder sister, Margaret, was killed. The lords of Scotland, assembling in a general council, at once arranged for the coronation of his little son, James V, born the previous year. Margaret, the Queen Mother, was made 'tutrix' of her son, but an invitation to act as Governor of Scotland was sent to John Stuart, Duke of Albany and heir to the crown should the issue of James IV fail. Albany was the son of Alexander Stuart, Duke of Albany, James III's younger brother, who had quarrelled with James and fled to France back in 1484. Alexander had married into the great French family of de la Tour d'Auvergne. His son John had wedded a lady of the same house, spoke French and 'was rather a Frenchman than a Scotsman'.* John 'arrived in Scotland in 1515, was made Governor in July of that year and held office till November 1524; but during that period he paid two visits to France—in 1517 and 1522'.

It is to Albany's credit that he made no effort to supplant his young cousin and that he kept good order. Nevertheless he 'stood definitely for France'. Soon after his arrival he 'expelled Margaret, who had lost prestige by her marriage with Archibald, sixth Earl of Angus', and was forced to flee to England.

There were thus two parties in Scotland, Albany's pro-French party and the Anglophil party revolving round Margaret and the Douglases.

Now let us turn back to France. Francis I had renewed the treaty of 1514 with England when he had come to the throne, but, despite this, his actions had been unfriendly to her, for he had interfered in Scotland and helped Albany to expel Margaret. Henry and Wolsey therefore determined to stir up trouble for Francis. They hired 20,000 Swiss mercenaries to serve under the Emperor Maximilian and reconquer Milan (which Francis now held). In the spring of 1516 Maximilian 'came down with the snows from the mountains' and marched towards Milan, but

* See *A History of Scotland* by J. D. Mackie, Pelican, 1964, p. 133.

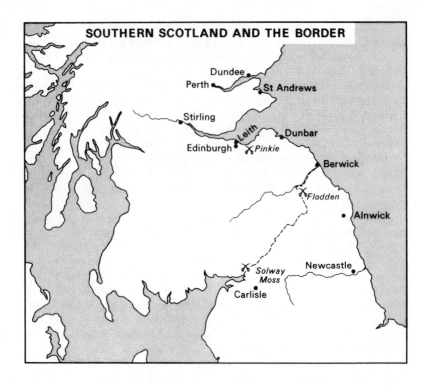

SOUTHERN SCOTLAND AND THE BORDER

when he got within sight of the French army, he suddenly turned round and went back. His reasons are not known. Probably he was, as usual, short of money.*

In 1516 Ferdinand of Spain died and Charles, his grandson, who had been governing the Netherlands since the previous year, became King of Spain and Duke of Naples. He was only a sixteen-year-old boy, and he decided that, to save Naples and gain a breathing space, he would make peace with the conquering Francis. Therefore he made the Treaty of Noyon, recognizing French rule in Milan.

Wolsey decided to make an attempt to overthrow this unwelcome treaty. Again Maximilian was to be the instrument. He paid the Emperor a sum of money to march down into the Netherlands and force his grandson, Charles, to dismiss his pro-French advisers. Maximilian pocketed the money, but proceeded to give his consent to the treaty!

But Wolsey was too sensible to alienate Charles. In 1517 he showed himself anxious to be friendly by lending Charles a substantial sum of money. Francis, alarmed by the 'threat of an Anglo-Burgundian *rapprochement*', withdrew his support from the Duke of Albany, who in this year visited France. The Auld Alliance was in fact renewed by the Treaty of Rouen, but only in terms 'rather disparaging' to Scotland. 'James was

---

* Maximilian was always short of money. Julius II once said that it was no use giving Maximilian any money, as he always wasted it in hunting the chamois.

64

promised a daughter of France, if there were one to spare after two Habsburg princes had made choice.'*

Wolsey reacted quickly to this estrangement between France and Scotland. In 1518, noting that Charles and Francis were already drifting apart (for already the Treaty of Noyon was showing signs of cracking), he invited a French embassy over to England. Amidst great festivities a treaty of alliance between France and England was signed. Tournai was to be handed back to France in return for a money payment. Henry's two-year-old daughter, Mary, was pledged in marriage to Francis' newborn son, the Dauphin.

But this was not the main treaty. A treaty of universal and perpetual peace, the Treaty of London, was also drawn up, to be signed later by all the great powers and twenty lesser powers, beside the Pope, whose legate, Campeggio, was already in London. This grandiose document outlawed war and set up a system of collective security by which any signatory, suffering aggression, could demand help from the others.

It is easy to dismiss all this as fraudulent nonsense, but it seems that Wolsey had some idealism in his character and was genuinely moved by the recent urgent calls of Erasmus, More and other humanists that war in Europe should be abolished.

In any case the signatories of the Treaty of London were soon jolted back to reality by a new danger. The Emperor Maximilian had sustained an apoplectic stroke and was known to be dying. Who would succeed him? Francis I was intending to make a bid for the imperial title, which was in the gift of seven German electors (three archbishops and four lay princes). Already he was spending huge sums in bribery. The traditional role of the Holy Roman emperors was to hold back the Turks, and who better than the victor of Marignano for this task? Strangely enough Henry was also tempted to stand for election. Maximilian seems to have planted the idea in his head, for the impecunious Emperor had long been trying to raise ready money by hawking the succession to his title round Europe (of course he could not really dispose of it).

In January 1519 Maximilian died. That summer an English mission was sent to Germany, if not to secure the title for Henry, at least to try and keep it out of the hands of Charles and Francis. Leo likewise wanted neither Charles nor Francis to triumph, for, since one ruled in Naples and the other in Milan, the papacy would in either case be overshadowed and weakened. But the issue was never in doubt. Charles was now Archduke of Austria (Maximilian's heritage), and, as a German prince he was bound to prevail over foreigners. He was elected unanimously in June 1519 with the title of Charles V.

Once more, it will be noted, Wolsey had failed. But at least he had ingratiated himself and Henry with the papacy. In the war of 1512–1514 they had come to the aid of Julius II against Louis XII. The 1516 expedition against Milan had been launched to save Leo from Francis.

* *Ibid.*, p. 134.

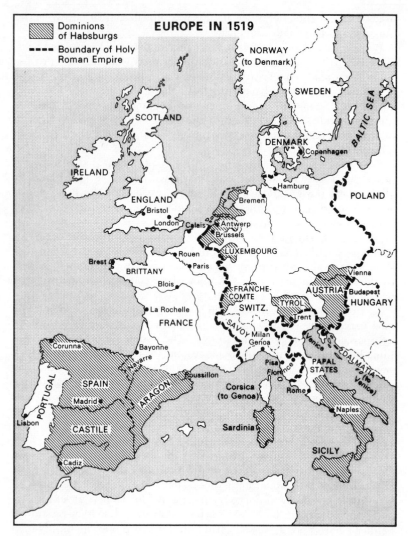

Dominions of Habsburgs

---- Boundary of Holy Roman Empire

NORWAY (to Denmark)

SWEDEN

BALTIC SEA

SCOTLAND

DENMARK

Copenhagen

IRELAND

Hamburg

POLAND

ENGLAND

Bristol

Bremen

London Calais Antwerp

Brussels

LUXEMBOURG

Rouen

Brest

Paris

BRITTANY

Blois

Vienna

FRANCHE-COMTE

AUSTRIA Budapest

TYROL

HUNGARY

La Rochelle

SWITZ.

Trent

FRANCE

SAVOY Milan

Genoa

Venice

DALMATIA (to Venice)

Corunna

Bayonne

Navarre

Pisa

PAPAL STATES

SPAIN

ARAGON

Roussillon

Florence

Madrid

Corsica (to Genoa)

Rome

PORTUGAL

CASTILE

Lisbon

Cadiz

Sardinia

Naples

SICILY

If the Spanish king was 'the Catholic' and the French 'the Most Christian', might not some such title be found for Henry in return for these efforts? As early as 1516 the title *Fidei Defensor* was mentioned, but it was not to be bestowed until 1521, when Henry wrote and presented to the Pope a learned treatise against Luther's teachings.

After Charles's election Francis felt himself more than ever hemmed in by his rival's dominions. To the south-west there was Spain, to the north-east Burgundy, to the east Austria and the Empire, to the south were Naples and Sicily. All these belonged to Charles. War was inevitable between the two great powers, Habsburg and Valois, and both looked to Henry for an alliance.

Wolsey stood for peace. In 1520 he invited Charles over to England for a conference with Henry at Canterbury. A few days later Henry and Wolsey crossed to France and met Francis at the Field of Cloth of Gold. The two sovereigns hated each other cordially, but they made a great pretence of amity at this 'last and most gorgeous display of the departing spirit of chivalry'. A fortnight later Henry met Charles again, at Calais, to finish the business that they had left undone at Canterbury.

At these meetings Wolsey made it clear that he stood by the Treaty of London. If either power attacked the other, England would come to the help of the one attacked. Thus he hoped to stave off war.

But, despite Wolsey's efforts, throughout the year 1520 relations between France and the Empire worsened. Border incidents multiplied, fighting broke out and it was soon obvious that Francis was the aggressor. Charles called upon England to discharge her treaty obligations, but Wolsey still strove to arbitrate. In 1521 he met a French delegation at Calais. Then he went to Bruges to meet the Emperor, who was adamant in his demands for support. Henry was also urging Wolsey towards war.* Moreover, in 1520 the Duke of Albany, now returned to Scotland, was being urged by Francis to make trouble on England's northern border. He failed (the memory of Flodden, says Mackie, was 'too recent'), but there was a definite threat here to England.†

In August 1521 Wolsey made a last desperate effort. He convened a diet or conference at Calais, which was attended by the French and Imperial chancellors and the Papal Nuncio. All was futile. War was already raging in Italy and on the Pyrenees. Reluctantly, Wolsey departed to Bruges and at last signed a treaty with Charles, promising war on France. If by the spring of 1523 Francis had not made peace with Charles, Charles was to invade France from Spain, while Henry invaded from Calais at the head of 40,000 men. The alliance was to be cemented by the marriage of Charles to Henry's five-year-old daughter, Mary, when she attained the age of twelve. (This was the occasion on which Charles promised Wolsey his support at the next papal election.)

Leo X had also made an alliance with Charles to drive the French from Milan; so once more Wolsey is found on the same side as the papacy.

Why did the English government abandon its role as mediator and 'commit itself to plunge into a continental conflict that concerned it so little'? Probably Wolsey was on this occasion obeying his master's voice. Wolsey alone would hardly have committed England to war on such a scale, since it must sooner or later mean asking Parliament for money. After his experience of Parliament in 1515 this was the last thing he would want. Henry, on the other hand, was worried by a new problem, that of the succession to the throne. Henry and Catherine had been married twelve years and there was only one child, and Catherine was thirty-six years old. In 1519 Henry had called physicians over from Spain to

* See J. J. Scarisbrick, *op. cit.*, Chapter 4.
† *A History of Scotland* by J. D. Mackie, p. 134.

examine Catherine. In 1521 he had executed the Duke of Buckingham, a remote cousin of Edward IV's, because his servants had talked indiscreetly about his claim to the throne. These things are an indication of the King's anxiety. When the infant Mary had been pledged to the Dauphin in 1518, Henry was still hoping for a son by Catherine. By 1521 this hope had faded. Marrying Mary to Charles, the most powerful prince in Christendom, was the one way of insuring her peaceful succession (at the expense admittedly of some loss of England's independence). But Charles, who was twenty-one, would need a lot of persuading to wait seven years for Mary. Henry therefore had to pay a high price— the promise of 40,000 men. This then is the probable explanation of England's desertion of a policy of neutrality, rather than the promise of support for Wolsey to gain the papal throne.*

Accordingly, in 1522 and 1523 English armies marched from Calais, ravaging the French countryside, while to the north the Scots once more took the field in support of their old ally, France. But on neither side was any big battle fought, and Wolsey was in dire straits to collect the money to pay for these campaigns.

Meanwhile in 1521 Leo X had died and, far from supporting Wolsey's candidature, Charles had persuaded the cardinals to elect his old tutor, Adrian VI. But Adrian lasted little more than a year, dying in 1523. It was time for Charles to fulfil his promise to Wolsey. 'He did so by writing letters from Spain to recommend Wolsey's election and retarding their transit until the election was over.' The cardinals chose an Italian, Clement VII.

The years 1522 and 1523 had seen the failure of the allied invasion of France (though in 1523 Suffolk, marching from Calais, got within fifty miles of Paris), but they also saw Charles's complete success in Italy, the French armies being driven out of Milan.

Great things were expected of England by the Imperialists in 1524, but Wolsey did nothing. Pollard and other historians have insisted that his inactivity was owing to pique that he had not received Charles's support for the papal crown. More likely his motives were financial. The efforts of these two years had exhausted the King's resources. Nearly £400,000 had been spent on the war in 1522 and 1523. Over £350,000 of this had been raised in forced loans. More could hardly be raised in that way. Accordingly, in 1523 Wolsey called the only Parliament which met during his chancellorship. As we have already seen (p. 59), he got much less than he asked for.

Charles was told then in 1524 that he could expect little help from England. In fact Wolsey was pursuing a double policy. On the one hand he received a secret French embassy; on the other he talked of attacking France if his allies (particularly the rebellious Duke of Bourbon) could

* See R. B. Wernham, *op. cit.*, pp. 100–102. Professor Scarisbrick takes rather a different view. He believes that Wolsey felt himself bound by the Treaty of London to go to war with Francis, who was the aggressor.

first defeat the French armies. 'There is strong evidence', states Professor Scarisbrick, that Wolsey had imposed this double-headed policy 'on a king who was straining to fight.' By the end of August Bourbon had won victories, but Wolsey was sick of the whole war and swore 'a great oath that he wished he had broken his arms and his legs when he stepped on shore to go to Bruges' to sign his treaty with Charles in 1521.

1524 was also the year when Albany was turned out of Scotland by Margaret Tudor, who, with the aid of English money, installed her twelve-year-old son James as ruler (July). The Anglophil party was thus once more in power in Scotland and the Franco–Scottish threat to England ceased to exist. This provides another reason for Wolsey's inactivity this year. There was no need for further war.

The Pope, Clement VII, who resented Charles's triumphs in Italy, was also turning towards France, and in 1524 he came to terms with Francis. Wolsey in this year began secret talks with Clement.

The year 1525 opened with a resounding victory of Charles's troops over those of Francis at Pavia in northern Italy. The French king was captured fighting at the head of his army.

Henry received the news of the victory with joy. Now the Great Enterprise could go forward. Now Henry himself would lead an army into France and claim his rightful crown (for during the Hundred Years' War the English kings had been crowned kings of France and the title had never been renounced). An English embassy was sent to Madrid to suggest a joint invasion of France and her dismemberment between England and Spain. It met with cold response. Charles was penniless and anxious for peace. He had no desire to redraw the map of Europe and thereby add to Henry's power. Wolsey likewise discouraged Henry's warlike ambitions. Nevertheless, he was told to go ahead and collect money for an invasion of France. Parliament was not sitting, and his attempt to levy an Amicable Grant on all men of property met with opposition. Reluctantly Henry gave up his Great Enterprise and 'allowed Wolsey to resume negotiations with France'. Hence in 1525 a treaty was made 'which put an end to three years of confused and wretched war between England and France'. Francis agreed to pay Henry 100,000 crowns a year during the latter's life-time.

Charles then proceeded to snub Wolsey by breaking off his betrothal to the Princess Mary and marrying instead Isabella of Portugal, who brought him a dowry of a million crowns (1526). Meanwhile he had extracted from Francis the Treaty of Madrid (1526) in which France gave up all claims to Milan and even surrendered the Duchy of Burgundy to Charles.

Henry was bitterly disappointed by the failure of his marriage scheme. According to one authority, 'the jilting of Princess Mary by Charles in 1525 marked the great turning point in Henry VIII's reign'.* By this he means that hitherto Henry had stayed close to Spain and to the

* R. B. Wernham, *op. cit.*, p. 111.

papacy. Now he was to begin to loose England from these ties. Indeed, hitherto, all his schemes had revolved around Mary's succession. Now that this seemed doubtful, he brought out from 'the decent obscurity in which he had been hitherto kept' his one and only illegitimate son. The six-year-old boy borne to him by Elizabeth Blount was paraded before the court and created Duke of Richmond. He was, moreover, given precedence over all the peers of the realm including the Princess Mary. He was even made Lord Lieutenant of the North and Lord Lieutenant of Ireland. Henry's intention was plain. In his anger with Charles he was going to make Richmond his heir.

Pollard makes much of Wolsey's folly in having helped Charles to 'a threatening supremacy in Europe'. But whom did Charles threaten? Surely not England but France, for Italy was too far away to be of concern to England, and in fact Wolsey had no interest in it until the 'divorce' became an issue. In any case Wolsey probably knew that Francis had merely signed the Treaty of Madrid to gain his freedom and had no intention of keeping it.

We have noted that Clement resented Charles's victories in Italy. In 1526, 'after months of burrowing and cajoling, a league was formed at Cognac, composed of France, the Papacy, Venice, Milan and Florence' against Charles V. Wolsey 'had a large share in the creation of this league, but to the surprise, then the dismay and finally the anger of its members, refused to become a participant',* though he did in the end contribute 30,000 ducats. His plan was to play the 'honest broker' and let others do the fighting (which promptly broke out in northern Italy). Then when Charles had been taught a lesson, a general peace could be signed (as in 1518) and everyone would be grateful to him and to Henry.

But things did not turn out quite as Wolsey hoped. In May 1527, while he was busy signing a new Anglo–French treaty at Greenwich amidst 'feasts, jousts and disguisings'—a treaty which was to include a marriage between Mary and a member of the French royal house—a large Imperial army marched down from Lombardy and sacked Rome with appalling slaughter. Clement VII narrowly escaped death by fleeing along a tunnel which led from the Vatican to the castle of St Angelo. Now he was a prisoner in Charles's hands (as the French King had been two years earlier).

The situation was particularly awkward for Wolsey, as Henry had just decided that he wanted to divorce Catherine of Aragon and marry Anne Boleyn. How was Wolsey to advance his schemes for a European peace, when Charles, the chief partner in such schemes, was being offended by news of insults to his aunt? And how was the Pope to be persuaded to allow the divorce when he was under Charles's thumb?

It was important for Wolsey that the Pope should be rescued. Hoping to achieve this by diplomacy, Wolsey crossed to France (with a train

* Quoted from J. J. Scarisbrick, *op. cit.*, p. 142.

of nearly a thousand horsemen) and met Francis at Amiens. He hoped to persuade him to make peace with Charles and secure the Pope's release. If this failed, Wolsey planned to set up a sort of caretaker papacy at Avignon (where the popes had lived for a time in the fourteenth century) with himself as temporary Pope, Clement, in his captivity, consenting. Alas, both plans failed. Francis was unwilling to fall in with Wolsey's peace plans, and Clement, hearing of the Avignon scheme, forbade any of the cardinals to go there. Worse still, Wolsey learned that, in his absence, the King (who now supped regularly with Anne Boleyn's father) had sent a messenger to Rome to make his own terms about the divorce. This was a 'grievous blow for Wolsey'. Henry obviously no longer trusted him and was working behind his back. Wolsey hurried home (September 1527) 'to find Henry closeted with Anne and willing to summon him for audience only with her approval'.*

But was all lost? If diplomacy had failed to bring Charles to terms, what about war? England would join the League of Cognac after all. In January 1528 the English herald delivered a declaration of war to the Emperor at Burgos. As usual, in Wolsey's later plans, 'there was no intention of active campaigning'. Henry and Wolsey well knew that war with the Netherlands would damage the wool trade; so they 'quickly concluded a commercial truce with Margaret, Charles's regent in the Netherlands'. The fighting would take place south of the Alps, and England would merely supply money and encouragement.

Wolsey, however, was too optimistic. The continued success of Spanish arms in Italy eventually convinced Clement, now released from captivity and back in the ruined city of Rome, that his best hope was friendship with Charles. 'I have quite made up my mind', he said to a friend 'to become an Imperialist and to live and die as such.' In fact, by 1529, the League of Cognac was breaking up. In July 1529 Francis bowed to the inevitable and made peace with Charles at Cambrai. 'Wolsey was carefully excluded from all share in the negotiations.' The 'arbiter of the destinies of Europe' saw all his dreams collapse, and what hope had he of gaining the divorce when Emperor and Pope were in such close accord?

Pollard stigmatized Wolsey's foreign policy as a 'brilliant fiasco', but he underrated the difficulties with which the Cardinal had to deal.

The reader may well ask, 'Would Wolsey not have been wiser to have imitated Henry VII and kept out of European wars altogether?' Indeed he might. But, remember, he served an adventurous master, while Henry VII had only himself to please. Also, once he had secured the marriage of his daughter to James IV, Henry VII had no threat from Scotland to worry him. Wolsey had such a threat, for Henry VIII had already broken the peace with Scotland before Wolsey came to power. Wolsey may thus have felt it essential to have a war with France as long as she held to an alliance with hostile Scotland. It is plain that Wolsey kept

* *Ibid.*, p. 162.

up the pressure on France as long as there was a hostile party in power in Scotland, that is from 1515 to 1524 (with a break in 1518–1520). He had his eyes fixed, not, as Pollard supposed he should, on Italy, but on the countries of the Auld Alliance.

But in truth it is only in the years 1514–1521 that we can properly speak of 'Wolsey's foreign policy'. It was then that he scored his two great triumphs, the treaty with France of 1514 and the Treaty of London of 1518. After 1521 it would appear he was playing Henry's dynastic game, seeking to secure first Mary's peaceful succession to the throne, and then, when that seemed a forlorn hope, the 'divorce' of Catherine, so that Henry could make a new marriage and at last beget a son.

The 'Divorce'

When Henry married Catherine of Aragon a few weeks after his accession to the throne, he had required a papal dispensation, for she was his brother, Arthur's, widow. Julius II had granted the dispensation, but there was some doubt whether, by canon law, it was legal for a pope to do so. All would have been well if the marriage had been fruitful, but it was not. One after another Catherine's babies were still-born. The only one that survived was a girl, Mary, born in 1516.

Now in *Leviticus*, 20 v. 21, we read, 'And if a man shall take his brother's wife, it is an unclean thing ... they shall be childless.' Henry came to believe that there was a curse on his marriage; that in fact it was no marriage at all and that he was being punished for living in sin. He badly needed a son. In those days a disputed succession was a terrible danger to a country. There was no precedent for a queen ruling England, except Matilda back in the twelfth century, and her reign had been anything but successful. Henry had long been worried about the insecurity of the succession. In 1526 Catherine was forty-two and could hope for no more children; then at the end of the year he fell in love with Anne Boleyn, daughter of a 'rich knight of City origins' who had married the sister of the Duke of Norfolk. Henry determined to discard Catherine and marry Anne.

The first step was taken in 1527 when Wolsey secretly summoned Henry before his legatine court to explain why he was living in sin with his brother's widow. But it was only a preliminary move. The Pope alone would be able to declare the marriage void. Before anything else could be done the news arrived that Rome had fallen and the Pope was a prisoner in the hands of Charles. This was a terrible blow for Henry, for Charles was Catherine's nephew, and the Pope would not now be able to do anything to offend him.

In 1528 Clement granted a commission to Campeggio (an Italian Cardinal) and Wolsey to set up a special legatine court and try the case in England. But he gave Campeggio instructions to 'delay as much as possible'. It took Campeggio three months to reach England from Rome. When he did arrive (in the autumn) he did nothing all winter but talk.

Catherine, meanwhile, was gaining the sympathy of all by her sorrowful dignity and straightforward refusal to sign away her rights and enter a convent.

It was not until June 1529 that the two cardinals opened their court ay Blackfriars. Meanwhile, Charles had triumphed in his war with France and grown too powerful for the Pope to defy him. Catherine appeared before the court and appealed from its jurisdiction to Rome. Clement, who had decided he had no choice but to be friendly with Charles, now grown so great, accepted the appeal and revoked his commission to hold the legatine court. News of the revocation reached England about the same time as did news of the Treaty of Cambrai. The two events between them sealed Wolsey's doom.

The fall of Wolsey

In his fury and disappointment Henry turned on Wolsey. By a writ of *praemunire* he was brought before the Court of King's Bench and accused of breaking a statute of 1392 which forbade anyone to introduce into England papal bulls which would usurp the King's authority. Wolsey realized that he could do nothing against the King. Undoubtedly, as Papal Legate he had broken the statute. Already the King had sum-moned a Parliament to meet in November, and an Act of Attainder passed by it would have cost Wolsey his head. So he hastily submitted. He was stripped of nearly all his wealth (including his two great palaces) and forced to yield up the Lord Chancellor's seal.

Yet he was allowed his liberty, and in 1530 he was ordered north to his province of York (which he had never yet visited) to take up his duties as Archbishop. He departed sadly, but was beginning to take an interest in his duties when his enemies struck again. Some letters were intercepted from his physician, one Agostini, to the Roman Curia. It seems that he had been asking the Pope to excommunicate Henry in the hope that the subsequent rebellion would restore him to power. He was arrested and charged with treason. His enemies, however, were to be cheated of the final reckoning. On his way south he fell ill, and died at Leicester Abbey, lamenting, 'if I had served God as diligently as I have done the King, he would not have given me over in my grey hairs.'

It was an aristocratic clique, led by the dukes of Norfolk and Suffolk, which thrust him from power and then hounded him to his death. They hated him as a base-born knave who had ousted them from their rightful places in Henry's counsels. Anne Boleyn was their instrument. Three years later, having failed to solve the problem they had inherited from him, they would in turn be elbowed out by another base-born minister, Thomas Cromwell.

5 Luther, Anti-Clericalism and the Years of Crisis (1529–1531)

Martin Luther

Since the next period of Henry's reign is often referred to (perhaps erroneously) as the period of the English Reformation, it behoves us to look now at the true Reformation, the revolt against the Catholic Church in Europe.

Wycliffe, the 'Morning Star of the Reformation', has already claimed our attention (*see the Introduction*). We have noted that the persecution of his followers, the Lollards, had merely driven his doctrines underground, not extinguished them. Recent research has shown that 'in the thirteen years before Luther' (that is before 1517) 'there were nearly four hundred prosecutions for heresy in England, leading to death by burning in at least twenty-seven cases, and the majority of those convicted could be described as Lollards'.* Lollardy then was still alight, albeit as a flickering flame.

But the Reformation is usually dated from 1517. In that year a Dominican friar called Tetzel was travelling round Germany 'selling' indulgences for the Archbishop of Mainz. It was a belief of the Catholic Church that money paid to the Church could absolve the payer from having to do his full penance for sin. Also, it could purchase for the payer's deceased relatives some alleviation of their sufferings in purgatory (a place where the dead were obliged to abide for a time until good enough to enter heaven). The money was needed for the rebuilding of St Peter's in Rome, for Julius II had pulled down the old Gothic cathedral and had commissioned a new building in the modern Renaissance style.

At Wittenberg University the professor of theology was a young friar of thirty-four, named Martin Luther, son of a Saxon miner. Luther was horrified that ignorant men should be encouraged to think that a worthless piece of parchment could absolve them from the penalties of sin. He wrote out ninety-five theses, or subjects for argument, and nailed them up on the door of Wittenberg church. One of his theses was, 'Every truly contrite Christian has plenary remission of sin and punishment even without letters of pardon'. He did not expect this action to have any great results. Scholars of this period delighted in the intricacies of logical debate, and he probably foresaw only an interesting theological argument (though he felt very strongly on these matters). Instead his action was to set all Germany aflame.

* See *Tudor and Stuart Britain* by Roger Lockyer, Longmans, 1964, p. 50.

74

Luther's theses attracted great interest. As the controversy spread, Luther was driven to develop his arguments in a number of 'powerfully written pamphlets'. His basic idea, which he got from St Paul, was 'justification by faith', that is that a man is not saved, as the Catholic Church believed, by good works (which often meant pious observances, acts of charity, pilgrimages, etc.), but by the faith within him. A great historian has written of Luther, 'He found such comfort in this idea ... and he grasped it with such energy that it has transformed the world.' *

Luther also taught that the Pope and the Catholic Church could err, that the only true authority was the Scriptures, and that a man could approach God direct in his prayers without the intervention of a priest. 'If the Pope acts contrary to the Scriptures', he wrote, 'we are bound to stand by the Scriptures.'

John Hus of Bohemia had been burned in 1415 for holding just such ideas as these, but Luther successfully defied authority in the shapes of both Emperor and Pope, and proceeded to win half Germany to his idea.

Luther's ideas soon spread to England, and particularly to Cambridge, where Erasmus had already led the way by attacking the more superstitious part of the Church's teachings (relics, pilgrimages, and the monastic life). By the 1520s a group of Protestant dons was meeting there at the White Horse Tavern, which acquired the nickname of 'Little Germany'. Its leaders were Thomas Bilney and Robert Barnes, the latter a friar who belonged to the same order as Luther. Two others were Miles Coverdale and William Tyndale, both of whom were to become famous as Bible translators, while a fifth was Hugh Latimer of Clare College.

Tyndale was horrified at the crude superstitions of many simple people. 'Thousands', he wrote, 'while the priest pattereth St John's gospel in Latin over their heads ... cross so much as their heels and the very soles of their feet, and believe that if it be done in the time that he readeth the gospel (and else not) that there shall no mischance happen to them that day.'

Tyndale felt that the only way to cure the superstitions of the people was to give them a good English translation of the Bible. He asked permission of the Bishop of London to undertake such a translation. When this was refused, he fled to Germany, and by 1524 had completed a translation of the New Testament, which by 1526 had been printed and was circulating in England. Then he began on the Old Testament.

Henry did nothing to encourage Lutheranism. In fact in 1521 he wrote a treatise attacking Luther's ideas, which earned for him from the Pope the title of *Fidei Defensor*, a title which still appears on British coins. Tyndale's New Testaments were among other Lutheran books publicly burned at St Paul's in Wolsey's presence in 1526.

Yet Lutheranism continued to grow. As the old rhyme says,

Turkeys, heresy, hops and beer
Came into England all in one year.

* *Lectures on Modern History* by Lord Acton, Macmillan, 1906.

The year was 1527. We hear in that year of two Essex Lollards travelling to London to meet Robert Barnes, and showing him some old manuscript copies of parts of the Lollard Bible. Barnes in turn sold them a copy of Tyndale's translation of the New Testament. Thus the old and the new Protestants were meeting and 'between 1520 and 1530 there developed a spiritual revolt of whose strength Wolsey, who showed himself contemptuous, was utterly unaware'.

Henry VIII's character

It is time we took a closer look at the character of the extraordinary man who now occupied the English throne. It was Professor Pollard's opinion that the ruin of Wolsey was not solely owing to his failure to get a divorce for Henry, but was rather the natural result of the development of Henry's great egotism.* Henry had always excelled at everything he undertook. As a young man he had been supreme in athletics. 'He was content with such exhibitions as prancing before the ladies between every course in a tourney, or acting as pilot on board ship, blowing a whistle as loud as a trumpet, and arrayed in trousers of cloth of gold.' As he grew older, however, 'the athletic mania wore off'. He became absorbed in architecture. Here also he excelled. 'From his own original designs York House was transformed into Whitehall Palace, Nonsuch Palace was built, and extensive alterations were made at Greenwich and Hampton Court. A generation later a writer described him as " the only Phoenix of his time for fine and curious masonry".'

But after a time he got tired of architecture. Then came the divorce. It presented such difficult problems, became such a challenge, that he became utterly absorbed in politics. This was Wolsey's undoing. The pupil became greater than the master, and would not brook the master as rival. Pollard states, 'The divorce and the insuperable obstacles which he discovered in attaining the end he thought easy at first, did more to harden Henry's temper than any bodily ills. He became a really serious man, and developed that extraordinary power of self-control which stood him in good stead in later years.'

In 1529 Henry was still on the right side of forty. Still in the full vigour of manhood, 'his physical graces were the marvel of those who saw him for the first time'. The new Venetian ambassador thus described him this year, 'In the Eighth Henry God has combined such corporal and intellectual beauty as not merely to surprise, but to astound all men. ... His face is angelic rather than handsome, his head imperial and bold, and he wears a beard, contrary to the English custom.' It was a strong combination, this bluff, open-hearted, handsome exterior and the watchful, secret eye that, as another commentator has it, 'marked what was going on without appearing to mark it, kept its own counsel until it was time to strike, and then struck as suddenly and remorselessly as a beast of prey'.

* See *Henry VIII* by A. F. Pollard, Longmans, 1951 edition, p. 191.

To all this must be added a lively and enquiring mind, an intellect trained under the new influence of the Renaissance (the first of English sovereigns so to be), which could wrestle with deep theological questions (his book against Luther had so impressed Leo X that he had 'read five leaves without interruption' and had remarked in admiration that 'other men which hath occupied themselves in study all their lives cannot bring forth the like') and had composed several masses and a song for the lute. Had Henry been at school today in England, he would have been not only captain of cricket and rugger, but also head prefect and a promising candidate for an open scholarship to Oxford or Cambridge. A more talented man has never sat on the throne of England.

But what was happening in this active mind at this critical moment in the reign? First of all Henry was moving against the Church. As his latest biographer, Professor Scarisbrick, has written, 'In the autumn of 1529 a momentous thing happened. Henry VIII threw in his lot with anti-clericalism, which would never have made full progress without him.' Having dismissed Wolsey from his post as Lord Chancellor, he replaced him with Sir Thomas More, a layman, a 'semi-Erasmian' and 'the author of the most shocking book yet written in England, namely *Utopia*'. From time immemorial the Lord Chancellor had been a bishop. Similarly the privy seal had been held in Henry's reign by three bishops in succession. Now it was entrusted to the hands of Anne Boleyn's father, the Earl of Wiltshire. Obviously, Henry had decided it was time to weaken the Church.

Other men who stayed high in Henry's favour at this time and acted as his advisers were the dukes of Norfolk and Suffolk (the latter of course his brother-in-law) and Stephen Gardiner, the new Bishop of Winchester, whose views on theology were very similar to Henry's.

Anti-clericalism

The English people of the early sixteenth century 'thought little of priests'. Nor was this attitude of mind peculiar to the English. European literature of the later Middle Ages is full of stories ridiculing priests. We find such stories in Boccaccio as well as in Chaucer. 'The hero of one discreditable adventure after another turns out to be a monk or a clerk in secular orders.'* The higher clergy were disliked because of their wealth and ostentation, the lower because of their greed, low morals and ignorance, for very few of the lower clergy were well educated.

The Church in England was enormously wealthy, and this wealth was concentrated in the hands of the larger monasteries, the bishops and a few other incumbents. 'The Church held probably about one third of all land in England, and the incomes of great abbeys like Glastonbury or St Albans, and of bishoprics like Winchester and Durham, exceeded the revenues of the greatest temporal lords.' Moreover the Church had

* See G. R. Elton, *op. cit.*, from which I quote repeatedly in this section.

the reputation, perhaps born of jealousy, of being either an inefficient or else a rapacious landlord. Many thought that society could ill-afford to carry 'this uneconomic burden, this vast institution which absorbed so much man-power, sterilized so much wealth, took so much and gave back so little'.*

Tithes (the one tenth of a farmer's produce which had to be given to the Church, stacked away in the tithe-barn alongside abbey, priory, rectory or vicarage) were a standing grievance. So were payments for the probate of wills and mortuary payments, the latter being 'demanded even of the poorest before a body could be buried in consecrated ground'

Beside all this, the Church courts were powerful and thoroughly disliked. Presided over by bishops and their officials and archdeacons, these courts could try not only clergy but also laymen, if the cause concerned wills, marriage, heresy or breaches of morals. Also they enforced the financial demands of the Church. Hence a great many laymen came in contact with these courts, whose jurisdiction was notoriously expensive, dilatory and corrupt. 'Of all the clergy, the archdeacon in his court and the summoner travelling around the country to serve summons on often innocent people, were probably the most hated.' It was not unknown for people to be excommunicated for no good reason at all, merely so that the archdeacon could get his fee.

'All in all, men were tired of being ruled or badgered by priests.' The parish clergy commanded little respect, not only because they were ill-educated (being 'unable to understand and sometimes even to read the Latin of the services'), but also because they were wretchedly poor and of peasant stock. The higher clergy were worldly and 'practised those abuses against which pope after pope and council after council had issued their edicts'—to wit, pluralism (the holding of more than one benefice), non-residence, simony and nepotism.†

The monasteries, as we saw in the Introduction, were in decline, many of them being more than half empty. Monastic life was no longer respected. 'Abbots and priors lived the life of the rural gentry with whom they consorted, administering their estates, hunting, dining and occasionally drinking.' Often monks took their vows when they were mere boys, too young to understand the meaning of them (Erasmus had particularly objected to this habit). Afterwards they found it impossible to forsake the world.

'The best spirits of the age'—men like Bishop Fisher who was to die for the papacy—desired reform, but the Pope was an Italian prince, wrapped up in his worldly affairs, the English bishops were often occupied with the King's business, and even Wolsey himself had failed to do anything in the way of reform.

* J. J. Scarisbrick, *op. cit.*, p. 243.
† For a definition of these terms see the section on 'Wolsey and the Church' in Chapter 4.

When the Church would not put its own house in order, was it not time for the state to do so instead?

Henry summons Parliament

In the autumn of 1529 Henry summoned Parliament (this is the great Reformation Parliament which was to last until 1536 and accomplish one of the greatest revolutions in English history). His object in summoning it was to bring pressure on the Pope to grant his divorce. He well knew that Parliament would be anti-clerical in temper, and would aid him in his new policy of hostility to the Pope. Clement had given Henry the weapon he needed when he summoned him to Rome to plead his divorce there (see the last chapter). This had been an insult to England. Hitherto, most Englishmen had been sympathetic to Catherine, whom they regarded as a good and injured woman. But Clement's action had aroused patriotic feelings of resentment against the Pope, especially since he was known to be dominated by a foreign prince (Charles). The Breach with Rome was perhaps the inevitable result of Charles's victories in Italy. While Englishmen could tolerate papal interference in England when the pope's policy was merely Italian, when that policy became Spanish, activated by one of the great powers of Europe, tolerance was no longer possible. (Of course the need for the divorce was a powerful catalyst for bringing these changes about, and accelerated the Breach.)

As soon as Parliament met, the Commons 'fell upon the clerical estate' and passed three anti-clerical bills, the third of which forbade pluralism and non-residence. It was altogether a new thing for Parliament to make rules for the conduct of the clergy. Hitherto, this had been done by Convocation. Here was a direct attack upon the independence of the Church. Naturally, the bishops and abbots in the House of Lords blocked the bills. Henry intervened and cleverly persuaded the Lords to allow a joint committee of the two houses to decide the matter. Thus the Lords were more or less tricked into passing the bills. Fisher, Bishop of Rochester, had spoken out most boldly against them.

But these 'mutterings of the storm fell on deaf ears at Rome'. Clement was too much in Charles's power to think of granting the divorce. He made no move.

After its first session Parliament was prorogued for a year. Meanwhile, Henry was busy with a new scheme. In the summer of 1529 he had gone for a progress through the country, and had stayed a day or two at Waltham. Here Stephen Gardiner was lodged at the house of a gentleman who had a clergyman called Thomas Cranmer as tutor to his son. This Cranmer was an old Cambridge acquaintance of Gardiner's, and the two got to talking of the King's 'divorce'. Cranmer, who was a fine scholar, came out with the suggestion that, instead of appealing to the Pope as to whether the dispensation was valid, Henry should appeal to the doctors of divinity in the various universities of Europe. Gardiner took the suggestion to the King, who was delighted with it (declaring that its author 'had the sow by the right ear'). Cranmer and Henry became friends, and Cranmer began a career which was to take him to the heights of power and then to the stake. He was a shy and diffident man, the very opposite of Wolsey, and yet he had physical courage and a certain firmness of character of which he was going to have great need in the future.

In the year 1530 a mission which included Cranmer was sent by Henry to visit the universities of Europe. The investigation it made was very thorough. Libraries were scoured and numerous scholars interviewed and questioned. In the end eight universities, including Paris and Bologna, gave judgments in Henry's favour. Of course a great deal of bribery had been used by Henry and counter-bribery by Charles, to gain verdicts.

Henry's hope in all this was that such a weight of learned opinion would persuade the Pope in his favour, if the marriage case were tried at Rome. But, as the summer of 1530 wore on, it became obvious that Clement, now friendlier than ever with Charles, was not going to give judgment for Henry. Hence the King changed his tactics. He began to urge upon the Pope the view that by ancient English custom no Englishman could be cited in law outside his homeland. The Pope was not impressed.

Henry's active and vigorous mind was by now taking him down very progressive paths. He was delving into old manuscripts, using his own and his servants' scholarship to study the history of papal and kingly power. Already by 1529 he seems to have convinced himself that 'the only power which the clergy had over laymen was absolution from sin. Even papal power was severely restricted'.* He had read William Tyndale's *Obedience of the Christian Man* (brought to him by Anne Boleyn), which asserted the rights of princes to the undivided allegiance, body and soul, of their subjects. In May 1530 he startled a conference of bishops and representatives of the two universities by telling them that he would cause the New Testament 'to be by learned men faithfully and purely translated so that he might deliver to his subjects' (who were reading too many Lutheran books) 'the clear waters of truth'. He then issued a proclamation to this effect.

Henry's agents in Rome in 1530 were set the task of hunting out papal decretals, conciliar decrees, letters of Innocent III (who lived in the thirteenth century), anything which would help Henry to appeal against the Pope's decisions and prove his (the Pope's) powers overrated.

There is little doubt that, by 1530, Henry had decided that he would break with Rome. He just lacked the nerve to do it. 'Twice in 1530 . . . Henry called a gathering of notables to court to ask them whether they would agree that he should disregard Rome and have the divorce settled once and for all in England by the English clergy; and on both occasions

---

* See his conversation with the imperial ambassador, mentioned in Scarisbrick, *op. cit.*, p. 246.

he met refusal.'* 'In November 1530 he told the imperial ambassador that the right of convoking a General Council' (i.e. a council of all the bishops in Europe, as had occasionally met in previous centuries) 'lay with the secular princes, not the pope, and that the latter was no more above a Council than he was above princes; that it would be doing God's service to take away the clergy's temporal possessions; that he had no need of a Council, for, like any prince, he would redress the evils of his own country without intervention from above'.†

In 1531 Henry decided to increase his pressure on the pope. The method he adopted was to accuse all the English clergy of a breach of the Statute of Praemunire (a fourteenth-century statute) for having 'exercised the jurisdiction of the Courts Christian in the realm' (in other words the church courts were illegal, because established by the pope without the King's permission, and all the clergy had broken the law in having used them). Faced with this indictment and the threat of legal proceedings, which might have led to the forfeiture of all their property, both convocations quickly submitted and bought their pardons (Canterbury for £100,000 and York for £18,000). But Henry wanted more than this. Archbishop Warham was summoned to a Council meeting and told that in the text of the clerical grant (the resolution passed by Convocation, granting the money) Henry should have been styled not just 'King and Defender of the Faith', but also 'protector and only supreme head of the English Church'. Faced with this new demand, however, Convocation plucked up its courage and insisted on adding to the new title the saving clause, 'as far as the law of Christ allowed'.

By 1531 then Henry had probably made the momentous decision to break with Rome. He must, however, feel his way cautiously. He needed to guide and educate popular opinion towards his own advanced ideas. He needed to get rid of one or two bishops, particularly Warham and Fisher, and, most of all, he needed a minister, more sympathetic to his ideas than Sir Thomas More, less bone-headed and harder working than Norfolk or Suffolk and a little less cautious and conservative than Stephen Gardiner. Such a man was Thomas Cromwell, who in 1531 'moved into the centre of policy-making'.

* J. J. Scarisbrick, *op. cit.*, p. 292.

† Professor Elton has called the years 1529–1532 the 'Years without a Policy'. Professor Scarisbrick differs from him. On p. 295 of *Henry VIII* he writes, 'These then were not years without a policy, but years without a successful one.' In other words Henry already knew in broad terms what he would do, but was waiting for the climate of opinion in England to alter, so that he would be sure of support.

6 Thomas Cromwell and the Breach with Rome

Thomas Cromwell

Thomas Cromwell was of humble origins. His father was a small business man of Putney, a 'jack-of-all-trades' and a man of 'doubtful honesty'. Thomas left home at eighteen and for ten years led a wandering life. 'He learnt soldiering probably in the French army in Italy, banking in Florence and business methods in the Netherlands.' Before he was thirty he was back in England. 'Having made a good marriage, he devoted himself to law, business and moneylending, and about 1520 entered the service of Wolsey.' * He was a man of powerful intellect, cold and calculating, with a lawyer's mind. He sat in the House of Commons in 1523 and again in the Reformation Parliament of 1529, when he took a part in the anti-clerical debates and in 1530 defended Wolsey when a bill attacking him was brought into the House by his enemies. Perhaps this loyalty to his master commended him to the King. At any rate by the end of 1530 he was sworn in as a Councillor and by 1533 had gained the King's full confidence and was his chief Councillor. He was then about forty-eight. In 1534 he was made Principal Secretary.†

The breach with Rome

'The parliamentary session of 1532 made it plain that a new temper had taken hold of the government. The uncertainties and futilities of the last three years were to give way to a definite plan and purpose.' So writes Professor Elton, and he attributes the change to the fact that Cromwell was now guiding the King's affairs. Certainly, Cromwell was a great help to Henry. Whether, however, he was the originator of the policies now carried through seems doubtful. Professor Scarisbrick's verdict is that 'he neither worked alone nor was he the true initiator of these royal undertakings'.‡

The Commons began by drawing up with Cromwell's help a document called the 'Supplication against the Ordinaries', which listed their grievances against the clergy. This, having been approved in debate,

* I am quoting from *The Earlier Tudors* by J. D. Mackie.
† For centuries British historians presented Cromwell as a man 'devoid of pity and conscience', a veritable ogre, actuated by the lowest passions in his attacks upon the spoils of the Church. Recently, however, the Cambridge historian, Professor G. R. Elton, has shown him as a superb administrator, 'the most remarkable revolutionary in English history' and a man who, though 'ruthless in affairs . . . lacked cruelty'. Elton's view has prevailed and scores of text-books have been put out of date by it.
‡ J. J. Scarisbrick, *op. cit.*, p. 304.

was presented to the King, who accepted it and sent it on to Convocation. When the bishops there rejected it, the King brought forward demands that Convocation was in future to make no new canons (laws) without the royal consent, and that the existing canon law was to be submitted to a committee appointed by the King. The canons approved by this committee would alone be valid. Convocation, confronted by an alliance of King and Commons, could only yield, but the upper house of Southern Convocation did so only after a bitter fight. Unfortunately, Fisher was ill and seven other bishops absent; so it was a minority, a mere 'rump', which granted to the King the clergy's 'precious freedom of legislation', and then only after half-veiled insinuations from Henry that it would be treason to refuse. The document which Convocation drew up is called the 'Submission of the Clergy'. Notice it made the Church dependent not on Parliament but on the Crown. The day after Convocation's surrender Sir Thomas More, a good Catholic, resigned the chancellorship which he could no longer in conscience hold.

Cromwell now proceeded to draw up (possibly with his own hand, for he was a fine lawyer) a series of great statutes, which would bring the English Church right outside the Pope's power.

The first of these was already being debated while the clergy were being brought to heel. It is usually called the First Act of Annates (1532). Annates (or first fruits) were payments made by new bishops to Rome when they succeeded to their sees. They comprised one third of the see's annual revenue. The act proposed to abolish them, and in case, in retaliation, the Pope should refuse to consecrate new bishops, it stated that bishops could be consecrated by an English archbishop. A clause was inserted saying that the act would only come into operation when the King should confirm it by letters patent. This was because Henry hoped that Clement would take the act as a threat and yield on the question of the 'divorce'.

But Clement did no such thing. Instead he threatened Henry with excommunication if he should proceed with the 'divorce'.

In August 1532 Warham, the Archbishop of Canterbury, died. This was the most tremendous piece of good fortune for Henry and Cromwell. In fact, had not the good archbishop been so old, one might be tempted to guess that they had poisoned him! After much hesitation they selected as his successor Thomas Cranmer. It was in some ways a strange choice, but there was method in it. Cranmer had been turned out of his fellowship at Jesus College, Cambridge, for being married. His first wife had died, and he was now in Germany on the King's business, and had just married again, this time to the niece of a Lutheran divine. He was known to be sound on the question of the 'divorce', believing that the Pope's dispensation had been against canon law. Moreover, during a sojourn at her father's house, he had become a great friend and supporter of Anne Boleyn. He was just the man then for Henry's and Cromwell's purpose.

Clement does not seem to have known about Cranmer's new marriage, for he confirmed him in his new office without a murmur, so that Henry now had an Archbishop of Canterbury who would do his will, and yet was indisputably a genuine archbishop. Henry must have known that Cranmer had strong Lutheran leanings, but he was desperate to get his 'divorce', and even the fact of Cranmer having a wife did not put him off. There was need for haste for by the end of 1532 Anne Boleyn was with child.

The pregnancy of Anne is of the utmost importance in the sequence of events, for it stampeded Henry into the action against the Pope which he had so long been contemplating but had hitherto hesitated to take. Why did Anne, who had resisted Henry so long, now yield to him? It is of course impossible to say with certainty, but in the summer of 1532 Henry had begun to treat Anne as his queen. He had bestowed on her the title of Marquess of Pembroke (not 'marchioness' for it was a title in her own right) and lands to the value of £1000 per annum, while in October she accompanied him to France to all intents and purposes as his queen. Perhaps Anne felt that, having gone so far, Henry could not now draw back. Incidentally, although Warham died in August, the nomination of Cranmer as archbishop was not made until January 1533, *after* Anne's pregnancy had been discovered.

In January 1533 Henry secretly married Anne. Soon afterwards Cromwell introduced into Parliament his next great statute, the Act in Restraint of Appeals. It forbade appeals in testamentary and matrimonial causes from the archbishops' courts to Rome. Thus it would be impossible for Catherine to appeal to the Pope against an annulment of her marriage. This great statute* so obviously meant a rupture with Rome that the Commons were quite reluctant to pass it, lest it should lead to reprisals from the Emperor. But Henry persuaded them, and Charles was too beset with his other troubles to take any action.

The stage was now set at last for the 'divorce'. In April southern Convocation, defying Rome, voted with only 25 dissentients that a marriage like that of Henry to Catherine 'was impeded by divine law, which no pope could dispense'. Northern Convocation followed suit. Fortified by these pronouncements (and by the 'determination' of the universities), in May Cranmer set up his Archbishop's Court in a priory at Dunstable and pronounced judgment that Henry's so-called marriage with Catherine had never been valid. A few days later he pronounced that Henry was legally married to Anne. In June Anne was crowned in Westminster Abbey, riding 'in triumph through the City of Westminster, carried on a litter under a canopy of cloth of gold, with her marvellous black hair pouring down onto her shoulders'.† Her child was due in September and the astrologers assured Henry that it would be a boy. But, alas, they were wrong. To Henry's bitter disappointment Anne's baby turned out to be a girl. She was christened Elizabeth.

After the Dunstable judgment the Pope excommunicated Cranmer

* Professor Elton calls it 'Cromwell's masterpiece in statute-making'.
† The description is Professor Scarisbrick's.

and drew up a bull of excommunication against Henry, but did not as yet execute it. He hoped Henry would take Catherine back.

Henry needed to justify his defiance of the Pope, so that he should not appear to his people as a heretic. There was a strong movement afoot in Europe at this time to call a General Council of all the Church bishops to settle matters of doctrine and deal with various well-known abuses. The advocates of a General Council maintained that it would have an authority superior to that of the Pope. Henry let it be known that he supported this movement, that he would appeal to a General Council if the Pope did excommunicate him, and that he regarded the Pope as a usurper whose power over the Church was unwarranted. In 1534 he issued an order that the Pope was to be known henceforth in England as the 'Bishop of Rome'. Thus he managed to make it appear that he was a good Catholic, but one who believed that the Pope should have less influence.

The year 1534 also saw a series of acts which put the coping stone on Cromwell's great ecclesiastical revolution. The Second Act of Annates confirmed the first one, and 'laid down the procedure for the election of bishops and abbots'. Another act ordered the payment of first-fruits and tenths (papal taxes) to the Crown, while the Act of Supremacy declared that the King 'justly and rightfully is and ought to be Supreme Head of the Church of England'. Also an Act of Succession was passed declaring the Princess Mary to be illegitimate and making the children of the new marriage heirs to the throne.

The Act of Succession included a requirement that the King's subjects take an oath to observe it. All men of consequence were expected to take this oath. Nearly all did, but Sir Thomas More and John Fisher, Bishop of Rochester, refused. They were put in the Tower.

It must not be thought that Henry had met little opposition from the clergy. In the early stages of the revolution they opposed him stoutly. For instance the First Act of Annates had been opposed by all the bishops and two of the abbots in the House of Lords, and had only been passed after Henry himself had been down to Parliament three times. But each year death removed members of the old guard of bishops and Henry replaced them with men more inclined to his way of thinking. 'Death— above all Warham's . . .—served Henry well.' Those bishops who still stood out against him were bullied into compliance by being put on charges of *praemunire* and threatened with the Tower, until only Fisher was left.

Cromwell now saw that there was something lacking in the existing law to carry through his revolution against papal power. The refusal of the oath of succession did not carry the death penalty. In the autumn session of 1534 therefore he got Parliament to pass the Statute of Treason. It made it treason to deny the King's supremacy in the Church by spoken word as well as by deed or writing. Thus the expression of opinion alone was treason. A 'bloody law' indeed, as Cromwell's accusers one day were to tell him.

Next year (1535) 'Cromwell used the recent Acts to make some notable examples'. The new Pope, Paul III, who had just succeeded Clement VII, infuriated the King by making Fisher a cardinal. Henry remarked that when the red hat arrived Fisher 'would perforce wear it on his shoulders'. Fisher was accused before a London jury of stating that the King was not Supreme Head of the Church. He was found guilty and beheaded. Three priors of the Carthusian order had already been hanged for the same crime. Now it was the turn of Sir Thomas More, a scholar 'whose name and fame were known through Europe'. He was the most kindly and human of men, and his life had been an example of gracious living. Moreover he was an old friend of Henry's, and the King had often strolled with him in his garden at Chelsea in friendly conversation. He made a brilliant defence, but was found guilty and beheaded.

Henry's show of force was sufficient. 'No leader emerged to challenge the policy of the Crown.'

Today we remember More, but at the time it was the killing of Fisher, a prince of the Church, which shocked the people.* Paul III had at first been inclined to come to terms with Henry, but, on hearing of Fisher's death, he drew up a second bull of excommunication, though, like the first one, it was not at once put into effect, for the simple reason that, Charles V being embroiled with the Moors in Tunis, there was no secular power available to enforce it.

The end of Anne Boleyn

By the year 1535 Henry was beginning to tire of Anne Boleyn. She had borne him only one child and that a girl. He desperately needed a son. Already he had his eye on Jane Seymour, daughter of a Wiltshire knight. Jane was brought to court and her relations given high titles. But little could be done while Catherine of Aragon was alive, for to annul the Boleyn marriage would raise awkward questions about the validity of the earlier union. Moreover, any marriage by the King within the lifetime of Catherine was a standing insult to Spain. Henry desired to be on better terms with Charles who at this time was at the height of his power. But in January 1536 Catherine conveniently died. A few weeks later Anne miscarried. It was now essential to find a new queen.

In the spring of 1536 evidence was prepared to incriminate Anne of adultery with several young men about the court. Certainly Anne had

* J. J. Scarisbrick's *Henry VIII* has a fine passage on Fisher, p. 331, which I here quote: 'Fisher had been a relentless opponent of Henry since 1527, standing across every path the king tried to follow, unmoved by threats, undaunted by his growing loneliness, busy in Convocation and Parliament, tireless in his support of Catherine, and, after he had said all he had to say in so many books on the divorce that he could not later remember exactly how many he had written, speaking out from the pulpit. Before his final imprisonment he had endured one confinement, several verbal warnings, two charges of treason. Unlike Thomas More, Fisher became increasingly bold and blunt the further Henry advanced, and in 1533 had taken the supreme step of appealing secretly to the emperor to use force against the King, a most remarkable, desperate action.'

been indiscreet. Perhaps in her intense desire to bear a son, she had been guilty. At any rate she had few friends about court except Cranmer, and he served the King before all else.

Suddenly Henry struck. Five men were arrested and accused of adultery with Anne (one was her own brother!). One of them confessed under torture. The rest denied the charge. All were condemned to death. Anne was brought to trial before a special commission of peers. Though denying everything she was found guilty and executed (by a headsman specially brought over from Calais). 'Two days before she died a court presided over by Cranmer at Lambeth reached the astounding conclusion that Henry's adultery with her sister' (Mary Boleyn had once been his mistress) 'had rendered the marriage void from the start'. Within a fortnight Henry had married Jane Seymour. At least no one could deny the legitimacy of the progeny of this marriage, for both Henry's previous queens were dead when it took place.

The dissolution of the lesser monasteries

Cromwell's biggest problem, like Wolsey's, was to find the money to carry on the King's government. The fall in the value of money (*see* Chapter 17) had continued. The buying power of English coins declined and the King's income stretched even less far. Meanwhile, the excommunication of the King was alarming. Both Spain and France were considerably greater powers than England and both were Catholic. What if the Pope should ask one of them to attack England and depose Henry? Henry needed ships and coastal fortresses and he needed them quickly. Where was he to get the money to pay for them? The monasteries owned vast lands and much valuable plate. Once the bastions of civilization in a barbarous world, they had now (it was believed) outlived their usefulness. Moreover, the monastic life was out of fashion. Erasmus and other writers had taught people to be scornful of it. Most of the monasteries were more than half empty. The monks were believed to live comfortably and to spend little on charity. They had the reputation of being rapacious landlords.

Whether the monasteries were really in a bad state and no longer useful is a big question which we cannot discuss fully here. Protestant historians in recent years have certainly been too sweeping in their condemnations. A Catholic counter-attack has been led by Dom David Knowles whose three-volume work, *The Religious Orders in England*, has become something of a classic. In this third volume, *The Tudor Age*,* he argues that with their daily doles of 'broken meats' (left-overs from the monks' tables) and the maintenance of boys in local grammar schools, the monasteries probably spent as much as ten per cent of their income on charity.

Many monasteries kept a great number of servants. For instance at

* Cambridge University Press, 1959, pp. 265–266.

Rievaulx in Yorkshire there were 102 servants to 22 monks. In the lesser monasteries the proportion of servants to monks was about three to one. But, as David Knowles points out (pp. 261–262), not all these by any means were domestic servants. Many were agricultural labourers (known as 'hinds'). Many were specialists working in the bakery, brewery, storehouses, furnaces, etc. Many would have been engaged when the monasteries were less empty (before Erasmus's attacks began).

That the monks were often spiritually corrupt is probably true. But the Carthusian houses presented an important exception. The London Charterhouse at Smithfield showed its metal in 1535 when its prior, John Houghton (together with two other Carthusian priors), was imprisoned and finally executed for refusing to take the oath acknowledging the King's Supremacy. They were followed by three monks of the London Charterhouse who were chained by the neck and legs to posts for a fortnight 'without the possibility of moving' before being likewise tried, condemned and executed. Finally two years later, ten monks of the same house, who had held out against all Cromwell's efforts to make them renounce the authority of the pope, were put in a ward of Newgate prison and starved to death. As they lingered in their cell, chained without possibility of movement, Margaret Gigs, adopted daughter of Sir Thomas More, bribed her way into the prison disguised as a milkmaid and fed them with her own hands from a basket of food she had brought with her. She was soon discovered and forced to leave the ten monks to die.*

Other Carthusian houses were not so staunch in their faith, but they also produced men willing to resist the oath of supremacy.

Whichever view we take, the Protestant or the Catholic one, the fact remains that Cromwell was intent on getting rid of at least the lesser monasteries. Many of them did not come under the archbishops but took orders from some other house on the Continent (an irritant this to Cromwell with his tidy lawyer's mind). How then could he touch them? The answer was simple. Henry himself was now Supreme Head of the Church and in this capacity he appointed Cromwell as his Vicar-General (January 1535) and ordered him to examine and reform the Church.

Cromwell began by appointing commissioners in each diocese to assess the wealth of the Church. They worked hard and soon produced a sort of 'sixteenth-century Domesday Book' called the *Valor Ecclesiasticus*, listing all Church property. Later in the year he sent round visitors to all the monasteries to report on their financial and moral state. The visitors (five in all) worked fast. Two of them visited a hundred and twenty monasteries in the north in two months. Some districts, including the whole of Lincolnshire, seem to have been missed out.

What Cromwell wanted, and what he got, was evidence to shock the Commons into passing a bill to dissolve the monasteries. The visitors reported some immorality and loose-living, and a lot of general laxity

* See Dom David Knowles, *op. cit.*, pp. 235–236.

in the observance of rules. It was sufficient for Cromwell's purpose. Before the visitation was finished he introduced a bill into the Commons to dissolve the lesser monasteries, those with an income of less than £200 a year. These were the ones least likely to be able to organize resistance. 'The property was to go to the Crown. The heads of the houses were to receive pensions,' and the rest of the monks were to be given the option of either entering larger houses or becoming secular clergy, when vacant livings could be found for them.

The Dissolution Act was passed in March 1536. Soon afterwards Parliament set up a new Court of Augmentations to deal with the mass of complicated business which would arise. The officers of this court were sent round to make surveys of land, take inventories of lead, gold, silver and precious stones, and see that the monks were properly settled.

The Pilgrimage of Grace

'By the summer of 1536, a time when Henry was riotously happy, celebrating his third marriage amidst incessant music, pageants and warm days on the river, there was grumbling unrest in the Midlands and the North. In October it burst into rebellion.'* The government was taken by surprise. The rebellion, which began in Lincolnshire, but spread to Yorkshire and the whole North, shook Henry's power severely.

The North at this time was the conservative area of England. Its people were loyal to the old feudal families, and resented the increasing power of Cromwell and the central government in London. In Lincolnshire it was suspected that the King had designs on the parish churches as well as on the monasteries ('Soon his hand shall be in everyone's pocket'). The rising was touched off 'by an inflammatory sermon preached by the Vicar of Louth'. The King's tax-collectors and monastery commissioners were the first people attacked. Many of the gentry joined the rising, making the demands 'that the King should suppress no more abbeys, should impose no more taxation, should surrender Cromwell to the people, and get rid of heretical bishops' (Cranmer, who was becoming more and more Lutheran, had promoted Hugh Latimer, a Cambridge Protestant, to be Bishop of Worcester).

Henry sent a rough reply to the Lincolnshire rebels (describing them as the commons of 'one of the most brute and beastly shires in England'), and on hearing it read out by his herald, they hastily dispersed, but by then the rising had spread to Yorkshire and indeed to the whole North. Robert Aske, a Yorkshire lawyer, son of a knight, appeared as its leader. Many gentry and even some nobles joined it and soon the rebels had captured York, and had 30,000 men at Doncaster, 'most of them well-armed and on horseback'.

The rebels took as their banner the 'five wounds of Christ', and described their movement as a Pilgrimage of Grace, but, as in Lincolnshire,

* J. J. Scarisbrick, *op. cit.*, p. 339.

the York rebels had many grievances beside religious ones. Enclosure of land for sheep farming (*see* Chapter 17) was one of them; others were the exactions of landlords and the general rise in prices.

Unlike the Lincolnshire rebels, who were on the whole ready to accept the Royal Supremacy, 'Aske, after some debate, called for England's return to obedience to Rome.' As in Lincolnshire, however, the Yorkshire rebels demanded that 'the advance of heresy should be halted, that the heretical ... bishops should be cast out (especially Cranmer), that Cromwell and Rich and other base-born councillors should be supplanted by men of decent birth, that ... the leading figures in the suppression of the religious houses should be punished.'*

Henry called on the Duke of Norfolk, the best soldier of the time, to quell the revolt. He was living in 'sulky semi-retirement', being jealous of Cromwell, but he responded to the King's call, and soon had quite a large, though ill-equipped, army. Feeling too weak to fight, he parleyed with the rebels at Doncaster Bridge and arranged a truce, while their demands were submitted to the King.

When Henry heard this news he was furious. But what could he do? Many of Norfolk's men sympathized with the rebels. Lord Darcy had surrendered Pontefract Castle, and more and more knightly families and their tenants were coming in. Obviously feeling was strong against upstart Cromwell with his 'villein blood'.

Henry played for time. He suggested another meeting between the rebel leaders and Norfolk. A 'great council' of the 'Pilgrims' met at York to consider the King's answer, and drew up articles demanding among other things a 'free Parliament', in which the influence of the King's servants in the Commons was to be reduced, greater freedom of speech, and the cessation of royal interference in elections. They also demanded that spiritual matters should be dealt with by Convocation, not by Parliament.

In December there was another meeting between the rebel leaders and Norfolk at Doncaster. This time Aske seems to have been very impressed by Norfolk's word, the Duke promising that he would present the articles to Parliament, and that the rebels would have a 'full and free pardon'.

When he heard the Lancaster herald read the promise of a pardon, Aske tore off his badge of the five wounds, declaring that he would 'wear no badge but the King's'. He then persuaded his followers, with some difficulty, to disperse.

The crisis was over. A few further risings (which Aske tried to prevent) enabled Henry to break his word and execute over two hundred of the rebels, including Aske, who was hanged in chains at York, and Lord Darcy, who was beheaded on Tower Hill.

Henry had been very lucky. 'The King was saved not so much by the loyalty of his friends as by the loyalty of the rebels. Time and again

* See J. J. Scarisbrick, *op. cit.*, p. 340.

Aske refused to take advantage of his opponents' weakness and held back the hotheads who wanted to march boldly southwards.'* Moreover, 'Rome was ready to intervene. As soon as the news arrived that the North was up, Reginald Pole' (a Yorkist nobleman living in Rome) 'was made a cardinal and sent to Flanders ... to muster support for the Pilgrims and maybe to come to England at the head of a military force'. But Pole was dilatory. He did not arrive in the Netherlands until 1537. Henry was also lucky in that Charles and Francis were quarrelling at the time of the rebellion.

One result of the rebellion was that the vague authority of the 'King's Lieutenant and Council in the north parts' was replaced by a properly constituted Council of the North. It was to carry on the King's Government in the five counties of Yorkshire, Durham, Northumberland, Westmoreland and Cumberland. Although its first president was a bishop and two earls were members, it was mainly composed of middle-class men, knights and lawyers, who were paid a regular salary and kept in close touch with the Council at Westminster. It had great powers and on the whole used them well, so that the North was now really pacified and reduced to obedience, at least for a time.

Moves towards an Erasmian position

Since Cranmer had been promoted to Canterbury, other advanced thinkers had received high office in the Church. In 1535 Hugh Latimer was made Bishop of Worcester, and Nicholas Shaxton Bishop of Salisbury. Now both of these were more than Erasmians. We have seen (in the previous chapter) that Latimer, a Cambridge man, was one of those Lutherans who gathered about Barnes and Bilney in 'Little Germany' in the twenties. Shaxton was also a Lutheran. Probably, when monasteries were being dissolved, it was helpful to have such men on the episcopal bench. Also at this time Cromwell was looking for support against the Catholic powers from the German Protestants, and this was one way to get it.

Henry, himself inclined to be an Erasmian, had a personal liking for both Cranmer and Latimer, and he did not stand in the way of their reforms, which as yet were not Lutheran, but only in the line of the best practices of Catholic humanism.

In 1534 Convocation petitioned the King to sanction the issue of an English Bible. Tyndale, working in the Netherlands, under the protection of the Merchant Adventurers, had already completed his fine translation of the New Testament and of the first books of the Old. But in 1535 he was arrested by the city authorities of Antwerp and, eighteen months later, strangled and burnt as a heretic. Those parts of the Bible he had completed are preserved with only a few changes in our Authorised Version, and 'no one has ever questioned that they are the work of

* See J. J. Scarisbrick, *op. cit.*, p. 342.

a genius and a principal moulder of the character of modern England'.
Tyndale's work was carried on by another Englishman in exile, Miles Coverdale, an ex-friar, who worked in Switzerland. The whole Bible, thus completed and printed in Zurich, was allowed into England in 1536—a major date surely in British history. In 1537 Cranmer approved a new version in which the parts by Coverdale had been improved by John Rogers, who published abroad under the alias of 'Thomas Matthew'. It is thus called 'Matthew's Bible'. This was finally reprinted in Paris, by Henry's order, in 1538, so that a Great Bible would be available for every parish church.

In 1536 Henry and Cromwell took a very cautious step towards religious reform. 'The doctrine of the Church was in sore need of definition.' Argument was waxing hot throughout the land. Convocation, presided over, to its own amazement, by Cromwell's (i.e. the Vicar-General's) proctor, drew up an official statement of faith, 'the Ten Articles'. They were definitely Lutheran in hue. 'They mentioned only three sacraments, baptism, penance and the sacrament of the altar, denounced the abuse of images, warned men against excessive devotion to the saints and against believing that "ceremonies have power to remit sin" or that masses can deliver souls from purgatory.'* Part of the Ten Articles follows the Augsburg Confession, the great statement of Lutheran theology, almost verbatim. It was followed in 1537 by the Bishop's Book, a publication produced by Convocation after long debates, which was equally Lutheran in outlook. Henry consented to the Ten Articles and to the Bishop's Book, which was to be read to the people on Sundays. Why, since he lived and died a good Catholic, did he do so? One reason is that he was angling for an alliance with the Protestants of Germany and wished to please them. But it does also appear that his active mind was influenced by the numerous Protestant writings which were being printed in England about this time. Then too it was a period when both Cranmer and Cromwell had great influence over him and both of them were Protestant. Professor Scarisbrick writes, 'that Henricianism was merely "Catholicism without the pope" will not do ... there can be no doubt that the Henrician Church took long strides towards the Reformers and that the English Protestantism which came to full flower in the next reign had many roots in this one.'† Nevertheless, I think we must admit that Henry's views were always closer to those of Erasmus than to those of Luther.

'Cromwell, acting as the Supreme Head's deputy, followed the Ten Articles with instructions to the clergy to preach against the usurped power of the Bishop of Rome, to discourage the veneration of images and relics and the making of pilgrimages, to teach children the Lord's Prayer, creed and commandments in English, and to place an English Bible in every church.'‡

* See *Henry VIII* by A. F. Pollard, 1951 edition, p. 303.
† J. J. Scarisbrick, *op. cit.*, p. 399.
‡ See *The Tudor Age* by J. A. Williamson, second edition, Longmans, 1957, p. 155.

All these things had been recommended by Erasmus, who during his lifetime (and he only died this year) was regarded as a good Catholic. Two years later (1538) Cromwell went further and issued injunctions ordering not only a Great Bible to be purchased and placed in every church, but also the public reading in English every Sunday of the Lord's Prayer, creed and commandments, and the removal of all shrines to which pilgrimages and offerings were made. Many tombs and shrines were thereupon destroyed, including the immensely wealthy one of Thomas à Becket, which yielded 'two great chests of jewels' to the King's Treasury.

The dissolution of the greater monasteries

Many monks and friars had been implicated in the Pilgrimage of Grace, and after it the abbots of Kirkstall, Whalley and Jervaux were executed, and the lands of their abbeys confiscated. After the fall of these three great northern abbeys, the dissolution of the others 'continued piecemeal in the next four years'. Some abbots, seeing the way things were going, voluntarily surrendered their abbeys, making the best terms they could with the government. Others, like those of Reading and Glastonbury, resisted and were executed on charges of treason.

In 1537 Cromwell sent round his commissioners again to take surrenders of abbeys, and in 1539 an Act of Parliament was passed legalizing all surrenders and vesting the property forfeited in the Crown. The last abbey surrendered in 1540.

With the abbeys fell the friaries, much poorer houses, usually located in towns. All that remains of many of these today are streets called 'Blackfriars' or 'Greyfriars' and a few crumbling stones.

The results of the dissolution

The dissolution of the monasteries was undoubtedly one of the most barefaced pieces of robbery ever indulged in by a British government. Yet the monks were not badly treated. About thirty ex-abbots became bishops within a few years of the dissolution. Others received good pensions. Monks and friars were either given livings in the church as secular clergy or pensioned off, and the pensions, though small, were at least paid right up to the death of the last pensioner early in the seventeenth century.

Much of the land was sold by the Crown to wealthy merchants, nobles or gentry, who sold the lead off the roofs (if the Court of Augmentations had not already done this) and allowed the buildings to fall into decay, using the walls as a quarry for the building of their new manor houses (often called 'The Abbey). Thus these beautiful buildings were allowed to become ruins, with a few notable exceptions like Bolton Abbey in Yorkshire, where the monastic church became the parish church, or the six abbeys mentioned below whose churches became cathedrals for new dioceses. The noble ruins of abbeys are hence familiar sights today in

Britain, suitable now only for picnics on summer days (for it was the abbeys in the heart of the countryside which could not perforce be used as churches).

Of course the dissolution meant a great increase in the revenues of the Crown. One historian estimates an increase of £100,000 a year, which would mean that Henry's income was doubled; but Henry's needs were so pressing that about three quarters of a million pounds worth of land had to be sold in the last eight years of his reign, and the annual revenue he retained from monastery lands was only about £40,000.

Not all the money was wasted or used to take up the slack of falling money values. Six new bishoprics were founded—Oxford, Chester, Gloucester, Bristol, Peterborough and Westminster (of these all but Westminster have survived). New chairs were endowed at Oxford and Cambridge in Greek, Hebrew, Theology, Law and Medicine, and a great deal of money was spent on defence, lest the Catholic powers should attack the new Reformation England. The coasts were fortified with 'low-built, thick-walled stone castles', and the fleet was rebuilt, several vessels being broken up and replaced by more modern, formidable ships. In fact Henry left to his successors a powerful, up-to-date navy. But a great deal of the King's new treasure was dissipated in the wars with Scotland and France towards the end of his reign.

It has been argued that the dissolution cemented the Royal Supremacy on England and made a papal restoration well nigh impossible, because so many families of gentry came to hold monastic lands and thus to have a vested interest in Protestantism. It is true Mary was unable to restore monastic lands, much as she wanted to, but on the other hand she did restore the Pope's power in England. Nor did all the families who held monastic lands adhere to Protestantism. Some, like the Russells, earls of Bedford, certainly did, but the earls of Worcester remained staunch Catholics even though they held large monastic estates. Probably many Catholics came to share Erasmus's belief that monasticism was bad, and to sympathize with Henry's actions against it.

That the gentry class was strengthened by the dissolution there can surely be little doubt. The men who bought monastery land often bought it on a tenure not liable to wardship, that is to say they owed no feudal dues to the King for the land. This gave them a sturdy independence. Moreover, they usually bought it with its monastic advowsons, that is the right to appoint the clergy to certain neighbouring parishes.* Here we see then the growth of that sturdy class of squires, economically independent of the Crown, yet with power over the Church, which was to play such a great part in the history of seventeenth-century England.

* See *The Crisis of Parliaments* by Conrad Russell, Oxford University Press, 1971, p. 118

7 Cromwell's Other Policies.
His Fall and Achievement.
Henry's Last Years

The union with Wales

Nothing is more astonishing to us, when we study Thomas Cromwell, than his extraordinary energy. Amongst all the other business of the year 1536 he found time to steer through Parliament an act which was to determine the government of Wales right up to the present day.

Wales at this time was divided into two parts. In the north-west was the Principality of Wales, which included the area conquered by Edward I from Llewelyn back in the thirteenth century, and comprised six counties. The rest was composed of marcher lordships, about one hundred and thirty in number, where the king had only indirect control, and where each petty lord professed to wield the powers of the Welsh prince his forbears had at one time displaced. Actually, fifty or so of the lordships had by this time come into the king's direct possession, either by inheritance from the House of Lancaster or conquest of that of York. But the remainder administered laws of their own, and it was easy for criminals to escape from one lordship to another where they could not be touched. We hear of heiresses being abducted and forcibly married, of juries refusing to convict obvious criminals, of witnesses absenting themselves from law courts out of fear, and of lords misusing the old laws of Hywel Dda to surround themselves with body-guards of lawless ruffians for whom they pretended to stand surety. The king's jurisdiction in theory extended to these areas through his Council at Ludlow, where first Arthur and later Mary had ruled as Prince and Princess of Wales respectively.

Cromwell's first move (in 1534) was to strengthen this Council of Wales and the Marches by putting Rowland Lee, Bishop of Coventry and Lichfield, one of Wolsey's old henchmen, in charge as its President, with instructions to be very strict.

Backed up by a 'burst of legislation' applying to Wales from Parliament, Rowland Lee *was* very strict. In fact he proved 'an extreme severe punisher of offenders', and is said to have hanged in all 5000 evildoers.

But once the area was reduced to order, Cromwell decided upon conciliation and his Act of Union of 1536 abolished the marcher lordships altogether, setting up seven new shires, and enlarging five others (including the three English border counties that came under the Council of Wales). Henceforth Wales was to send MPs to Westminster, one from each shire, and one from each shire town. Welshmen were to become

JPs and administer the law in petty and quarter sessions, while the king's judges were to travel in circuit throughout all Wales instead of only in the Principality. The English common law was to extend to all Wales, and Welshmen were in every way to be equal under the law to Englishmen.

This statesmanlike act was welcomed in Wales, and certainly made the Welsh more loyal than ever to the Tudors, a most necessary state of affairs, when we consider the long, exposed Welsh coastline, so close to Catholic Ireland. The western approaches were a danger point to Reformation England, as who should know better than the son of that Henry Tudor who had himself invaded through Wales? *

Ireland

Cromwell dealt with Ireland with the same energy that he dealt with Wales, but the problems there were far greater. Garret More's long life had ended in 1513, when he was killed in a skirmish. He had come as near as any man since the Conquest to being accepted as king of all Ireland. His son, the new Earl of Kildare, was made Deputy by Henry.

It was soon obvious that the new earl was not as strong as his father. The government lost power and authority. The Pale dwindled in size and became more and more Irish. Complaints began to arrive at Westminster against Kildare's rule.

In 1520 Henry sent over the Earl of Surrey as lieutenant instead of Kildare. Surrey had an army of 1100 men, but he soon discovered it was not enough. He told Henry he would need 6000 to pacify the country, but Henry could not afford such an army and, after two years, Surrey was removed and Kildare was restored.

But Kildare had many enemies. His rivals, the Butlers, earls of Ormond, were relations of Anne Boleyn, and, in her period of favour, this told against him. In 1533 the Council at Dublin (some twelve men who were mostly pro-English) complained to Cromwell about Kildare. In 1534 the Earl was summoned to England and lodged in the Tower. He left his son, Thomas Fitzgerald, in charge in Ireland. But 'Silken Thomas', a handsome youth of twenty-one, was rash and hot blooded, and, being told (falsely) that his father was dead in the Tower, 'the victim of a cruel and heretic king', he rose in rebellion. Cromwell sent over Sir William Skeffington as Deputy with the largest army seen in Ireland for some time. Aided by the Butlers, he crushed the rebellion, and in 1534 Silken Thomas surrendered and was lodged in the Tower (where his father had now truly died). In 1537 he was executed at Tyburn together with five of his Geraldine uncles, it being Cromwell's (and Henry's) desire to exterminate the whole Geraldine race.

Thus was the power of the Geraldines broken and Ireland learned to fear Cromwell as she was to fear his namesake a hundred years later.

* For a good account of the Act of Union see *A History of Modern Wales* by David Williams, John Murray, 1934.

After this, Henry and Cromwell tried to fasten the English Reformation on Ireland. The Irish Parliament was persuaded, with some difficulty, to repudiate the pope, to acknowledge the king as Supreme Head of the Irish Church, and to suppress the Irish abbeys. Abbey lands were useful in bribing the king's enemies and Ireland was reduced to some sort of order; but four years after Cromwell's fall, the first Jesuit mission appeared in Ireland and the 'island of saints' once more turned her eyes towards Rome.

The danger from the Catholic powers

In 1535, after the execution of Fisher and More, the new pope, Paul III, had prepared a bull of excommunication and deposition against Henry. He knew that there was no hope of getting Henry's subjects to act upon it, but hoped that Francis or Charles or both might dethrone Henry. But Charles and Francis were always at loggerheads, and indeed towards the end of 1535 the death of the last Sforza duke of Milan led to further enmity between them, for Charles held that the duchy of Milan now lapsed to him as its feudal overlord. Francis was determined to take it from him, and war broke out in the following year. Watching all this, Paul III saw that the time was inopportune for the publication of his bull, and he kept it in suspense.

Nevertheless the situation was dangerous, for where was England to turn for help if the great powers should combine against her? Cromwell looked for an alliance with the Protestant princes of Germany, and in 1533 and again in 1535 English missions were sent to Germany to 'survey the possibilities of co-operation'. Henry, however, a more skilful and experienced diplomat than Cromwell, was more cautious. He did not want to alienate Charles and refused to fall in with Cromwell's plan of an alliance with the Schmalkaldic League, a league of German Protestant princes, who were Charles' enemies.

Once Catherine of Aragon and Anne Boleyn were dead (1536) Henry saw no reason why he should not be on good terms with Charles. Meanwhile, it was obviously to his interest to keep Francis and Charles at loggerheads. This he did by offering his hand in marriage to ladies on both sides, for Henry was now a widower again, his third wife, Jane Seymour, having died in 1537, soon after giving birth to a boy, the Prince Edward. But neither party could supply him with a suitable bride, and the French ambassador was not pleased with his suggestion that he should choose one from a bevy of beauties to be paraded at Calais. 'The ladies of France,' he pointed out, 'were not to be inspected like ponies.'

The dissolution of the monasteries and the spoiling of the shrines caused great satisfaction among the Lutherans of Germany. As Spain and France drew together (for in 1538 Charles and Francis came to terms and made a truce), some alliance between England and Germany seemed advisable. 'English envoys were sent to Germany with this purpose in the spring of 1538, and German divines journeyed to England to lay the foundation of a theological union,' but 'to the three points on which they desired further reform in England, the Communion in both kinds,' (the congregation to have the cup as well as the bread) 'the abolition of private masses and the enforced celibacy of the clergy, Henry himself wrote a long reply, maintaining in each case the Catholic faith.' *

In December 1538 Paul III, horrified by the same things which pleased the Lutherans, decided to promulgate the bull of excommunication against Henry. The time was opportune, as Charles and Francis were at peace. Cardinal Pole was despatched to Spain and France to call their rulers to a crusade against England. David Beaton was made a cardinal and sent home to Scotland to rouse James V.

Things were now looking really serious, and Henry looked to England's defences. The coast was fortified (stone from dissolved monasteries being dragged there to build block-houses), a fleet of 150 sail concentrated at Plymouth, the militia mustered and beacons prepared.

Charles and Francis, however, made no move—Charles because he had enough on his hands with the Turks and Lutherans, Francis because he feared to move without Charles.

Henry's alarm had two results. First, there was a spate of executions among the surviving nobles of the White Rose—Courtenays, Nevilles and Poles. Two of Reginald Pole's brothers were executed, while his old mother, the Countess of Salisbury (daughter of that Duke of Clarence who was murdered in the Tower) was attainted and placed in the Tower, to be executed two years later.

The second result of the crisis was that a new Parliament was called in 1539 and passed the Statute of Six Articles. This was really a panic measure, intended to show the Catholics of Europe that a crusade against England was quite unnecessary. It asserted six Catholic doctrines which were not to be repudiated on penalty of death. These were transubstantiation (the doctrine that the bread and wine in the mass actually changed into the body and blood of Christ), communion in one kind (bread only for the congregation, not bread and wine), the continuance of the bar against marriage of priests, the continuance of private masses (sung for particular people's souls), the perpetual observation of religious vows, and the use of confession.

This Act represents a retreat from that Lutheran position which Henry and Cromwell had taken up in 1536. Henry was a realist, and niceties of religious practice mattered to him less than the safety of the realm.

The Protestants, who were becoming hopeful that England was progressing their way, were of course shocked by the Act of Six Articles. Bishops Latimer and Shaxton both resigned their sees and spent a year in prison. Cranmer, who had spoken against the Act in the Lords, was compelled to send his wife abroad for a time.

---

* See *Henry VIII* by A. F. Pollard, p. 306.

But the 'whip with six strings' as the Protestants called it, was not severely enforced, and Cromwell, the friend (up to a point) of the Protestants, still remained in power.

The Act of Proclamations

In 1539 Parliament passed another act which should here be considered. This was the Statute of Proclamations, which ordered that proclamations by the King, provided they did not conflict with the common law and did not involve loss of life or forfeiture of goods or liberty, should be obeyed as though they were acts of Parliament. This act was once wrongly considered by historians to have marked the pinnacle of Henry's despotism. Recent examination of it, however, has convinced their successors that it was an innocuous and tame affair, which did little or nothing to increase the King's power. Professor Joel Hurstfield in a famous pamphlet entitled *Was there a Tudor despotism after all?** has pointed out that it was intended to be much more. We know that the bill, as originally drafted, and of which no copy exists, ran into a lot of resistance both in the Lords and the Commons and was drastically amended. Moreover, the preamble of the act shows that it was intended to be a more sweeping measure. Professor Hurstfield believes that the original bill was a real attempt to establish a Tudor despotism, that it was something akin to Germany's Enabling Law of 1933 by which the Reichstag gave Hitler the right to govern by proclamation for four years. It is significant that the act was repealed by Somerset in 1547 and that John Aylmer (a future bishop of London) in 1559 described those who opposed the bill as 'good fathers of the country and worthy of commendation in defending their liberty'. So perhaps here was an attempt by Henry and Cromwell to establish a despotic kingship.

The Cleves marriage

Meanwhile Henry was still busy looking for a wife. An English embassy in Germany had the idea of a marriage with the Duke of Cleves' sister, Anne. Now the Duke of Cleves was not exactly a Lutheran. Like Henry, he was 'betwixt and between' the new and old faiths. But he was brother-in-law to the Elector of Saxony, the greatest Lutheran prince in Germany. The marriage would thus give Henry a useful alliance with the Protestants of Germany against the Catholic powers.

After long negotiations, Hans Holbein, Henry's court painter, was despatched to Germany to paint the lady's portrait and, the result being satisfactory, the betrothal was made. But, alas, when Anne arrived at Rochester, Henry, who had hurried down to meet her, found her plain and dull. 'I am ashamed that men have so praised her as they have done, and I like her not,' was his verdict.

* Transactions on the Royal Historical Society, 1967.

However, there was no backing out now, especially as the foreign situation was still threatening. Henry valiantly went through with the wedding with his 'Flanders mare', as he rudely called her, but the marriage was never consummated and three months later he was finding scruples of conscience that it had been invalid because Anne had already been engaged to another man. But by this time he no longer needed his German Protestant alliance, for Francis and Charles were already falling apart.

In July 1540 Convocation and Parliament both declared the marriage null and void, and Anne was given two country houses and pensioned off with £500 a year. She made no complaint.

The fall of Cromwell

In June 1540 the captain of the guard arrested Cromwell at the Council table, 'as he sat there, amidst his enemies, about the royal business'. While Norfolk and Southampton tore the insignia of the garter from his neck, 'he flung his cap on the ground with a passionate cry of despair. "This then", he exclaimed "is the guerdon for the services I have done! On your conscience, I ask you, am I a traitor?"'*

In the Tower Cromwell broke down and begged for the mercy he had never shown to others. He was kept alive to testify in the divorce proceedings between Henry and Anne of Cleves. Then, a bill of Attainder having been passed through Parliament against him, he was beheaded at Tyburn amidst general rejoicing. The Treason Act which he had himself drafted in 1534, enabled Parliament to decide that the things he had done were treasonable.

Thus fell the second and greater of Henry's two great ministers, each having learned the slender value of a Tudor's gratitude. On the very day of Cromwell's execution, Henry, with callous indifference, married Catherine Howard, a niece of the Duke of Norfolk.

The fall of Cromwell is usually attributed to Henry's anger with him about the Cleves marriage. Such an interpretation, however, does not fit the facts. First, Henry was fully aware of all the negotiations going on with the Duke of Cleves. He was as much responsible for the marriage as was Cromwell.† Second, the Cleves marriage was made in January, Cromwell's fall did not come until June, and meanwhile, in April, he had been given a peerage (Earl of Essex) and made Lord Great Chamberlain of the Household—surely signs of royal goodwill.

The whole thing is a mystery. It appears that his enemies, Stephen

---

* See *A Short History of the English People* by J. R. Green, Everyman, which is still very readable, nearly a hundred years after its publication, and still probably, despite Trevelyan and Feiling, the best history of England in one volume.

† Incidentally, it is also false that Holbein's portrait misled Henry by flattering Anne. Although we do not have the original portrait, there is a portrait by Holbein in the Louvre, based on the other, which shows Anne admirably to be what she was, a quiet, shy girl, who 'spent most of her time sewing, was not highly educated' and was not likely to be 'inclined to the good cheer of this country,' as one of Henry's agents had reported.

Gardiner and the dukes of Norfolk and Suffolk, used Catherine Howard to persuade Henry of the existence of some imaginary plot in which Cromwell was involved (much as Norfolk had used his other niece, Anne Boleyn, to get rid of Wolsey). They seem to have convinced Henry that Cromwell was a *sacramentary* (member of a sect which denied the Real Presence in the Eucharist) and that he had aided heretics. The main accusation in the Act of Attainder passed against him was that of heresy.

Two days after Cromwell's execution, three well-known reformers, including Robert Barnes, the Lutheran, were burned at Smithfield after being condemned by Act of Attainder. In their last speeches they showed that they were quite bewildered by their condemnation, and only supposed it must have been for heresy because they were being burned! Moreover, the same day three Catholics, supporters of Catherine of Aragon, were executed for no known reason. It appears possible that Norfolk and his friends invented such an elaborate conspiracy that six innocent men (beside Cromwell) had to die to make the whole thing convincing.

About eight months after Cromwell's death, Marillac, the French ambassador 'reported that Henry was gloomy and malevolent; that he suspected that his very ministers had brought about Cromwell's destruction by false accusations and "on light pretexts" ... that he now knew that Cromwell had been the most faithful servant he had ever had.' *

Cromwell's achievement

Professor Elton has said of Cromwell, 'In eight years he engineered one of the few successful revolutions in English history, and he achieved this without upsetting the body politic.'† The revolution which Cromwell brought about was not only the substitution of the king for the pope as Supreme Head of the Church of England, but also the establishment of a new concept of national sovereignty. In Cromwell's Act of Appeals (which he probably drafted himself) we read, 'This realm of England is an Empire'. By the word 'Empire' he meant a sovereign national state, free from the authority of any foreign potentate. Thus is discarded not only the authority of the pope but that of the emperor of the Holy Roman Empire, who was regarded in medieval times as overlord of all the kings of Christendom. The statute goes on to make it clear that the ruler of this 'Empire' receives his authority directly from God. When we remember that Burgundy, a country as populous and rich as England, had passed at this time under the control of Spain, the value of this new concept of sovereignty is plain.

Cromwell's achievement then was to increase the power and status of the king. But Professor Elton is careful to show that it was not a despotic

* Quoted by J. J. Scarisbrick, *op. cit.*, p. 383. This book gives a clear discussion of the reasons for Cromwell's fall. It is the only book I know which does.
† See *England under the Tudors*, p. 159.

monarchy that Cromwell created. The old idea of the 'Tudor despotism' has now been rejected by historians. It was the 'King in Parliament' that Cromwell exalted, or, when he acted in an executive capacity, the 'King in Council'. For Cromwell was himself a lawyer and a House of Commons man. His rule strengthened the common law as Wolsey's had weakened it. The statutes of the 1530s 'opened up a great and important new field' to the common law courts, which had the task of enforcing them. The attitude of judges to Parliament changed. They began to obey statute law more carefully, having a greater respect for it.

Thus Cromwell's rule enhanced the power of Parliament and of the common law. 'Wolsey had used Parliament as rarely as he could.' Cromwell used it so much that he transformed its place in the English constitution. No less than two hundred public acts were passed by it during his eight years of power. Because he used it so much Cromwell took great care to manage Parliament. He interfered in elections, trying to ensure that men sympathetic to the king's policy should be elected, himself attended the Commons regularly, organized opinion, drafted bills, and, when made a baron in 1536, continued to sit by special provision in the lower House for another three years. Professor Elton calls him England's 'first Parliamentary statesman'. Yet it should be pointed out that the growing wealth of the gentry was bound to be reflected in a more powerful House of Commons. Cromwell merely moved with the times and used the instrument he found to hand. Nevertheless, this resulted in Parliament taking a much more modern shape in his eight years of power. Its sessions became longer. It asserted its privileges more clearly. It became more important.

But consolidation of the king's power is the real key to Cromwell's achievement. Not only did he sweep away the pope's authority, but also he attacked various 'franchises and semi-independent rights within the borders of the realm itself'. Thus in 1536 he got Parliament to pass an act 'for recontinuing certain liberties and franchises heretofore taken from the Crown'. This act ended in particular the independence of the County of Durham, the only great palatinate which had survived (apart from the Crown lands). Judges in it were in future to be appointed only by the king, and all writs in it were to run in his name. We have seen that by the Act of Union Cromwell had done the same thing to the marcher lordships of Wales and the border. It was all part of his policy of consolidation of the king's power. 'Cromwell wished to turn the Empire of England into a properly consolidated state, governed throughout by the King in Council and subject to the legislative sovereignty of the King in Parliament.'*

Administrative reforms

'Cromwell was an administrator of genius.' He was also a reformer of administration. Under Henry VII the household departments, Ward-

---

* G. R. Elton, *op. cit.*, p. 179.

robe and Chamber, had increased in importance and handled more and more of the Crown's revenue. The trouble with this arrangement was that it demanded a strong king. After Henry's death there was a decline in the efficiency of government, at least until the coming of Wolsey. Cromwell 'spent much time and thought on reorganizing the machinery of administration'. He took business away from the household and gave it to a set of bureaucratically organized courts or departments of state, each with its seal, its regular meeting place, and its own specialized officials. Thus, while the Exchequer still administered customs and parliamentary taxation, and the Duchy of Lancaster still looked after Lancastrian lands, the Court of General Surveyors took over the Crown lands acquired under Henry VII and Wolsey, the Court of Augmentations the monastic lands, the Court of First Fruits and Tenths revenue obtained from the Church, and the Court of Wards the Crown's feudal income. Some of these were actually set up after Cromwell's fall; all were planned by him.

Cromwell himself co-ordinated all these departments by taking the post of Principal Secretary in 1534. His action foreshadowed the future. Wolsey was the last minister to head the government as Lord Chancellor. The Chancellorship 'had too many judicial and routine duties attached to it for Cromwell's purposes'. As Secretary he could pry into every corner and control everything, and Elizabeth's chief ministers followed his example by taking this office. Cromwell transformed the office of Secretary from that of the king's private servant into that of a great officer of the realm.

The other administrative reform achieved by Cromwell was the formation of the Privy Council. Previously there had been an inner ring of advisers who followed the king, while the outer ring remained in London and met daily. Cromwell gave this inner ring a real standing and shape. He provided it with a clerk and a minute book. It became known as the Privy Council, and we hear for the first time of 'ordinary' councillors—Councillors who are not members of the Privy Council. Nevertheless, it is after Cromwell's fall (when there was no longer an all-powerful minister to monopolize the control of affairs) that the Privy Council emerges as an omnicompetent body. 'For the first time since the beginning of the reign it supervised the whole of royal affairs, issuing letters in its name and insisting that despatches be directed to it as a collectivity and not to any individual member thereof, exchanging correspondence between its two halves when it broke up into the Council attendant upon the King (when the latter went on progress) and the Council in London.'*

To sum up Cromwell's achievement, I cannot do better than quote from Professor Scarisbrick (p. 303 of *Henry VIII*):

'Far from being the ruthless Machiavellian of legend, Cromwell was a man possessed of a high concept of the "state" and national sovereignty,

* J. J. Scarisbrick, *op. cit.*, p. 426.

and a deep concern for Parliament and the law; an administrative genius; one who may have lacked profound religious sense (though instinctively favourable to some kind of Erasmian Protestantism), but something of an idealist nonetheless. That the 1530s were a decisive decade in English history was due largely to his energy and vision. He was immediately responsible for the vast legislative programme of the later sessions of the Reformation Parliament—a programme not rivalled in volume and moment until the nineteenth or even twentieth centuries. He oversaw the breach with Rome and the establishment of the Royal Supremacy. He effected a new political integration of the kingdom and imposed upon it a new political discipline by making war on local franchises and the intrenched bastard feudalism of the northern and western marches, handling the final incorporation of Wales into English political life and giving Ireland a foretaste of determined English overlordship. He directed the immense operation of the dissolution of the monasteries. He was either the direct or posthumous founder of the two courts (we would say ministries) of Augmentation and First Fruits, which handled the new income from the dissolved religious houses and the secular Church, and the two courts of Wards and Surveyors, which were designed to exploit more efficiently the crown's feudal rights and lands. Indeed, he left a deep mark on much of the machinery of central and local government. Finally, he was the first royal servant fully to perceive the power of that young giant, the printing-press, and, when the time came to launch a large-scale propaganda campaign on behalf of the new order, supervised the first effort of an English government to shape public opinion.'

Cranmer declared that Cromwell's death deprived Henry of 'such a servant in wisdom, diligence, faithfulness and experience, as no prince in this realm ever had'. Modern historians would be inclined to agree.

Henry's last years, 1540–1547

After Cromwell's death Henry 'took counsel from various angles'. On the one hand Norfolk and Gardiner, the Catholics, advised him, but he also listened to Cranmer and Edward Seymour, the Earl of Hertford, Jane Seymour's brother. In fact there was no strong Catholic reaction despite the King's marriage to Catherine Howard. Henry preferred to steer a middle course.

Henry was fond of his new young wife whom he nicknamed his 'rose without a thorn'. He became rejuvenated, rose before six and attended more carefully to business. He grew once again gay and cheerful.

His happiness was short-lived. In 1541 the Privy Council was informed that Catherine Howard, before her marriage, had had immoral relations with more than one man. To conceal such a story would have been dangerous for the councillors; yet 'none cared for the task of enlightening' the King. At last Cranmer was persuaded to do it. Henry was heartbroken, but enquiries showed that the Queen had been secretly meeting

5 Thomas Cromwell by Holbein

6 Embarkation of Henry VIII from Dover by an unknown artist. The ships are carracks of Henry's new design, equipped with cannon. The forts are of Italian design

one of her old lovers even after her marriage. Such conduct amounted to treason, and Catherine was condemned by Act of Attainder and executed (1542). A year later Henry married his sixth and last wife, Catherine Parr, a widow of thirty who had Protestant sympathies.

Scotland was growing important for Henry because of the succession question. In 1540 the Prince Edward, Jane Seymour's child, was only three, and not expected to live long. Mary and Elizabeth had both been declared illegitimate (in any case women were not regarded as fit to rule). The next in succession was James V of Scotland, son of Henry's elder sister, Margaret Tudor.

Henry had early perceived that friendship with James was important, for it would be difficult to defend his anti-papal kingdom against the Catholic powers if Scotland were to remain Catholic. But James, as he grew to manhood in the thirties, had inclined to the Catholic party in Scotland, had rejected Henry's requests for a meeting, and had finally gone off to France and married Mary of Guise, a strong Catholic, member of the greatest Catholic noble family of France.

Henry had borne a good many insults from James, and, when in 1541 war broke out again between Charles V and Francis, he saw it was a good opportunity to avenge himself. He had some excuse since James had promised to meet him at York in 1541 and Henry made the weary journey north only to find James had not turned up. The redoubtable Norfolk was launched with an army against Scotland. His campaign was a failure, but a Scottish raid which followed it led to an English victory at Solway Moss, 1542.

On hearing the news of this defeat, James 'collapsed into moaning and grief'. Within a month he was dead, leaving only a baby daughter, Mary, known to history as Mary, Queen of Scots.

Henry underestimated the Scottish people. He renewed Edward I's claim of feudal overlordship over the Scottish Crown, and planned to marry his son Edward to the Scottish baby queen. The pushing of these claims stiffened Scotland's resistance and brought her old ally, France, to her rescue. In 1543 a French expeditionary force arrived in Scotland. Henry had already made a secret alliance with Charles, and he now declared war on France.

1544 was a year of great military activity. One is surprised at the vigour and efficiency of the Tudor government mobilised for war. No doubt this was largely due to Cromwell's administrative reforms.

An amphibious expedition was launched against Scotland. The command of 12,000 troops was given to Lord Hertford, Norfolk being regarded as an old man, no longer fit for independent command. Lord Lisle, the Lord Admiral, conveyed them from Newcastle with a strong naval squadron in support. Leith and Edinburgh were captured and sacked, and the whole expedition marched back to Berwick, arriving there with the loss of only forty men.

Meanwhile, a vast army of 36,000 men was mustered at various ports in the South and conveyed across to Calais. It is noticeable that the

English infantry was still armed with long-bows and pikes. The long-bow had, however, reached its last days, and it was considered necessary to hire 6000 German mercenaries, armed with hackbuts, a form of fire-arm. Henry, who had an ulcer on his leg, accompanied the expedition on a litter. He laid siege to Boulogne, and captured it after two months, during which his 60-pounder cannon battered its walls and a new weapon, a mortar which fired exploding shells, destroyed its houses.

At this point, however, Charles V suddenly deserted his ally and made peace with Francis. Things looked serious and Henry hurried home to organize England for defence. The year 1545 was one of terrible anxiety, for Francis concentrated an army and a fleet of 150 sail at Le Havre (including twenty-five fighting galleys brought from the Mediterranean). The English fleet, held at Portsmouth, was smaller, but of better quality. Every available seaman was called up, while on land the lords-lieutenant mustered the shire-rolls, and men waited with bow, bill or pike to fall in when the beacon fires should give the warning. 'The people were totally for the King.' A 'benevolence' (or tax on land, without Parliament's consent) was asked for by the Privy Council, and willingly paid. 'If this be too little,' wrote one contributor, 'His Grace shall have more.' Even peace-loving Cranmer raised a troop of artillery for the defence of Kent.

At midsummer the invasion was hourly expected, and the King and his Council moved down to Portsmouth. When the French fleet arrived, however, it was beaten off in the Solent by the British ships, while a small force which was landed on the Isle of Wight was easily mopped up. Then, after an indecisive engagement off the Sussex coast, the French fleet returned to Le Havre, its crews sorely depleted by disease.

The war had already cost Henry nearly half a million pounds. In 1546 he bluffed Francis into making peace. The French agreed to pay two million crowns over a period of eight years, at the end of which Boulogne should be restored to them. Henry's strong navy had once more paid him dividends.

The Scots, however, still controlled by a Catholic government, refused to make peace on Henry's terms. The one hopeful sign (for Henry) was the growth of Protestantism in Scotland. A certain George Wishart, with his disciple John Knox, was preaching Geneva Protestant doctrines and making many converts. When the Government arrested Wishart and burnt him for heresy, it only led to still more conversions.

Henry's death

Meanwhile Henry's health had been growing worse. Though only fifty-five he had worn himself out with excessive exertions. As the ulcer in his leg grew worse 'he became unable to take exercise, and would not at the same time moderate his hearty eating and drinking. His corpulence grew into a crippling handicap.' He knew that he could not last

106

long and had already begun to plan for the period of his son's minority. A religious civil war such as that which had already rent Germany was his greatest fear. The country was divided, as was his Council with a Protestant and a Catholic party each manoeuvring for power. On the one hand there were Bishop Gardiner, and the Duke of Norfolk and his son the Earl of Surrey, all of whom would declare for the pope if the occasion offered. They were opposed by Cranmer, Hertford and John Dudley, Viscount Lisle, son of Henry VII's grasping minister, executed in 1510.

The Protestants seemed to be gaining ground. In 1545 Parliament, to raise money, had dissolved the chantries, transferring their endowments to the King. The chantries were places where priests sung masses for the souls of dead men in purgatory. Their dissolution was a complete reversal of the Act of Six Articles.

The Earl of Surrey took alarm and foolishly began to speak openly that his father should be Regent when the King should die. He (Surrey) assumed, on account of his descent from Edward I, royal arms to which he was not entitled. Henry saw these moves as dangerous, and in December 1546 Surrey and Norfolk were arrested. The son was tried by a London jury for treason, condemned and executed. The father was placed in the Tower, and an Act of Attainder passed by Parliament against him. On the very morning in January 1547 when he was due to die, the King himself passed away, and so the sentence was not carried out.

Henry's last action, the striking down of the Howard family, ensured that his son should inherit the throne, for the Catholic party might well have preferred Mary. So the dying King controlled affairs right up to the end. An act of 1543 had settled the throne on Edward, Mary and Elizabeth in that order, and had given the King the right of altering the succession by testament. In his will Henry affirmed the succession of his three children, but stated that, in the unlikely event of none of them having heirs, the Stuart line of Margaret Tudor should be excluded, and the throne should descend to the heirs of his younger sister Mary, who, as will be remembered, had married eventually the Duke of Suffolk.

The influence of Catherine Parr in these last years is of the utmost importance. She was a moderate Protestant and greatly admired Erasmus. In her widowhood, before marrying Henry, she had received Reformers like Latimer and Coverdale at her house, and, as Queen, she 'became the centre-piece of a humanist circle', as Cromwell had been in his time. But her greatest contribution was in the education of the royal children. It was probably due to her influence that, at the end of 1543, all three of them came together for the first time in their father's household. Mary was now grown up and too old to change greatly, but Elizabeth was only ten, and she and Edward must have been much influenced by their new step-mother and the notable humanists whom she engaged as their tutors.

Moreover, Catherine, whose habit it was to hold daily Scripture classes with her ladies-in-waiting, spent much effort in trying to persuade Henry to finish the revolution he had started and purge the Church of England 'clean from the dregs of Rome'. Gardiner watched with horror and apprehension her growing influence upon Henry, and at one time was almost successful in having her arrested. In Henry's last years Protestantism had spread from the universities and a few *avant-garde* London churches and had penetrated every level of society including the Court. Whether Henry himself was tinged with it or whether he just listened to Catherine as a tolerant, loving and indulgent husband, it is impossible to say. Women have always been influential in religious matters, and it is fascinating (but probably unprofitable) to speculate upon the powers they have exerted in history behind the scenes. But there is no doubt at all that Protestant England stands in debt to the last of Henry's queens.

The last seven years of Henry's reign, with its expensive wars, had left the country in a bad state financially. Since 1542 about £800,000 worth of crown lands (mostly old monastic property) had been sold, great amounts had been borrowed at high interest on the Antwerp money market, and, worst of all, the coinage had been debased, a procedure which is always fatal to trade and confidence.

All this was a bad legacy for the next reign. Yet those historians who condemn Henry for his poor government in these last years are perhaps unfair to him. Times had been troublous. The Counter-Reformation (that great movement in Europe in which the Catholics fought back to regain all they had lost) was getting into its stride. Catholic Scotland and France in combination were undoubtedly a terrible threat to England, and Henry was perhaps wise to strike out at them as he did. At least he remained to the end a king beloved as well as feared by his people. In some ways he was more astute even than Cromwell. He avoided the great danger of religious civil war. He kept friendly with Charles V at a time when the Netherlands trade was so valuable to his kingdom. He steered a careful course among the innumerable rocks and shoals of religious and personal rivalries. He drove himself right to the end to carry out his duties, and in 1545 he rallied the country behind him in its hour of danger.

His numerous marriages have given posterity a false picture of him. He was no Bluebeard following only his own lusts. In fact his court was much less libertine than that of his rival, Francis I. Nor was he ever dominated by a woman. For long he was remembered and regretted as 'Bluff King Hal', who had been the embodiment of Merrie England. 'Brutal, crafty, selfish and ungenerous' he may have been, but he also had great courage, a fine intellect and an instinct for ruling, and, on the whole, he served his people well. He was buried, at his own request, beside Jane Seymour in the choir of his college at Windsor.

8 The Swiss Reformers and the reign of Edward VI

Zwingli and Calvin

To understand the reign of Edward VI, it is necessary to look once more at the Reformation in Europe and see how it was progressing. Luther's ideas had conquered most of Northern Germany and had spread to Scandinavia. But his writings were not ideally suited to make things clear to the people of western Europe. There was a certain Germanic fogginess about Luther, a ponderous style in which the outline of the ideas got blurred by the strength of feeling. His writings lacked that Latin clarity which in a future period might distinguish Mozart from, say, Wagner. Soon rival and clearer thinkers were coming forward to challenge the Catholic Church in western Europe. The first (a contemporary of Luther's) was Ulrich Zwingli, the people's priest in the Great Minster at Zürich. His ideas were much the same as Luther's. He attacked Indulgences, the power of the pope, clerical celibacy (he himself married, as did Luther), the practice of fasting, monasticism, the excessive ritual of the Catholic Church. Soon he had converted the city fathers and people of Zürich and made the city a centre of Protestantism.

Like Luther, Zwingli laid stress on the direct relations between man and God, that is that any man can pray to God on his own without getting a priest to help him. Like Luther he believed in justification by faith. But, whereas Luther believed anything was allowable in the service, provided it was not contrary to the Word of God (and thus allowed the wearing of vestments by the minister because nothing in the Bible explicitly forbade the wearing of vestments), Zwingli believed that the whole service should be sanctioned by Scripture. He thus developed a much simpler service. Not only were vestments disallowed, but all images and stained-glass windows were removed and even organs discouraged, because they are not mentioned in the New Testament. The last supper was celebrated not on an altar but on tables in the nave. The ministers faced the congregation, wore ordinary clothes and carried the bread round on large wooden trenchers to the people sitting silently round the tables. There were no hymns (unlike in the Lutheran service) but only metrical versions of the psalms, for hymns would have been unscriptural.

Moreover, Luther and Zwingli differed fundamentally in their interpretation of the doctrine of the Eucharist. Luther had rejected with scorn the Roman doctrine of transubstantiation, that the bread and wine were actually changed in the service of the mass into the body and blood of Christ. But he could not forget the words of Jesus (*Matthew* 26 : 26 and

Mark 14 : 22), 'Take, eat; this is my body.' He therefore came to believe that, although the substance of the bread and wine remained unchanged, the body of Christ was there, along with them, 'as the fire enters into the iron when it is heated'.*

Zwingli on the other hand preferred Luke's wording, 'This is my body which is given for you; this do in remembrance of me.' (*Luke* 22 : 19). He thought that when Jesus said, 'This is my body' he was speaking metaphorically, as when he said, 'I am the door' or 'I am the vine', that he meant in fact, 'This is a sign of my body.' To Luther then the communion service was a sacrament (perhaps what our modern generation would call a 'happening'). He believed in the Real Presence of Christ at the service. To Zwingli salvation was a spiritual experience and ceremonies were unimportant The communion service was purely commemorative.

Both Luther and Zwingli agreed the civil power should control the church, for had not Paul said, 'the powers that be are ordained of God' (*Romans* 13 : 1)? But, whereas in Luther's Germany this meant control by a prince, in Switzerland it meant control by a city council, a body in which (at least in Zürich and Basle) smaller craftsmen, organized in powerful gilds, had much influence. Zwingli's church therefore was more democratic in organization than was Luther's.

Zwingli was killed in a battle between the Catholics and Protestants of Switzerland in 1531, but Henry Bullinger carried on his work in Zürich, while his ideas spread down the Rhine valley to Strasbourg (a great trading centre) where Martin Bucer became the leading reformer. Bucer had an influence outside Strasbourg, for instance in the German state of Hesse. He also had an influence upon the greatest of all the reformers, the Frenchman, Jean Chauvin, known to history as Calvin.

Calvin was born in France in 1509 and studied Latin and theology at the University of Paris. He intended to become a priest, but changed his mind and moved to the University of Orléans to study law. Here he was influenced by the ideas of Luther and Zwingli and indeed by the French reformer, Lefèvre, who had already translated the Bible into French. His conversion to Protestantism took place through no hard struggle, as had Luther's, but quite suddenly. He later wrote, 'As if by a sudden ray of light I recognized in what an abyss of errors I had hitherto been plunged.'

Soon the persecutions of Francis I forced Calvin to flee to Basle in Switzerland and there in 1536 he published the first edition of his great book, *Institutes of the Christian Religion*. Over the next twenty-three years he repeatedly revised and expanded the work, and it is certainly one of the most influential publications of the century. It was written in Latin but Calvin wished it to reach a larger public than that of Latin scholars and in 1543 he translated it into French. In 1559 it was translated into Italian and in 1561 into English.

* See *History of Europe, 1494–1610* by A. J. Grant, Methuen, 1931, p. 119, for this explanation of Luther's views.

Calvin's *Institutes* is an earnest sermon attempting to persuade readers of the existence of God and of the need of shaping their lives according to His will. Based on a deep knowledge of the Bible as well as of classical writers and the early Fathers of the Church, it is infused with its author's tremendous faith. It is as inspiring to read today as when it was first written. Here are a few extracts from it.*

(1) 'We are' he writes in the Prefatory Address to Francis I '(if you will) the mere dregs and off-scourings of the world . . . so that before God there remains nothing of which we can glory save only his mercy, by which, without any merit of our own, we are admitted to the hope of eternal salvation.'

(2) Here he insists on the existence of God: 'There is no nation so barbarous, no race so brutish, as not to be imbued with the conviction that there is a God. Even those who, in other respects, seem to differ least from the lower animals, constantly retain some sense of religion; so thoroughly has this common conviction possessed the mind, so firmly is it stamped on the breasts of all men.'

(3) Here he attacks the Catholic Church: 'All men promiscuously do homage to God, but very few fully reverence him. On all hands there is abundance of ostentatious ceremonies, but sincerity of heart is rare,' or again: 'Nothing therefore can be more absurd than the fiction that the power of judging Scripture is in the Church, and that on her nod its certainty depends. . . . As to the question, How shall we be persuaded that it came from God without recurring to a decree of the Church? it is just the same as if it were asked, How shall we learn to distinguish light from darkness, white from black, sweet from bitter? Scripture bears upon the face of it as clear evidence of its truth, as white and black do of their colour, sweet and bitter of their taste.'

(4) Here he speaks of knowing God: 'Until men feel that they owe everything to God, that they are cherished by his paternal care, and that he is the author of all their blessings, so that nought is to be looked for away from Him, they will never submit to him in voluntary obedience; nay, unless they place their entire happiness in him, they will never yield up their whole selves to him in truth and sincerity.'

(5) Here he extols the Bible: 'But in regard to the Holy Scriptures, however petulant men may attempt to carp at them, they are replete with sentiments which it is clear that men never could have conceived. Let each of the prophets be examined, and not one will be found who does not rise far higher than human reach. Those who feel their works insipid must be absolutely devoid of taste.'

(6) Here he talks of the elect and the damned: 'The will of God is, I confess, immutable, and His truth is always consistent with itself; but I deny that the reprobate ever advance so far as to penetrate to that secret revelation which Scripture reserves for the elect only.' Or again:

* Taken from a translation by Henry Beveridge, published, in three volumes, at Edinburgh for the Calvin Translation Society in 1845. There is no modern English translation in print at the time of writing.

111

'God therefore does not allow Satan to have dominion over the souls of believers, but only gives over to his sway the impious and unbelieving, whom he deigns not to number among his flock.' And this: 'If all is a gift of God, even the faith by which we appropriate the gift, then from all eternity God must have chosen some to life . . . and left others unredeemed.'

(7) Here he speaks of Providence (and how his faith shines through his words!): 'If one falls among robbers or ravenous beasts; if a sudden gust of wind at sea causes shipwreck; if one is struck down by the fall of a house or a tree; if another, when wandering through desert paths, meets with deliverance; or, after being tossed by the waves, arrives in port and makes some wondrous hair-breadth escape from death—all these occurrences, prosperous as well as adverse, carnal sense will attribute to fortune. But whoso has learned from the mouth of Christ that all the hairs of his head are numbered (*Matthew* 10 : 30) will look farther for the cause, and hold that all events whatsoever are governed by the secret counsel of God.'

(8) Here he speaks of Christian duty: 'How difficult it is to perform the duty of seeking the good of our neighbour! Unless you leave off all thought of yourself, and in a manner cease to be yourself, you will never accomplish it. How can you exhibit those works of charity which Paul describes unless you renounce yourself and become wholly devoted to others?'

(9) Here he speaks of the folly of worldly ambition: 'If we believe that all prosperous and desirable success depends entirely on the blessing of God, and that when it is wanting all kinds of misery and calamity await us, it follows that we should not eagerly contend for riches and honours, trusting to our own dexterity and assiduity, or leaning on the favour of men, or confiding in any empty imagination of fortune; but should always have respect to the Lord, that under his auspices we may be conducted to whatever lot he has provided for us.'

(10) Here he speaks of bearing the cross: 'Those whom the Lord has chosen and honoured with his intercourse must prepare for a hard, laborious, troubled life, a life full of many and various kinds of evils; it being the will of our heavenly Father to exercise his people in this way while putting them to the proof. . . . Hence it affords us great consolation in hard and difficult circumstances, which men deem evil and adverse, to think that we are holding fellowship with the sufferings of Christ; that as he passed to celestial glory through a labyrinth of many woes, so we too are conducted thither through various tribulations.'

It will be seen from some of the quotations above, particularly numbers 6 and 10, that one of Calvin's clearest ideas was that some are chosen for salvation and some are foredestined to damnation. This idea is usually called 'predestination' and is opposed to the Catholic doctrine of 'free will'. Calvin got it from Paul's epistles, which he greatly admired, and, far from giving him and his followers a fatalistic attitude, it made them the more earnest to deserve the blessings they felt were showered upon them. It also led Calvin to search for some new method of governing his church (when he came to organize it) other than Luther's method of simply letting the civil power take control and appoint bishops etc. For what sort of a church would it be which was controlled by other than God's elect?

Calvin was an unknown young man of twenty-six when he first published his *Institutes*. He soon moved from Basle to Geneva, and, after a short retirement to Strasbourg, he settled in Geneva in 1541, at the request of the city fathers, and made it the greatest centre of Protestantism in Europe. He was a tremendous organizer, and soon persuaded the city council to establish a series of regulations known as the Ecclesiastical Ordinances. These set up an elaborate system of church government, which consisted of pastors, elders, teachers (or doctors) and deacons. New pastors were chosen by the established pastors, though the city council could reject the choice. The elders were disciplinary officials and were chosen by the councils of the city in consultation with the pastors. Every week pastors and elders met together in a body called the Consistory, which had great power, and could punish people for moral shortcomings.

Calvin believed he was establishing a church (or rather *the* Church, for there was in Calvin's belief only one true church to which all the elect belonged) which should be an exact replica of the primitive church of the apostles. Like Zwingli's, Calvin's services were simple. There were seventeen services a week, five on Sundays and two on each weekday, and attendance on the sermon was compulsory for all. Many found Calvin's system an intolerable tyranny. Others found in it a clear road to the knowledge of God, a source of joy. John Knox called it 'the most perfect school of Christ that ever was on earth since the days of the apostles'. Soon Geneva became a place of refuge for Protestants fleeing from France, Scotland, Italy and the Netherlands, and the city grew greatly in size.

Luther's church, like Henry's and Elizabeth's, was controlled by the civil government which appointed the bishops. Luther's church therefore could only flourish where governments were friendly. Calvin on the other hand gave his church self-government and such a cellular structure that, like communism today, its congregations could spread even into hostile territory. Various congregations would communicate with each other and send representatives to synods—events which alarmed not a little the governments of sixteenth-century Europe! Soon Calvinism was making great inroads on France, Scotland and the Netherlands. Wherever it went it changed society, giving people not only a new faith, but also a new discipline, for Calvin's church, once established, claimed and asserted as much authority as that of Rome itself. Calvinism gave new life and vigour to the Reformation after Lutheranism had spent itself. It was more democratic than Lutheranism for the full congregation of an individual church (its elders and deacons) would issue a 'call' to a new pastor who would, of course, be an ordained minister of the Church.

Such was the Reformed Church which was to make the greatest impact on Europe, including England, for the next hundred years. It was not the only inspiration of the English Puritans, but it was their main inspiration, at least after the first decade of Elizabeth's reign.

Let us now return to events in England, where already Zwingli's ideas were making themselves felt.

The Duke of Somerset and Scotland

Edward VI was only nine years old when his father died. He had been brought up by Catherine Parr and already had Protestant leanings. He was an intelligent boy, devoted to his studies, but of weak health. A great deal of care was lavished on his education, and as he grew older, he became keen on Protestant theology and was something of a prig.

Henry had named in his will a set of executors who were to rule the country until his son should be old enough to take over. They were mainly Protestants and Norfolk and Gardiner were not among them. The executors soon decided they must have a regent to take over royal powers. They therefore appointed one of their number, Edward Seymour, the Earl of Hertford, as Protector of the realm. He was, of course, the King's uncle, and had shown his great abilities as a general in the Scottish campaign of 1544. He took the title of Duke of Somerset, while John Dudley, Viscount Lisle, became Earl of Warwick.

Somerset soon had plenty of trouble on his hands. The King of France, Francis I, died only two months after Henry. In his last years he had become rather weak, a pawn in the hands of women. His son Henry II, who succeeded him, was more vigorous and was determined to regain Boulogne without delay. Moreover, he had a son, the Dauphin Francis, whom he planned to marry to Mary, Queen of Scots. Since Edward VI's two half-sisters were both supposed to be illegitimate, might not Mary in the end succeed the sickly Edward on the English throne? Thus, a great Valois empire would come into being, stretching from Scotland to France and cutting the Habsburg Empire in two. As yet this was only a dream, but Somerset was aware of its dangers, and it made him the more determined to secure Scotland, with which, of course, England was already at war.

In 1547 the French succeeded in passing more troops into Scotland. They captured St Andrews from the Protestants, who had been rebelling against the Regent, and John Knox was taken away with many others to row as a slave in the French galleys.

Now the French were in the ascendant in Scotland, Somerset felt something must be done. He aimed at a union of the two countries by the marriage of Edward and Mary, but it was to be on equal terms. There was to be no more talk of English overlordship. There would be one country, 'Great Britain', protected by the sea and 'with mutual love for garrison'. The Scots, however, could not fail to think that the centre of gravity of this new country would be London not Edinburgh. Confi-
114

dent in the support of France, they refused to negotiate. Thereupon Somerset himself led an army of 18,000 men across the border and routed the Scots at Pinkie Cleuch (1547). This last great battle between the two kingdoms was decided, unlike Flodden, by firearms, though the bow still played its part. Somerset stopped the slaughter as soon as he could, for he had no desire to exasperate the Scots, many of whom had welcomed his forces.

'After Pinkie Somerset pursued the methods he had vainly urged on Henry.' Instead of sacking towns he garrisoned them, and then sent out emissaries with Bibles and anti-French propaganda to try and win over the people. In this way he may have done a lot of good, but in the end all his plans for Scotland came to naught. Mary was betrothed to the Dauphin Francis, and shipped off to France in 1548. Most of the garrisons had to be withdrawn in 1549 for use in the war with France, for Henry II was besieging Boulogne. For the next ten years Scotland was to remain under French influence.

It is hard to decide whether Somerset's policy in Scotland was wise or not. It did not achieve much, but it is difficult to see what else he could have done. Scotland was the key to the internal security of England. By its geographical position it could link the discontents of the conservative English north to the turbulence of Ireland. There were constant comings and goings between Scotland and the northern parts of Ireland. Since the Geraldine rebellion of 1534 these ties had grown still closer, and James V had encouraged them. As long as Scotland remained a client of France, the latter would have a back-door held open into England. It was in order to close that back-door that Henry had turned his attention to Scotland. Somerset inherited his policy and his war. That he failed to solve the Scottish problem does not mean that he was unwise to try.*

The growth of Protestantism

The Duke of Somerset, though not a strong Protestant, was sympathetic to Protestantism, and 'had a real hatred of persecution and terror'. His rule 'showed a tolerance and love of justice that were in marked contrast to the duplicity and bigotry of most of his contemporaries'.

Hence, when Parliament met in 1547 Somerset persuaded it to repeal the Statute of Six Articles and all the old heresy laws allowing religious persecution. The savage treason laws of Henry VIII were likewise repealed. 'Treason by writing and overt act remained, but treason by word of mouth was swept away.' A new Chantries Act was passed completely abolishing the chantries, and confiscating all endowments providing for prayers for the dead. The chantry priests who had been paid to sing the masses were pensioned off, and money was provided to pay for guild and chantry schools which otherwise might have perished, but the rest of the money went into the Treasury.

* See R. B. Wernham, *op. cit.*, pp. 140 and 149, for a clear statement on this subject.

115

Meanwhile, under Cranmer's influence (and Somerset's) the Church of England was moving in a Protestant direction. The main Catholic bishops, Bonner of London and Gardiner of Winchester, were removed from their sees, and imprisoned in the Tower. Eminent refugees from the Continent began to arrive, invited by Cranmer. Two who came from Strasbourg were Martin Bucer, Calvin's old friend, and the Italian, Peter Martyr Vermigli. Both were made professors of Divinity, the former at Cambridge, the latter at Oxford. Charles V had just defeated the German Protestants at the battle of Mühlberg and Germany was not a healthy place for Protestants. Luther had died in 1546, but his friend Philip Melanchthon was invited over, though he declined to come.

Most of these reformers were Zwinglians and under their influence Cranmer moved in a Zwinglian direction. 'Praise God', wrote a young English Protestant to Bullinger, the leader of the Protestants at Zürich, 'Latimer has come over to our doctrine of the eucharist and so has the Archbishop of Canterbury and other bishops who until now seemed to be Lutheran'.*

In 1549 an Act of Parliament permitted the clergy to marry, and Cranmer's wife began to appear in public.

So far only liberty had been given and things were becoming chaotic. 'Some parish priests observed old forms, others new.' The government was bound to act, if only because not to do so was to lay itself open to a charge of insincerity. All men at this time, Catholics and Reformers alike, believed there was only one true church. Since the king's government was allowing reform, it had better show that it knew what it was doing and lay down the exact degree of reform.

Cranmer had long been working on an English Prayer Book (he was a great scholar and spent most of his time in his study). It was a translation of the old Catholic *Use of Sarum* but also owed something to Protestant services, and the communion service was, on the whole, Lutheran. It is the basis of our Prayer Book today, and Cranmer's language is of course very beautiful. An Act of Uniformity of 1549 required the exclusive use of this book. Mild penalties were laid down for priests who refused to use it, but none at all for laymen who did not attend services. The book, as published, was hardly able to content its author who, as we have noted, had recently become more Zwinglian, for a majority of bishops in the House of Lords insisted on modifying it in a Catholic direction.

The fall of Somerset

The new Prayer Book was to come into use on Whitsunday, 1549. It was greeted by risings in Cornwall and Devon. In those days the Cornish language, which is akin to Welsh, was still in use, and the Cornishmen complained that they could not understand the new English service

* See Owen Chadwick, *op. cit.*, p. 120.

which was 'like a Christmas game' to them. There were also social under-tones to the rebellion, the peasants resenting the new order of landlords grown rich on monastic lands. Plymouth was captured and Exeter besieged by the rebels. The Council despatched Lord Russell with an army mainly composed of the militia of the nearby counties and 300 Italian mercenaries, and the rising was fairly easily quelled. A rift had now grown up in the Council between Somerset and the Earl of War-wick. Somerset was for conciliation and kindness to the rebels, but War-wick and his friends overruled him and ordered Russell to punish the leaders ruthlessly.

While Russell was putting down the western rising, a far more serious outbreak occurred in Norfolk. It was caused not by religious grievances but by social and economic ones.

As already noted in Chapter 4, the high price of wool in the fifteenth and early sixteenth centuries had led to much enclosure of common and arable strip land for sheep farming. The question is discussed more fully in Chapter 17. Suffice it to say here that many enlightened people (from Sir Thomas More on) believed that enclosure was an evil, that it led to poor men losing their livelihood and wealthy men growing wealthier. Governments from the Yorkists onwards had tried to prevent the process, chiefly because it led to a discontented peasantry, but also because arable land, it was believed, bred plenty of sturdy labourers for the army in wartime, while sheep pastures did not. A few shepherds could look after a great many acres of sheep pasture, so that conversion to sheep-farming led to depopulation of the countryside.

When Edward VI's reign opened, Hugh Latimer, erstwhile Bishop of Worcester, and himself a yeoman's son, had begun to preach against the social evil of enclosure. John Hales, a Member of Parliament and a personal friend of the Protector, began to write and talk about reme-dies. They and their followers were known as the 'party of the common-wealth' (meaning they cared for the general good).

Somerset sympathized with the views of these reformers, and, after a few riots in the southern counties in the spring of 1548, he issued a proclamation against enclosures, and appointed commissions to examine the problem and see if the law could be enforced.

These commissions met opposition from the landlords, while many members of the Council itself, including the Earl of Warwick and his friends, were opposed to any action.

But Somerset pressed on. Besides being a kind-hearted man, he was inclined to be arrogant and self-righteous. His own wealth in land was vast and recently acquired, mainly from the Church. When his policy was opposed he declared, 'Maugre the devil, private profit, self-love, money, and such like the devil's instruments, it shall go forward.'

In May 1549 Somerset issued a second proclamation against enclosures, and in June, four days after the outbreak of the Western Ris-ing, he gave a general pardon to all those who had taken the law into their own hands and thrown down fences. The peasants of Norfolk, much aggravated by their landlords' opposition to Somerset's commissioners, and feeling that the Protector was on their side, now broke out into rebellion. They found a leader in Robert Ket, a well-to-do tradesman. About 12,000 small farmers and peasant cultivators marched under him to Norwich, throwing down fences as they went, and camped on Mousehold Heath north of the city. Ket regarded his gathering not as a rebellion but as a demonstration in favour of the law, and he offered to help the Protector enforce the law. He ruled his army for six weeks, helped by an elected council, and kept good order and discipline. There was no religious motive behind the rising, for Protestantism was strong in East Anglia. In fact the rebels held regular services on the Heath using the new Prayer Book.

Actually the articles of complaint presented by the Norfolk rebels hardly mention enclosure at all. As we shall see (in Chapter 17) enclosure was not going on at all fast in the middle of the century, and Norfolk was not a county much affected by it at any part of the Tudor period. The main agrarian grievances of the rebels were two-fold. First they objected to rack-renting (the raising of tenant farmers' rents and copyholders' fines as prices rose) and optimistically suggested rents should be fixed at the 1485 level. Secondly, they complained of loss of commons rights owing to the lords of the manor pasturing too many of their beasts on the commons.

We are thus left with the paradox that a rebellion, caused by the commonwealth party preaching and writing against enclosure, took place in an area where enclosure was not a grievance and never had been since 1485.

Somerset sympathized with the rebels, but could not countenance their actions. An army of ten thousand, already mustered for the western rebellion, and commanded by the Earl of Warwick, was sent against them and routed them with much slaughter. Ket and over fifty other leaders were taken and hanged.

Warwick and most of the other Councillors had long been dissatisfied with Somerset's rule. Now that he had an army at his back, Warwick took his chance. He allied himself with the Catholics in the Council and prepared to arrest Somerset. Somerset, realizing what was happening, moved with the King to Windsor and tried to rally the people to his side. He was popular enough and many joined him, but Russell and Warwick both had armies, including some mercenaries, and both declared against him. He had no choice but to surrender (October 1549) and he was placed in the Tower.

Somerset is usually described in history books as a weak but good man. 'Weak' he certainly was, at any rate not strong enough to control the rough and turbulent nobility of Tudor England. It is harder to be sure about the 'good'. He was what in modern parlance is termed a 'do-gooder'. In his attempts to help the people there was a streak of self-righteousness, a lofty superiority to those in the Council whom he regarded as being more selfish. He made a bid for popularity in an age

118

when popularity did not matter. The people came to love him; yet his actions brought them few benefits and much harm. He established a Court of Requests in his own house to deal with poor men's causes. Thus he showed himself at once kindly and arbitrary. The legend of the 'good duke' was one he carefully cultivated. Yet in doing so he lost the confidence of the landed class, which was of course the governing class, and so his rule ended in disaster. It would have been well if he had remembered the simple truth that the rightness or wrongness of any action depends upon its foreseeable consequences. His economic policies were unwise, for he twice debased the coinage (in 1547 and 1549).

The mid-century crisis

On the other hand, it is only fair to Somerset to point out that there was an economic crisis building up in the two short years of his rule. Henry VIII's war expenditure in his last years had been very great. Wars had become expensive as firearms replaced the bow and ships became bigger and coastal fortresses more sophisticated. As pointed out in the last chapter, Henry had been forced to sell large amounts of monastery lands, to borrow heavily in the Antwerp money market and to debase the coinage. All these things were an evil legacy for Somerset. The debasement of the coinage particularly had severe economic repercussions, for it led to an unhealthy stimulation of England's cloth exports to Antwerp. As the pound sterling was debased, its exchange value fell from twenty-seven Flemish shillings in 1542 to twenty-one by 1547 and fifteen by 1551. The same number of Flemish shillings would thus buy much more English cloth, and cloth exports to Antwerp suddenly increased (by fifty per cent in the ten years before 1547). Such rapid expansion put all sorts of strains on the national economy. The old clothing towns with their strict guild rules could no longer cope with the demand, and the cloth industry began to move out of them into villages or into unincorporated towns like Newbury. This caused new problems and tensions—unemployment in the old towns and new, unpopular 'bosses' in the new ones. Moreover, with a growing demand for cloth the demand for wool increased and sheep farming became suddenly more profitable (just at the time when landlords were feeling the pinch owing to the lower value of their rent money). Naturally landlords tended to enclose land and to put more sheep on the common pasture, besides desperately trying to increase their rents to recoup the lower value of their money.

All this amounts to a real mid-century crisis, to be aggravated incidentally (after Somerset's fall) by the sudden slump in the Antwerp market in 1551.* The widespread rebellions of 1549 then (for there were risings in Oxfordshire and Yorkshire as well as in Cornwall and Norfolk) were not provoked merely by Somerset's unwise policies. They were also caused by deep-seated economic and social strains. As the news of this

* See Chapter 17, the sections on 'Woollen Manufacture' and 'Overseas Trade', for a fuller account of these matters.

widespread unrest reached France, Henry II declared war on England (in August 1549). Somerset was then faced with a new problem. Some of the men drafted from the county militia to serve in Scotland (where Somerset was preparing a new invasion) and Boulogne, turned aside to help Ket and the Western rebels. In fact the social and religious strains we have noted had made the county militia no longer reliable. Somerset had to call on noblemen and gentry with their retinues to crush the rebellions, beside the mercenaries he had already hired for his Scottish war. About 300 Italian mercenaries were used against the Western rebellion and about 1000 Germans against Ket.*

The rule of Warwick

The Earl of Warwick was now the most powerful man in England and the Council elected him as its Lord President. He has been described as 'a good soldier and a politician of diabolical cleverness'. He did not take the title of Protector, since the office had fallen into discredit. Most men expected him to initiate a Catholic reaction, since the Catholics had helped him to power. Instead he decided to rely on the Protestants. Perhaps this was because London and the home counties were by this time Protestant and their wealth outweighed that of the rest of England. Also, there was much plunder still to be had from the Church, and Protestantism would give him the opportunity to confiscate Church lands and distribute them as favours to his followers. But in any case what was the alternative? To go back to the old Catholic ways of Henry VIII would have meant restoring Gardiner to office and bringing back to power such great noblemen as the Earl of Shrewsbury (who had been prominent in the Scottish war), the Earl of Southampton (an ex-Lord Chancellor) and even perhaps the Duke of Norfolk himself from the Tower. These conservative noblemen with their great wealth and immense social prestige would have made 'an upstart Dudley seem very small beer'.† Henry VIII could have controlled them, but it is doubtful if Warwick could have. Finally it must be remembered, young Edward was already a strong Protestant and one day he would probably take control.

In the four months after Somerset's fall, therefore, Warwick carefully manoeuvred the Catholics out of the Council. By February 1550 five of them were under arrest. They were replaced by Warwick's supporters. Gardiner was still in the Tower and had been deprived of his see of Winchester. The great historian Pollard wrote, 'The unrecorded struggle between the Protestants and Catholics in the Council at the end of 1549 was a turning point in English history.'

Since the Treasury was empty, one of Warwick's first actions was to make peace with France. A treaty early in 1550 handed back Boulogne in return for the payment of 400,000 crowns. The Scots captured at St

* See *Tudor Rebellions* by Anthony Fletcher, Longman, 1968.
† See R. B. Wernham, *op. cit.*, p. 193.

Andrews were to be released (a shrewd move this, which pleased the Scottish Protestants immensely, and led to John Knox taking up residence in England). Warwick also withdrew from Scotland those of Somerset's garrisons which had not been captured, and ceased opposing the marriage of Mary, Queen of Scots to the Dauphin. Henry II's designs in Scotland thus went forward unopposed for the time being. This was a pity no doubt, but Somerset's ambitious foreign policies had been too expensive.

Warwick's religious policy

In 1550 and the following year four Catholic bishops were deprived of their sees, and two other sees fell vacant. The six vacant bishoprics were filled with Protestants. Thus Nicholas Ridley replaced Bonner at London, John Hooper became Bishop of Gloucester, while Miles Coverdale, the Bible translator, took over Exeter. Both Hooper and Coverdale 'had long been exiles on the Continent, were warm adherents of Zürich, and disapproved of ancient episcopacy while they were being consecrated bishops'.* Hooper was even lodged in the Fleet prison for a time to force him to withdraw his objections to the ceremony of consecration. Thus Warwick's government drove the Church of England towards Protestantism as Somerset's had gently led it.

As each Protestant bishop was appointed, he was forced to surrender most of the lands and revenues of his diocese to the government, or even to Warwick and his friends (it is hard to distinguish the two). Thus, when Coverdale got Exeter it was worth only £500 a year instead of, as previously, over £1500. Tunstall, the much respected Catholic Bishop of Durham, was deprived of his see in 1552, and an act of Parliament was introduced (it never became law) to give most of the diocese lands to Warwick to give dignity to his new title of Duke of Northumberland.

Thus, the wealth of the bishoprics followed that of the monasteries and the chantries into lay hands. It is now that the Church was 'really ruined'.

Meanwhile the Council had ordered all remaining church altars to be removed and replaced by a simple wooden table. Church stained-glass windows were smashed, tombs broken up and statues removed, on the ground that they encouraged idolatry. 'In 1551 the confiscation of church plate was ordered except for the minimum required for carrying out services.'

What did Archbishop Cranmer think of all this? Of much of it he approved, for he had reached a thorough Zwinglian position himself, but the pace was a bit hot for him and, when he seemed to be dragging his footsteps, Warwick wrote to William Cecil, the new Secretary of State, 'For Heavens sake make Knox Bishop of Rochester; he will be a whetstone to Cranmer, who needs one.' The appointment was never made, but it would have been an interesting one.

* See Owen Chadwick, *op. cit.*, p. 120.

Cranmer, never satisfied with his first Prayer Book, was busy revising it. The communion service was changed to make it purely commemorative. Vestments worn by the officiating priest were much simplified. The service in fact became almost purely Zwinglian, though Cranmer insisted that communicants kneel when taking the sacrament (to the great disgust of Knox and other advisers).

This Prayer Book was enforced by the Second Act of Uniformity of 1552, which was stricter than the first act in that there were penalties laid down for both clergy and laymen who did not comply with it. In fact everyone had to attend church on Sundays, and the service had to be in accordance with the new Prayer Book.

After the publication of his Second Prayer Book Cranmer devoted himself to the definition of doctrine and his Forty-Two Articles of religion were published in 1553, but were never submitted to Parliament nor even to Convocation. In fact Warwick's method, in line with those of the Swiss reformers, was for the civil government to control the Church, pushing the bishops more and more into the background.

Warwick maintains his power

Warwick's position was somewhat precarious. A majority of the Privy Council could have unseated him at any time as Somerset had been unseated. His only firm supporters were the extreme Protestants, who hailed him as a true reformer 'that most faithful and intrepid soldier of Christ' (as one of them called him). But the extreme Protestant party was not strong in the Council, and here he relied upon the lavish distribution of bribes from confiscated Church lands to keep his supporters loyal. Also he was at pains to obtain an ascendancy over the King, that 'young Josiah', as the Protestants called him, referring to the young King of Judah who, according to *II Kings* Ch. 23, 'put down the idolatrous priests ... and the images and the idols and all abominations'. Edward VI believed that Warwick was a sincere Protestant, and, in the simplicity of his youth, trusted him.

Nevertheless, Warwick had thought it expedient to release Somerset from the Tower early in 1550 and reinstate him in the Council. He was after all the King's uncle, and it might please the reformers to be generous to him.

But Somerset was always a danger to Warwick. To the people he was still the 'good duke'. Warwick's pro-French policies were not popular, nor were his extreme religious measures. He relied upon the support of a faction in order to keep in power. The noblemen who had helped him quell the 1549 rebellions had been encouraged to keep in being, paid by government money, the troops of horsemen they had raised at that time. Moreover, many of them had been granted permanent commissions as Lords-Lieutenant to take over the county militia from the sheriffs. They thus had quite strong military forces available for an emergency, and, since the economic state of the country was going from bad to worse, there was need for such forces to keep down the perpetual unrest of the countryside.

In October 1551 several of these noblemen were rewarded with higher titles, while knighthoods were distributed lavishly among Warwick's lesser followers. He himself took the title of Duke of Northumberland. 'Backed by armed faction, controlling the Council and possessing a remarkable influence over the boy-King', in December 1551 Northumberland (as we must now call him) felt strong enough to arrest Somerset, who had been intriguing against him. He was tried before a court of peers on a trumped-up charge of treason and executed in January 1552, just before Parliament met, 'among impressive scenes of popular sorrow'.

Commerce and exploration

Meanwhile the economic situation was getting worse. In 1551 the cloth export trade to Antwerp suddenly collapsed. The market had become saturated and prices slumped. Moreover, owing to successive debasements of the coinage, foreign traders were refusing to accept English coins. Thousands of weavers found themselves out of work.* Northumberland tried desperate remedies. He changed the nominal value of the shilling to six pence at a single blow (this only created chaos). He sold crown lands worth £150,000. In the end he made the wise move of appointing Sir Thomas Gresham, a member of the Merchant Adventurers and 'conversant with the cloth trade and the subtle questions of exchange' as economic adviser.

Gresham was to make his mark in the reign of Elizabeth. He did, however, take one important step now, and that was to take away the privileges of the Hanseatic League, which was still handling a large amount of British cloth exports. In February 1552 its charters were revoked and 'the German merchants were thenceforward to be reduced to the condition of unprivileged foreigners'. Thus, British merchants were rid of an unfair competition.

It will be remembered that we first met Northumberland when as Viscount Lisle he was Lord Admiral and took charge of the naval force which accompanied the Scottish expedition of 1544 (*see* Chapter 7). He had now resumed the office of Lord Admiral, and his sea connections and knowledge enabled him to initiate British exploration overseas, and thus to take the first step in the founding of the British Empire.

We saw in Chapter 2 that Henry VII had been interested in John and Sebastian Cabot's attempts to find a route to Asia sailing westward. Sebastian returned from his 1508 voyage to find Henry VII dead, and, getting little encouragement from his son, he took service under the king of Spain (1512) and for forty years English exploration languished, chiefly because the incredible prosperity of the wool trade made it unnecessary to seek new markets.

* See also Chapter 17, the section on 'Overseas Trade'.

After years of responsible work under the Spanish government, Sebastian Cabot, now an old man, had returned to England in 1548, invited by some English councillors, and, when Northumberland came to rule, he made use of Cabot's knowledge to set afoot expeditions which would find new markets for British woollens, which were no longer selling so briskly at Antwerp.

The first of such expeditions was launched in 1551. It was led by a naval officer, Thomas Wyndham, and was to Morocco, where the Portuguese held a monopoly of the trade with Europe. Wyndham was successful, to the indignation of the Portuguese, in establishing a British–Moroccan trade, and in 1553 he followed up his success by a voyage to the Gold Coast, again with Northumberland's support. Although Wyndham lost his life, this expedition also opened up a new trade (in gold and ivory) for the London merchants who backed it.

These, however, were small triumphs. A far greater project was the exploration of a new route to the Orient. Portugal controlled the route round the Cape of Good Hope, which her navigator, Vasco da Gama, had discovered in 1497. Spain controlled the more difficult route round the southern end of South America. With Cabot's advice it was therefore decided to explore the North-east Passage, the route which was supposed to exist round the northern coast of Asia.

In the winter of 1552–1553 Northumberland formed a joint-stock company. Councillors, courtiers and merchants subscribed, and in 1553 three ships set out under Sir Hugh Willoughby and Richard Chancellor. Willoughby rounded the north of Norway, but was forced to winter in Lapland, where he and all his men perished. Chancellor, however, made his way into the White Sea and reached the port of Archangel. Thence he travelled to Moscow and presented his credentials to the Russian Czar, Ivan the Terrible, returning to England in the summer of 1554. The result of this voyage was the formation in 1555 of the Muscovy Company, which developed a thriving trade with Russia. Hitherto, the only way Russia had obtained European goods was overland from the Hanse merchants.

Chancellor died on his next voyage to Archangel in 1556. The North-east Passage was not discovered for another three hundred years. But Northumberland had inaugurated that expansion of British overseas trade which we usually attribute to the reign of Elizabeth.

The death of Edward VI

Though he made some contribution towards aiding English commerce, in the broader realm of foreign policy Northumberland's rule ended in failure. He had tied England to a French alliance and in the end it let him down. In 1552 the French king, Henry II, had a short, victorious war against Charles V. Allied with the German Protestants, he invaded Germany and captured Metz, Toul and Verdun, three imperial bishoprics. Charles appealed for English help under the treaty of 1543, but

124

Northumberland refused to make a move. Now was shown the folly of his pro-French policy. The triumphant Henry, realizing that Edward was a sickly youth and that soon England might be ruled by the half-Spanish Mary, began to plan an attack on England aided by Scottish arms. Northumberland's mismanagement had certainly made England a tempting prey. Her fleet was run down, her coastal defences under-manned, her foreign mercenaries disbanded, her finances in disorder and her people hopelessly divided over religion. Probably only Charles's renewal of the war with an attack on Metz in October 1552 saved England from an invasion that autumn.*

When spring arrived in 1553, Henry II found Northumberland was doing his work for him (the work of preventing Mary's succession). He therefore made no hasty move. Mary was heir to the throne under Henry VIII's will. A good Catholic, she had refused throughout her brother's reign to put away her priests. Obviously, Northumberland could expect little favour from her if Edward were to die. When therefore, early in 1553, Edward fell ill and it was apparent he would not live long, Northumberland decided upon a desperate plan. To secure himself in power he would marry his remaining unmarried son, Guildford Dudley, to Lady Jane Grey, elder daughter of the Duke of Suffolk, and descended (by her mother) from Mary, Henry VIII's younger sister.

The Suffolk line, it will be remembered, had been mentioned in Henry's will, but only after Mary and Elizabeth. Now Mary and Elizabeth were to be passed over (Elizabeth because Northumberland was not sure of her) and Frances, Duchess of Suffolk, Henry VIII's niece and Jane's mother, who was still alive, was to be excluded as well. What legal excuse could there be for this? It seemed that Northumberland hoped that Jane's marriage would speedily bring forth a boy and then all the females could be logically passed over (because they were females) in favour of this child. Thus in the first draft of Edward's will 'the male heirs of Jane' were allotted the succession, and only when it was apparent that the King would not live long enough for a male heir to be born, was Lady Jane herself inserted in the will.

At any rate the fifteen-year-old Jane was (most unwillingly) married to Guildford Dudley in May 1553. The King was persuaded to will her the throne on the ground that thus he could save the country from a Catholic reaction, and a great many councillors and other notables were bullied into signing the letters-patent, altering Henry VIII's will.

Hardly had the document been signed by the leading men of the realm before the King died (July 1553).

All Northumberland's carefully-laid plans miscarried. The country did not relish a disputed succession. It was plain for all men to see that Lady Jane had no right to the throne. A king's will could not change the succession unless Parliament decreed it, and here Parliament had not been consulted. In fact it had been dismissed in March 1552 to stop

* See R. B. Wernham, *op. cit.*, p. 206.

it interfering with the plan. So, when Northumberland proclaimed Lady Jane Queen in London, there was little enthusiasm shown. Meanwhile Mary, acting with great resolution, had avoided Northumberland's troops and taken herself to Norfolk, where the Catholic Howard family held great lands. When she set up her standard, men flocked to it, while Northumberland found his followers deserting him. Even the Council changed sides when its members saw which way things were going. Mary, with a large army, marched on London and entered it in triumph on 3 August. Northumberland was lodged with Lady Jane Grey in the Tower, and the latter's brief reign was over.

9 The Reign of Mary

A cautious beginning

Mary was thirty-seven years of age when she ascended the throne. Her life had been an unhappy one. Declared a bastard at the age of seventeen, she had not been allowed to marry, and had seen her mother disgraced and her religion abused. Surprisingly she had remained a 'kindly, well-intentioned woman', yet with none of Elizabeth's understanding of men. Simon Renard, the Imperial Ambassador told his master, Charles V, 'I know the Queen to be good, easily influenced, inexpert in worldly matters and a novice all round.' Half Spanish herself, she was a great admirer of Spain and an ardent Catholic. She had her father's strength of character and his stubbornness, but none of his ability to govern and to compromise.

It was Mary's determined aim to restore the papal authority in England. But at first she moved cautiously. She cleared the Tower of its prisoners, including the Duke of Norfolk (an old man now), the three Catholic bishops, Gardiner, Bonner and Tunstall (who were restored to their sees) and young Edward Courtenay, a descendant of Edward IV, who had been imprisoned by Henry VIII.

Gardiner was made Lord Chancellor and became the Queen's chief minister.

Northumberland was of course executed, but Mary showed clemency to others in the plot against her. Lady Jane Grey and her husband, though condemned to death, were given a respite of execution and kept in the Tower, as was Cranmer. Ridley, Latimer and Hooper were imprisoned, the first for conspiring with Northumberland, the second for preaching when forbidden and the third for being in debt to the government. In fact there was a great outing of Protestant Bishops and a substitution of Catholic ones, Mary presumably exercising her rights as Supreme Head (a title she of course detested).

A great many leading Protestants, including Knox and many

foreigners, fled to the Continent. Gardiner made no attempt to stop them. There were about eight hundred in all, and some of them helped to form the nucleus of the Church of England when they returned to England in the reign of Elizabeth.

Under the influence of the restored bishops the mass had been reintroduced in many churches. Under the existing law this was illegal, and Mary's first Parliament, when it met in September 1553, proceeded to regularize the situation. It passed an act repealing nearly all Edward VI's religious statutes, and providing that public worship should be conducted as in the last year of Henry VIII's reign. Cranmer's Prayer Book was thus abolished. Mary wanted Parliament to go further and restore the papal supremacy and give back monastery lands, but these things it refused to do. Monastery lands were by this time widely distributed, having been sold and resold, and there must have been few members of Parliament who did not own or lease a portion.

The Queen's marriage

Mary was intent on marrying a Spaniard, and had already let the Spanish ambassador, Renard, know that Charles V's son, Philip, would be acceptable. This was a wonderful windfall for Charles, whose affairs recently had not prospered. The Protestants of Germany had made common cause with Henry II, King of France, and the French armies had inflicted severe defeats on the imperial troops. Growing old and gouty, Charles was thinking of retirement, but the prospect of his son's marriage to the Queen of England gave him new life and hope.

The Spanish marriage did not appeal to the British people, however. Spain was immensely greater than England, and men feared that England might become, as had the Netherlands, a mere province of the Spanish crown. The Commons protested against the marriage and urged that the Queen marry an Englishman—only to receive an angry answer. Even Gardiner disliked the idea, and suggested the Queen should marry Edward Courtenay, now created Earl of Devonshire. But, since coming out of prison, Courtenay had begun to make up for the lost years by 'a career of debauchery abhorrent to the Queen's strict mind'.

The Queen was determined to have her way and in January 1554 the Spanish embassy arrived (snowballed by the youth of London as it rode through the streets) and a treaty was speedily drawn up.

Compelled to accept the alliance, Gardiner made the best bargain he could. All offices in church and state were to be conferred by Mary and could only be held by Englishmen. If Mary died childless, Philip was to have no further interest in England. The laws and customs of England were to be preserved intact, and the country was not to be involved, except by her own choice, in Spain's wars.

But even while the treaty was being negotiated, rebellion broke out in Kent. It was led by Sir Thomas Wyatt, a 'ruffianly though valiant

127

soldier' and was directed against the Spanish marriage. Wyatt received arms and money from France, but he was forced to rise before he was quite ready because the conspiracy, which was nation-wide, was betrayed to Gardiner by Courtenay (who was in the plot but got 'cold feet'). Thus other risings in Devon, the Welsh border and the Midlands (the last led by Lady Jane Grey's father, the Duke of Suffolk) hardly got going at all.

Wyatt, however, came very near to success. A force of the London trained bands, led by the Duke of Norfolk, was sent against him, but deserted to him in a body. He then marched on London. Mary behaved with great spirit and rallied the citizens of London by a speech at the Guildhall. Wyatt was thus unable to cross London Bridge, but he moved up-stream, crossed the Thames at Kingston, and moved down on the City, scattering the first force that was sent against him. But when he finally reached the City the gates were closed, and, with a royal army behind him, he lost heart and gave himself up.

Wyatt's was the closest-run of all the Tudor rebellions. Its motives were partly religious and this shows the strength of Protestantism in London and the south-east. Lady Jane Grey and her husband, though innocent of complicity, were both now executed. Lady Jane was only sixteen and died 'a martyr to the dynastic ambitions of her kinsfolk'. She was a sweet and gentle girl, though perhaps not devoid of ambition. Her father, the Duke of Suffolk, was likewise executed, as were Wyatt and a hundred of his followers.

Elizabeth, to whom Wyatt had written (though she had not replied) was suspected of complicity and placed in the Tower. The Spanish ambassador urged her execution, but Paget and some of the Protestant lords who had quelled the rebellion (for Mary still used several of the councillors who had held office under Edward VI) stood up for her, and in two months' time she was released. There was in fact no evidence against her.

Mary learned nothing from the rebellion. She insisted on going ahead with her marriage. A new Parliament was called in the spring of 1554 and gave its approval to the marriage treaty, but when bills were introduced to revive the heresy laws and the Act of Six Articles the Lords threw them out 'mainly because they feared heresy charges against owners of church property'.

It seemed that both religions were to be allowed to exist side by side. Without the heresy laws Mary had no power to compel conformity. She had to be content for the moment with the expulsion of about 1500 clergy from their livings on the ground that they had taken wives.

In July Philip arrived at Southampton and the royal marriage took place three days later at Winchester, Gardiner officiating. Philip in his cold way did his best to appear gracious, and his attitude together with the cart-loads of Spanish gold he had brought for Mary's dower, did something to lessen the national displeasure.

128

7 Queen Mary by Antonio Moro. This is a portrait which reveals Mary's soul. Elizabeth was careful never to allow such 'psychological penetration' in her portraits, and all of them show her as a regal symbol, a queen, not as a private person

With Philip established on the throne beside her, Mary was able to press ahead with her plans for a reconciliation with Rome. In the autumn of 1554 she summoned her third parliament. To make sure it would co-operate she exerted a certain amount of pressure on the officials in charge of elections. They were to choose members 'of a grave and Catholic sort'. As a result only forty per cent of old members were re-elected. This Parliament was to show itself in consequence much more Catholic than the first two of the reign.

The Pope's chosen instrument of reconciliation was Cardinal Pole. Reginald Pole was the grandson (through his mother, the Countess of Salisbury) of the Yorkist Duke of Clarence, 'the ill-fated brother of Edward IV'. He had been allowed to go abroad by Henry VIII when he had declared himself in opposition to Catherine of Aragon's divorce. Since then he had lived in Rome, loudly denouncing the evils of Henry VIII and Edward VI. He was an honest, sincere man, a devout Catholic, but utterly devoid of moderation and caution. A fellow-cardinal wrote of him 'He is a truly learned prelate, very virtuous and indeed of holy life; but he does not understand the first thing about the conduct of affairs.' Julius III now appointed him papal legate in England.

Charles V, well aware that Pole's immoderate enthusiasm might ruin everything in England, did his best to delay his arrival and sent Renard to Brussels to warn Pole that the restoration of monastery lands was not to be thought of. Pole reluctantly agreed, though he did not like bargaining with heretics.

Pole arrived in England in November, soon after Parliament had met. A week later both houses petitioned to be received once more into the Roman Church, and Pole performed the ceremony of absolution and reconciliation with the Queen and both houses kneeling before him.

In the mood of 'pious rapture' which followed this return of the realm to Rome, some formidable acts of Parliament were passed. The terrible heresy laws of the fifteenth century, which allowed burning as a penalty, were revived. All Henry VIII's statutes against papal authority were repealed; but ex-Church lands were declared to be under the protection of the common law.

Philip was probably responsible for this last, wise measure. He was a far better politician than Mary and knew when to move cautiously so as not to arouse resentment.

It was at the time of the meeting of this, her third Parliament (November 1554), that Mary became convinced she was with child. What if she were to die in childbed (she was after all thirty-nine years old)? To both Philip and Mary the solution seemed to be that Philip should be crowned King of England so that he might be able to carry on the government. But both houses of Parliament refused to countenance the idea.

Philip had tried, in his rather stiff way, to make himself popular. He drank English beer; he punished sharply any of his Spanish suite who were guilty of brawling with the English; he distributed pensions among nobles and councillors. Yet he made no attempt to learn the English language, and his attitude to English economic interests was far from satisfactory. He refused to throw open the valuable Spanish American trade to English merchants and even frowned on their trading in West Africa against the Portuguese monopoly. Worst of all he supported the privileges of the Hansards against the Merchant Adventurers (whom he thought of as rivals to his own Netherlands merchants).

These actions naturally caused resentment, but what really worried Englishmen about Philip was that he might obtain the crown and get control of the country altogether. Great hopes were centred upon the succession of the Princess Elizabeth, an event which Philip would, of course, oppose with all his might.

The persecutions

Those members of Parliament who re-passed the heresy laws probably had little idea how savagely they would be put into force. After all, these laws were part of the ancient Church system, which was now being restored. It was the Queen who decided that Protestantism must be stamped out by terror. She acted with the best of motives. Men's bodies must be burned now, if their souls were not to suffer in eternal torment. Cardinal Pole agreed. Gardiner, who died in November 1555, was inclined to be merciful after a few examples had been made, while Philip who burned thousands in the Netherlands, tried to dissuade Mary from her task for political reasons. He saw that it was he and the Spaniards who would get the blame. Also he feared revolt.

The first victim was John Rogers, a canon of St Paul's and editor of the so-called 'Matthew's Bible'. He was burned at Smithfield in February 1555. Hooper was burned soon after in his old diocese at Gloucester. Ferrars, Bishop of St David's, was burned at Carmarthen, while Ridley and Latimer died in the town ditch at Oxford, where the Martyrs' Memorial stands today. Latimer, eloquent to the last, spoke the words to Ridley which were soon to ring round England and prove a true prophesy: 'Be of good comfort Master Ridley, and play the man. We shall this day light such a candle by God's grace in England, as I trust shall never be put out.'

Cranmer's case was more difficult. He had been appointed by the Pope and only the Pope could degrade him. In February 1556 this was done, and he was handed over to the civil government to be burned.

But then for a month he was kept in suspense. His enemies knew that a full recantation would be of great value to their cause, for men honoured Cranmer and respected his opinions. As was hoped, he broke down and signed several recantations of his Protestant views. He was nevertheless condemned to death, and, when the morning came on which he was to be burned at Oxford, he was required to make a final
130

speech of recantation in St Mary's Church. The story is well-known that his courage came back to him, that, to the consternation of his enemies, he repudiated all he had written and declared he would plunge first into the fire the hand which had so falsely written. And so it was. Cut short in his speech by the angry doctors, he was led out to be burned and did indeed hold his right hand in the flames that it might suffer first. So died an Englishman who was loved by high and low alike, a gentle scholar whose love of language comes down to us still in the gracious cadences of our liturgy. 'The Protestants drew courage from his end.'

Pole replaced Cranmer as Archbishop of Canterbury. The burnings went on. By the end of the reign they numbered three hundred. Mostly they took place in the south-east and in East Anglia where Protestantism was strong. Bonner, in his diocese of London, was most active of all.

Apart from the leading divines, it was not the great and wealthy who suffered. Only nine 'gentlemen' are listed as having been burned. The majority were poor people—'weavers, apprentices or widows' (for sixty women were among the victims). Their bravery and steadfastness swung popular opinion towards Protestantism as the self-seeking Northumberland's church reforms had never done. 'The steadfastness of the victims ... baptized the English Reformation in blood, and drove into English minds the fatal association of ecclesiastical tyranny with the see of Rome. ... Five years before the Protestant cause was identified with church robbery, destruction, irreverence, religious anarchy. It was now beginning to be identified with virtue, honesty and loyal English resistance to a half-foreign Government.' *

From his refuge in Geneva Knox wrote his *Blast of the Trumpet against the Monstrous Regiment of Women*, denouncing the Queen as Jezebel and predicting the day of vengeance. John Foxe, also an exile, wrote a more powerful book still. His *Book of Martyrs*, published soon after Elizabeth's accession, 'recorded in loving and gruesome detail' the lives and deaths of Mary's victims. It became a best seller and stirred men's hearts with its pathetic descriptions of the last hours of the Protestant martyrs— propaganda, if you like, but propaganda which contained much solid truth.

Mary's tragic end

One hope the Protestants still had. Mary's pregnancy, loudly and rashly announced to the world in 1555, proved to be a false alarm. Instead she was ill with the disease of dropsy which finally killed her, and her heir was the supposedly-Protestant Elizabeth. At Frankfurt, Zürich, Basle and Strasbourg the Protestant exiles (who included five English bishops and many bishops-to-be) could afford to wait, knowing their turn must surely come.

Mary had other troubles. In August 1555 her unloving husband,

---

* Owen Chadwick, *op. cit.*

Philip, called away on urgent business, left her to go to the Netherlands. His father, Charles V, was about to abdicate his sovereignty over the Netherlands, Spain and Italy, and Philip was to succeed him.

Deserted by her husband, and aware of the growing hostility of her people, Mary received little comfort from her fourth Parliament which met in October 1555. It would only grant her one subsidy, and a bill to restore first-fruits and tenths to the pope was only passed in a modified form, and then only after the Commons had been locked into their House by the Queen's order, 'as if they were a jury which had failed to agree'. Several members were committed to the Tower in complete disregard of their right of freedom from arrest while Parliament is sitting.

Gardiner died soon after Parliament had met, and Pole became Mary's chief adviser, a position for which he was quite unfitted. Meanwhile, affairs in Europe had taken a disastrous turn. In May 1555 Paul IV had been elected Pope. He was a Neapolitan and, as Cardinal Caraffa, had played a leading part in the extirpation of heresy from the Church. He disliked Cardinal Pole, whom he knew well from the latter's long residence in Italy, but his special antipathy was towards the Spanish, whom he desired to expel from his beloved Naples.

In January 1556 Philip became King of Spain and ruler of its Italian dependencies. Paul IV lost no time in allying himself with France against the new Spanish King, and when, in September 1556, Philip launched an army under Alva against the Papal States to combat this new alliance, the Pope in fury excommunicated him.

Mary, loyal daughter of the Church, thus found herself in the pitiable position of being married to an excommunicated king, and having to choose between support of her husband or of the Holy Father. In 1557 Paul aimed another blow at her when he deprived Pole of his position of *legate a latere* and then summoned him to Rome on suspicion of heresy.

In March 1557 Philip visited England, not, as his fond wife hoped, in order to be with her, but solely to persuade the government to enter the war against France. It is true that Henry II had given the British plenty of provocation for such a war. He had done his best to persuade Scotland to attack England, had aided English exiles, had even plotted to marry Courtenay to Elizabeth, so that together they might supplant Mary and Philip on the throne. But hatred of France in Britain was now being matched by hatred of Spain, and there was great disgust in the country when Mary acceded to Philip's request and in June 1557 declared war on France.

The fears held by so many Englishmen at the time of Mary's marriage had now been realized. Despite the careful terms of the marriage treaty, England had been dragged into war to forward Spain's interests, a war incidentally for which she was in no way prepared.

With difficulty a force of 7000 men was raised and despatched to the Netherlands in July. A month later a Spanish general defeated the French at the great battle of St Quentin. Paris lay at his mercy, but, instead of marching upon it, he hesitated. Henry II, an able strategist, at once withdrew his forces from Italy under their brilliant general, the Duke of Guise, and concentrated them in the north of France. In dead of winter Guise devised an attack on the last British possession in France, left over from the great gains of the Hundred Years' War. Calais was invested by land and sea and stormed successfully in the first week of the new year, 1558.

It was a grievous blow to Mary, who is supposed to have declared that, when she died, 'Calais' would be found written on her heart. In fact to the British nation it was probably a blessing in disguise. Calais had outlived its usefulness to trade, as the location of the wool staple, and its loss would turn the minds of ambitious English governments away from Europe to the overseas possessions which would one day form the beginnings of the British Empire.

For the moment though it was a great blow to British prestige and confirmed Englishmen in their hatred of Mary's government and of all things Spanish.

In the last few months of her reign Mary made some attempt to restore her country's finances and rebuild its navy. But time was running out for her. By the autumn of 1558 she was very ill and confined to her chamber in St James' Palace. Pole also was ill, for Paul IV's treatment of him had 'cut him to the heart'. They both died on the same day, 17 November 1558, and the Londoners lit bonfires when they heard the glad news. The nation's agony was over.

The case in favour of Mary

Can nothing good be said about 'Bloody Mary's' policies? To answer this one must first remember that it was her early death which caused the failure of her Catholicizing policy. In 1553 'the body of committed English Protestants was much smaller than in France, the Southern Netherlands or Bavaria, and all these were turned by persistent government persecution into Catholic countries and have remained so to this day'.* Had Mary lived, would she not have been hailed by historians as the great queen who kept England Catholic? It is also her misfortune that the history of her reign has usually been written by Protestants.

Her persecutions are almost all that is remembered of Mary. Yet many more heretics were burned in France about this time than in England, while the Netherlands counted their victims in thousands.

Mary has been accused of having no religious policy but repression and of failing to discover the Counter-Reformation. This is hardly fair. As Professor Dickens has pointed out † she had to rely on the bishops and other church officials who had served her father. In order to train a new generation of clergy, more suited to her purpose, she gave the University of Oxford (Cambridge she distrusted) a large benefaction of

* See Conrad Russell, *op. cit.*, p. 134.
† *Lollards and Protestants in the Diocese of York*, Oxford University Press, 1959.

former monastic property. Pole was made Chancellor of the university and he revived the canon law faculty which had been abolished by Henry VIII, bringing in a scholar from Padua (where he had spent much of his exile) to guide it. The English Catholics in exile in Elizabeth's reign, such as Cardinal Allen, who excite our admiration, were all products of Marian Oxford. Conrad Russell points out, 'Had Mary lived another fifteen years she would have had as brilliant a bench of Catholic bishops as any in the history of the country.'

Moreover, Mary's financial administration was on the whole good. Her Lord Treasurer, the Marquess of Winchester, helped by Sir Thomas Gresham, was quietly efficient. There was some check on administrative corruption, the expenses of the household were cut and the administration of the Crown lands was much improved, so that they brought in £70,000 a year, more than double what they had yielded at the beginning of the reign. In 1558 a new Book of Rates was issued, in which duties were increased by an average of seventy-five per cent. Hitherto, cloth had escaped lightly and the weight of export taxation had rested on raw wool. The annual revenue from customs rose from £25,000 at the beginning of the reign to £80,000 and the end.* Thus Mary's reign 'checked the decline towards bankruptcy that had set in during the last years of Henry VIII' and 'left Elizabeth relatively solid foundations on which to build'.

Mary's greatest misfortune was that she produced no children. Hence there lay across her reign the shadow of a Protestant succession. This shadow became longer and darker as the reign proceeded and all hope of the Queen's pregnancy disappeared.

Finally, it is worth noting that, whereas later generations of Protestant Englishmen, brought up on Foxe's *Book of Martyrs* (and the innumerable text-books which have followed it), have learnt to think of her as 'Bloody Mary', contemporary Englishmen disliked her less for this and more for her Spanish marriage, her pro-Spanish policies and her loss of Calais. The opposition of her fourth Parliament was most marked, and it was caused chiefly by fears of an unnecessary war and dislike of her too-powerful Spanish consort.

10 The Counter-Reformation

The reforming popes

Since Elizabeth's reign was one long fight against the Counter-Reformation, the forces of revived Catholicism in Europe, it is necessary to study this movement in order to understand the reign.

Clement VII, the Pope who had had to deal with Henry VIII's

* R. Lockyer, *op. cit.*, p. 130.

divorce, died in 1534 and was succeeded by Paul III, a Pope who was bent on reform. Everyone, Catholic and Protestant alike, realized that the Church needed reform. Its abuses were too glaring to be neglected. Simony, pluralism, non-residence and nepotism were rife, and all the world knew it. Moreover, the Lutherans in Germany had split away from the Church and no longer even pretended to want reconciliation with it. Something had to be done, and done quickly.

Paul III began his work by appointing a number of first-rate cardinals. Among these were Reginald Pole (whom we have seen at work in England), Contarini and Caraffa. (He even offered the red hat to Erasmus, who refused it.) Amongst all this galaxy of talent it was soon evident that there were two schools of thought. Pole and Contarini were the leaders of the humanist party, which wanted conciliation with the Protestants, a reduction of the powers of the papacy, less discipline, clerical marriage, and the granting of the communion cup to the laity. Their views for a time looked like triumphing. At Ratisbon, in 1541, they almost found agreement with some leading Protestant divines (including Melanchthon and Bucer) upon the doctrine of justification by faith. Perhaps if Erasmus, the greatest of the humanists, had been alive, the moderates might after all have prevailed and the Church been reunited. But he had died in 1536.

Caraffa and the conservative party came into their own after the failure of the Colloquy of Ratisbon. They believed in fighting the Protestants, refusing all concessions, sticking to the medieval traditions of the Church, which put the clergy above the laity, the pope above kings.

In 1542 Contarini died. Caraffa and his friends came to the fore. They persuaded Paul III to found an Inquisition (a court to deal with heresy) similar to that which already existed in Spain. By the bull, *Licet ab Initio*, six cardinals (including Caraffa) were appointed as Inquisitors-General. All Catholics were to be subject to their authority. 'They were given power to imprison on suspicion, to confiscate property and to execute the guilty. . . . Caraffa would not wait for a grant from the papal treasury, but bought a house which he fitted with offices and dungeons and shackles.' *

The Roman Inquisition had no effect outside Italy, for the Catholic sovereigns of Europe had their own courts for the suppression of heresy and did not want papal interference. In Italy it was 'successful and disastrous'. It blotted out the few pockets of Lutherans which existed in Naples and elsewhere, but it also suppressed much humane thinking, especially when Caraffa ascended the papal throne as Paul IV in 1555.

Paul IV was seventy-nine years old when elected. Yet throughout his short reign he was busy with reform. He published an Index of forbidden books, which included all the works of Erasmus and even the *Decameron* of Boccaccio. There was a great burning of books throughout Italy. In

* Owen Chadwick, *op. cit.*, p. 270.

Venice 10,000 volumes were burned in one day. Paul even commissioned a painter (nicknamed 'the Trouserer') to clothe some of the naked figures in Michelangelo's paintings on the ceiling of the Sistine Chapel. 'Italian humanism, colourful and eccentric, ... could hardly survive the new rigours of clerical government.'

Books were not the only things to be burned by Paul IV. In Rome he used the Inquisition with such energy that there was almost a reign of terror there. Many heretics were burned, many imprisoned. 'Even if my own father were a heretic', declared Paul, 'I would gather the wood to burn him.' In Venice and other cities where the Holy Office had branches, there were many trials and some executions. No wonder that, when Paul died, the Roman people threw his statue into the Tiber and 'released seventy prisoners that he kept in the Inquisition'.*

Yet some of Paul's reforms were much needed. For instance he drove back to their sees all but ten or twelve of the 113 bishops whom he found living in Rome. He took such care in selecting new bishops that at one time fifty-eight bishoprics stood empty.

Paul died in 1559, but other reforming popes followed him. In general the popes of the sixteenth century from Paul III onwards were earnest men, interested in reform, determined to cleanse the Church of its slackness and worldliness. They form a marked contrast to the Renaissance popes who had been worldly, artistic, gay and corrupt. There was a new spirit abroad in Italy. Italian painters and writers turned towards religious subjects, depicting sacred scenes and writing sacred poetry. 'Learned Italy was returning to the piety of the Church.'

The Council of Trent

The Inquisition gave the popes a powerful instrument of control over Italy, but it had little or no power outside Italy. History showed that the way to cure a split in the Church was to call a General Council of all the chief bishops and abbots—an Ecumenical Council, as it was called.† It was thus that John Hus's heresy had been crushed in the early fifteenth century. Paul III therefore called such a Council in 1536. Owing to various difficulties, such as the opposition of Francis I of France, it did not meet until 1545. Then it met at Trent, a neutral town, as it were, which was geographically in Italy but politically within the bounds of the Empire (Pope and Emperor were, as usual, at loggerheads).

Despite many difficulties, the Council of Trent did make some important decisions on dogma. For instance it decided that the Scriptures were not the only source of truth, but that the traditions of the Church were equally to be so regarded. It considered Luther's doctrine of justification

* See Lord Acton, *op. cit.*, Chapter 5, on 'The Counter-Reformation'.
† I do not know a better brief account of the Counter-Reformation than that in A. J. Grant's *A History of Europe, 1494–1610*, from which much of the information in this section is taken.

by faith and decisively rejected it. Likewise it affirmed the doctrine of free will, and rejected that of predestination, which Calvin was preaching vigorously at this time in Geneva. The value of good works as a means of salvation (which the Protestants denied) was affirmed.

These decisions made it even harder for the Protestants to be reconciled to the Church. They disappointed the Emperor Charles V. 'Charles' dream of an assembly representing all believers, reaching decisions on both doctrine and reform which would win universal acceptance and restore peace to Christendom, was not to come true.'* Nevertheless the Council had given Catholics a clear idea of what the Church's doctrines were—a platform, as it were, on which they could take their stand. Moreover, in 1562 the Council reassembled and passed some resolutions on reform. Bishops were to have only one diocese and were to reside in it. Monks were to stay in their monasteries. 'The financial abuses connected with Indulgences were abolished.' Some of these were pious hopes, but some did result in improved behaviour by churchmen. Especially effective was an order that the bishop of any diocese where no university existed should establish a seminary to train boys and young men for the priesthood. It took some years for the order to take effect, but, when it did, it removed one of the chief complaints of the Protestants—that Catholic priests were so uneducated that they were incapable of preaching and that they mumbled the mass without understanding its words, as though it were some magic formula.

The Society of Jesus

Perhaps even more important to Catholicism than the Council of Trent was the formation of the Society of Jesus. This was a religious order founded in 1540 by a Spanish nobleman called Ignatius Loyola.

Loyola had been a soldier until wounded in both legs in the wars against France (1521). A cripple from then on, he had spent the next two decades of his life preparing himself for the great work he felt he had to do. He spent a year at Manresa near Barcelona, 'praying for seven hours a day, flagellating himself three times a day, rising at midnight for prayer, leaving his hair and nails uncut, begging his bread'. He spent seven years at the University of Paris, studying philosophy and theology. He took, with the six disciples he had gathered about him, the vows of poverty and chastity. Most of all he practised what he called 'Spiritual Exercises', which consisted in prolonged contemplation of the miseries of sin, the furies of Hell, the mercies of Christ etc.

At last in 1540 he was ready for his task. He applied to the Pope to found a new order and the Society of Jesus was formally accepted in a papal bull.

Two things were especially remarkable about the Society and distinguish it from all orders that had preceded it, whether of monks or

* This quotation is from *The Emperor Charles the Fifth* by Royall Tyler, Allen & Unwin, 1956, now unfortunately out of print.

of friars. The first is the extraordinary insistence which Loyola put upon discipline. His Society was divided into ranks like an army. There were six ranks in all—novices, scholastics, lay brothers etc., leading up to the General at the top (Loyola himself in the early years). Each member of a lower rank had to obey any orders given to him by those above him promptly and unquestioningly. 'The Jesuit under orders is to be as a staff in a man's hand, and so entirely without will of his own that he is to resemble an inanimate corpse.' So rigid was the discipline that it was said that a Jesuit writing a letter, if given an order by one of higher rank, would stop in the middle of a word to go and execute it.

The second remarkable thing about the Order was that it had no definite routine laid down (as had monks) nor narrowly defined objects (as had friars). According to the Constitutions included in the Bull of 1540, it existed 'for the advancement of souls in Christian life and doctrine and for the spread of the faith'. Thus the Society was a flexible instrument in the hands of its General to be put to any use he saw fit (in the furtherance of its general aims), provided the pope agreed with it.

Its activities took, under Loyola's guidance, two forms. First, it was busy in sending out missionaries, not only to countries like India, Japan and China which had hardly been touched by Christianity before, but also to European countries, whether Catholic or Protestant. Secondly, it was active in education. Numerous schools and colleges were founded by it all over the world, and many of them still flourish today. The education given in them was (and is) of a high standard, and soon wealthy and noble families from many countries were sending their children to Jesuit schools.

'In 1540 the Society was still a little group, primarily for education and pastoral work among the poor. By 1556, when Ignatius died, it had more than a thousand members and had become one of the powerful forces in the Catholic world, by its ministry not to the poor but to the upper ranks. ... It began by teaching the urchins of the Roman slums. It ended by teaching princes and princesses.' *

The Order spread rapidly, first to Italy and Spain; then Catholic bishops invited Jesuit fathers to work in southern Germany (1542). At this time the cause of Catholicism in all Germany seemed lost. Protestantism was still spreading in Catholic areas like Austria, Bavaria and Bohemia. North Germany had of course long been lost. The Jesuits tackled the situation by reforming the Church. With the help of the pious Prince Albert of Bavaria they altered the state of affairs wherein 'the clergy were often illiterate, the monasteries often like country inns, the vicarages commonly contained a concubine and numerous progeny ... and ... there were many drunken priests'. Thus the tide of Protestantism was turned back, and not in southern Germany only; the Jesuits were also very successful in Ireland, Poland and the southern part

* See Owen Chadwick, *op. cit.*, which contains a long and valuable chapter on the Counter-Reformation.

of the Netherlands. In the reign of Henry II they received legal recognition as a community in France.

The historian, Macaulay, summed up the achievements of the Counter-Reformation in the following magnificent passage:

'Within fifty years from the day on which Luther publicly renounced communion with the Papacy and burned the bull of Leo before the gates of Wittenberg, Protestantism attained its highest ascendancy, an ascendancy which it soon lost and has never regained. Hundreds who could well remember Brother Martin a devout Catholic, lived to see the revolution of which he was the chief author, victorious in half the states of Europe. In England, Scotland, Denmark, Sweden, Livonia, Prussia, Saxony, Hesse, Würtemburg, the Palatinate, in several cantons of Switzerland, in the Northern Netherlands, the Reformation had completely triumphed; and in all the countries on this side of the Alps and the Pyrenees, it seemed on the point of triumphing.... At first the chances seemed to be decidedly in favour of Protestantism; but the victory remained with the Church of Rome.... If we overleap another half-century, we find her victorious and dominant in France, Belgium, Bavaria, Bohemia, Austria, Poland and Hungary. Nor has Protestantism in the course of two hundred years, been able to reconquer any portion of what was then lost.'*

The second half of the sixteenth century then saw a very different Catholic Church than that which had existed in the days of Henry's 'divorce'. This ancient institution had staged a remarkable revival. Its torpid limbs had revived. It was no longer easy to ridicule as in the days of Erasmus. Its clergy were imbued with a new spirit. Its scholars were as learned and sincere as the leading Protestant divines. It was once more the Church Militant, marching against the enemy, and even daring to advance into fields into which the enemy had never yet penetrated. It was confident and forward-looking. This was the Church with which the Protestant Elizabeth would have to cope.

The political Counter-Reformation

'The name of Counter-Reformation is loosely applied not only to the movement for Catholic reform,' already described, but to 'the political revival of the Catholic powers of Europe', particularly Spain. Spain was unique among European powers in that she had had her own Counter-Reformation, as it were, before the Reformation had ever taken place. Back in the days of Isabella and Ferdinand, grandparents of Charles V, the Spanish Church had been reformed under the leadership of Cardinal Ximénez. Between the years 1495 and 1517, setting a high example himself, Ximénez, as Primate of Spain, reformed the clergy and religious houses of Spain. 'He enforced poverty among the monks and friars; dissolved religious houses which failed to conform to his standards ...

---

* Macaulay, *Essay on Ranke's History of the Popes*, 1840.

compelled incumbents to reside in their benefices, to expound the Scriptures and to educate children; and created the University of Alcalá, designed to train scholastic theologians and the clergy. . . .'* Long before Luther protested against Indulgences, Cardinal Ximénez had forbidden them to be preached in Spain.

The result of all this was that, when the Reformation came, Spain was proof against Protestant propaganda and Protestantism made no headway there. Although the ideas of Erasmus were accepted in Spain (until about 1530, when the Spanish Inquisition began to frown on his works), those of Luther got no recognition there whatsoever.

Spain then was the Catholic power *par excellence* in the sixteenth century. But in the reign of Charles I (the Emperor Charles V) she was so hampered by the opposition of France that she could do little to hurt the Protestant states of Europe. It is only after Charles's abdication in 1556 that Philip II brings the long war with France to an end in 1559. Then the new Spanish king, 'devout, determined, austere, spending long hours on his knees before the statues of saints, living in the Escorial rather as a monastery than as a palace, ruling the Church of Spain as tyranically as Henry VIII ruled the Church of England, identifying heresy with treason to the established authorities, wealthy with the gold of Peru' (thus Chadwick describes him), then, I repeat, he was in a position to concentrate his wealth and power upon the destruction of impudent little Protestant states like England, especially since, as we shall see, France was soon to be hopelessly torn by civil war (1562–1593).

This then is the political Counter-Reformation, a dedicated crusade by Philip II, in alliance with other Catholic monarchs, to defend the Catholic Church and overthrow Protestantism by force. Although he had not inherited the Habsburg lands of Germany, Philip had got the rest of his father's great empire. His possessions included Spain, the Netherlands, Milan, Naples, Sicily, Sardinia and all the Spanish colonies in the Americas. He wielded a formidable power, and Elizabeth came to the throne just at the moment when its full impact was about to be felt.

11 The Reign of Elizabeth. The First Ten Years

The young Queen

Elizabeth was twenty-five years old when she ascended the throne. 'Comely rather than handsome', she was tall in stature with fine eyes and a commanding bearing. Her childhood had been unhappy, for her mother, Anne Boleyn, had been executed when she was only two and

* Owen Chadwick, *op. cit.*

140

8 Elizabeth I from a painting by Nicholas Hilliard. (From a private collection)

a half, and she had been declared a bastard. But there had been compensations. Her step-mother, Catherine Parr, had been kind to her, and she and her half-sister, Mary, had been treated at court as the King's 'dearest children' equally with Edward.

Her education had been extremely thorough. Born 'in the full flush of Renaissance enthusiasm', when it was the fashion to educate women as thoroughly as men, she had been the pupil of that great schoolmaster and scholar, Roger Ascham. She grew up able to speak French and Italian 'as well as she does English', and well-grounded in Latin and moderately so in Greek. She seems to have been quick and intelligent and to have had a real love of learning.

But her best education had been in the hard school of experience. Mary's reign had been a difficult time for her. As heir presumptive to the throne, she had been the centre of plots. She had spent weeks in the Tower accused of complicity in Wyatt's rebellion. Amongst all such political intrigues she had learned to hold her tongue, and to screen her thoughts, to pick her way cautiously, and to rely on herself alone. By the time she came to the throne her character was formed of tempered steel.

One of her first steps was to appoint William Cecil as her Principal Secretary. Cecil, who was to serve her faithfully for forty years, was thirty-eight years old at this time. A Protestant with a Cambridge background, he had been private Secretary to the Protector Somerset and Secretary to Northumberland. In Mary's reign he had kept out of trouble by conforming to the Catholic religion. He was a man who never allowed his heart to rule his head. As a minister he was to show a capacity for work, a care for detail and a grasp of affairs which amounted to genius.

The danger to the realm

As already indicated Elizabeth came to the throne at a time of great danger from the Catholics. Henry II of France 'bestrode the realm like a Colossus'. In Scotland Mary of Guise was Regent. In France her daughter Mary, Queen of Scots, was Dauphiness, having married the Dauphin Francis. Henry II, the King of France, ruled largely on the advice of the Guise brothers, Francis, the Duke, and Charles, the Cardinal. The large Guise family was immensely wealthy in estates and church benefices. One historian describes it as 'one of the two spearheads of the Counter-Reformation' (Philip II being of course the other), for its members were strongly Catholic, indeed usually fanatically so.

The Catholics, of course, regarded Elizabeth as illegitimate. To them the true heir to the English throne was Mary, Queen of Scots, granddaughter of Margaret Tudor. To many observers it seemed unlikely that Elizabeth's regime would last more than a few months. The Catholics would surely overthrow it. The country was in any case in a bad state, 'its finances in disorder, its fortresses defenceless, its military forces negligible', except for the navy which was still able to dominate the Channel.

Yet in this dark picture there were some rays of light. One was the popularity of the young queen, who was everywhere acclaimed with enthusiasm. In particular the City of London received her most joyfully when she visited it, for all were captivated by her gracious manner.

Another ray of light was the attitude of Philip II of Spain. He was of course hostile to the Guises, and not averse to making friends with Elizabeth, who might yet turn out to be a Catholic (for so far she had skilfully disguised her Protestant leanings). Philip was even thinking of a marriage with Elizabeth, the most eligible widower in Europe to the most eligible spinster (and for a short time she kept him guessing).

Amidst all these dangers Elizabeth picked her way most carefully. If there was to be opposition in England it would come from the Catholic bench of bishops. Fortunately Pole was dead and five other bishoprics stood vacant at Mary's death. By the end of the year four more bishops had died. 'That accursed Cardinal', complained the Spanish ambassador, 'left twelve bishoprics to be filled, which will now be given to as many ministers of Lucifer.' Although his figure was too high, he was correct in his judgment that Elizabeth would move in a Protestant direction. She had not really much choice, being born of a marriage abhorred by the Catholic Church.

On Christmas day 1558 she ordered the officiating bishop at the royal chapel to omit the elevation of the host at the service of the mass. When he refused she walked out of the service. A month later at the opening of her first Parliament, she bade the abbot and monks of Westminster as they met her in broad daylight with tapers burning, 'Away with those torches! We can see well enough.'

Meanwhile the Protestant exiles in Germany and Switzerland were arriving in large numbers. Only Knox was not allowed to come, for he had just published his *First Blast of the Trumpet against the Monstrous Regiment of Women*. This was aimed at Mary of Guise and other Catholic female rulers, but it did not exactly please Elizabeth.

The Church Settlement

After much wrangling Elizabeth's first Parliament passed in 1559 the two great acts which brought into existence the Church of England as we know it today—the Acts of Supremacy and Uniformity. In the debates the main opposition to change came from the Upper House which included a solid phalanx of Catholic bishops. Two bishops in fact were put in prison because of their fierce opposition. The Lower House was by no means subservient either, and three drafts of the Act of Supremacy had to be prepared before both houses could be persuaded to pass it.

Professor Neale argued convincingly that in 1559 the government had to change its plans. It had originally intended to pass only an Act of

142

Supremacy. This would have left the communion service more or less a Catholic mass as in the days of Henry VIII. The intention was to go forward by easy stages and introduce a Protestant prayer book later on in the Queen's second Parliament, after Convocation (purged no doubt of Catholic bishops who would have refused to take the oath of supremacy) had agreed to it. But the plan miscarried. The bitter opposition of the bishops in the House of Lords to the Act of Supremacy and the determinedly united front of the Protestants in the House of Commons told Elizabeth she must make a clean sweep of Catholic bishops and rely upon the only alternative—a bench of Protestant divines including some newly arrived from exile on the Continent. Also, the temper of the Commons convinced her that the country was more Protestant than she had believed.*

At any rate at Easter (says Professor Neale) the Queen changed her mind (the signing of the Treaty of Cateau-Cambrésis with France which had just taken place doubtless made her feel more secure) and the Act of Uniformity was introduced. It brought in a prayer book which had never been discussed by Convocation, a fact which was to cause difficulties later on.

Let us now look at these two great acts. In its final form the Act of Supremacy asserted that all clergy and holders of office under the Crown must take an oath recognizing the Queen as 'the only supreme governor of this realm, as well in all spiritual and ecclesiastical things as temporal'. The use of the phrase 'supreme governor' instead of 'supreme head' as used by Henry VIII and Edward VI was intended to soften the blow to Catholic consciences. Also there was a feeling among members that a woman could not be supreme head of a church. After all a woman could not be a priest.

The Act of Supremacy was followed by an Act of Uniformity establishing the second Prayer Book of Edward VI (with some modifications) as the basis of worship. The modifications were in a Catholic direction. For instance the petition to be delivered from the tyranny of the 'bishop of Rome and all his detestable enormities' was struck out of the litany. The communion service was made a little more like that of Edward's first Prayer Book. By this compromise Elizabeth hoped to win over the Catholics (who were still probably a majority in the country).

In fact she resisted a good deal of pressure from the returning émigrés Protestants, who would have liked to establish the New Jerusalem of their dreams with the latest reformed worship of Zürich, Geneva etc.

The Act of Uniformity stated that everyone had to attend church on Sundays and holy days. The penalty for not doing so was a fine of one shilling.

The Marian bishops, all but one (Kitchen of Llandaff), refused to have anything to do with the supremacy oath or the new prayer book. One by one they were deprived of office, some being sent to the Tower,

* See *Elizabeth and her Parliaments*, Volume I by J. E. Neale, Cape, 1953, Chapters 1 and 2.

others allowed their liberty. Great efforts were made to win over the aged and much-respected Tunstall, Bishop of Durham, but he remained staunch to his faith to the end. The persecuting Bonner, whom Elizabeth disliked, died in prison.

The lower clergy were not so staunch and the great majority accepted the new prayer book quite readily, while on the whole the laity followed the clergy's lead. Thus England became gradually Protestant, the North being the area which stood out longest for the old religion.

Why did the Pope not excommunicate Elizabeth at once? Paul IV would probably have done so had he lived, but he died in 1559. Pius IV, his successor, was more cautious, and Philip II, the only monarch in Europe who might have put a bull of excommunication into execution, constantly warned him not to move because he did not want a conflict with England at this moment. Also, there was always hope that Elizabeth would return to the fold of her own accord, a hope she kept alive by various artful devices like the use of candles in her private chapel, whispered remarks to the Spanish ambassador and a pretence of great ignorance in matters of doctrine!

The empty bishoprics were filled with moderate men, when suitable ones could be found. Matthew Parker, a cautious scholar, was made Archbishop of Canterbury. He had been one of the society known as 'little Germany' which had gathered round Barnes and Bilney at Cambridge in the early days of the English Reformation. A friend of Cranmer, Latimer and Ridley in their day, he had never succumbed to the new ideas of Calvin, as had so many English Reformers. It was Parker who drew up the Thirty-Nine Articles which were adopted by Convocation in 1563 and became the basic doctrine of the Church of England.

Bishop John Jewel of Salisbury soon published his *Apology* showing that this Church of England was no new church but the old church of Christ rid of the 'multitude of your traditions and vanities' which had crept into the Catholic Church in the Middle Ages. 'We have planted no new religion', he wrote 'but only have renewed the old that was undoubtedly founded and used by the apostles of Christ.' The Apology was widely read throughout Europe, and most bitterly attacked by the Catholics there.

The establishment of the Church of England was not the least of Elizabeth's many great achievements. It has stood the test of time wonderfully well. But it was not achieved easily. In fact the first ten years or so were years of hard struggle for all concerned. The bishops found Catholicism formidable in its passive resistance. They had behind them all the resources of the state, including the church courts. They controlled the printing presses. Yet their letters and reports to Cecil and Parker and to their friends abroad alternate between hope and despair. Parliament gave them much help. The penalty originally imposed on those in key positions who refused the oath of supremacy was to be disabled from holding office under the Crown for life. But in 1563 Parliament went further and required the oath of supremacy to be taken by all university

144

graduates, schoolmasters, lawyers and MPs, and the penalties for refusing to be made more severe—loss of all goods and imprisonment.

There was much to be done by these busy Protestant bishops in these early days. 'They administered the oath, they reported on who was hostile to and who supported the religion established by law; they ordained ministers, they licensed preachers and saw that those who could not preach read the homilies setting forth the teaching of the Church. Clergy had to be disciplined and churchwardens prodded into activity. Four times a year all with the cure of souls were required to preach that "all usurped and foreign power" had no warrant in God's word. Schoolmasters had to be approved and to take the oath, books had to be licensed, and children had to be taught the catechism of the new church. Thus the formidable machinery of the church and of the state was directed against the Roman religion, which in these early years was seen as the main danger to the Church of England.'*

Fortunately for the authorities the Church of Rome gave English Catholics little leadership. One reason for this probably was that the Pope had greater matters on his mind. Little England was after all an unimportant part of Europe. Who was to know that she would soon be challenging mighty Spain herself? Deprived of a strong lead from Rome, the Catholic gentry played a passive part. They kept quiet and made themselves inconspicuous. Priests likewise, though they might celebrate the mass in private, were inclined to conform outwardly. After all the penalties for refusing to use the prayer book were severe—loss of all benefices for a second offence.

Foreign affairs: Scotland

In 1559 France and Spain brought their long series of wars to an end at the Treaty of Cateau-Cambrésis. England, as the ally of Spain, was represented at the peace conference, and Elizabeth instructed her envoys to try and regain Calais. However, the French government was adamant, and Calais had to be surrendered. Moreover, during the deliberations Philip announced his intention of marrying Elizabeth of Valois, eldest daughter of King Henry II of France. His period of dalliance with Elizabeth of England was thus over. In a tournament held to celebrate the royal wedding Henry was killed by a lance thrust in the eye. His eldest son, Francis, thus became king at the age of fifteen and a half (as Francis II). As we have noted, he was already married to Mary, Queen of Scots, and so her uncles, the Duke of Guise and the Cardinal of Lorraine, now became the real rulers of France. Since their sister, Mary of Guise, ruled in Scotland, the danger to England was still great.

But Mary of Guise's government was far from popular with the Scots. They resented French domination as much as the English had resented Spanish domination in Mary's reign and Protestantism in Scotland was

* Patrick McGrath's *Papists and Puritans under Elizabeth I*, Blandford, 1967, p. 56.

growing fast. In 1557 the Scottish Protestants had secured the support of a number of nobles and bound themselves together in a Covenant for the defence of the gospel, calling themselves 'The Congregation'. Elizabeth, eager to stir up more trouble for Mary of Guise, in 1559 allowed John Knox to pass through England back to his native Scotland. Knox's fiery preaching soon set all Scotland alight. At Edinburgh, Perth, Scone, Stirling and Linlithgow the crowds ran riot, attacking monasteries and churches, pulling down images and in many cases the abbey buildings themselves. In Perth alone three friaries and a monastery were gutted. 'Down with the nests' Knox had cried, 'and the rooks will fly away'. 'The ancient abbey church of Scone, where Scottish kings had been crowned for hundreds of years, perished among the ruins.'

All through the summer months the destruction continued, with the government hesitating to stop it. Then in October 1559 the Lords of the Congregation, as the Protestant nobles had come to call themselves, raised the standard of revolt at the market cross of Edinburgh and declared the Regent deposed.

Elizabeth and Cecil watched these events anxiously from England. At first they gave only secret help, sending money and munitions to the rebels. But it was soon evident that the French would crush the rebellion quite easily. It was time to move. An English fleet was therefore sent north to the Firth of Forth (where the port of Leith was besieged by Covenanters), and an army of 6000 men was assembled on the border.

Only when Elizabeth had heard from the Netherlands that Philip II was too bankrupt to intervene, and from France that the French government was in difficulty with a Huguenot conspiracy known as the 'Tumult of Amboise', did she order this army to march.

It attacked Leith without success, but the French saw themselves hopelessly outnumbered and in 1560, after the death of Mary of Guise, made the Treaty of Edinburgh. By it the French garrisons were to be withdrawn from Scotland and government was to be handed over to a Council, partly chosen by the Queen, partly by the Lords of Parliament. 'For the first time in history an English army recrossed the border sped on its way by the cheers and gratitude of the Scottish nation.'*

Later in the year 1560 the Scottish Parliament met and passed laws abolishing the authority and jurisdiction of the pope in Scotland. 'Mass was forbidden and orders were given to enforce a Protestant confession of faith.' Thus was the Reformation established in Scotland.

The marriage question

Elizabeth had not married in her sister's reign, because she would have had to make a political marriage and probably one with a pro-Spanish bias. When she became Queen, it was assumed she would marry and provide an heir. Suitors were pressed on her from all quarters—not only

* G. R. Elton, *op. cit.*, p. 278.

Philip of Spain, but the King of Sweden's eldest son and the Emperor's two younger sons. Elizabeth rejected them all. Obviously she was not forgetful of her sister Mary's disastrous political marriage. As for marrying an Englishman, there were objections to that as well, for whoever she chose, his rivals at court would feel themselves slighted, and so bad feeling would be stirred up. When in 1559 the Commons petitioned her to marry, she returned an evasive answer and even alarmed them by suggesting she might 'live and die a virgin'.

Then in 1559 her heart began to play a part in the matter. When Cecil returned from Scotland after concluding the Treaty of Edinburgh, he found to his horror that Elizabeth had become infatuated with Lord Robert Dudley, the son of the ill-fated Duke of Northumberland. Dudley was a fine-looking fellow, tall and handsome, an expert jouster. Unfortunately, he was married, though he saw little of his wife, Amy Robsart, for Dudley, being Master of the Horse, lived at Court, and Amy at their house in Berkshire. Soon rumours were going about that Dudley was to poison his wife and marry the Queen.

In September 1560 Dudley's wife was found dead at the foot of a staircase in her country house, her neck broken. The debate still goes on today whether Amy Robsart was murdered or committed suicide. A coroner's jury returned a verdict of 'death by misadventure', and absolved Dudley of all blame, but public opinion persisted in believing that it was murder, and all over Europe the Catholics gloated, and the Protestants were plunged in gloom, for, if Dudley had murdered Amy Robsart, it was presumably with Elizabeth's connivance. Elizabeth gradually came to see the danger to her reputation, and at last ended her dalliance with Lord Robert. Cecil once more took control of her policies, and the ship of state once more proceeded on an even keel. But it was not till the summer of 1561 that the crisis was fully passed.

The expedition to Le Havre

Late in 1560 the boy-king Francis II of France unexpectedly died (leaving Mary a widow at the age of eighteen). He was succeeded by his brother, Charles IX. Charles being a minor, his mother, Catherine de Médici, became Regent, and the Guises were ousted from power. At first these events seemed to be to England's advantage. The Guise threat in France, as in Scotland, had passed away. But in 1562 violence broke out all over France between Huguenots and Catholics. The Duke of Guise left his retirement in Lorraine and rode into Paris at the head of his retainers to put himself in command of the Catholics. The Protestant leaders fled from Paris and raised the standard of revolt in the provinces. France had begun the series of civil wars which were to plague her on and off for the next thirty-one years (1562–1593).

The Huguenots soon found themselves hard-pressed, and appealed to Elizabeth for help. She drove with them a hard bargain—too hard a bargain. In return for the loan of troops she was to have Calais back

147

and as a pledge for it Le Havre was to be at once handed over. In their extremity the Huguenots agreed to these humiliating terms and a British expedition occupied Le Havre. But this had the unexpected result of bringing the civil war to a halt. Rather than see France dismembered Catherine de Médici offered the Huguenot leaders generous peace terms, which they accepted. Then all Frenchmen together rose in their wrath to drive the hated English out of France. After a heroic defence by its English garrison, Le Havre was retaken and Elizabeth forced to make terms. Her intervention in France had been as disastrous as her Scottish intervention had been successful. But then Scotland was by this time a mainly Protestant country. France was not.

Mary Stuart

We have seen that, on the death of her husband, Francis, Mary Queen of Scots was left a widow at the age of eighteen.

Mary was, in every way, the opposite of Elizabeth. She had been brought up since the age of six in the somewhat sheltered atmosphere of the French Court. She had never had to struggle with adversity, as had Elizabeth. She was not an intellectual like Elizabeth, but was emotional and womanly, 'violent in her attachments and equally violent in her hates', a rather empty-headed girl who loved music, dancing and gaiety and had been thoroughly spoilt. Yet in times of trouble she was to show great spirit, and her face, which seems ordinary enough in her portraits, must have been mobile in expression, for she was bewitching to men. Men meant much in Mary's life, particularly good-looking ones, and in the end a man was to be her downfall.

Mary might never have returned to Scotland if her husband, Francis, had lived. But, now that he was dead, she decided to go back, and arrived in 1561.

The Scottish people received her without enthusiasm. She was known to be a papist and they had had enough trouble from French papists. She soon made it clear, however, that she was not going to interfere with the religious settlement in Scotland. Thus even the Protestant nobles were soon won over to her and flocked to Court. Only John Knox, Minister of St Giles in Edinburgh, remained hostile and suspicious.

While Mary had no ambition to interfere with religion, there was one ambition which lay close to her heart, and that was to establish her right to be regarded as heir-presumptive to the English throne. The Treaty of Edinburgh had contained a clause stating that Francis and Mary should abstain 'for all time coming' from using the style and arms of England and Ireland. This clause she now sought to have altered, but Elizabeth would not agree. At Mary's urgent request a meeting was arranged between the two queens in 1562, but the outbreak of civil war in France made it inexpedient for Elizabeth to show herself too friendly to a daughter of the House of Guise, and the meeting never took place.

It was obvious that Mary would marry again. Elizabeth was naturally anxious that it should not be to some great Catholic prince of Europe. She pressed her, therefore, to have Lord Robert Dudley, her own discarded suitor. In 1564 Lord Robert was created Earl of Leicester, no doubt to make him a more suitable match.

But Mary was not one to marry against her own inclinations. In 1564 the Catholic Earl of Lennox returned to Scotland from exile in England, and was soon followed by his nineteen-year-old son, Lord Darnley. Darnley was directly descended from Henry VII's elder daughter Margaret Tudor, for after the death of her first husband James IV, Margaret had married again and had had a daughter who had married the Earl of Lennox. Mary found Darnley attractive, and doubtless his claim to the English throne gave him an added attraction as a prospective match. So she decided to marry him, and despite frantic objections from the English Court, did so in July 1565.

The Scottish Protestant nobles, led by the Earl of Murray, had refused to agree to the Darnley marriage and had left the Court in anger. They had then been outlawed, and when Mary and Darnley collected troops and occupied Edinburgh, they fled across the border into England where, lacking help from Elizabeth, they lived for a time in poverty.

How different the history of Scotland (and indeed England) would have been if Darnley had been a fine character! Alas, he was not. Professor Black describes him thus: 'an addict to drink and boon companions, promiscuous in his relations with women, violent in temper, unstable, volatile and quite incapable of business'. Mary's infatuation for the callow youth soon cooled and was replaced by an attitude of scornful neglect. She came more and more to turn for companionship to her private secretary, an Italian called David Riccio.

Riccio had come to Scotland in 1561 at the age of twenty-eight in the train of the Duke of Savoy's ambassador. Mary had wanted a bass singer to complete a quartet and had prevailed upon him to remain in the country. Soon he had been promoted to the post of French Secretary (to deal with her French correspondence). Thus he became her favourite, and, scandal said, her lover.

Doubtless Riccio's presence brought to Mary a breath of the Renaissance and the *joie de vivre* which she had known in France. Scotland had as yet been hardly touched by the Renaissance. It was a land of dark, gloomy castles, of barons who knew of no pastimes but hunting, drinking and war. Mary must have craved for the gracious living she had known in France, for the sparkling conversation and the music and dancing which enlivened the evenings. Riccio doubtless knew something of the latest Italian plays and music and could talk to her of things she loved. It is impossible to tell whether or not he was her lover, but Mary became pregnant and Darnley was tortured with suspicions that the child was not his.

The murder of Riccio was plotted by Darnley and the Protestant lords (those in exile and those in Scotland). The Protestants hated Riccio, not only as an upstart but also as an emissary of the Pope, which they

149

imagined him to be (Mary's policies recently had taken on a more pro-Catholic tinge). Once Riccio was out of the way, Darnley was to gain the 'crown matrimonial', which Mary had refused to give him, and which would secure for him the privileges of royalty even after Mary's death. Murray and his fellow exiles were to be restored to their lands and titles, for it was expected that the shock of the murder would either kill the Queen or so throw the government out of gear that Darnley would take over power (Mary being perhaps openly condemned by the Kirk as a strumpet). Such, as far as we know, were the aims of the plotters; their motives were jealousy and personal animosity. The nobles of Scotland were not used to going cap-in-hand to ask favours of a base-born foreigner.

On the evening of 9 March 1566 Riccio was sitting at supper with Mary and Lady Argyll in Mary's boudoir in Holyrood House (the room adjoined Mary's bedroom). Darnley and a number of other lords, one of them in full armour, suddenly entered the room. Riccio clung terrified to the Queen's skirts, but was dragged shrieking from the room and despatched with daggers in an outer chamber.

The murder of Darnley

Mary recovered quickly from the shock of Riccio's murder. She pretended to forgive Darnley and persuaded him to desert his fellow-conspirators and flee with her from Holyrood where she was practically a prisoner. Then she admitted Murray who had appeared in Edinburgh soon after the murder, to her Council, detaching him from the other conspirators.

All seemed to be settling down in Scotland, especially when in June 1566 the Queen gave birth to a baby boy, christened James. The only fly in the ointment was Darnley, who, being hated by all the great nobles and treated with contempt by the Queen, was a man with a grievance—'brooding, suspicious, disgruntled, rebellious'. He corresponded with the Pope, posed as the champion of the Catholics and talked of leaving the country for Flanders. Mary was eager to get rid of him and divorce was suggested, but this would have been harmful to the baby prince. At a conference of the Council at Craigmillar Castle, one of the councillors (Lethington) made the sinister suggestion that, if she left it to her councillors, they would find a way of getting rid of Darnley!

Meanwhile Mary, passionate as ever, had found the lover she craved for, the Earl of Bothwell, 'a glorious, rash and hazardous young man' of about thirty. The fact that Bothwell was recently married does not seem to have prevented Mary becoming his mistress.

Now the scene was set for the next act of the tragedy which is the life of Mary Stuart. At the end of 1566 Darnley fell ill of smallpox. He recovered, but on the way back to Holyrood was taken to Kirk-o'-Field, a house on the outskirts of Edinburgh. Here Mary visited him, but on the night of 9 February 1567 she left to attend a masque at Holyrood.

That night Kirk-o'-Field was blown up and the body of Darnley was found in the garden, apparently strangled.

All Scotland believed that Bothwell was the murderer. Yet Mary took no steps against him. It was Darnley's father, the Earl of Lennox, who brought him to trial, but the court was so packed in favour of the accused that Lennox did not even dare to attend as accuser. So Bothwell was acquitted, and soon Mary promoted him to a dukedom.

Was Mary privy to the murder of her husband? This we shall never know. The celebrated Casket Letters, produced by Murray four months after the murder gave 'evidence' of her guilt. But they may have been forgeries. What seems fairly certain is that Mary knew a plan was going forward against Darnley and did nothing to warn him or protect him.

It was in any case Mary's actions *after* the murder which cost her her throne. In April she allowed herself to be kidnapped by Bothwell and carried off to Dunbar. Bothwell then obtained a divorce from his wife (himself being declared the adulterer) and in May he married Mary in Edinburgh by Protestant rites.

This was too much for the other Scottish lords. They were not prepared to lie quiet while the 'insolent Bothwell, enemy to many and friend to few, took the Queen and the Kingdom for his reward'. They revolted, with the righteous wrath of the Scottish people to support them. In June Mary was captured and brought to Edinburgh amidst shouts of the people to 'burn the whore'. Bothwell fled to Denmark to die there some eleven years later. Mary was taken to Loch Leven Castle to be out of the way of the Edinburgh mob who were clamouring for her blood.

While Knox and his fellow clerics threatened 'the plague of God to this whole country and nation' if the Queen were spared the punishment due to her, and while Elizabeth, no less incensed, demanded through her ambassador, 'What warrant have they in Scripture to depose their prince?' Mary was persuaded in July 'under threat of public trial . . . defamation of character and possibly death' to sign her abdication in favour of her infant son. Three days later James was crowned in Stirling and it seemed the career of Mary, Queen of Scots, was finished.

But it was not easy to keep Mary under lock and key. She was so beautiful that some young man in the castle was bound to fall in love with her. So it happened. In May 1568, helped by a youth of the castle household, Mary escaped. She raised an army among the Catholic Hamiltons, but was swiftly defeated by Murray's army, and after a tremendous ride (92 miles 'without stopping or alighting') reached the English border and threw herself upon the mercy of Elizabeth.

Elizabeth's dilemma

Elizabeth was in a quandary. To restore Mary by force of arms would not only mean a costly war, but would put the Catholic party back in power in Scotland. To hand her over defenceless to her enemies in Scotland would be to countenance rebellion and encourage treason—

impossible for a queen even to contemplate. To send her abroad to France would possibly lead to the renewal of the old French policy of interference in Scotland.

In the end Elizabeth decided to keep Mary under restraint. She was moved from Carlisle to Yorkshire and an enquiry was held at York into the question of why she had been deposed. Mary herself did not appear before this tribunal or 'conference' as it was called, but she was induced by various vague promises to send a representative. Murray attended and, after long delays, being at last assured that Mary was not to be restored as Queen, produced the famous Casket Letters, which had been found in a casket belonging to Bothwell and which purported to have been written to him by Mary. If these letters were not forgeries, they certainly proved that Mary had been guilty of the murder of Darnley for love of Bothwell. It is impossible today to judge whether they were forgeries or not, for the originals have disappeared and only copies remain. Many historians believe they were genuine. The English councillors (many of them Catholics) who saw them seem to have regarded them as genuine. Their existence gave Elizabeth an excuse for not restoring Mary to the Scottish throne and for keeping her a prisoner, but the fact that they were not published meant that many Catholics in northern England and Scotland still looked hopefully to Mary as a 'magnet for their discontents', which they might not have done had they known the full enormity of her crimes.

Eventually the York Conference was moved to Westminster. So many lies were told before it by so many people that it was impossible for the commissioners to come to any conclusions. In the end, declaring that nothing had been proven against Mary, Elizabeth dismissed the conference. The Queen of Scots was kept a prisoner in Tutbury Castle in Staffordshire, and lived to plague her hostess and sister-queen almost as much as she was plagued by her. Elizabeth would probably have been wiser had she let Mary go to the Continent, for there she would have been treated with cold contempt, the Catholic world having long since decided that this sensual and passionate woman was more of a liability to it than an asset. During her long imprisonment in England she was always the centre of plots.

12 Strained Relations with Spain

The drift from the Spanish alliance

Friendship with Spain had been a main aim in British foreign policy since the accession of Henry VII. In his reign we have the marriage between Arthur and Catherine of Aragon. Henry VIII, in the main, carries on the policy, and it culminates in Mary's reign with the Queen's marriage to Philip.

There were two main reasons for this lasting alliance. The first and more important was the cloth trade between England and the Netherlands, which created a bond between the two countries (and of course the Netherlands had been united to Spain on the death of Ferdinand of Aragon in 1516). The second was the hostility of both countries towards France.

In the 1560s the Anglo-Spanish alliance began to weaken. Religion was the main reason for this. Philip was a fanatical Catholic, the very spearpoint of the Counter-Reformation. Elizabeth and her countrymen were swiftly becoming Protestant. The Spanish had become unpopular in England during the reign of Mary, when, as we have seen, the name of Spain was linked (wrongly as it happens) with the religious persecutions. But it was the Spanish treatment of the Netherlands which really turned Englishmen against Spain in these years.

In 1559 the conclusion of the Treaty of Cateau-Cambrésis enabled Philip to leave the Netherlands and return to Spain. He left his half-sister Margaret of Parma, as Regent, but he was inclined to treat the Netherlands as a mere province of Spain (which his father Charles V, a Burgundian by birth, had never done), and he left an army of 3000 Spanish veterans there to keep order. The Burgundian nobles were not used to being treated as servants of Spain. Several of them were Lutherans, several Calvinists (for Calvinism was now spreading rapidly among the townsmen and the lesser nobility), and they particularly disliked the Cardinal de Granville, President of the *consulta* or royal committee which dealt with Netherland affairs. De Granville was a Burgundian, but 'as devoted to the Spanish crown as any Spaniard'.

Margaret had orders from Philip to take the advice of de Granville's committee, which thus usurped the functions of the Council of State, the council of great nobles, which normally governed the country and advised the duke.

As soon as Elizabeth saw that there was unrest in the Netherlands she began to stir it up secretly. She did not want the Netherlands absorbed by Spain. These seventeen provinces with their vigorous political institutions, their thriving towns, their wealthy and powerful merchant families, controlled the river mouths of the Rhine and the Scheldt and so commanded some of the best harbours in Northern Europe. That Catholic and Counter-Reformationary Spain should control these (so close to England's shores) was not to Elizabeth's liking to say the least of it. Hence the campaign against de Granville was fomented by pamphlets printed in England and distributed by English agents. We know (from his ambassador's letters) that Philip knew all about this and it certainly affected Spanish policy towards England.

We have noticed that fear of France was a major cause of the friendship between England and Spain. But from 1562 onwards this cause ceased to operate, for France had become involved in civil war and had ceased to be a threat to anybody.

As Calvinism spread in the Netherlands, it found leaders among the minor nobility, men like Louis of Nassau, younger brother of the powerful Lutheran noble, William of Orange. When in 1566 some of these presented a petition to the Regent Margaret (thus earning their nickname of the *Gueux* or 'beggars'), she was somewhat intimidated and relaxed the orders against preaching which Charles V had made. The outburst of preaching which followed caused riots. In four days the 'Calvinist Fury' led to the looting and destruction of some 400 monasteries and churches. The cathedral of Antwerp, rich in medieval art, was badly damaged.

Philip was indignant, but he loved to conceal his purpose. He pretended to yield, while preparing to strike hard. The Inquisition was withdrawn. A general amnesty was granted.

The Duke of Alva

In 1567 Philip sent his best general, the Duke of Alva, to the Netherlands with a fine, well-equipped army of 19,000 men. Alva saw no difficulty in his task. 'I have tamed men of iron,' he remarked, 'I shall soon have done with these men of butter.'

Margaret of Parma did not welcome Alva's arrival and after it soon resigned, so that Alva became Regent as well as Governor-General.

Alva was wholly devoted to King and Church and he ruled the Netherlands ruthlessly, blotting out local institutions where they opposed him. Soon he united people of all classes and faiths against him. His emergency council known as the 'Council of Tumults', or more commonly the 'Council of Blood' claimed 1800 victims in three months, including two of the leading nobles of the realm. Thousands fled abroad from its persecutions. It has been calculated that in the six years of Alva's rule (1567–1573) no less than 60,000 refugees came to England, many bringing with them skills such as cloth-weaving, which were of great assistance to the English economy.

William of Orange, the most powerful noble in the Netherlands, emerged as the hero of his people. In 1567 he fled from Alva's wrath to Germany (where he had lands), raised an army and returned, but was easily defeated by Alva. In 1568, with Huguenot support, he tried again, but was again defeated.

Thus by 1568 Alva had triumphed. The Netherlands lay prostrate beneath his hand. Only in the northern coastal provinces was there some defiance. Many Dutch Protestants bought themselves fighting ships and took to the sea as privateers, attacking Spanish shipping and disrupting Alva's supply lines. They called themselves the *gueux de mer* or 'sea beggars'. Already many Huguenot gentlemen were engaged in the same occupation.

Elizabeth's attitude to the rebels in the Netherlands was by no means entirely friendly. On principle she did not like rebels, and she did not particularly like Calvinists, for her own were beginning to give her trouble. When the Dutch Calvinists started wrecking churches in 1566 she was careful not to help them, but she gave a warm welcome to the 30,000 or so refugees who had arrived by the end of the year, giving them permission to settle, practise their trades and worship in their own Calvinist conventicles.

Alva's rule in the Netherlands of course aroused great hostility and suspicion in England. The fact that he allowed English Catholics who had fled from Elizabeth's government to enlist in his armies, made him appear as the leader of a Catholic crusade. Naturally, these *émigrés* clamoured for the overthrow of Elizabeth. Alva had to be stopped; yet war with Spain was out of the question. Elizabeth therefore moved cautiously.

She began to allow money raised from Flemish refugees to flow into the Low Countries. Volunteers (mainly Flemish refugees) were allowed to go and fight against Alva. Most important of all perhaps she allowed privateers, sea beggars like La Marck, who flew the flag of Orange, to load ordinance and munitions in English harbours.

Privateering in the Channel had been a cause of friction with Spain before Elizabeth began to encourage it. The Channel swarmed with freebooters who preyed mainly upon the Flemish and Spanish ships sailing between Spain and Antwerp. Some were French, some English, but the fact that the English coast had better harbours than the French made them use the former. Thus Philip blamed England for the deprivations to his trade, though in fact, until 1567, the English Privy Council did its best to put the privateers down. Only when Alva's power threatened to crush all resistance did Elizabeth cautiously begin to allow the Sea Beggars to use English harbours. They operated mainly from Dover and by 1570 they numbered over a hundred sail.

Decline of the Netherlands trade

It is important here to note the decline in the Netherlands trade which took place in the 1560s, for without this occurrence Elizabeth would never have been able to adopt an anti-Spanish policy, a luxury which the former Tudors had been unable to enjoy because of their dependence on that trade. De Granville had been eager to weaken Protestant England by any means in his power, and in 1563 he used the excuse of an outbreak of plague in England to forbid the import into the Netherlands of English cloth. Elizabeth at once retaliated by forbidding all imports from the Netherlands. The Merchant Adventurers, who handled all cloth exports, now had to find a new vent for their goods. They tried Emden in north Germany without much success and by 1564 they had

155

24,000 unsold cloths on their hands. Then, fortunately, de Granville was recalled by Philip, the quarrel patched up and Antwerp reopened to English trade.

Elizabeth's government now granted a new charter to the Merchant Adventurers which extended their field of trade to Germany as well as the Netherlands, and strengthened their monopoly. When therefore the Calvinist Fury made Antwerp unattractive for trade in 1566, they were able to establish themselves in Hamburg, whose merchants gave them a ten-year trading charter in 1567. This Hamburg charter was a real break-through for English trade. It reduced England's dependence on Antwerp and gave English foreign policy a new freedom of manoeuvre, since no longer was it necessary to be friendly with Spain.*

Also, about this time England had become independent of the once-powerful Hanseatic League, for the growth of power of Denmark and Sweden in the middle of the century shattered the Hanse monopoly of the Baltic trade and let in rival Dutch, German and English shipping. By 1560 England's trade with Baltic lands was being carried mainly by English ships. This meant not only a new vent for English cloth, but also that England was independent of the Hanseatic League for her vital imports of timber and other naval stores.†

The sudden freeing of England from economic dependence on Antwerp and the North German Hanse came only just in time, for the Duke of Alva's arrival in the Netherlands was to cause great interference with the Antwerp trade and bring it almost to a halt as we shall soon see. This north-eastward shift of trade was incidentally of greater importance than the south-westward movement of English trade which we noted in Chapter 8, when we saw Northumberland encouraging trade with Morocco and West Africa, for the latter was on a smaller scale.

Further friction with Spain

Elizabeth likewise encouraged the West African trade, and, when Portugal protested, she said she would not recognize Portuguese sovereignty except in lands where Portugal was in effective occupation. This was also her attitude to the Spanish government when it attempted to prevent English merchants trading with Spanish America. Since Spain lacked a navy of ocean-going ships which could control the Atlantic, here was a great opportunity for English merchants such as John Hawkins of Plymouth. In 1562 he secured a cargo of negro slaves from the Portuguese in West Africa, took them across the Atlantic, and sold them to the Spanish planters in Hispaniola, who were very short of labour. The Spanish colonists welcomed Hawkins' venture, but the government in Madrid let it be known it did not approve. Nevertheless, Hawkins, who had made a good profit, repeated his voyage in 1564. This time he took

* See R. B. Wernham, *op. cit.*, for a clear account of these events.
† See Chapter 17, section on 'Overseas Trade', for a further account of these matters.

an armed flotilla and the Queen herself lent him a ship. Again he made a handsome profit.

In 1567 he set off on his third voyage with no less than seven well-armed ships, one of them commanded by a young captain called Francis Drake. The Spanish government was now thoroughly on the alert, and the Spanish colonists had been warned of trouble if they took Hawkins's wares. He was obliged therefore to sack half a town before he could force the Spanish to buy his slaves, and in September 1568 he was forced to put into the harbour of San Juan de Ulloa to refit. Three days later a large Spanish fleet appeared outside the harbour of San Juan with the Viceroy of Mexico on board. Hawkins made terms with the Spaniards who agreed not to molest him if he allowed them to enter the harbour. But once inside, the Viceroy broke his word and attacked the English. Hawkins and Drake escaped with three of the ships. The other four, with over a hundred men aboard, were lost.

The news of San Juan de Ulloa reached England at the beginning of December 1568, and caused much indignation. It may have had something to do with Elizabeth's next action. Later in the month a Spanish fleet loaded with bullion from Genoan bankers and bound for the Netherlands was forced to shelter from Channel pirates in Plymouth and Southampton. Elizabeth, discovering that the bullion was still the property of the Genoese, decided to borrow it herself.

It so happened that Philip had just appointed a new ambassador to England, Don Guerau De Spes. De Spes, a most fanatical Catholic, had already contacted Mary, Queen of Scots (recently arrived in England) and his head was full of wild plans of raising revolt in England and placing Mary on the throne. When he heard of the confiscation of the Genoese treasure, he at once, without bothering to learn all the details, wrote to Alva urging immediate reprisals. Alva for once acted precipitately and laid an embargo (without Philip's permission) on all English property in the Netherlands. When news of this action reached England, the Council at once issued orders for the confiscation of all Spanish property in England. Thus there was a stoppage of trade between the two countries, which in fact was to last five years. Fortunately the Merchant Adventurers had at Cecil's bidding in 1567 made a ten-year agreement with the authorities at Hamburg for full trading privileges, so there was still an outlet for British cloth to the continental market.

The Rising of the Northern Earls

The arrival of Mary Queen of Scots in England and the quarrel with Spain brought to a head discontent which had long been growing against Cecil's rule. The old nobility resented Cecil as an upstart and they disliked his policies. As in the days of that other upstart, Thomas Cromwell, it was the Howard family which took the lead (in the plot that developed) in the person of the Duke of Norfolk, though he was rather unwillingly pushed into this position by the Earl of Arundel and other great lords,

157

such as the earls of Northumberland and Westmorland. The absence of a successor to Elizabeth made the old aristocracy feel insecure. Indeed most Englishmen felt the Queen was neglecting her plain duty. She was 'selfishly and wantonly letting the morrow take care of itself', because she would not be there to see it. Elizabeth was now thirty-five. She had recently rejected her most eligible suitor, the Archduke Charles of Austria, against the advice of many of her councillors. Cecil's policy, moreover, seemed to be leading England into war with Spain.

Norfolk, Arundel and the rest wanted a reversal of this policy. Some of them wanted Mary Stuart to marry the Duke of Norfolk and beget an heir apart from her Scottish son. Norfolk and Leicester were of this way of thinking, the plan having been first suggested to them by the Scottish commissioners at the York conference to settle Mary's future. Others, like Arundel, Northumberland and Westmorland were opposed to the marriage as they considered Norfolk to be a Protestant. They wanted the restoration of the old religion and Mary to be placed on the English throne at once. (This was clear treason.)

It was the latter group which, through an Italian banker named Ridolfi, got in touch with de Spes, the Spanish ambassador, and asked for Spanish help. De Spes told Philip that the English people were on the verge of rebellion, and that, if the Netherlands trade stoppage was enforced, there would be revolution. He wanted Alva to seize the English cloth fleet bound for Hamburg, and precipitate war. Alva, however, regarded de Spes' hopes as over-optimistic, and did nothing.

Cecil got wind of the plot (from Leicester, who at one time was in it). Elizabeth thereupon interviewed Norfolk and flatly forbade his marriage to Mary. In September 1569 Norfolk left the Court without permission, and in October he was arrested together with Arundel and two other lords.

Then the Earl of Sussex, President of the Council of the North, ordered Northumberland and Westmorland to repair to Court. Expecting to be arrested, they rebelled (perhaps Cecil summoned them in the hope that they would).

The North was still strongly feudal. The great families of Percy (Northumberland), Neville (Westmorland) and Dacre owned most of the land between Yorkshire and the border and even the authority of the Crown was exercised mainly through their members as lords-lieutenant, JPs and so on. Moreover, feudal law-courts were still powerful here, whereas elsewhere they had given way to royal jurisdiction. Since agricultural land was poor in these areas, employment in one of the great households was an important part of the economy. Men spent their lives in the service of a lord, and it was commonly said of the Northumbrians that 'they knew no prince but a Percy'.

Moreover, the North was Catholic. Elizabeth's new Prayer Book was disliked there, and her bishops found it impossible to enforce the new worship. Recusancy fines were not collected, for the JPs were themselves usually Catholics.

The arrival of Mary in this Catholic area provided a focus for discontent. The earls soon had thousands of enthusiastic followers. They marched to Durham and celebrated mass in the cathedral there, 'treading the Prayer Book underfoot'. Then they occupied Hartlepool as a port of entry for Alva's forces (which de Spes had promised them without Alva's authority). They planned to rescue Mary from Tutbury, but she was hastily moved south to Coventry.

The Earl of Sussex had few loyal forces in the North and could only hold out in York, but Elizabeth despatched an army from the South, and, when this drew near to Durham, the earls gave up hope, disbanded their foot-soldiers and fled with a few horsemen across the Scottish border.

Murray, the Scottish Regent, had stood firm for Elizabeth and kept watch on the border, but now, in January 1570, he was assassinated by a Hamilton, and this enabled the Scottish Catholics to raise their heads. They sent reinforcements to support Leonard Dacre, who, believing himself about to be arrested, had decided belatedly to join the rebellion. Fortunately, Elizabeth's army reached Carlisle first and prevented these reinforcements crossing the border.

Elizabeth took a stern retribution from the North. Nearly 800 people were executed, one from each town or village which had contributed to the rebellion. Land confiscations were so extensive that the feudal structure of the north was broken down, and the Council of the North under a new president really took over the government of the area in the Queen's name.

Elizabeth punished the Scottish Catholics who had attempted to help the rising, by sending punitive expeditions across the border, burning and destroying several castles. She also sent a force to Edinburgh to help the Protestant Party under the Earl of Morton and secured the election of her nominee, the Earl of Lennox (Darnley's father) as Regent.

Elizabeth excommunicated

Elizabeth's religious policy was proving successful. Many English Catholics had drifted into the Church of England. Those who held out had got into the habit of conforming outwardly, but secretly receiving the mass in their own homes. This state of affairs did not suit the great reforming Pope, Pius V. Encouraged by the stories he heard of the growing discontent in Northern England, in February 1570 he published a bull excommunicating and deposing Elizabeth.

When news of the bull reached England (in May) it caused the government some alarm. Norfolk was released from the Tower as a gesture of goodwill, and Cecil even approached Mary to discuss the terms of her restoration. But it soon became evident that Pius had released his bull without any temporal support. Neither France nor Spain were going to move (in fact Philip was annoyed that the Pope had not consulted him before issuing the bull). The English Catholics, having just been

159

thoroughly crushed, were in no mind to rebel again, and most of them comforted themselves with the fact that technically the bull was incorrect, as it referred to Elizabeth having claimed the 'supreme headship' of the Church, which in fact she had not. Nevertheless Elizabeth thought it prudent to call a Parliament (her fourth) in April 1571, and at her instigation it passed an act making it treason to introduce a papal bull into the country or to assert that she was not the rightful queen. From now on Catholics were carefully watched by the government. They were thought of as possibly treasonable people, whereas hitherto they had been regarded as normal and friendly to the state.

The Ridolfi Plot, 1571

Though the Pope had no army, he could still join in a conspiracy. The indefatigable Ridolfi was soon busy with another plot. He hoped to overthrow Elizabeth and seat Mary on the English throne by means of a Catholic rising in England combined with Spanish landings on the east and west coasts. He visited Italy in 1570 to get the Pope's approval. Then he contacted Mary Queen of Scots to get hers. Norfolk was more difficult to persuade, but eventually he was won over, as of course was the Spanish ambassador, de Spes. In 1571 Ridolfi visited Brussels, Rome and Madrid. Philip gave him some encouragement, but Alva opposed the plan vigorously, pointing out it would fail and only drive England into the arms of France.

Meanwhile Cecil had got wind of the plot. All through the summer of 1571 he was patiently collecting evidence. Only when he had enough did he arrest Norfolk. De Spes was ordered to leave the country. Norfolk was tried by his peers and executed. Ridolfi escaped, being safe overseas. The chief result of the plot (apart from the execution of Norfolk) was the damage it did to the popularity of Mary Queen of Scots.

The Treaty of Blois

Now that Alva appeared to be triumphant in the Netherlands, the growing power of Spain was becoming alarming to both France and England. Charles IX of France aspired to strike a blow at the Habsburgs as his father and grandfather had done before him. His opportunity came in 1570 when there was a lull in the civil wars and the Treaty of St Germain was made with the Huguenots, giving them liberty of worship. Coligny, the Huguenot leader was called into the King's councils and the idea grew of France joining the Protestants of Europe in an alliance against the Habsburgs. England was to be drawn into the alliance by a marriage between Elizabeth and the Duke of Anjou, who was the French King's brother and heir to the French throne.

The English government, somewhat shaken by the rising of the Northern Earls, and feeling in need of friends, looked with sympathy on the idea. If Elizabeth were to marry and produce an heir the plots in favour

160

of Mary would cease. Sir Francis Walsingham, the English ambassador in Paris, was entrusted with the negotiations.

It was soon evident though that there could be no marriage, for Anjou, a strict Catholic, insisted that he should be allowed freedom of worship in England. This Cecil, now created Lord Burghley, would have granted, but the Queen would have none of it. 'I am persuaded', wrote Leicester sadly to Walsingham, 'that her Majesty's heart is nothing inclined to marry at all.'

Nevertheless, as 1571 drew to its close, there were more reasons than ever for a French alliance. The Ridolfi plot with its Spanish machinations alarmed the English, while the victory of the Spanish fleet over the Turks at Lepanto had brought Philip to the very height of his power.

Hence in April 1572 a defensive treaty was signed at Blois between England and France. Each country agreed to come to the assistance of the other if attacked by a third power.

The descent on Brill

'Some three weeks before the Treaty of Blois was concluded' (that is in 1572) 'a revolution broke out in the Netherlands which upset all the calculations of the diplomatists, plunged France into one of the gravest crises in her history, and shook the Anglo–French alliance to its foundations.'* It happened thus. Elizabeth decided that the *gueux de mer* led by La Marck, the accredited admiral of the Prince of Orange, were becoming too disorderly and were a danger to British shipping besides being a cause of Spanish hostility to England. Therefore in March 1572 she issued a decree forbidding them to use English ports any more. Expelled from Dover La Marck sailed east and descended at night upon the little Dutch port of Brill and captured it. This was the signal for the outbreak of revolt all over the northern Netherlands. Soon Flushing, a fine deep-water port commanding the entrance to the Scheldt (and thus to Antwerp), was in the patriots' hands, and William of Orange was declared Stadtholder of Holland, Zeeland, Friesland and Utrecht.

It seemed that Alva's days in the Netherlands were numbered. William advanced with reinforcements from Germany. The French government, much influenced by the Huguenot leader, Coligny, allowed a Huguenot army under William of Nassau to advance into the southern Netherlands.

What was Elizabeth to do? At this crisis in the affairs of the Protestants, while the London crowds rejoiced that Alva was being driven out, she and Burghley thought little of the independence and freedom of the Dutch and much of the danger of French occupation of the Netherlands ports.

Sir Humphrey Gilbert was despatched to Flushing with a force of 'volunteers' with instruction to hold it at all costs against the French.

* *The Reign of Elizabeth* by J. B. Black, second edition, Oxford University Press, 1959, p. 155.

161

But Alva, despite reverses, was not finished. He attacked the Huguenot army and drove it back into France. Orange also was forced to retreat into France, and the southern Netherlands remained firmly in Alva's hands.

The massacre of St Bartholomew

Many people at the French Court, particularly Catherine de Medici, the Queen Mother, and members of the still-powerful Guise party, were watching Coligny's policies with growing dismay. Having obtained an ascendancy over the King, Charles IX, Coligny seemed likely to involve France in a full-scale war with Spain, a war for which she was in no way prepared. In August 1572 Paris was full of Huguenots who had come up for the marriage of Henry of Navarre to Margaret of Valois, the King's sister (Navarre was a Huguenot). The marriage was intended to bring peace to war-torn France. In fact it was to bring at its outset, bitterness and strife.

The traditional interpretation of the events that followed is that Catherine, who was partly Italian and thus perhaps familiar with murder as an instrument of policy, decided to have Coligny assassinated. But this version has been questioned by N. M. Sutherland,* who points out how much Catherine's reputation has been blackened by 'the hardy legend of the wicked Italian queen'. (In fact Catherine was more than half French.) Bearing this in mind we must approach the following account with caution. On 22 August, while returning to his lodging, Coligny was shot at from a neighbouring window and quite badly wounded in the hand and arm. Charles IX, unaware that his mother was behind the deed, ordered an enquiry. Catherine then told him that there must be no enquiry for she herself was the perpetrator of the deed, and, since the Huguenots were already pointing accusing fingers at her, the only course was to destroy Coligny and the other leaders of the party 'before the inevitable revelations came out'. Charles IX reluctantly agreed. Then various Catholic leaders, including Henry of Guise, were told of a bogus plot to kill the King and were thus persuaded to help get rid of the Huguenot leaders.

Shortly after midnight on St Bartholomew's day, 24 August, the killing began. Guise supervised the murder of Coligny. Navarre and Condé were spared, being of royal blood.

But it did not stop there. The mob in Paris, seeing what the government was up to, began the indiscriminate slaughter of Huguenots in Paris. Then the fever spread to provincial towns like Rouen. In a few days many thousands of Huguenots were killed, while panic-stricken survivors streamed into England from Dieppe.

'Catholic Europe did not hide its satisfaction' at the appalling atrocity. The Pope, Gregory XIII, declared himself better pleased than by fifty

* *Catherine de Medici and the Ancien Régime*, Historical Association pamphlet, 1966.

162

Lepantos, and ordered a *Te Deum* to be sung at St Peter's. Charles IX was regarded in Italy as having brought off a great piece of strategy (although historians today believe the massacre was not planned at all). Philip II gleefully referred to the 'long dissimulation' of his most Christian brother.

Protestant countries on the other hand 'were struck dumb with amazement and horror at the cruelty and barbarity of the deed'. In England the people were appalled and the Queen told the French ambassador that France had been 'guilty of the most heinous crime since the days of Jesus Christ'.

At first the English government thought that the massacre was a prelude to full-scale attack by the Catholic powers on Protestant Europe. But, when the French government continued to appear friendly, and Catherine de Medici even resumed negotiations for the marriage of her fourth son, the Duke of Alençon, to Elizabeth, it became reassured. The Treaty of Blois was not broken off, and only secret help was given to the Huguenot stronghold of La Rochelle in the west of France.

The renewal of the Netherlands trade

Nevertheless, the general feeling of the English Council now was that France could not be trusted, and that it would be wise to become reconciled to Spain. In any case the stoppage of the Netherlands trade had caused something of an economic depression in England. Spain also was eager for a resumption of trade. Therefore in 1573 negotiations were opened with Alva. Soon an agreement was reached, damages for the depredations of 1568 were decided upon, and trade was reopened. Elizabeth showed she was sincere in her intentions by sending a strong fleet to sea to clear out the privateers from the Channel, which it successfully did. Once more the rich Flanders trade was allowed to flow.

The years 1573–1585 were years of marked prosperity in England. Partly this was caused by the stream of refugees which had been arriving both from France and the Netherlands. The Flemings settled mostly in Norwich and Colchester and introduced new varieties of cloth manufacture, known as the 'new drapery'. The Huguenots settled mainly in London and many of them were silk-weavers.

One indication of the new prosperity was that the public debt (which Elizabeth had inherited) was much decreased. In the Parliament of 1576 the Chancellor of the Exchequer was able to announce that the internal debt (moneys owed to Englishmen) had been entirely paid off. The Queen was able to borrow at this time from foreign bankers at eight or nine per cent interest, whereas Philip of Spain had to pay over twelve per cent. His endless wars were proving costly. The Northern Netherlands revolt was still in full swing, although the massacre of St Bartholomew had of course ended all Huguenot help from France, and caused Alva's complete triumph in the south.

Elizabeth renewed the Treaty of Blois in 1574, when Charles IX died

163

and his brother, Anjou, succeeded as Henry III. 'Her aim was to keep the French alliance in being in case of war with Spain, and at the same time to take care that the Huguenots were not destroyed in case France and Spain should combine against her.' * Hence her secret help to beleaguered La Rochelle.

In 1573 Sir Francis Walsingham was recalled from the French embassy and made a privy councillor and the Queen's Principal Secretary, Burghley becoming Lord Treasurer. Walsingham, a Cambridge man, was a keen Protestant. He had fled abroad in Mary's reign, and had learnt to regard the Catholic cause as that of the powers of darkness, an attitude which had been strengthened by his experience as resident ambassador in Paris during the massacre of St Bartholomew.

By 1575 then things seemed to be set fair for Elizabeth. Spain had become more friendly with the renewal of trade. France had renewed the Treaty of Blois and her prince, Alençon, was suitor for Elizabeth's hand in marriage. The conservative opposition at home had been crushed, and prosperity was increasing. Moreover, Alva had been removed from office in the Netherlands (in 1573) and replaced by the much milder and more conciliatory Requesens. The war in the Netherlands was a stalemate, which suited Elizabeth. The Huguenots in La Rochelle were holding out (which also suited her). Scotland had settled down at last after the alarms of 1570 and was firmly under the control of its new Regent, the Earl of Morton.

Above all, England was at peace.

13 Religious Opposition to the Church Settlement. The Approach of War

The Puritan movement

Many English people were dissatisfied with the Church of England. They believed the religious settlement had not gone far enough. As Calvinism spread in Europe the people of England felt its influence. Calvin's church governed itself by popularly elected councils; it did not take orders from a civil government. The Church of England seemed to these people (who were nicknamed Puritans) to be not strict enough. It was too much like the old Church of Rome. Was not its Prayer Book little more than a translation of the old Roman Catholic service book? It had too much matter-in-the-service, too much ritual. The wearing of vestments, the use of an organ, the chanting of set prayers, the ring in marriage, the

* See J. A. Williamson, *op. cit.*

sign of the cross in baptism, the kneeling in holy communion, the excessive number of holy days; were not all these things the 'dregs of Popery'? Had not Jesus said 'God is a spirit, and they that worship him must worship him in spirit and in truth?' There is no doubt these early Puritans were sincere and much troubled in conscience.

It was not only Calvinism which influenced the Puritans. Many Englishmen (perhaps 800, if we include their families) had fled abroad in the days of the Marian persecution and had come under the influence of various centres of European Protestantism—Zürich, Frankfurt and Strasbourg beside Geneva. They were composed mainly of 'gentlemen, clergy, merchants and young men studying for the ministry'. Returning to England, they welcomed the setting-up of the Church of England, but regarded it only as a first step, a beginning. Surely the Queen must go on and establish a church more in line with the 'best reformed churches' of Europe. Six of these exiles became bishops (Jewel and Grindal were two of them). Some of them sat in Elizabeth's first Parliament. Professor Neale has estimated a 'vital core of at least twelve and probably sixteen' returning emigrés in this Parliament.* They included Sir Anthony Cooke, William Cecil's father-in-law (whose daughter, Mildred, also a strong Protestant, had great influence over her husband) and Nicholas Bacon, who became Elizabeth's Lord Keeper.

The Geneva exiles, those 'wolves from Geneva', as one of the Marian bishops had called them, seem to have arrived a little later than the others and they did not get the promotion in the Church that the others got, perhaps because of Elizabeth's dislike of John Knox. They were thus inclined to form a sect apart of 'godly' men, more radical in their ideas than the others, more intent on fundamental changes. It is noteworthy that Elizabeth did not invite over the great leaders of the reformed churches on the Continent, men such as Peter Martyr, who had been invited over in Edward VI's reign and would have been glad to have had an invitation now.

A number of great nobles had Puritan leanings, the earls of Leicester, Huntingdon, Bedford and Warwick for instance. They could help the Puritan clergy by making them chaplains in their households, presenting them with livings and then protecting them from the persecution of bishops, or getting them lectureships at the universities. Without the support of such patrons the Puritans would not have exerted anything like so much influence.

The Puritan movement received a boost by the publication of the Geneva Bible in England in 1560. Its explanatory notes were Calvinist in tone. The bishops brought out their own version, the Bishops' Bible, in 1568, but it was the Geneva Bible which sold best until the production of the Authorised Version in 1611.† In 1561 Calvin's *Institutes of the Christian Religion*, that most convincing of all books of the Reformation,

* J. E. Neale, *op. cit.*, p. 57.
† See Patrick McGrath, *op. cit.*, p. 82. I am much indebted to this book for details in this section.

was published in an English translation. Thus, although Calvinism got off to a slow start in Elizabeth's reign, it soon began to overtake the other reformed churches in its influence.

Elizabeth had no love of Calvinism. It was a religion which inevitably weakened the power of the crown. 'Calvinists, like Catholics, asserted the supremacy of the spiritual over the temporal power, and if they thought it was the will of God, they were prepared to challenge the authority of the prince.' They had already shown their ways in Scotland by opposing Mary of Guise.

The dispute between the Puritans and the Church began in 1559 over the question of the vestments prescribed for the clergy by the royal Injunctions. In 1563 the agitators petitioned Convocation to make a clean sweep 'of obnoxious practices'—the wearing of vestments, the use of the sign of the cross in baptism, kneeling at communion, the use of organs in the service and the observation of holy days. The petition was rejected by only one vote.

Meanwhile great disorder prevailed in the Church. Some minsiters used a surplice, others did not. In some churches the communion table stood in the middle of the chancel, in others 'altarwise a yard distant from the wall'. In 1563 the Queen, who was worried and irritated by the whole business, told the archbishops of Canterbury and York 'to take effectual measures that an exact order and uniformity be maintained in all external rites and ceremonies'. In 1566 therefore Parker, the Archbishop of Canterbury, issued his *Book of Advertisements*, laying down fixed rules for the conduct of the service. The sacraments of baptism and holy communion were to be carried out in the way laid down in the Prayer Book. A 'comely surplice with sleeves' was to be worn in the service by the minister. The parish was to provide 'a decent table standing on a frame for the communion table' and it was to be covered with 'a fair linen cloth'. The Ten Commandments were to be set upon the east wall 'over the said table'. All communicants were to receive the sacrament kneeling.

The attempt to impose conformity met with some resistance in London, where Parker had already got the Bishop of London to suspend thirty-seven recalcitrant ministers. Throughout the country, however, the bishops supported Parker, though some of them in rather a lukewarm manner. Zwinglian bishops (Grindal, Jewel, etc.) looked to continental reformers such as Bullinger of Zürich at this time, and many earnest letters passed to and fro, as they sought guidance as to what they should do. But Bullinger and the other Zürich leaders counselled caution and so none of the English bishops resigned. Had they done so it would have 'split the Church of England wide open' and set Elizabeth's government a real problem.* The attitude of these Zwinglian bishops (there were at least five of them left) was that it would do the Church no good if they were to resign—better to stay and try to reform it from the inside.

* *Ibid.*, p. 96.

Yet the 'godly' ministers who objected to Parker's Advertisements were not quite on their own. The Zwinglian bishops, in their various dioceses, were inclined to be kind to them and to disregard their illegal practices. Also, as has already been pointed out, powerful lay patrons were able to protect their favourite ministers and find them livings, chaplaincies and lectureships, while a number of town corporations were sympathetic to Puritan beliefs. Even Cecil himself (no doubt urged on by his Puritan wife) was not altogether on Parker's side. Thus a small number of passionately earnest men, believing they were doing the Lord's work, kept alive the spirit of nonconformity, and indeed made it grow.

Deprived of the leadership of the bishops, the Puritans (it is now the word first begins to be used to describe those who wished to purify the service) found a stalwart leader in Dr Thomas Cartwright, professor of divinity in the University of Cambridge. His writings were hard to combat, for he argued with great learning that Anglican Church government with its bishops appointed by the civil power had no basis in scripture. In 1570 he was deprived of his professorship and in 1574 fled abroad to avoid arrest.

Meanwhile the House of Commons had been growing steadily more Puritan. In 1571 a member called William Strickland introduced a bill for the reform of the Prayer Book 'so as to have all things brought to the purity of the Primitive Church'. The bill got a first reading and there was a good deal of support for it, but the Queen, regarding it as a plain invasion of her prerogative, had Strickland brought before the Privy Council, and he was forbidden to enter the House. This roused such a storm of protest in the Commons, that the Queen climbed down and Strickland was allowed to return but no more was heard of the bill. A year later Elizabeth informed the Commons through the Speaker that 'henceforth no bills concerning religion should be received into this House unless the same should first be considered and liked by the clergy'.

Blocked in the Commons, the Puritans began a bitter pamphlet warfare. Cartwright returned briefly from the continent to help wage it. His chief antagonist was John Whitgift, Regius professor of divinity at Cambridge. London was the chief stronghold of the Puritans, and the Bishop of London complained to Burghley 'The city will never be quiet till these authors of sedition ... be removed from the city; the people resort to them as in popery they were wont to run on pilgrimages.'

In 1575 Archbishop Parker died, and the Queen appointed Edmund Grindal to succeed him. Grindal was a reforming bishop, who had been in exile in Mary's reign, but it is not correct to label him a Puritan, for he had no sympathy with those clergy who refused to carry out divine service as laid down.* He did, however, believe that, if the Church of England was to survive, it must have a learned and responsible body

* *Ibid.*, p. 150.

of preaching clergy. The custom had grown up, particularly in London and the south-east, of holding meetings in private houses to hear sermons and discuss them. Laymen as well as clergy attended these 'prophesyings', as they were called, but clergy alone were allowed to speak. The local bishop was always informed and usually he appointed a moderator to conduct the meeting. The object of these 'exercises' (another name for them) was 'to train a godly and learned ministry'. Unfortunately, in the 1570s Puritans had managed to use these meetings to put forward their own views, and in 1576 the Queen decided the time had come to suppress them. She therefore instructed Grindal to do so. Grindal replied in a long letter that he had consulted his fellow bishops and they had decided that 'exercises' were profitable to the Church and should continue. He seems to have been quite sincere in his desire to follow his conscience in the matter, and begged the Queen to allow bishops and divines to judge of all matters touching religion, as she referred legal matters to her judges. Elizabeth, however, was adamant. 'It may well be that she judged the situation better than her archbishop.' The Puritans certainly constituted a real danger to her Church Settlement. In 1577 she ordered Grindal to be confined to his house and sequestered from exercising his temporal powers. In other words he was suspended from office.

'The drive against the Puritans went on,' and an attempt (only partly successful we think) was made to suppress prophesyings. Despite her title of Supreme Governor of the Church, Elizabeth was far from being all-powerful in church affairs. In many parishes laymen had the right of appointing the clergy. In others they had control of tithes and could appoint 'lecturers' in addition to the clergy, paid by the money they collected.

At the end of the 1570s Puritanism had become more formidable and was challenging the authority of the bishops, a thing it had not done in the 1560s. Two centres of Puritan thought were Oxford and Cambridge, particularly the latter. The Chancellor of Cambridge was Lord Burghley, who had a good deal of sympathy with the Puritans (being married to a Puritan wife). The Chancellor of Oxford was the Earl of Leicester, who was a great patron of Puritans and had persuaded the university to license John Field, a leading Puritan, as a preacher.

In the early 1580s the Puritans, and especially the Presbyterians, began to organize themselves into a series of *classes* and synods on the model Calvinists had developed in Europe. A *classis* was a conference of local clergy, perhaps twenty or more, who would meet regularly and secretly in private houses to discuss the scriptures and talk about their common problems. One *classis* corresponded with another, whether it be John Field's powerful London conference or some *classis* in Suffolk or Cambridge (for the movement was mainly situated in the south-east of England). The London group was also in touch with sympathizers in Scotland and the Netherlands (which were both of course strongly Calvinist countries). Here then were the beginnings of a national Presbyterian system, though the classical movement was as yet small and not very important. Probably the dedicated Calvinists among its members were a minority.*

But while 'Puritan influence was spreading, the resistance of the establishment was stiffening'. The older generation of bishops who had been in exile in Mary's reign was dying off, and Elizabeth replaced them with men who were not at all sympathetic to Puritanism. In 1583 Archbishop Grindal, who had never been restored to power, died and was replaced by Whitgift, himself the leading opponent of the Puritans.

Soon after his appointment Whitgift, after consulting the bishops and the Queen, issued a series of orders aimed at both Puritans and Papists. These laid down that no one was to preach or hold services unless he put his signature to three articles, which stated (1) that he acknowledged the royal supremacy, (2) that he agreed the Book of Common Prayer contained nothing contrary to the Word of God and that he would use it at all services, (3) that he agreed the Thirty-Nine Articles were agreeable to the Word of God.

To enforce these rules Whitgift set up a new Court of High Commission with himself as President. Many clergy found that they could not bring themselves to sign the three articles and between 300 and 400 were forced to resign.

But, as already pointed out, the Puritans had friends as well as enemies in high places. Influential men were annoyed when they found their favourite preachers being dragged before an ecclesiastical court. In 1584 some ministers in Essex appealed to the Council after being deprived of their livings. Thereupon eight privy councillors (including Burghley himself) protested to Whitgift, pointing out that, while 'lewd, evil, unprofitable and corrupt' clergy were immune, the people might be deprived of 'diligent, learned and zealous' ones. In the face of this opposition Whitgift modified the wording of the submission required to the three articles, and most of the deprived clergy were restored.

The Puritans were active in the Parliament of 1584–1585,† but, when they failed to achieve anything there, they turned once more to the printing press (both legal and illegal) to forward their ideas. The Privy Council thereupon decided that more must be done to control the press and in 1586 a Star Chamber decree (issued in the Queen's name) ordered the Archbishop of Canterbury and 'others of the Privy Council' to take action. All printing presses were to be registered with the Stationers' Company. Unregistered presses were to be destroyed. Printing presses were to be allowed only in London and its suburbs, apart from one in Cambridge and one in Oxford. No books were to be printed unless first approved by the Archbishop of Canterbury or the Bishop of London.

By the early 1580s, however, Elizabethan Puritanism had reached its high-water mark. The Church of England was settling down. It no longer

* *Ibid.*, p. 211.
† See Chapter 16, section on 'Elizabeth's Parliaments'.

appeared to be a temporary expedient as when Elizabeth first ascended the throne. As already noted, the Marian exiles who had become bishops were mostly now dead, and the new generation of bishops had little inclination towards Geneva.

Roman Catholic, Anglican and Calvinist all had one thing in common. They demanded that everyone join their churches, and brought disciplinary powers to bear on those who refused. They had no thought of toleration, of each man going his own way. Everyone was to be compelled to be a good Christian.

At Cambridge, 'that deep well of non-conformity', about 1582 there appeared a group of men who talked of each congregation going its own way without any central guidance or authority. Their leaders were Robert Browne and Henry Barrow, and they preached with such fervour and wrote with such force that for a time they became 'the spearhead of Elizabethan Puritanism'. Browne's teaching, however, was anathema to the government and in 1583 two members of his sect were hanged for denying the royal supremacy. The Brownists were the first of the English Independents or 'separatists' who were to grow so much in influence that in the next century they were to be the backbone of Cromwell's army and thus become rulers for a time of all England. Baptists, Congregationalists, Quakers and many other churches are today their heirs.

Whitgift with his High Commission Court (first set up in 1580) broke the back of the Elizabethan Puritan movement; and after the Armada Puritanism lost some of its patriotic appeal, for, while the enemy is knocking at the gates, those who attack him most vigorously are likely to win popular acclaim.

The Catholic influx

As has already been pointed out, in the early years of her reign, Elizabeth's religious policy had been very successful in winning converts from Rome to the Anglican faith. Moreover, those Catholics who remained true to their faith had mostly begun to compromise with their consciences, to attend Anglican service on Sundays in order to avoid being fined, and to hold masses, when a priest could be secured, in the privacy of their houses. Meanwhile, the drift from Rome continued and the Catholic cause in England appeared to be a lost one.

A new element entered the situation when in 1568 an English exile called William Allen founded a college for English Catholics at Douai in the Netherlands. Here young men were given a good education, and at the same time were taught that it was their duty to return to England to work for the salvation of souls, and, if necessary to seek martyrdom in the work. The Douai College was soon forced by the Governor of the Netherlands, Requesens, to move to Reims in France. In 1579 another college was formed in Rome and this came under the sway of the Jesuits and soon produced a number of men eager for martyrdom.

The colleges became so popular that the English government became
170

alarmed at the number of students fleeing overseas, and tried to check the stream.

The first 'seminarists', as the Douai students were called, began to arrive in England in 1574. About a hundred are thought to have come before the Jesuit mission arrived in 1580. They seem to have had some success. Undoubtedly they raised the morale of English Catholics and gave them a self-confidence they had previously lacked. The authorities in England took alarm. There appeared to them to be something of a Catholic revival taking place. Catholic books were being circulated, some printed abroad, some printed secretly in England. By 1578 three of the Douai priests had been captured and executed as traitors.

Their situation was not helped by the actions of Gregory XIII who had succeeded Pius V in the chair of St Peter in 1572. Gregory, like his predecessor, was determined to win back the Protestant countries to Rome, by force if necessary. 'The destruction of Elizabeth and all her works was the master purpose of his life.' In 1579 he rashly patronized a mad attempt by an Irishman called Fitzgerald to land troops and arms in Ireland and stir up rebellion there. Fitzgerald's force was easily destroyed, but, when the first Jesuit missionaries from Rome began to land in Britain in 1580, they found the government thoroughly alarmed and in no mood to treat them as other than traitors.

The leaders of the Jesuit mission were Edmund Campion and Robert Parsons. They began by holding a secret 'synod' in Southwark, which was attended by many priests. Here they explained their mission and pointed out that the Pope did not approve the widespread belief that Catholics might attend Anglican services 'without detriment to their souls'. Then they set out separately, travelling through the shires of England, stopping at numerous gentlemen's and noblemen's houses, celebrating mass, strengthening and encouraging the faithful, and always teaching that it was the duty of good Catholics not to compromise with the Anglican Church. Parsons also set up a secret printing press in London.

In July 1581 Campion, a noble character who had deeply endeared himself to all he met, was arrested, and Parsons was forced to flee overseas.

The missionaries always insisted that they were not inciting people to rebel, but were carrying out a purely spiritual task. Nevertheless Campion was tried for treason (after having refused under torture to incriminate others), convicted and hanged at Tyburn. On the scaffold he declared, 'We are dead men to the world; we travelled only for souls.' He was hailed as a martyr, and his death led to the production of several fine poems. Here is one:

> God knows it is not force nor might,
> Nor war nor warlike band,
> Nor shield and spear, nor dint of sword
> That must convert the land:
> It is the blood of martyrs shed,

It is that noble train,
That fights with word and not with sword,
And Christ their capitaine.

Parliament reacted to the invasion by passing in 1581 stricter recusancy laws. The fine for not attending church was raised from one shilling per Sunday to £20 a month, an enormous sum in those days. Even larger penalties were fixed for saying or attending mass.

These penalties were made even more crippling by a statute of 1586 which stated that those who were convicted of not attending church would continue to pay the £20 fine twice a year without further indictment. Only gentry families were prosecuted under these acts (they would be the only ones capable of paying), but some of these (less than 200 probably) must have suffered grievously, for no less than £36,000 was collected in fines over a period of five years. Some families paid over £2000 in these five years. It is not surprising that the Catholic gentry plotted in the next reign to kill the king and seize power, for the recusancy fines meant their ruin.

The invasion of Jesuits and other missionaries continued. The Douai College sent 438 priests to the English mission before 1603. By this date there were also similar colleges at Lisbon, Madrid, Seville and Valladolid. To these 'trained, zealous, courageous men, Roman Catholicism in England owed its continued existence'. Between 1577 and 1603 '123 priests were executed and some sixty men or women who had been guilty of harbouring or assisting them.' Another fifty or so Catholics died in prison.

It was not a great persecution by continental standards, but it caused great anger in the Catholic countries of Europe.

Many English Catholics, probably the majority, did not approve of the activities of the Jesuits. They believed that it was possible to be a good Catholic and yet loyal to Elizabeth. When the crisis came and the Armada sailed, the people, Catholic as well as Protestant, stood solid behind Elizabeth.

The achievements of the Jesuits and other seminarists was that they 'stopped the rot'. They did not turn men back from Protestantism, but they prevented more going over to it. We have the figure of 8570 recusants (those who refused to go to church) in England in 1603. Probably another 100,000 attended occasionally to avoid fines. Up and down the country today may be found manor houses containing 'priest's holes', reminders of the days when Catholic squires kept alive the religion of their forefathers.

Was Elizabeth's government justified in putting to death these brave men who always declared their aims were religious and not political? It is hard to give an answer to this question. Remembering the situation on the continent and the march of the Counter-Reformation, one can only admit that the government had plenty of provocation. Perhaps that does not entirely excuse it.

172

In the Netherlands the war dragged on. William of Orange's strength lay in the two coastal provinces of Holland and Zealand. It was practically impossible for the Spanish to invade these from the land side, as they consisted mainly of islands. Nor was a sea invasion possible, for the rebel navy was already more powerful than that of Spain and was increasing every year.

In 1576 Requesens died and Philip appointed Don John of Austria as Governor in his place. Don John, an illegitimate son of Charles V, was a notable warrior and very ambitious. He was famous as the victor of Lepanto, the great naval battle against the Turks in 1571. He was now only thirty years of age.

Don John was a long time arriving in the Netherlands. In the interval of ten months between Requesens' death and his arrival, the Spanish troops in the Netherlands mutinied for lack of pay. There was a reign of terror in the Flemish provinces, culminating in September in the 'Spanish Fury', wherein about 7000 citizens of the city of Antwerp were slaughtered.

This appalling massacre drove the southern provinces into the arms of the North, and, when Don John arrived in January 1577, he found all seventeen provinces for once united against Spain.

Don John was no disciplined public servant like Alva, but an emperor's son with an eye on a kingdom for himself. His aim was to make himself strong in the Netherlands, then cross to England, rescue Mary Stuart and marry her. He had imbibed these ideas in Italy, for Gregory XIII never ceased to dream of his *empresa* against England. It is doubtful if Philip approved of them, for he gave Don John instructions to work for reconciliation and peace.

For a time Don John did work for peace. Then suddenly in 1578 he attacked and defeated the army of the States-General.

Repeated requests by the States-General to Elizabeth for help brought only promises. Despite Walsingham's and Leicester's urgent demands for war, Elizabeth as usual preferred to work by diplomacy. In despair the States-General turned once more to France where there was a party led by the King's brother, the Duke of Alençon (now created Duke of Anjou), which believed in Coligny's old policy of helping the Dutch rebels. In August 1578 a treaty was signed between Anjou and the States, giving the former the title of 'Defender of Belgian Liberty'. Soon an army under Anjou was on Netherlands' soil.

At this point of crisis Don John suddenly died of the plague. Elizabeth thereupon 'executed one of her swift and unexpected changes of front in foreign policy—she revived the Alençon (Anjou) marriage policy'. Her object in doing this was doubtless to distract Anjou from his designs in the Netherlands. She pursued the courtship so vigorously that even her own ministers believed she was serious. In 1579 the Duke actually visited England. The Queen got on well with him, and playfully called him her 'frog'. It was obvious, however, that the country was against the marriage. Puritan pamphleteers raged against it. Her Council was divided and so the Queen (it seems reluctantly) shelved the project. She was after all, forty-six, and Anjou was some twenty years her junior.

In 1580 Philip had a tremendous stroke of luck. The throne of Portugal fell vacant and he was the legitimate heir. He marched in an army under the Duke of Alva to make good his claim. All went without a hitch and he found himself suddenly 'master of the gold of Africa and the spices of the East', for the Portuguese Empire included at this time Ceylon and Brazil, parts of West and East Africa, as well as trading stations in Malaya and India.

Meanwhile in the Netherlands Spain was once more triumphant. Don John had been replaced by Alexander Farnese, Duke of Parma, son of an illegitimate daughter of Charles V. He turned out to be 'the ablest and most astute of all Philip's soldier administrators, and a brilliant diplomatist to boot'. Within six months he had detached the Catholic provinces of the south from their alliance with the seven Calvinist northern provinces. When Anjou renewed his advance into the Netherlands (in 1581), Parma defeated him. Anjou was not the dedicated warrior that Parma was. In November 1581 he visited England to renew his courtship with Elizabeth (and was again much encouraged by that fickle lady). In 1582 he was back in the Netherlands, and it was said that he had taken to 'tennis, riding, running at the ring, and hunting the otter with spaniels, while Parma was capturing cities'.

The states never trusted Anjou and his sovereignty was so hedged about with restrictions that he found his position unbearable. In 1583 he made a treacherous attack on several Flemish cities in order to establish his power. This failed and made him so unpopular that he left the Netherlands for good. A year later the young Duke, who had carried with him the hopes of so many people, died. Elizabeth's contribution to his campaigns had been to give him some £20,000 or so. Her long dalliance with him had enabled her to exercise some control over his actions.

Scotland

We left Scotland, in the last chapter, under the firm rule of the Regent Morton. His power was shaken in 1578 when two earls managed to drive him from power and declare the King, James VI, aged twelve, now of age and able to govern. Morton recovered his position of power in 1579, but the revolution had caused a revival of the hopes of the Guise party in France, and in 1579 there arrived in Scotland a person who was to cause great trouble for the Protestant party. This was Esmé Stuart, Seigneur d'Aubigny, nephew of the Earl of Lennox, and thus first cousin to Darnley, James's father. Esmé was a young man with 'polished French manners which screened a subtle if not profound mind'. He came 'as the secret agent of the Guises to win the friendship of the young King

174

of Scots and to promote the cause of France, of Catholicism and of Mary Stuart'. He soon acquired an ascendancy over the King who was tired of Morton and his other dour advisers. James loaded Esmé with honours and titles, making him, among other things, Earl of Lennox. From now on the young King was surrounded by evil companions. He fell into bad habits and acquired a taste for oaths and bawdy jests. His association with Lennox probably contained a sexual element.*

Under Lennox's leadership a confederacy was formed to overthrow Morton. In 1580 he was arrested, and in 1581 'despite Elizabeth's frantic efforts to save him', executed.

Elizabeth was furious. She thought of war, but in the end withheld her forces. After a year of plot and counter-plot, during which a Jesuit mission was admitted into Scotland, James was suddenly seized by Protestant nobles while he was hunting near Perth (the 'Raid of Ruthven'). The Protestants thus regained power and Lennox fled to France.

Twelve months later, however, the Catholics, led by the Earl of Arran, a friend of Lennox's, were back in power. By this date (1583), James was seventeen and was beginning to assert himself. He was a most vain young man and 'esteemed himself superior to all other princes'.

One result of the Raid of Ruthven was to convince the Guises that 'Scotland was a harder nut to crack than they had imagined'. A plot was therefore hatched with Mendoza, the Spanish ambassador, to land a Spanish army under the Duke of Guise's command in England and put Mary on the throne. Walsingham's spies, however, stumbled on the plot while watching the suspicious movements of a certain English Catholic gentleman, Francis Throckmorton. Throckmorton was put on the rack and confessed all he knew. Mendoza thereupon was expelled from England (1584), the second Spanish ambassador to be so treated in the reign. He left, swearing vengeance on England.

In 1586 the situation in Scotland righted itself in England's favour. The Protestant nobles, after much scheming, came back to power and James was induced to sign the Treaty of Berwick with England. This was a mutual defence treaty and included a clause giving James £4000 a year out of the English Exchequer. He thus became the pensioner of England and in return promised to make no alliances prejudicial to England.

War draws near

Two events in 1584 brought war between Spain and England closer. One was the death of Anjou (already mentioned). Since Henry III had no children, Henry Bourbon, King of Navarre, was now heir to the throne, and he was a Huguenot. The Catholic princes, nobles and gentlemen of France had recently formed themselves into the Catholic League,

---

* See *James VI and I* by D. H. Willson, Cape, 1956.

under the leadership of Henry, Duke of Guise. The League was determined that no heretic should sit on the throne of St Louis and it now made a treaty with Philip of Spain, both sides agreeing to extirpate heresy in France and the Netherlands. Thus the worst had happened for England. The two spearpoints of the Counter-Reformation, Philip and the Guise family, so long at enmity, had drawn together. Inevitably in 1585, France was once more plunged into civil war, the Catholic League being opposed to Navarre and the Huguenots. This is sometimes known as the 'War of the Three Henrys'.

The second event of 1584 which brought war closer was the assassination of William of Orange. Philip had put a price on his head in 1580 and now he was murdered for gain in his palace at Delft. His death (and that of Anjou) left the Dutch leaderless at a time when Parma was steadily advancing and closing his grip on Antwerp.

'The time had come for Elizabeth to bestir herself.' In 1585 she at last made a treaty with the Dutch. In return for the temporary cession of Flushing and Brill, she would send over an army to serve in the Netherlands until the end of the war. In December Leicester set sail with 6000 foot and a thousand horse. The years of hesitation were over.

14 Elizabethan Seamen. The Tudor Navy

Exploration

Grenville, Drake, Hawkins, Frobisher, Gilbert, Raleigh—what names they are in English history! Gentlemen of Devon all (except for Frobisher who came from Yorkshire)! Did ever a single county make so great a contribution to the history of England in so short a space of time? The reason for the pre-eminence of Devon in seamanship in this period seems to have been the discovery of Newfoundland by John Cabot and the Bristol men back in the 1490s (*see* Chapter 2). The Newfoundland cod-fisheries were soon attracting west country sailors and by the middle years of Henry VIII's reign 'Newland fish' was a common article of trade between England and her neighbours. Devon with its situation in the west, its numerous good harbours, its fishing traditions, sent out the deep-sea fishers who learnt the art of navigating the oceans.

William Hawkins (the elder) of Plymouth was the first Devon man to engage in regular oceanic trade. About 1530 he began trading with Brazil (which belonged to Portugal) bringing home the valuable 'brazil wood' which contained a dye useful to cloth-makers. This trade was of course frowned on by the Portuguese.

About the same time Hawkins began to trespass on another Portuguese monopoly, and trade with the Guinea coast of West Africa, bringing home mainly ivory.

176

We have seen (in Chapter 8) that Northumberland encouraged exploration and trade in West Africa, and round the north of Norway. He relied much, as we saw, on the advice of Sebastian Cabot. Another of his advisers was a young geographer called John Dee. Dee was a great authority on medieval exploration (by Europeans and Arabs) in Asia. He was also a skilled mathematician and an astronomer of note. It was largely his enthusiasm that, after Northumberland's death, kept alive in England the interest in exploration. In the sixties and seventies he was well known in court circles, wrote memoranda on exploring projects, had interviews with the Queen and her councillors, and gave mathematical and cartographical instruction to sea captains like Frobisher and Drake. Dee 'became the prophet of the north-east passage and later of the fabled southern continent—the great *Terra Australis Incognita* supposed to lie to the south of the Pacific Ocean and to stretch from Cape Horn to the East India islands'.*

Dee was not the only geographer in Elizabethan England. There were many others. In fact Elizabeth's reign saw 'an astonishing output of geographical literature, some of it original but most of it translated from the works of Italian, Spanish, Flemish and German writers'.

One of the writers, Sir Humphrey Gilbert, was also a sailor. Gilbert was one of a trio of Devon gentlemen who had similar careers, for he was Raleigh's half-brother and cousin to Sir Richard Grenville. Born near Dartmouth, he was educated at Eton and Oxford. In 1566 he went to Ireland as a captain to take part in the constant warfare 'which proved so remarkable a nursery of soldiers, adventurers and colonisers'. Soon he became Governor of Munster, was knighted and became MP for Plymouth. We have met him (in Chapter 12) campaigning in the Netherlands in charge of a band of 'volunteers' in 1572. After this he lived in retirement for five years near London, and it was probably then that he wrote his *Discourse for a Discovery for a New Passage to Cathay*, advocating the exploration of a new trade-route round the north of North America (the famous North-west Passage). This was widely circulated in manuscript and had much influence.

But it was Dr Dee's advocacy of the search for *Terra Australis* which first attracted action. Bible students believed that somewhere in the South Seas lay Ophir which is mentioned (in *I Kings* 9:28) as the place from which Hiram, King of Tyre, 'fetched gold'. Marco Polo, the thirteenth-century Venetian explorer had written of 'wonderfully wealthy lands in the ocean to the south-east of China'.

A Spanish expedition from Peru had recently discovered 'Solomon's Islands' and reported that a continent lay beyond them. In 1574 Sir Richard Grenville and a group of Devon gentlemen applied to the Queen for a patent to explore the southern seas beyond the Straits of Magellan. The patent was granted, but then revoked, for Elizabeth had just

* See G. R. Elton, *op. cit.*, which has a chapter on 'Seapower'. James A. Williamson is an even greater authority on this subject (see his *The Tudor Age* and *The Age of Drake*).

patched up her quarrel with Spain, and she was afraid that Grenville (who had some record of privateering) might turn aside to plunder Peru.

The next project was inspired by Humphrey Gilbert's book. A London merchant named Michael Lok joined forces with Martin Frobisher and planned an expedition to search for the North-west Passage to Cathay. The government gave permission and in 1576 Frobisher set off. He was a tough, rugged Yorkshireman, who as a boy had sailed with Thomas Wyndham on his Gold Coast voyage, and in the sixties had gone privateering in the Channel having obtained a commission from the Huguenot leaders. He was known and feared as a strict disciplinarian.

Frobisher rounded the southern point of Greenland and discovered a bay (now named Frobisher Bay) just north of Hudson Strait. He believed he had discovered the entry to the North-west Passage, and on his return great enthusiasm prevailed in London, particularly as one of his crew had brought back some black stones which were believed to contain gold. Two more expeditions led by Frobisher set forth in 1577 and 1578, but they deteriorated into mining operations on the Canadian coast instead of geographical explorations. They brought back loads of rocks (some of which were in the end used for building a road in Dartford, Kent!) but no gold, and the company which had financed them went bankrupt. In fact Frobisher did discover Hudson Strait, but in the general disappointment this was scarcely noticed.

In 1580 the Muscovy Company organized an attempt to find the North-east Passage (round the north coast of Siberia). 'Of all the voyages of the period none was more elaborately prepared nor more carefully thought out.' Its leaders were Arthur Pet and Charles Jackman. After a weary battle for two months with ice, fog, rain and contrary winds, they had to give up. Other attempts to find the North-west Passage were begun in 1585 by John Davis of Dartmouth, 'prince of Elizabethan navigators'. He made three voyages in all, in 1585, 1586 and 1587 respectively. Eventually he reached latitude 73°N. He established the fact that Greenland was separate from America (the strait between them is now named Davis Strait). But, when he turned west at last into open sea, he ran into contrary winds and was compelled to turn back. By careful observations he had cleared up the geography of the east coast of Baffin Land, and the way he had pointed out was 'much later to prove the right one' (*see map* p. 183). Davis never had the backing that Frobisher had, but he was a most persistent mariner in his miserable little ships.

The Levant Coast trade which English merchants had enjoyed in the fifteenth century had declined and virtually ceased by 1550 because of Turkish sea power and general lawlessness in the eastern Mediterranian. But the Spanish victory over the Turks at Lepanto in 1571 opened up new opportunities. In 1578 some London merchants sent an envoy to the Sultan's court and the Sultan agreed to grant trading privileges to English merchants in the Turkish empire. In 1581 the Turkey Company was formed and was granted a charter by the Queen (it later changed
178

its name to the Levant Company). It soon began to prosper, bringing home the 'sweet wines of Candia' (Crete), olive oil and dried currants.

Since all other routes to the east had failed, the Turkey merchants planned to open up trade with India (and perhaps beyond) by the overland route through Syria. In 1583 they despatched John Newbery and Ralph Fitch to explore the route. They reached Agra in central India and presented a letter of credence from Queen Elizabeth to the Great Mogul. Then Newbery turned back (and perished on the way home), but Fitch pushed on to Bengal, then to Pegu in lower Burma and finally to Malaya. He arrived home in 1591 through India and Syria, bringing with him some wonderful travellers' tales after his nine years of wandering, but little hope of conducting an overland trade with India. The Indo-European trade at this time was of course in the hands of the Portuguese who used the Cape of Good Hope route.

The Caribbean—Hawkins and Drake

We saw, in Chapter 12, that John Hawkins of Plymouth (who was son of that William Hawkins who had traded with Brazil in the 1530s) had begun in 1562 to conduct a triangular trade in slaves, taking them from the Portuguese in West Africa to the Spanish colonists in America. We also saw that, after great initial success in this trade, Hawkins struck disaster at San Juan de Ulloa in 1568.

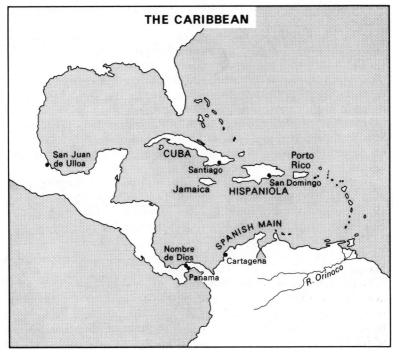

THE CARIBBEAN

The treacherous attack on Hawkins's fleet at San Juan ended all possibility of peaceful trade with the Spanish empire. Hawkins now deserted the Caribbean. He took to privateering in the Channel, building up a formidable fleet of some sixteen ships, large and small, which he kept at Plymouth and which the Queen relied upon to protect the south-west coast in times of emergency. With him in this venture he had other wealthy men and he had the backing of the Earl of Leicester at court.

Among several captains whom Hawkins employed in privateering was Francis Drake. Drake was born near Tavistock in Devon of yeoman stock in 1541. His father was a clergyman and became chaplain at Chatham dockyard which was the main base of Elizabeth's navy. From his father he inherited an ardent Protestantism, which was to make him in time the most persistent and enthusiastic of all English captains in fighting the Spaniard. He was apprenticed as a boy to the coasting trade and thus differed much in his education from Raleigh, Grenville and Gilbert, all of whom went, as gentlemen's sons, first to universities, and then, to learn a smattering of law, to Inns of Court. He was related to John Hawkins and thus came to command a ship in the ill-fated San Juan de Ulloa expedition of 1567–1568.

Hawkins now employed him, together with other captains, to make occasional raids on Spanish treasure ships in the Caribbean, as they collected the treasure for the two annual trans-Atlantic sailings from San Juan de Ulloa and Nombre de Dios. Drake thus became acquainted with 'the run of the treasure traffic', and soon began to plan a more ambitious raid.

In 1572 he set off with two small vessels and seventy men (equipped as usual by Hawkins and his friends) and attacked Nombre de Dios without much success. Then he landed on the Panama Isthmus and, with the help of a Huguenot crew who were also raiding, he captured a convoy of mules carrying Peruvian treasure to Nombre de Dios. In 1573 he returned to Plymouth with £20,000 of gold.

Drake's reputation was made, but it was a bad moment to annoy the Spanish for Burghley was just patching up peace with them after the five-year trade-stoppage. Drake therefore disappeared from view for two years.

In 1576 John Oxenham, one of the men who had accompanied Drake in 1572–1573, tried to repeat his exploit. His expedition ended in disaster. He was captured and hanged by the Inquisition at Lima, while most of his men ended their days as slaves in the Spanish galleys.

The cruelties of the Inquisition and the ruthless methods of Spanish administrators in the New World were major causes of the growing hatred of Spain by the English at this time.

Drake had espied the Pacific in 1572 and had become aware of the defenceless nature of the Spanish shipping in those waters. He and others now revived the project which Sir Richard Grenville had been forced to abandon of entering the Pacific by the Straits of Magellan, a route which incidentally the Spanish had abandoned as too dangerous (they
180

used the overland route across the Isthmus of Panama). Times had changed since 1573 and friendship with Spain was no longer considered so vital. The government therefore smiled on the scheme, which was in fact a semi-state undertaking with Leicester, Walsingham and the Queen herself contributing. Drake, rather than Grenville, was chosen to lead the expedition. Ostensibly the plan was to search for *Terra Australis*, but, before Drake left, he was conducted by Walsingham to a secret interview with the Queen, who authorized him to attack the Spanish possessions in the Pacific, but 'the Lord Treasurer', Burghley, 'must not know it'. Presumably it would be much easier for Burghley to tell the Spanish ambassador that Drake had acted without permission, if he thought he really had!

The expedition set sail in December 1577 with four vessels. The largest, the *Pelican* (soon to be rechristened the *Golden Hind*) was only 120 tons. Thomas Doughty, a friend of Drake's, was second-in-command. When they reached the coasts of Patagonia Doughty stirred up a mutiny. Drake 'court martialled Doughty himself, condemned him, took communion with him and then executed him with his own hands—so that no man but himself should be accountable to Heaven for the deed'. Drake then burned Doughty's ship and proceeded on his way. He passed through the Straits of Magellan in sixteen days and then met appalling weather in the Pacific. His little fleet was scattered and driven southward. Here they discovered nothing but open sea. There appeared to be no *Terra Australis* after all, and the idea emerged that the land south of the Straits of Magellan was only an island not the tip of a vast continent. (It is, of course, indeed the island of Tierra del Fuego.)

One of Drake's three remaining ships was now lost with all hands; another turned for home. Only Drake himself in the *Golden Hind* sailed north when the weather grew calmer (it was now November 1578). The whole of the Spanish Pacific Empire now lay at his mercy. He proceeded along the coast, entering ports and capturing ships, until at last he captured a treasure ship bound for Panama, which yielded as much silver and gold as he could conveniently carry. Hearing from prisoners that Oxenham and his men had been captured, he avoided Panama and sailed north, hoping to find the western end of the famous North-west Passage. He passed what is now California (claiming possession of it by the name of New Albion!), and having reached beyond latitude 40°N, decided that the North-west Passage was too far north and he had better turn westwards and return by the Cape of Good Hope route. This he did, experiencing many dangers on the way. He reached Plymouth in September 1580, the first Englishman, and only the second man, to circumnavigate the globe. His first question to some fishermen he met off the English coast was, 'Is the Queen still alive?'.

The amount of treasure this expedition realized has never been revealed. It is thought to have been well over £400,000, and therefore considerably greater than the annual revenue of the English crown at this time. The government appears to have kept half of it. The rest was

181

divided among the expedition's backers. Drake himself became a rich man and bought himself Buckland Abbey in Devon. The treasure was 'an enormous accession to the country's fluid capital'. It enabled Elizabeth to conduct a more vigorous foreign policy and was in general a spur to trade and industry at this vital moment in English history.

Drake became a national hero. The Spanish ambassador clamoured for his head, but Elizabeth ordered the *Golden Hind* round to the Thames and knighted Drake upon the deck of his own ship.

Colonization

Various writers had been urging for some time that the English should plant colonies in North America. The idea had got about that England was over-populated (after all unemployment and vagabondage were rife). Colonies would take away the surplus population. Then there was the fact that Spain and Portugal had colonies. Natural pride demanded that England should also have some. It was generally believed moreover that 'the country weakened itself and strengthened its neighbours by buying goods from them. ... English settlers might produce wines and silk, dyestuffs and naval stores, hitherto obtained from the continent of Europe.'* Such were the arguments put forward.

Sir Humphrey Gilbert was the first to act. In 1578 he obtained a royal patent, authorizing him to plant settlements in North America. He made some sort of an expedition that autumn, but met with no success. In 1583 he at last sailed with 260 men for Newfoundland, and formally took possession of the harbour of St John's. Then he explored southwards, but he had no luck. One of his five ships had already deserted; another was sent home with the sick, and a third was now wrecked. Sadly Gilbert turned for home with his remaining two ships. One, the *Squirrel*, was only 10 tons. Gilbert chivalrously insisted on sailing in her. One night there was a great storm. Gilbert was seen by the men of the other ship in the stern of his little frigate, a book in his hand. He shouted joyfully to them 'We are as near to heaven by sea as by land.' A little later the lights of the *Squirrel* disappeared. She had foundered. The story of Gilbert's death made a great impression on his countrymen.

It was Gilbert's half-brother, Raleigh, who carried on his work. Born in 1552 at a farm-house in Devon which may still be seen,† Raleigh came of gentle stock and had some Cornish (i.e. Celtic) blood in him. He was sent at the age of sixteen to Oxford, but in 1569 volunteered to fight with the Huguenots in France. After this he completed his education at the Temple Inn. In 1578 he sailed with Gilbert on a privateering voyage and perhaps on his colonizing voyage later in the year. In 1580 he went to Ireland as a captain of foot, and came to the notice of the Queen a year later, when he was sent home with despatches for the government. His tall and handsome person, quick wit and good manners

* See J. A. Williamson, *op. cit.*
† Hayes Barton near Budleigh Salterton.

182

caught Elizabeth's eye, and it is now probably that the incident of the cloak, spread across the puddle, for the Queen to step on, took place.

At any rate Raleigh became a great favourite. The rewards showered upon him were out of all proportion to his services. He was given Durham House in the Strand and the monopoly of granting licences to tavern-keepers.

In 1584 he obtained a patent to plant a colony further south on the North American coastline than where Gilbert had made his attempt. He at once sent out a reconnaissance party which found what was believed to be an ideal site on Roanoke Island off what is now North Carolina.

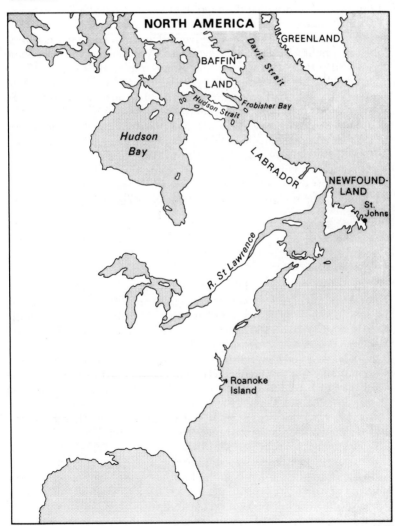

Raleigh, a born flatterer, decided to name his colony Virginia. The Queen insisted that he should stay at court; so his cousin, Sir Richard Grenville, took command of the colonizing expedition which was despatched in 1585. The colonists were set ashore on Roanoke Island under the command of a certain John Lane, Grenville promising to return with supplies in a year's time.

The colonists did not prosper. Unfriendly Indians and a lack of plentiful food were too much for the settlers, and, when Drake visited them in 1586 on the way back from his mighty raid on the West Indies, they persuaded him to take them home. A fortnight later Grenville arrived with ample supplies to find the colony deserted. He left a token force of fifteen men to preserve the English claim and sailed away.

In 1587 Raleigh and his associates sent out another expedition. They found a deserted stockade and evidence that the fifteen men had been killed in a fight with Indians. Nevertheless a settlement was once more formed (this time with women and children as well as men). After a time John White, the leader, was prevailed upon to go back to England for more supplies. He departed reluctantly. The next year was Armada year and the relief fleet for the colony was forbidden to sail, as its ships could not be spared. It was not till 1591 that White was able to return, and he found the colony deserted. There was no evidence of a fight, and it is not known today what happened to the colonists.

There were no further attempts at colonization in Elizabeth's reign. Nevertheless Gilbert and Raleigh, Grenville, Lane and White were the pathfinders for the great British colonial movement of the next century.

Later voyages

There were other voyages into uncharted oceans after Drake's great circumnavigation of 1577–1580. There was Thomas Cavendish, a Suffolk man, who followed Drake's path almost exactly. He passed through the Straits of Magellan in 1587 and arrived back at Plymouth in 1588, having captured immense treasure on the way.

Both Drake's and Cavendish's long voyages had a double intent. They were not only out to plunder Peru. They also hoped to open up trade with the Spice Islands and Cathay. In fact Drake actually picked up three tons of cloves in the Moluccas on his voyage home in 1579.

In 1591 Cavendish tried again, but without success. He died at sea. By now the Spaniards were arming their Pacific ships, and raiding Peru was becoming too difficult.

Next came an attempt by some London merchants to open up trade with the Portuguese colonies in the East, using the Cape of Good Hope route. They sent out expeditions in 1591 and 1596. Both failed disastrously, but were the forerunners of the East India Company, founded in the following decade. The Dutch were up to the same game, and John

Davis, the hero of the North-west Passage, took service with them in 1596 to learn the navigation of the route.

To the Spice Islands via the Straits of Magellan or via the Cape of Good Hope—which was the better route? The Plymouth men favoured the former, the London men the latter, and in the end it was the London school of thought which prevailed.

In 1595 Raleigh sailed on the most hair-brained scheme of all. The Spaniards believed that somewhere up the Orinoco lay a fabulously rich city ruled by Eldorado, the gilded king. For how else could one explain the fact that the natives of Peru were rich in gold yet had no gold mines? Raleigh found out about this belief and himself led an expedition up the Orinoco in 1595. He got quite a long way, but was eventually stopped by water-falls. Returning to England he published in beautiful prose (for Raleigh was a fine scholar) his *Discovery of Guiana*, arguing that by the discovery of this city England's revenue might be increased ten-fold to bring it level with that of Spain.

There is not space in a book such as this to tell of all the other voyages of Elizabeth's reign. It is important to mention, however, that the sea-dogs obtained a worthy chronicler. Richard Hakluyt was a clergyman from a family on the Anglo-Welsh border. He became a geographer of some standing and in 1582 published his first book, *Divers Voyages*, describing John Cabot's voyage among others. In 1589 he published *The Principal Navigations, Voyages and Discoveries of the English Nation*. This was enlarged into three volumes in 1599. Hakluyt wrote magnificent prose and took infinite trouble to collect his data, even going down to the quay-side to get first-hand accounts by mariners just arrived. His book was widely read and he taught Englishmen to believe that England's destiny lay over the oceans.

The Navy

The British Navy dates from Yorkist times. Medieval kings of England relied for protection on merchant ships. By ancient tradition merchant vessels and seamen were at the king's disposal in time of need. The owners were compensated, but they could not refuse to lend their ships. Likewise the crews were paid, but they could not refuse to serve.

The medieval fighting ship was simply a merchant ship with wooden castles fitted fore and aft. In all the major English ports were to be found castlewrights who specialized in fitting these structures. The method of fighting was to grapple and board and to discharge light missiles (arrows, and later, shot from hand-guns) at short range. Every war-ship carried soldiers, who did the fighting, the mariners' task being simply to lay their vessel alongside the enemy. The higher the castles the greater advantage, obviously, in short-range fighting, for you looked down on the enemy and he had no shelter from your missiles.

It was Edward IV who first realized the need for a royal navy. He was doubtless impressed by the way Warwick the Kingmaker had used his private fleet to his own advantage in the late years of Henry VI's reign. By 1481 Edward had built up a powerful fleet of sixteen ships. But only four of these were left to Henry VII, and they were little more than merchant ships. Henry relied chiefly on hired merchant vessels, but he had a nucleus of 'King's ships' and in 1509 there were five of these including the *Regent* of 600 tons, carrying 225 light guns (the largest fired a mere quarter-pound ball), and the *Sovereign*, rather smaller with 141 guns. Henry also developed Portsmouth as a naval base (with the Navy's first dry-dock). This enabled his warships to operate for considerable periods in the Channel without returning to their main bases in the Medway and Thames estuary. Moreover, he assembled near these bases at Greenwich and Woolwich stores of guns, ammunition and bows and arrows, so that hired merchant ships could be speedily transformed into useful fighting ships. Hence, although he had few ships, he could probably produce quickly more fire-power than any other monarch in western Europe.

Henry VIII took a great interest in the navy, and by 1515 had built it up to a fighting strength of 27 ships, including the prestige ship the *Great Harry* of 1500 tons.

Henry VIII's ships were carracks, a Mediterranean type of vessel with high castles at bow and stern and of very broad beam (the proportion of beam to length of the average carrack was one to two and a half). They usually carried 200 to 300 small-calibre guns 'which fired chain and canister to sweep the opposing decks'. The forecastle and poop provided the accommodation for the soldiers and were excellent for short-range fighting. The objective of these ships in war was not to sink the enemy, but rather capture him.

In the French war of 1512–1514, however, an incident occurred in which two combatant ships were lost by fire while grappled together. This 'caused Henry VIII to improve the carrack by installing a tier of heavy guns low down near the waterline, so that his ships could batter and sink the enemy without grappling'.*

Since the thirteenth century the administrative officer in charge of the navy had been known as the Clerk of the King's Ships. In the 1520s the enlarged fleet needed more administration, and new officers were added. One was the Treasurer of the Navy, another the Comptroller of Ships (who dealt with the provision of materials). Towards the end of the reign these three together with three other Principal Officers came to sit regularly as the Navy Board. All six were nearly always combatant officers who had served at sea and would be expected to do so again in a crisis.

Thus Henry VIII laid the foundations of an administrative structure which was to last right up to 1832.

Henry VIII also encouraged the Trinity House gild of Thames pilots

---

* See James A. Williamson, *op. cit.*, Appendix II on 'The Navy'. Most of the quotations in this section are from it.

'to chart, buoy and train pilots for the tricky navigation of the Thames estuary and the waters southward past the Goodwins to the Channel'. This made it easier to move the fleet from its main Thames and Medway bases to the advanced Channel bases he and his father had developed at Portsmouth and Falmouth. Even so his lofty carracks could not easily manoeuvre against the wind, and his great interest in Boulogne was because it would provide a harbour on the windward side of the Channel (especially desirable now that Francis I had built the mighty naval dockyard of Le Havre).

In the middle of Henry VIII's reign there was a lull in naval building, Wolsey's French wars being over. But in the late 1530s, when the threat of invasion by the Catholic powers grew serious, another intense period of building began, the money being provided by the wealth of the monasteries. Now the old carracks were replaced with new ones equipped with big guns. Thus the *Great Harry* of 1500 tons, which had been too large for shallow coastal waters, was replaced by the 'new-builded' *Great Harry* of only 1000 tons—still a monster by the standards of the times.

To this latter period also belongs the building of that long chain of coastal fortresses which remain today to remind us of the determination of Henry and the dangers of a breach with Rome. Not only the southeast harbours were thus protected, but the Isle of Wight, Portsmouth, Falmouth and the northern ports such as Hull and Scarborough. No wonder Marillac, the French ambassador, declared in 1539 he thought England 'well prepared'. No wonder also that the richer monasteries, which had been spared in 1536, went the way of the lesser ones. A monk's head carved over the gateway of St Mawes fort near Falmouth reminds us whence the stones for these fortresses came.*

It was this new fleet of Henry's which fought the French war of 1543 to 1546. Its greatest service was the foiling of the invasion threat of 1545. When Henry died, there were fifty-three ships in the Navy, most of them built during the previous twelve years, and twenty-five of them over 200 tons.

Henry also built new dockyards on the Thames at Woolwich and Deptford, Portsmouth dockyard, the one his father had used, being too close to France for safety.

Edward VI's and Mary's reigns were times of decline for the Navy. Corruption crept in. Money which should have been spent on the upkeep of ships went astray, so that by the end of Mary's reign 'a number of decayed ships were sold at break-up prices, and it became difficult to turn out even a moderate force for Channel service'. Northumberland, who was himself Lord Admiral, had done something to halt the decline and had built Chatham dockyard, which under Elizabeth was to replace Portsmouth as the headquarters of the Navy. Nevertheless, by the end of Mary's reign a fleet hardly existed except on paper.

'In the first twenty years of Elizabeth there was a good recovery in

* The reader is referred to R. B. Wernham, *op. cit.*, for a valuable account of naval affairs (look in the Index under 'ships').

fighting efficiency.... Elizabeth did not in this period increase the number of her ships, but she did build or buy new vessels to replace those left hopelessly decayed by Mary.' Nevertheless in this period there was still a good deal of peculation and graft going on in the dockyards, Sir William Winter, Master of the Ordnance and Surveyor, being the chief culprit.

In the early 1570s the Spanish had begun to abandon the carrack and build galleons. The carrack was clumsy and top-heavy—unfit for the oceans. The galleon was a lower, slimmer ship, faster and more weatherly. The propertion of its beam to its length was about one to three and a half as against the carrack's one to two and a half. It carried heavier guns and, although it retained the high poop, it had no castle in the bow. It relied on the broadside rather than boarding when in action.

England was rather slow to follow Spain's lead. Burghley was well aware that all was not well with the Navy, but, until Sir John Hawkins came to advise him, he had not the technical knowledge to put things right. Hawkins was an ocean seaman who fully understood the superiority of the galleon over the carrack. 'On his last West Indian voyage he had taken one of the Queen's great ships, the 700-ton *Jesus of Lübeck*, and twice she had nearly foundered at sea,' while it was to repair her defects that he had to put into San Juan de Ulloa with such disastrous results (*see* Chapter 12).

After San Juan Hawkins retired from the sea and married the Treasurer of the Navy's daughter. Thus he 'gained inside information of what was going on in the dockyards under Winter's control'. The Queen and Burghley had come to know and trust him, and in 1577 he wrote a report revealing to them the corruption and extravagance that was going on in the Navy Board. In that year his father-in-law died, and Burghley appointed him as Treasurer in his place.

This appointment was a turning point in the history of the Navy. Up to then the outlook of the Tudor Navy had been limited to the coastal waters of Northern Europe. 'No Tudor fleet had ever been more than a few days' sail from Portsmouth or Chatham.' The carrack-built ships, moreover, took to the sea only in summer. Winter work was undertaken by smaller craft. Hawkins saw the need for ships which would attack the Spanish treasure-fleets far out in the Atlantic or raid the ports of Spain—galleons in fact. He set about providing them. It was a hard struggle. For the first seven years Sir William Winter and the rest of the Navy Board opposed him at every step. He was short of money and had to resort to cutting carracks in two amidships and building centre portions to lengthen them, while at the same time reducing the amount of superstructure. Thus were galleons improvised. They were actually better than the Spanish galleons, because Hawkins insisted on less superstructure.

In 1585, however, a new Lord Admiral, Lord Howard of Effingham, was appointed. He backed up Hawkins and also brought about a reconciliation between him and Winter. Now that Britain was at war with

Spain, more money was made available and the building of new galleons went on apace. The result was that a fine fleet of twenty-five modern fighting ships of over 100 tons and eighteen ocean-going pinnaces, was available to fight the Armada. It was this fleet of Queen's ships which took the brunt of the fighting in 1588.

15   The War with Spain

The scope of the war

For the last eighteen years of her reign (1585–1603) Elizabeth was at war with Spain. She had not sought the war. In fact she had striven desperately to avoid it. It was one of her greatest achievements that she had been able to delay its outbreak for so long. Had it come twenty, or even ten, years earlier, England would have had neither the economic nor the naval strength to survive it. As it was, the strains on both were tremendous.

The war was not fought only at sea. For these eighteen years the government maintained an army in the Netherlands, including garrisons at Flushing and Brill. Between 1589 and 1596 expeditions were sent to France to help Henry of Navarre (now become King Henry IV) fight the Catholics. Thirdly, Ireland became the biggest battlefield of all, when rebellion broke out there in 1595 and 'joined hands with the national enemy'.*

Elizabeth and her ministers have been accused by historians of conducting the war badly, of frittering away England's resources on useless continental expeditions, of refusing to take the offensive at sea (as both Hawkins and Drake wished), of continual hesitations and procrastinations and cheese-paring economies.

Such critics are inclined to forget the tremendous difficulties under which the British government laboured. First of these was the man-power problem. The population of England and Wales at this time was probably about three and a half million—perhaps a quarter that of France and less than a half that of Spain. Where then could England get the men to fight her wars? There was no standing army. The old feudal levy could no longer be relied upon. Mercenary armies were too expensive. Volunteers were few and uncertain. There remained the county militia. 'All Englishmen between the ages of sixteen and sixty were liable to muster once a year for a review of the forces available, a check on equipment and training.' The best of the militia, the 'trained bands', were kept at home to defend the realm. When an expedition was going abroad, the lords-lieutenant of the counties were asked to raise men from the militia and send them to the ports of embarkation. Thus each new

---

* See G. R. Elton, *op. cit.*, Chapter 13, to which I am much indebted.

expedition started off as a bunch of raw recruits, 'pressed men who did their best to desert on the march to the ports'. In the later stages of the war, criminals, prisoners and vagabonds had to be recruited. The total number of men available from the militia at any time was little over 100,000. These had to be victualled, armed and paid by the primitive methods of sixteenth-century government.

The Navy also suffered under difficulties. It was almost impossible to provide water and victuals sufficient to keep a fleet at sea for more than two months, for the sailing ships of these times carried large crews and had little storage space. Then bad weather was always a menace. The primitive rig of the time made it hard to sail close to the wind. In a gale ships were forced to run before the wind, and thus fleets were often scattered, and if caught on a lee shore, wrecked. 'There was only one Armada simply because three others, sent in the 1590s, were driven back by storms before they got into English latitudes.'

Finally, the war was expensive and the British government was always short of money. Infantry could no longer be sent into action equipped with long-bows. They had to have muskets, calivers (light hand-guns) and pikes. The Netherlands campaigns alone swallowed £2,000,000 before Elizabeth died. The Irish rebellion certainly cost as much or more. Since the ordinary revenue of the Crown was somewhere between £200,000 and £300,000 a year, these were staggeringly large sums to find. Burghley began the war with a reserve of £300,000, but this was gone by 1588. Six Parliaments were called during the years of war and all granted subsidies with quite surprising readiness. Even so the government had to raise benevolences and forced loans, to borrow widely and to sell crown lands. By the end of the reign £800,000 worth of crown lands had been sold, and yet James I was left with heavy debts to pay.

In fact the war with Spain 'laid the foundation for that shaky financial position which the Stuarts were to find the biggest obstacle to autocratic government'. It is well to remember then, in judging the government's war effort, that, as G. R. Elton points out, 'shortage of money dogged every step'. It was fortunate that Spain's financial plight was, in some ways, worse.

The first three years of war

Before Leicester took his army over to the Netherlands, Drake was despatched with a force of twenty-nine ships and 2000 men to raid the West Indies. The expedition was financed by a joint-stock company for which the Queen supplied one third of the money and two fighting ships. Drake missed both treasure fleets, but captured and sacked Santiago, the capital of Hispaniola, and Cartagena, the capital of the Spanish Main. Philip was forced to restore these two towns and to divert money from Parma's army in the Netherlands in order to do so. The expedition was thus a great success. It cost the Queen almost nothing, for much booty was taken.

9 Mary, Queen of Scots, as a girl. Attributed to Clouet

10 Robert Dudley, Earl of Leicester. From a portrait of the Flemish School

Leicester was much less successful. He infuriated the Queen by accepting the title of Governor-General of the Netherlands without her permission. Then he quarrelled with the Dutch, got involved in political factions and wasted his supplies. His campaign included no military success, and is chiefly remembered for the heroic death of Sir Philip Sidney at the siege of Zutphen. Sidney was a fine lyric poet and was adored as a beautiful and ideal young man, much as another poet, Rupert Brooke, was adored at the opening of the First World War. Sir Philip increased the legend by the manner of his death, for, though mortally wounded, he refused a drink of water, and indicating a common soldier nearby spoke the words 'Give it to him; his need is greater than mine'. His body was brought home and buried in Westminster Abbey, the funeral procession being over a mile long.

Leicester's campaign had cost £126,000 and there was nothing to show for it. Fortunately, Parma remained inactive, being kept short of funds by Philip who had already decided to invade England before dealing with the Dutch.

The end of Mary Stuart

The assassination of William the Silent had made a great impression in England. Might not Elizabeth be the next? In 1584, at the instance of the Council, a document called the Bond of Association was circulated. It declared that if the Queen's life were attempted 'the signatories would revenge it to the uttermost, would prevent the succession of the person in whose favour the attempt was made, and would do their best to put that person to death'. Englishmen from all walks of life flocked to sign. In 1585 an Act of Parliament was passed including the second point— that the person in whose favour the attempt was made should not succeed.

Philip, watching all these things, made up his mind to invade. His great admiral, Santa Cruz, had long urged an invasion of England. Philip had hesitated, largely because he knew France would not like it, but also because an invasion could only help Mary, Queen of Scots, his rival. The Bond of Association altered the situation. It now appeared unlikely that Mary would survive a successful invasion.

Walsingham's spies soon found out that an invasion was being prepared. He and the rest of the Council were well aware that Mary's life had stood between England and a Spanish invasion. Now that this was no longer so, was it worth while keeping her alive? As long as she lived she was the centre of plots, a focus of discontent for the English Catholics.

Mary had long been kept under mild surveillance in Sheffield Castle. Now she was moved to the care of Sir Amyas Paulet at Tutbury Castle, and then, later in 1585, to Chartley Manor in Derbyshire. Paulet's instructions from Walsingham were to keep her a close prisoner. The Minister then got hold of a renegade Catholic, who agreed to arrange

191

facilities for Mary to smuggle out messages. The brewer at Chartley was persuaded to bring out packets of letters concealed in the household beer barrels. These were scrutinized by Walsingham's men and then replaced. Ingoing messages were likewise allowed to pass, apparently without interference. Mary fell into the trap. By the middle of 1586 a plot had taken shape. A young gentleman called Anthony Babington was the main conspirator. He wrote to Mary a full account of the plot which included the assassination of Elizabeth, and asked for her approval. After a long pause it came. The trap was sprung. The conspirators, Babington, a Jesuit-trained priest called Ballard, and others, were arrested and executed. Mary herself was brought to trial before a special commission of peers, privy councillors and judges in Fotheringay Castle. She defended herself with great spirit but was declared guilty of treason.

All this took place in 1586. Early in 1587 Elizabeth signed the death-warrant, but even so would give no order for it to be sent to Fotheringay. She was in an agony of doubt what course to take. Burghley took the matter off her shoulders, and, after a meeting of the Privy Council, it was decided to send the warrant without the Queen's permission. This was done and Mary was executed forthwith.

Great was Elizabeth's rage (real or simulated?) when she found out. The Secretary who had despatched the warrant was heavily fined and committed to the Tower. The rest of the Council trembled, but after a time the Queen's rage passed.

Mary was accorded a royal funeral in Peterborough Cathedral, but this deceived no one. In Scotland there was a great indignation, but after a time James VI allowed his ambitions for the English throne to overrule his feelings for a mother he could not remember. In France the uproar was greater and more prolonged. But Henry III had enough troubles of his own and did not want to add to them a war with England. Philip of Spain was probably secretly pleased. As for the Londoners, they rang the church bells and lit bonfires and held festivities which lasted a whole week, so great was their relief.

The Armada

While the tragic drama of Mary Stuart was played to its conclusion in England, Philip was busy with his invasion plans. Throughout 1586 and 1587 the west coast ports of Spain and Portugal were full of vessels being got ready for the enterprise. The admiral in charge, the Marquess of Santa Cruz, favoured a direct sea-borne landing. This, however, would have been too expensive. Philip's plan was to send a fleet which would secure command of the Channel, make contact with Parma in the Netherlands and cover the crossing to Kent of 30,000 veterans of his army.

Walsingham's spy system was fairly good by this time, and the British government was aware that preparations were going forward. The Spanish spy system was less good. The invasion was intended for 1587, and in April of that year Drake was sent with a strong squadron of ships to attack the Spanish ports. As he sailed down the Spanish coast he learned that a division of the Armada was in Cadiz and that its ships lacked guns. Boldly he sailed into Cadiz harbour, past the shore batteries guarding its entrance, and sank or destroyed some thirty ships 'including a great galleon built for Santa Cruz himself'.* Altogether he captured more than a hundred fishing and coastal cargo boats. Many of the latter turned out to be laden with cooper's stores, barrel staves particularly. Knowing the value of these in naval warfare, Drake had them all burned. Consequently, when the Armada sailed a year later, many of the casks used for storing water, wine, salt-meat, biscuits etc., turned out to be made of green staves and therefore faulty (for tight casks well-seasoned wood is essential). This caused much delay for most of the squadrons ran out of water twenty days out of Lisbon and the whole fleet was forced to put into Corunna to replenish supplies. Moreover, on the long voyage home round Scotland and Ireland supplies of food and water again ran low because of faulty casks, and many a ship came to grief on those uncharted coasts while seeking to find a harbour among the rocks to take on supplies. The loss of those barrel staves may have been an important factor in the Armada's defeat.†

After a brief stay at Sagres Drake sailed for the Azores. He had heard that a Portuguese carrack laden with spices, silks and ivory, was on its way back from the Far East (remember Portugal and Spain were now united under Philip II). He soon sighted and captured her and returned to Plymouth with his rich booty, having, as he said, 'singed the King of Spain's beard'.

As a result of Drake's exploit the Armada was delayed for a year. Drake and Hawkins would have liked to attack it again in port, but the Queen, even now still intent on peace overtures, would not allow them to. So the building and equipping was resumed in peace.

Early in 1588 Santa Cruz died, and Philip had no great sailor of high rank with whom to replace him. He appointed the Duke of Medina Sidonia, a grandee of unimpeachable character but one who had no desire for the task and who protested his inability to do it. 'I know by the experience of the little I have been at sea that I am always seasick and always catch cold,' he wrote to Philip, but was nevertheless given the command. In England the command of the fleet naturally went to the Lord Admiral, Lord Howard of Effingham, Drake being his second in command.

Three times in the summer of 1588 Lord Howard sallied forth from Plymouth towards the Spanish coast, hoping to repeat Drake's exploit of the previous year. Each time he was forced back by contrary winds. He was refitting in Plymouth after the third of these attempts, when, on 19 July, the Armada was sighted off the Lizard.

The Armada consisted of 130 ships 'of which it is reckoned that thirty-seven were of serious fighting value, the rest being transports and small

* See J. A. Williamson, *op. cit.*
† See *The Defeat of the Spanish Armada* by Garrett Mattingly, Cape, 1959, pp. 116–117.

craft'. Lord Howard probably had rather fewer large fighting vessels, for he had twenty-one Queen's ships of over 200 tons, and a few well-armed fighting merchantmen of the Turkey Company. Drake, Hawkins and Frobisher each commanded squadrons, Drake being Vice Admiral. The old idea that the Spanish had neglected artillery and were out-gunned has now been disproved. Medina Sidonia was indeed short of heavy, long-range guns capable of destroying ships, but he had insisted on a good supply of artillery, as well as powder and shot—more in fact than Santa Cruz had planned.

The British fleet had been surprised by the enemy's approach. Some of the Spanish captains urged Medina Sidonia to attack it in Plymouth, but his orders were plain—to sail up the Channel and make junction with Parma without seeking a battle. He therefore proceeded on his way in stately formation, all his ships keeping strict station and moving slowly, as his transports, crowded with soldiers (he carried about 20,000) slowed him down, and the winds were light.

Lord Howard skilfully brought his fleet out of Plymouth in about 24 hours, and worked it round to windward of the Spanish—a difficult manoeuvre. On 21 July he attacked, and was surprised by the tough resistance put up by the Spaniards and the weight of their broadsides.

Being unable to break up the Armada's formation, the British followed it up the Channel, capturing two galleons on the way. Three days later there was a heavy engagement off Portland Bill in which neither side lost a ship but much ammunition was expended. The day after this the Spanish lost another galleon off the Isle of Wight.

On 27 July both fleets had reached the Straits of Dover and the Span-ish dropped anchor in the open sea off the little port of Calais. From here Medina Sidonia was able to send messages to Parma asking him what he intended to do. The Spanish really needed a large deep-water port to effect the junction of their forces. The only suitable one was Flush-ing, but this was in Dutch Zealand and was held by an English garrison. Had Parma held it, probably the fate of England would have been sealed, for he could have prepared his invasion at leisure and waited his chance to cross, which must have come sooner or later.

At Calais Lord Howard anchored a mile to windward of the Spaniards. He was joined by Seymour's squadron of 30 ships, including five royal galleons, which had been helping the Dutch watch the Nether-lands coast where Parma's barges lay. Being short of ammunition and powder as well as food, Lord Howard determined to force an engagement right away. He had eight merchantmen prepared as fire-ships and about midnight on 28 July sent them drifting downwind upon the Armada.

The manoeuvre was successful. The Spanish captains slipped their cables and made off in confusion. Dawn found the Armada dispersed over miles of sea to the north-east, but Medina Sidonia and his squadron commanders skilfully got their big warships into formation again. Lord Howard attacked at once and the battle of Gravelines, as it is called, continued all day. The English squadrons worked separately under their

194

leaders and attempted to crush individual ships with their broadsides. By the end of the day the Spanish had lost four more large ships and had sustained much other damage and loss of life. The English fleet was intact. Being out of heavy round-shot the Armada was finished as a fighting force.

That night a strong south-west wind sprang up, and carried the Armada into the North Sea. Medina Sidonia decided to attempt to return to Spain round the north of Scotland. Lord Howard followed past the Firth of Forth, fearing the Spaniards might put into a Scottish port to refit. But Medina Sidonia had no such intention. As his fleet limped round the coasts of Scotland and Ireland, Atlantic gales took their toll. Many ships were wrecked. About thirty-five disappeared at sea without trace. Only about half reached the Spanish ports in September fit for further service. Medina Sidonia himself, having led his fleet conscientiously and well, reached Santander in September, 'semi-delirious from sickness and privation, and protesting feverishly to the king that nothing would get him to sea again'.*

The mood in England was one of gratitude and relief, when it was at last learned what had happened. Elizabeth had a medal struck bearing the words, 'Afflavit Deus et dissipati sunt'. Certainly the winds had helped, but we must look deeper to discover the reason for the failure of the 'Invincible Armada'. One point was that the English ships were more weatherly, could sail closer to the wind and were thus able to keep the weather-gauge. Thus they could attack when they liked and break off the fight when they liked. But Medina Sidonia did not need to win the six-days running battle up the Channel. He only needed to keep his fleet intact until it should reach Parma's forces. This he succeeded in doing. His fleet, drilled like an army, kept excellent formation. The two fleets fired off an incredible amount of round-shot without doing each other any real damage, for the few ships which the Spanish lost in those six days were crippled by accidents and not by English gunnery. Shortage of round-shot caused the Spanish defeat at Gravelines, for, while the English had replenished their round-shot during the six-days running fight, little boats coming out of English harbours with fresh supplies, Medina Sidonia's messages to Parma, begging for supplies of heavy cannon-balls, had met with no response.

Parma's actions throughout seem to show that he had little belief in the success of the enterprise. The barges he had prepared at Dunkirk were miserable, flat-bottomed affairs which could make no sort of a fight with warships. The shallow approaches to Dunkirk were patrolled by Dutch fly-boats under Justin of Nassau. These were small, shallow-draught warships which could easily sink Parma's barges. The junction between the Armada and Parma's army was supposed to be made at sea. Yet Parma could not get to sea because of the Dutch blockade, and the Armada galleons, having a draught of 25 to 30 feet, could not get

* See *Spain under the Habsburgs*, Volume I, by John Lynch, Blackwell, 1963, which gives a most interesting account of the Armada from the Spanish point of view.

into the shallow water round Dunkirk to clear away the Dutch fly-boats.

The Enterprise of England then was badly planned and doomed to failure. The fault was no one's but Philip's. That obstinate man seems to have closed his ears to Parma's complaints and forced him into a plan in which he had no faith. Medina Sidonia played his part manfully, but no one told him of the Dutch blockade and that all his efforts were bound to fail.

The English themselves did not understand the Dutch blockade and always kept a squadron to watch Dunkirk. 'There is not a Hollander nor a Zealander at sea', wrote Lord Howard the day after Gravelines, after he had ordered Seymour to resume his station off the Downs; but Justin of Nassau did not need to be 'at sea' in the English sense to maintain his blockade of Dunkirk.*

Elizabeth herself acted throughout the crisis with the greatest coolness and heroism. While London repaired its walls and called out its trained bands, the only considerable English army (perhaps 10,000 men) was assembled under Leicester at Tilbury. Elizabeth proceeded by barge down river and insisted on reviewing the troops without her usual body-guard of yeomen of the guard. Then she made her famous speech:

'I know I have the body of a weak and feeble woman, but I have the heart and stomach of a king and of a king of England too, and I think foul scorn that Parma or Spain or any prince of Europe should dare to invade the borders of my realm; to which rather than any dis-honour should grow by me, I myself will take up arms, I myself will be your general, judge and rewarder of every one of your virtues in the field.'

It was received with rapturous applause.

In Spain, though the King treated him kindly, most people blamed Medina Sidonia for the defeat, and, though he lived another twenty-two years, serving two kings in high office, he always bore a melancholy air and always blamed himself for the great catastrophe.

Philip was much shaken by the defeat, but within a few months he had pulled himself together and begun patiently rebuilding his fleet in order to try again.

The war at sea continues

How was the great victory over the Armada to be exploited? That was the question the British government now had to decide. Hawkins' and Drake's views on the matter differed. Hawkins wanted to mount a con-tinuous naval blockade of the Spanish coast right through the summer months. If six well-provisioned fighting ships, he argued, were stationed somewhere near the Azores, they could stop the treasure fleets and East India convoys from reaching Spain. After four months they could be

* I am indebted to Garrett Mattingly, *op. cit.*, for this account. The book is authorative and highly readable.

196

relieved by another six, the rest of the fleet being kept in the Channel. Thus Philip would be so starved of money that he would be forced to make peace.

Drake's idea on the other hand was to invade Portugal (which was believed to be ready to rebel against Philip), and set Don Antonio, the Portuguese Pretender, on the throne. The Azores would then be placed at England's disposal and the vast Portuguese empire be opened up to British merchants. Don Antonio was quite willing to fall in with this arrangement.

The Queen adopted Drake's plan, but with modifications. She wanted the forty odd ships returned from the Armada and known to be sheltering in Santander and other Biscay ports, destroyed first. Early in 1589 a great expedition was got together including 18,000 soldiers under the command of Sir John Norreys. Drake was to command the fleet, and, as there was little money in the Treasury, the whole thing was to be paid for by a joint-stock syndicate, the Queen contributing about one third of the finance.

In April the expedition sailed. It attacked Corunna and captured the harbour and part of the town, but there was only one Armada ship there, and the undisciplined troops soon drank themselves sick on the wine from the town storehouses. After a fortnight Drake held a conference of sea-captains, and it was decided that contrary winds made it unwise to sail for Santander. Drake used this as an excuse to disobey orders and do what he wanted (and what he thought would pay dividends to the syndicate)—make for Lisbon. This he did, but by this time the defences of Lisbon had been put in readiness. Drake landed Norreys and his army with Don Antonio forty-five miles from the city, intending to sail up the Tagus and meet him outside its walls with guns and supplies. In fact the twelve miles of river he had to negotiate proved too difficult; so the attack had to be abandoned. The Portuguese (good Catholics of course, although anti-Spanish) had shown no signs of joining their heretical would-be liberators, and, after some further raids, Drake was forced to return to Plymouth, having lost great numbers of men and accomplished very little.

The failure at Lisbon discredited the two commanders in the eyes of the government. Neither received another command for several years. But worse than this, it discredited the Navy and 'for years afterwards Elizabeth held back her deadliest weapon and spent her resources on armies on the continent'.

Hawkins continued to press the Council for a blockade of the Spanish coast, but only an intermittent blockade was allowed. The treasure fleets from the New World continued to reach Spain with the greatest regularity. By 1591 Philip, using this money, had managed to equip a new fighting fleet. Incidentally, it was in this year that Grenville in his little ship the *Revenge* was caught by a great Spanish fleet near the Azores, and fought the epic battle which led to his death and imperishable fame.

197

The war at sea between 1589 and 1595 was mainly fought by privateers. Merchants, courtiers and officials invested in the lucrative business and 'Spanish records recently discovered show an almost incredible concourse of small English vessels in West Indian waters' * in these years. The two main hunting grounds were the Caribbean and the vicinity of the Azores. Occasionally a really fat prize was secured, as when the great East Indian carrack, *Madre de Dios*, was taken near the Azores in 1592, bringing a profit, after the crews had their plunder, of £140,000.

Expeditions to the Continent

In 1589 the last of the Valois kings of France, Henry III, was assassinated. His successor was the Bourbon, Henry of Navarre, who was a Huguenot. The powerful Catholic League turned against him, and he appealed to Elizabeth for help. Elizabeth responded promptly (after all the League was the ally of Spain) and sent him £20,000, following it up with a small force of 4000 men under Lord Willoughby, which landed in Normandy. This force did not achieve very much except a breathing space for Henry, and after three months it was withdrawn. Willoughby had been Leicester's successor in the Netherlands command and he was now succeeded there by Sir Francis Vere, a fine fighting soldier, who ably assisted Maurice of Nassau against Parma.

In 1590 Henry won a victory over the League at Ivry and threatened Paris. Philip thereupon ordered Parma to strike in from the Netherlands and relieve Paris (which he did). It was a fine military manoeuvre, but, as Parma feared, it relieved the pressure on Maurice of Nassau, who now at last with the help of de Vere began to capture important towns and win victories. From this moment the salvation of the Dutch becomes virtually certain.

Early in 1590 Philip had renewed his treaty with the League, and, late in the year, he landed 3000 men in Brittany, to help the League. This was most alarming for the English, for Brittany with its fine ports was almost as good a jumping-off point for an invasion of England as the Netherlands.

Elizabeth reacted strongly. In 1591 she sent Sir John Norreys to Brittany with 3000 men, and, later in the year, the Earl of Essex to Normandy with 4000 men. Essex was recalled in 1592, not having achieved very much, but Norreys continued his campaign in Brittany for four years, desperately striving to prevent the Spanish from capturing the great port of Brest. In this he was successful. In 1594 with the help of a strong naval squadron under Frobisher he stormed and took the fort of Crozon which the Spaniards had built overlooking Brest (Frobisher was killed in this action). Meanwhile in 1593 Henry IV, despairing of capturing Paris otherwise, had changed his religion and attended mass at the abbey of St Denis at Reims. The cities and nobles of the League thereupon

* See J. A. Williamson, *op. cit.*

198

hastened to make peace with him and by 1595 he was left fighting only the Spanish. Norreys' force was thereupon withdrawn from Brittany, being no longer needed there.

The war at sea revived

Parma had died in 1592, and with Maurice of Nassau holding his own in the Netherlands and Henry IV master of nearly all France, the English government once more turned its attention towards the war at sea. Drake, now at last restored to favour, proposed a raid on Panama to cut the treasure route at its weakest point. A great expedition was prepared with Hawkins and Drake in joint command. It sailed in 1595 and was a disaster from the outset. The Spanish had warning and were well prepared. Hawkins and Drake co-operated badly, and Hawkins died before the Caribbean was reached. Drake failed in an attack on Puerto Rico, and then landed 700 men on the Panama Isthmus, only to have them beaten back to his ships in a matter of four days by a strong Spanish force. After this fever broke out among his men and Drake himself caught it and died. It was a sad end to the careers of these two great sailors, both grown somewhat rigid and set in their ways (Drake was fifty-five, Hawkins in his sixties).

In 1596 it became known that Philip was preparing another Armada, and the Queen was persuaded to equip an expedition to attack it in its home ports before it sailed. A fine fleet of almost 150 ships was prepared, forty-eight of them being warships. About eight thousand troops were collected, and the joint command was given to Lord Howard of Effingham and the Earl of Essex, Raleigh being a subordinate commander. The expedition sailed straight for Cadiz, destroyed or captured all the shipping in the harbour, and then captured the town. Essex wanted to install a garrison and remain in Cadiz, but Lord Howard persuaded him to stick to instructions, and Cadiz was sacked and burned, the civil population having first been sent out.

Professor Neale has a fine paragraph on the attack on Cadiz. 'Cadiz', he writes, 'was no failure, but a perfect example of that dashing, careless bravery upon which Fortune was prone to smile. Essex joyfully throwing his hat into the sea at the order to enter the harbour; Raleigh replying to the cannon shots from the Spanish fort with scornful fanfares of trumpets; the boyish competition to steal the lead and find a place in the bottleneck where the naval engagement took place; the reckless scaling of the town walls; all these were of a piece with the courtesy, humanity and generosity of Essex in his treatment of the people of Cadiz after its capture. They read like the pages of a romance, and even the Spaniards were moved to praise'.*

The expedition returned in triumph (to be met incidentally by complaints from the Queen that it had taken so little booty).

* *Queen Elizabeth I* by J. E. Neale, Cape, 1934.

Although Lord Howard was chiefly responsible for this victory, Essex gained much popularity from it. His bravery had always been acknowledged, and now it was believed to be accompanied by humanity, moderation and generosity. 'He became England's favourite', as he already was the Queen's.

Europe acclaimed a great victory. 'In Venice, such was Elizabeth's fame, people clamoured for her picture "Great is the Queen of England" they cried: "Oh, what a woman, if she were but a Christian!".'

'Four months after the sack of Cadiz the exchange at Florence published its periodical list of debtors who had failed to meet their obligations. Among them was the King of Spain.' Despite his bankruptcy, however, Philip despatched his Armada late in 1596. It was dispersed by storms off Cape Finisterre with great loss of life.

Although he was now a sick man, in 1597 Philip prepared yet another Armada. Essex thereupon persuaded the Queen (who doted upon him as upon a son) to give him the command of a new expedition to attack the Spanish ports. This time he was given complete command, and Lord Howard and Raleigh were his subordinates. He proved unequal to the task. Because contrary winds made it difficult to attack the Spanish ports, he sailed instead to the Azores, hoping to intercept a plate fleet. Here he quarrelled violently with Raleigh, his rival to the Queen's favour, and allowed the plate fleet to slip through his fingers. Meanwhile, Philip's new Armada had sailed and approached quite close to the undefended English coasts before being, as usual, dispersed by storms.

The failure of the Islands Voyage, as it was called, and the fright which she and her Council sustained when they learned of the approach of the Spanish fleet, determined Elizabeth to launch no more great naval expeditions, but rather to keep her fleet in the Channel.

In 1598, much to the disgust of Elizabeth, Henry IV made peace with Spain at Vervins. The Dutch, however, would not think of peace, as Spain would not grant them their independence. As for England, she was 'too deeply committed to withdraw without loss of honour'. Nevertheless there was a debate in the Council and Burghley advocated peace, only to be overruled by Essex and his friends. It was the last appearance of the old Lord Treasurer who had served his mistress so well for forty years. He died later in the year, and was soon followed to the grave by Philip himself.

Burghley's stature as a minister is hard to assess, for, like her grandfather Henry VII, Elizabeth kept much of the direction of affairs in her own hands. Professor Black calls him 'if not the brain at least the regulative balance in the Elizabethan government'. His counsel was usually given on the side of moderation and caution. He was a staunch Protestant, yet not as bigoted as Walsingham; an enemy of the Spaniard, yet not as rash as Leicester. As an administrator he was probably (in Tudor times) second only to Thomas Cromwell. To the Queen he was an old friend as well as a minister, and there is a touching story of her visiting him in his last illness and coaxing him to eat.

The conquest of Ireland

In the last five years of Elizabeth's reign 1598–1603, the war centred on the Netherlands and on Ireland. In the Netherlands a small British force under de Vere helped Maurice of Nassau conquer the whole of the North. In Ireland large expeditions had to be sent to deal with the rebellion begun by the Earl of Tyrone.

We last dealt with Irish affairs in Chapter 7, where we saw that Cromwell destroyed there the power of the Geraldines. Henry VIII exchanged the title of Lord of Ireland for that of King (1540) and 'continued the old policy of anglicizing the Irish chiefs by turning them into earls'.* The area round Dublin, known as 'the Pale', and the towns of the south and west (Waterford, Cork, Galway etc.) were the only parts of Ireland firmly held by the English government. In the rest, Irish Ireland, the only real authority was that of the tribal chiefs, or, as the English government preferred to call them, earls. The only one of these on whom Elizabeth could really rely was the head of the house of Butler, Thomas, tenth Earl of Ormond, for he had spent some time at her court in his young days and developed a 'passionate devotion to her'. The least reliable area, now that the power of the Geraldines was broken, was Ulster, where the O'Donnells and O'Neills held sway. Being very inaccessible, Ulster had remained practically 'in the savagery of the bronze age'.

Irish Ireland was always in a continual state of upheaval. 'Cattle raids, the burning of the countryside, the murder of its people' were common. Nowhere, outside the Pale, was there real peace and order.

At the beginning of Elizabeth's reign the Irish people were not very strongly Catholic, but some devoted Jesuit missionaries had by the middle of the reign changed this situation, and the Irish had become staunch for the Church of Rome, as, of course, they are today.

Elizabeth's task throughout her reign, was to conquer the country, for there was always some rebellion going on. She tried for a time to do it on the cheap. 'The forces at the disposal of Irish viceroys were as a rule amazingly small—a few thousand, and at times less. . . . One reads of forts garrisoned—and successfully held . . . by twenty or thirty men.' An endless guerrilla warfare went on between successive lords-lieutenant and the tribal chiefs. The country, being full of woods, hills and bogs, was difficult for armies to negotiate, and easy for the Irish to disappear in when defeated. That the English were not driven into the sea was owing to existence of the walled towns and the fact that the Irish were divided, and some could always be relied on to fight for the government. 'No single Irishman . . . ever rose to the concept, much less the fact of national resistance.'

In 1579 came the Desmond rebellion in Munster which the Pope tried to help with an invasion (see Chapter 13). It lasted for four years and at the end of it Munster was devastated. 'Outside the few towns there were no human inhabitants or domestic animals to be seen and . . . wolves

* The quotation, like many others in this section, is from G. R. Elton, *op. cit.*

201

ranged over the land.' The Earl of Desmond was killed in 1583 and his lands were confiscated and an attempt made to plant them with English colonists. Sir Walter Raleigh was the head of the syndicate which undertook to do the planting, and Sir Richard Grenville was one of its members. Ireland was to be treated as a colony. In the end about 1500 English settlers went over (among them the poet Edmund Spenser) but the venture was short-lived, as we shall see.

Ulster was the next trouble-spot. Hugh O'Neill, Earl of Tyrone, had been educated in England and 'trained in the modern methods of war with firearms'. In 1585 he returned to Ireland 'ostensibly a good friend to the English'. Not so was the other Ulster chief, Hugh O'Donnell, Earl of Tyrconnel. This young man (he was only nineteen in 1593) had been imprisoned for five years by the English in Dublin. He escaped and in 1593 raised a rebellion. After some hesitation O'Neill joined him, and, in 1594, having obtained some money from Philip of Spain, the two earls 'began ravaging beyond the borders of Ulster'.

In 1596 Philip set all Ireland alight by promising armed help and actually sending an Armada (the one which was dispersed by storms off Cape Finisterre). The prospect of receiving foreign help so excited the Irish that the Ulster rebellion spread to Connaught, Munster and even Leinster, so that in 1598 Elizabeth was faced with a full-scale Irish revolt.

It was now that the Munster colony begun by Raleigh and Grenville came to its end. The handful of settlers was driven out. Also on the Ulster border O'Neill won a great victory at Yellow Ford, the English losing over a thousand men.

The English government was forced into action. In 1599 the Earl of Essex was given the title of Lord Deputy and despatched with the 'largest and best equipped army' ever sent to Ireland (about 17,000 men). Anxious to redeem the failure of his Island Voyage, he had asked for the job, but the Queen, who had grown to doubt his ability, gave it to him reluctantly.

Essex's task was enormous. The Queen expected him to strike first at O'Neill, 'the keystone of the rebellion'. But the problem was supplies. In the wilds of Ulster he would find little food for his army; so he was forced to buy up cattle to drive with him. These proved 'neither strong enough to drive nor fat enough to kill after the winter scarcity'; so he was obliged to delay his campaign till midsummer. Meanwhile he decided to make a military progress through Leinster and Munster, reinforcing garrisons and pacifying the area. This took longer than he expected and his troops dwindled through desertion and sickness. When he returned to Dublin, he decided it was too late in the year and his forces too small to attack Ulster. He wrote to the Queen suggesting the attack be put off. Elizabeth was furious and wrote him a sarcastic letter demanding that he attack at once. At the end of August (he had arrived in April) he advanced to the Ulster border with less than 3000 men and at last made contact with O'Neill's army.

O'Neill avoided battle and kept Essex marching to and fro. Then he suggested a parley and Essex was unwise enough to agree. By talking to a rebel out of earshot of any witnesses, he gave his enemies a golden opportunity to call him a traitor.

A truce was fixed up. This was 'a sorry outcome to the great expedition for the conquest of Ulster'. The Queen's letters became more and more scathing. Believing that his enemies at court were poisoning the Queen's mind against him, Essex left Dublin without permission and returned to court to put his side of the case to the Queen. He was immediately arrested.

The fall and execution of Essex belong to another chapter. Although brave and popular he had not the experience nor the ability to deal with Ireland. But one cannot help feeling that better men than he would have failed in his place.

Elizabeth replaced him with a more solid, if less brilliant commander, Charles Blount, Lord Mountjoy. He was given the title of Lord Deputy and sent to Ireland in 1600 with a new army. He approached his task more cautiously. Instead of seeking battle he concentrated on fortifying and garrisoning as many points as possible and wearing out the enemy by destroying his crops and killing or detaching local leaders. It was slow work but the Queen backed him up better than she had Essex. Perhaps she realized he was better worth her support.

By 1601 Tyrone had lost a lot of ground. In September of that year the Spanish at last landed a force in Ireland. Four thousand men were put ashore at Kinsale in southern Munster. Mountjoy as usual acted with great energy. Swiftly concentrating his forces he laid siege to Kinsale, while an English squadron blockaded it from the sea. O'Neill and O'Donnell marched down from Ulster to raise the siege, but were heavily defeated by Mountjoy in a battle in which, though outnumbered, he showed 'great superiority in skill and dash'. O'Donnell thereupon fled overseas to Spain. The Spanish surrendered within a month, and O'Neill was left on the defensive, until he finally surrendered in 1603.

Thus was Ireland tamed. The task of settling the country was left to the reign of James I, for, before the surrender of O'Neill, Elizabeth was dead.

16 Elizabeth and her Parliaments. The Church of England. The Essex Conspiracy.

Elizabeth's Parliaments

Throughout the Tudor period Parliament grew in power. Henry VII as we noted, 'was not afraid of Parliament'. Yet Wolsey, at the height of his power, in 1523, was forced to withdraw discomfited when he entered the House of Commons to bully it into acquiescence. In Elizabeth's reign Parliament, and especially the House of Commons, grew still more in power, but yet remained inferior by far to that Parliament which in the Stuart period was to dispute with the throne the very core of government and power.

The House of Commons had also grown in size since the time of Henry VIII. This was partly owing to Henry VIII having granted representation to Wales by the Act of Union. (This had increased the county seats from 74 to 90 and added a number of borough seats.) But the chief cause of the growth had been the Crown's habit of creating new borough seats, usually with the object of increasing representation in areas friendly to its policy. Thus Henry VIII had added fourteen borough seats (besides the Welsh ones), Edward VI thirty-four, Mary twenty-five and Elizabeth was to add sixty-two. It is noticeable that, whereas Mary's new seats were in Catholic Yorkshire, Elizabeth's were mostly in Protestant Hampshire or the royal duchy of Cornwall. The consequence of these new grants was that the borough seats increased from 224 in Henry VII's reign (*see Introduction*) to 308 in Elizabeth's first Parliament and 372 in her last. Hence, by the close of the century the House was half as large again as it had been at the beginning.

Parliament under Elizabeth had a very imperfect control of the executive. For one thing it met seldom and for short periods. In a reign of forty-four and a half years it sat for only thirty-five months. Sessions were short and the intervals between them long and irregular.* Hence it was difficult for parties to develop or for strong leaders to emerge. There was always a number of privy-councillors in the House 'who assumed an informal leadership'. The Speaker was in theory the freely elected spokesman of the Commons, but in fact his nomination usually came from a privy-councillor and he was regarded by the Crown as partly a royal official (he was paid a salary), and was liable to be summoned by the Queen and reprimanded if he allowed too much criticism of the Crown to be voiced in the House.

It was already the custom for the Speaker to petition the Crown at the beginning of each session for recognition of certain privileges. These were (1) 'freedom of access for the House to the royal presence in all matters of urgency and importance'; (2) 'favourable construction of the Speaker's words when reporting resolutions of the House'; (3) 'freedom from arrest of members and their servants during the continuance of Parliament'; and (4) 'freedom of speech "in whatsoever was treated, propounded and debated in the house"'.

The Queen had her own ideas about (4) and regarded certain matters as 'outside the scope of popular debate', and fit only to be handled by herself and her Council. Such were her marriage, the succession question, religion and foreign policy.

*See J. B. Black, *op. cit.*, pp. 215–234 for a full discussion of Elizabeth's Parliaments.

The succession question was always a delicate one with Elizabeth. In 1559 she rebuked the Commons for 'presuming to ask her to marry'. In 1562 she fell ill of the smallpox and nearly died. This gave her people a fright, as there was no satisfactory heir. The Parliament of 1563 (her second) therefore presented petitions (from both houses) that she marry and 'permit the nomination of a successor'. She put the matter off with a sonorous but vague speech. In this Parliament forty or fifty active members appeared, mostly Puritans, who formed a sort of opposition to the privy councillors.

In 1566 this Parliament, which had been prorogued for three years, was recalled to grant supplies. The Speaker meanwhile had died, and the opposition (if we may so call it) had the temerity to divide the House on the question of a successor, almost but not quite ousting the official nominee. Then, when the subsidy bill was introduced, the Commons demanded that, before it was passed, the Queen give a more favourable answer to their three-year-old petition about the succession. The Lords backed up the Commons, and Elizabeth was for a time beside herself with fury. 'It is monstrous', she said, 'that the feet should direct the head.' After further agitation on the part of the Commons she sent down an order to them to cease discussion of the question at once. But this only resulted in them drawing up an address declaring their right of free speech. The address was never presented, for Elizabeth, realizing that she had gone too far, relented and withdrew her command. With relief and delight the Commons passed the bill. It was this ability to give way graciously when she found imperious commands were ineffectual, which enabled Elizabeth to avoid head-on clashes with Parliament.

Elizabeth's second Parliament was dissolved in 1567 and a third one was not called until 1571. We have already noted (in Chapter 13) William Strickland's attempt in that year to reform the Prayer Book and the Queen's reaction to it.

In this third Parliament appeared for the first time a young Puritan member from Northamptonshire, Peter Wentworth, who was soon to make his mark as an opponent of government policy. Wentworth was struck by the frequent rumours and messages which went through the House recording the Queen's wishes. He made speeches in 1571 and 1572 complaining of the matter, but it was not until 1575 that he was able to unburden himself with real eloquence. His speech of that year is, in Professor Elton's phrase 'one of the great classics of parliamentary oratory'. Here is one passage from it:

'Amongst others, two things do great hurt in this place, of the which I do mean to speak; the one is a rumour which runneth about the house, and this it is, take heed what you do, the queen's majesty liketh not such a matter, whoever preferreth it, she will be offended with him. ... The other: sometimes a message is brought into the house either of command-ing or inhibiting, very injurious to the freedom of speech and consulta-tion. I would to God, Mr Speaker, that these two were buried in hell, I mean rumours and messages. ... For we are incorporated into this place to serve God and all England and not to be time-servers . . . or as flatterers that would beguile all the world, and so worthy to be condemned both of God and man. . . .'

The speech contained a reference to the Queen as being, like others, not 'without fault'. Such language so shocked the House that Wentworth was not allowed to finish his speech, and was examined by a special committee of the House and committed to the Tower, where he remained a month.

In 1576 Wentworth attacked the bishops in the Commons, and the Commons drew up a petition to the Queen which complained of the 'ignorance and non-residence of the clergy' as well as the unsuitability of many of them to hold livings, they being 'infamous in their lives and conversation'. The Queen graciously undertook to confer with the bishops on the matter and in fact new canons were produced in this year to try and deal with the abuses named.

Parliament was to meet in November 1584, and the Puritans were very active in trying to influence elections, in lobbying MPs and in making 'surveys of the ministry' in which they hoped to show by examining the deficiencies of individual clerics how unsatisfactory was the state of the Church. When Parliament met, the Lord Chancellor, in granting the usual request for free speech, added the words, 'only she restrained the cause of religion to be spoken of among them'. This was optimistic on the Queen's part. Soon after Parliament met a group of Puritan MPs presented a petition to the House, signed by many gentlemen of their shires, complaining of the state of the Church and 'the restraint of so many worthy preachers'. Despite the Queen's warning the House heard the petition and a committee was appointed which drew up a scheme of reform and presented it to the Lords. The Lords replied that they would like to consult the Queen. They did so, but Elizabeth stood as firm as ever and replied that, while some of the complaints would be dealt with, others were 'not to be granted'. She also sent a message to the Commons via the Speaker who reported, 'She knows—and she thinks you know—she is the Supreme Governor of the Church next under God'; she believed that some matters needed reform and she would deal with these, but Parliament had been instructed not to meddle with them and they must stop any further proceedings. The Commons then dropped three bills concerning religion with which they had been dealing.*

Next came the Parliament of 1586–1587. In this the Puritans were again active and a member introduced a bill to abolish the Prayer Book and replace it by a Puritan book of discipline and worship. The House 'in that desperate year when the Queen of Scots was dead and when a Spanish descent on England seemed only too likely', was in a mind to listen, and it was agreed to have a reading of the proposed book the next day. When the Queen heard of this intention, she sent for the Speaker and ordered him to deliver up both book and bill. This he did,

* Patrick McGrath, *op. cit.*, p. 223.

but Wentworth thereupon drew up ten articles which he presented to the Speaker for the House's consideration. These articles were framed as a series of questions asking whether free speech was not essential that Parliament fulfil its duties, whether there was any body besides Parliament which could alter the laws of the realm, and whether the Speaker had the right to 'overrule the House in any matter ...'.

The Speaker was so alarmed by this document that he showed it to a privy councillor and in consequence Wentworth was again committed to the Tower, this time by the Queen.

The member who introduced the bill and others who supported it were likewise imprisoned, and the House made no protest at these flagrant breaches of its liberties. After all with the Armada threatening it was a bad time to 'rock the boat'.

Wentworth was thus silenced for a time, but not cowed. In 1591, having written a pamphlet entitled 'A pithy Exhortation to Her Majesty for Establishing the Succession', he was again committed to prison by the Council and remained there six months. In 1593 we find him agitating the succession question again both inside and outside Parliament (for the Puritans of course feared, of all things, the succession of a Catholic). Again he was committed to the Tower, where he remained until his death in 1597—a martyr in a great cause, and a true forerunner of the great Parliamentarians of the seventeenth century (Eliot, Pym, Hampden etc.) whose valiant stand for freedom has won for us the liberties we still enjoy.

Of the four matters which, we saw, the Queen disliked the Commons to discuss (marriage, the succession, religion and foreign policy), she was most successful with the first two. After all they were personal matters which even Councillors, meeting in private, would handle with caution. On foreign policy she achieved moderate success. The only important foreign policy debate was in 1587, on the question of whether the Queen should accept the offer from the Dutch rebels of the sovereignty of the Low Countries. This debate was quoted in the next century as a precedent for the Commons' right to debate foreign affairs, but at the time it aroused little dispute.*

Religion was the most conspicuous failure. It aroused strong passions and, as we have seen, the Puritans would not be silenced. It is hard to see what right the Queen had to forbid its discussion. After all, as Peter Wentworth pointed out, the 'banishment of the Pope and Popery' had been achieved by the House of Commons rather than by the bishops in the reign of Henry VIII. But, if Wentworth was right about that, he was wrong in claiming a *de jure* right of free speech. This the Commons had never had. Henry VIII had threatened with dire punishment MPs who spoke out of turn in the Commons. What is new about the Elizabethan House of Commons was that it formally claimed privileges which had hitherto been quietly assumed. It was becoming more conscious of its rights.

*See Conrad Russell, *op. cit.*, p. 221.

The power of the purse was of course the Commons' chief weapon. The strains of financing the great war with Spain were very great indeed. In the 1593 Parliament the Queen asked for three subsidies. This was a huge amount of money and Sir Francis Bacon, for once deserting the royal cause, suggested they should be spread over six years, for 'gentlemen must sell their plate and farmers their brass pots ere this will be paid'. The bill for the three subsidies only passed the House after debates which lasted twenty-four days.

The last Parliament of the reign met in 1601 and was the most turbulent. The Queen's habit of granting monopolies to courtiers to trade in some particular product came under discussion. There had been some discussion about this in the previous Parliament of 1597 but nothing had been done about the matter. Monopolies were a convenient and quick way for the government to raise money. In return for a substantial loan or gift, or in payment for a service, a man might gain by royal patent the sole right of exporting, importing, manufacturing or distributing some particular article, such as pepper or starch. Thus Raleigh had been granted a monopoly of the import of playing-cards (and incidentally the privilege of licensing all taverns for thirty years). Sometimes good came of the system, as it might give a boost to some particular trade or manufacture which otherwise would not flourish. When it was abused, however, as it often was, it caused great harm to honest merchants who found their labours suddenly rendered profitless.

As the debate proceeded a member read out a list of fresh patents issued since the last Parliament. It included currants, powder, cards, ox shin-bones, train oil, oil of blubber, aniseeds, sea-coal, saltpetre and many other articles. Another member then stood up and asked 'Is bread not there?', adding that, if something was not done, it would be there before the next Parliament.

When Sir Robert Cecil intervened in the debate, he was constantly interrupted, and complained that the House's behaviour was 'more fit for a grammar school than a court of parliament'.

At this point the Queen wisely intervened. Summoning the Speaker, she told him she would review the situation and at once abolish bad monopolies and suspend others until people had had a chance to sue against them in the courts. The Commons were over-joyed and at once agreed to send a deputation, headed by the Speaker, to express their gratitude. A touching meeting took place in which Elizabeth made a gracious speech, thanking them for preventing her from falling 'into the lap of an error, only for lack of true information'. Meanwhile a royal proclamation was issued withdrawing many monopolies and suspending others as promised.

It is worth mentioning here that Elizabeth and the other Tudors did not interfere in Parliamentary elections. The exception is Mary, who, as we saw, asked in 1554 for 'members of a grave and Catholic sort', but even her Parliaments were far from subservient. Elizabeth in 1584 asked the returning officers for members 'well-affected to the Queen' and in 1586 asked for the re-election of the last Parliament's knights and burgesses. In neither case is there evidence that her circulars had much effect. As we saw (in the *Introduction*), it was the landowners who influenced and controlled elections, and the Crown, as the greatest landowner of all, was able to ensure the election of a body of privy-councillors, who were backed up by members elected to seats controlled by councillors and courtiers. Thus a sort of unofficial government group of MPs did in fact exist.

Elizabeth's success in handling Parliament (in such marked contrast to the failures of James I and Charles I) was thus due to three things— the careful management of the House of Commons' debates by privy councillors, the tact and graciousness which she frequently displayed in crises, and finally the awe, respect and love in which she was held in her declining years.

The Church in the 1590s

'In the history of the Church of England the 1590s were a time of consolidation and mounting triumph.'* On the one hand the Catholics were becoming divided. On the other the Puritans were in retreat.

The English Catholics had remained loyal to their country at the time of the Armada. Many of them considered Philip to be no true instrument of God, but simply out for his own ends. The Jesuit Robert Parsons (whom we met in Chapter 13) had become Philip's adviser and propaganda expert on England. In 1594 he published a pamphlet urging the claims of the Spanish Infanta to succeed Elizabeth on the throne.† The book provoked an explosion of indignation among the 'seculars' (those who were not Jesuits) in the English seminary in Rome. Also at Wisbech Castle in Norfolk, where many priests were imprisoned, thirty seculars refused to follow the Jesuit lead.

In 1594 Cardinal Allen, the head of the English Catholics, died, and the seculars asked the Pope to appoint a bishop from their own ranks. The Pope refused and appointed instead an archpriest with Jesuit leanings. The English seculars refused to acknowledge his authority. Thus were the English Catholics hopelessly split.

As for the Puritans, they seemed to be 'running out of steam'. They made little showing in Parliament in the 1590s. After the defeat of the Armada, these extreme opponents of the Counter-Reformation, commanded less popular support. While Spain threatened, puritanism had been equated with patriotism. Now the situation had changed. Nevertheless in 1593 a member called James Morrice brought in two bills attacking the ecclesiastical courts and especially the 'tyrannical practices of the High Commission'. Elizabeth sent word to the Speaker (who had told her about the bills) that he should permit the reading of no bill

---

*G. R. Elton, *op. cit.*, p. 457.
† The claim came through John of Gaunt, whose second wife had been Constance of Castile. Their daughter, Catherine, married Henry III King of Castile.

concerning ecclesiastical causes. Such a command in earlier days would have stung the Puritan 'choir' into action. Now it moved no one. Morrice's bills were dropped and he himself imprisoned for a few weeks. In 1593 a stringent act of Parliament was passed against 'separatists' (whom we met in Chapter 13), and three of them—Barrow, Greenwood and Penry—were executed later in the year for writing pamphlets against the establishment of Church and State. Thereupon the London congregation which Barrow had organized moved to Amsterdam. Browne's congregation had already moved to Middleburg in Holland, though Browne himself returned 'uncomfortably' to the bosom of the Church of England. Thus began the movement which was finally to lead to the sailing of the *Mayflower* in 1620.

It must be remembered that in all the lands surrounding England—France, the Netherlands, Scotland—Calvinism was winning the assent of all reformers. Moreover, in Germany no state had dared to attempt a unity between Lutheran and Reformed. Elizabeth attempted it, but, despite her efforts, there remained two schools of thought in the Church of England—Calvinist and Episcopalian. For a time it was not clear what the non-Calvinist school was teaching. 'They were not Lutheran, for few of them accepted the Lutheran doctrine of the eucharist.... The Thirty-nine Articles, which reached their final form in 1571, and to which assent was demanded of the clergy, taught the classical doctrines of the Reformed Protestants, that men are justified by faith alone, that the grace of sacraments is received only by men of faith, that the Church can teach nothing which Scripture does not contain.'*

Neither Whitgift, the Archbishop of Canterbury, nor Bancroft, the Bishop of London, both great campaigners against the Puritans, had found it possible to answer Cartwright's contention that the Scriptures, being the authentic word of God, must be a better guide to the right ordering of the Church than the opinion of men.

From this dilemma the Church of England was rescued by a 'poor obscure English priest'. Richard Hooker was a fine scholar and became Master of the Temple in 1584. During his seven years in the post he engaged in a running controversy with his 'lecturer' or curate, William Travers, a strong Calvinist. Travers claimed that Hooker had no right to preach in the Temple until the congregation had issued its 'call'. Hooker refused the proposal and 'master and lecturer preached against each other's doctrines, Canterbury versus Geneva'. Thus Hooker's ideas crystallized and, when, in 1591, he moved to the country parsonage of Boscombe in Wiltshire, he began his great work in seven volumes, *Of the Laws of Ecclesiastical Polity*.

'The Calvinists contended that all things done in church must have positive warrant in Scripture.' Hooker argued that, though the Scriptures certainly revealed the way of salvation, there was a wide area of human behaviour where they gave no guidance and here human

---

*See Owen Chadwick, *op. cit.*, p. 213.

reason must take over. Where the Scriptures are silent, the Church has a right to make laws for her own well-being and government, provided she does not infringe upon or contradict the commands laid down in Holy Writ. Human society is always changing and a state or church may order whatever practice is edifying and expedient provided its order obeys the scriptural law or is in harmony with natural law.

Hooker wrote in beautiful prose and he had a humanist's respect for tradition. 'In those things', he wrote, 'whereof the Scriptures appointeth no certainty, the use of the people of God or the ordinances of our fathers must serve for a law.'

The first four volumes of Hooker's treatise appeared in 1593 and had an immediate success in England. Strangely enough it was acclaimed also in the intellectual circles of papal Rome. Pope Clement VIII agreed that it contained in it 'seeds of eternity'. Hooker's defence of tradition and of the revelation of the Church fathers appealed to Catholics.

Hooker hoped to unite the Church of England. He did not succeed. The gulf between the Puritans and the others was 'too wide to be bridged by any philosophic discussion'. But he strengthened the Church and gave it a doctrine and a philosophy clearer than those it had had before.

As for the Puritans they ended the reign weaker in the House of Commons but stronger in the homes of the people than they had begun it, and of course they could hope for better times when Elizabeth, their steadfast opponent, was dead and a king from Calvinist Scotland should rule in her place.

The Essex conspiracy

Robert Devereux, Earl of Essex, came of a family with strong connections in Wales and Ireland. He was heir of the vast lands of Sir Rhys ap Gruffydd in south-west Wales. His father, the first Earl, had led a disastrous attempt early in the 1520s to plant a district in Ulster. In the Armada year Essex was twenty-one. He was a gay, bold, ambitious young man who was already becoming a favourite of the Queen. Leicester, her old favourite, died in this year, and perhaps Elizabeth needed a man to idolize in his place, and also a man of high rank to do the sort of work a consort would have done. At any rate Essex, like Raleigh before him, got far more attention from her than was good for him, and soon began to suffer from an overweening conceit.

Anxious to prove himself in arms he ran away from court to join Drake's disastrous Portuguese expedition on 1589. As the older men died (Walsingham in 1590, Drake in 1595, Hatton, the Lord Chancellor, in 1591) Essex's star rose in the sky. In 1593 he became a member of the Privy Council. In 1596 he was joint-commander with Lord Howard of Effingham of the successful expedition to Cadiz. His chief rivals were Sir Robert Cecil, Burghley's second son, who became Secretary of State in 1596, and Sir Walter Raleigh (the latter Elizabeth never regarded as a statesman).

As Elizabeth grew older she seemed to be losing 'that firmness of grasp that had characterized her earlier rule'. Burghley died in 1598, and by 1599 the tension at Court was great, two rival groups having emerged, the one led by Essex and Sir Francis Bacon, the other by Cecil and Raleigh.

We saw in Chapter 15 the failure of Essex's expedition to the Azores in 1597, known as the Islands Voyage. After returning home from this, Essex took umbrage when the Queen created the Lord Admiral, Howard, Earl of Nottingham. His office and his title gave him precedence over Essex. Essex left court in a sulk and was only restored to good humour when Elizabeth made him Earl Marshal, which gave him precedence over the new Earl of Nottingham.

Essex frequently acted like a spoilt child. He seems to have had a theory that if he bullied Elizabeth enough, she would, in the end, as a mere woman, give him anything he desired. Once, after a furious quarrel, she boxed his ears, and he left the court 'in a tearing rage'.

In 1599 the Irish expedition was launched. Essex demanded that he should be allowed to lead it. With some misgivings Elizabeth complied. In many ways he was well suited to lead an Irish expedition. His extensive lands in south-west Wales gave him good opportunities to recruit officers and men. For many years he had been infiltrating his supporters into key positions on the Council of Wales and into Welsh sheriffdoms, undermining the authority of the Earl of Pembroke, the President of this Council, who was an invalid. Welsh adventurers, usually the younger sons of squires, had fought under him at Rouen, Cadiz and the Azores.* Some of them were Catholics or Puritans, in revolt against Elizabeth's middle way. They now gladly followed him to Ireland, for Essex was indeed the 'darling of Wales'.

Thus Essex gathered around him men who were willing to follow him through thick and thin, English as well as Welsh. In Ireland he behaved more like a prince than a mere general, conferring knighthoods without the Queen's permission, and indeed against her express orders.

When, in September 1599, Essex returned precipitately to Court, he was arrested for deserting his army without permission. For a time he was confined to his own house. Then in 1600 he was brought before a royal commission which suspended him from most of his offices for military disobedience. Allowed to go free, though forbidden to enter the Court, he brooded upon his wrongs, and gathered about him a crowd of officers, eager for power and advancement who had deserted from the Irish army. Essex was something of a Coriolanus, a noble character, devoid of meanness, kind to subordinates and incapable of guile or even common caution. Two or three noblemen joined him, including Shakespeare's patron, the Earl of Southampton, who had been with him in Ireland.

As he brooded at Essex House in the Strand, 'despair grew on him'.

*See *Studies in Stuart Wales* by A. H. Dodd, University of Wales Press, p. 81.

He began to correspond with James of Scotland, offering support for his succession, and hinting that the Cecil party was planning to put the Spanish Infanta on the throne after Elizabeth's death. He also corresponded with Mountjoy in Ireland, begging him to come over with his army and 'free' the Queen. Most foolish of all perhaps 'he gave vent to disparaging remarks about the Queen, calling her "cankered", her mind being "as crooked as her carcase"'. In February 1601 the Council at last took notice of his schemings and summoned him to attend. He thereupon gathered together his friends, about 200 strong, arrested the four privy councillors sent to find out what was going on, and sallied forth, his party armed with swords, to raise the City. Riding up Fleet Street and Ludgate Hill and crying 'For the Queen, For the Queen: The Crown of England is sold to the Spaniard! A plot is laid for my life!', he met with no support, only blank amazement.

A force was sent from the Court to arrest him and he quickly surrendered. Nine days later he was brought to trial before a court of his peers for treason. Even in this extremity he bore himself proudly. 'What booteth it to swear the fox?' he contemptuously asked, when Raleigh was sworn in as a witness. When he was found guilty and 'the dreadful traitor's death pronounced', he merely said, 'I think it fitting that my poor quarters, which have done her Majesty true service in divers parts of the world, should now at the last be sacrificed and disposed of at her Majesty's pleasure.'

Returned to the Tower, his spirit at last broke under the ministrations of the chaplain he had asked for. To Cecil and three other councillors whom he had asked to see, he made a full confession. 'This man' (the minister) 'in a few hours hath made me know my sins unto her Majesty and to my God; and I must confess to you that I am the greatest, the most vilest, and most unthankful traitor that ever has been in the land'.*

He who had courted popularity all his life asked for a private execution rather than a public one. He was executed in Tower yard and met his end humbly and devoutly. He was only thirty-four.

But the people of London had not forgotten him. They almost lynched the executioner on his way home from the execution. They sang ballads in his honour:

Sweet England's pride is gone!
Welladay! Welladay!

At court there was a 'strange quiet' for a time and 'it almost seemed as if the soul of Elizabethan England had departed'. Even eighteen months after his death visitors were being shown the spot where the 'brave hero' was beheaded and the shields which he had presented to the Queen when tilting.

---

*Quoted in *Queen Elizabeth I* by J. E. Neale.

213

The Queen, after Essex's death, was not yet finished. She continued to enjoy dancing and hunting. In 1601 she dealt with her last Parliament, as we have seen, with masterly skill. But by Christmas 1601 she was growing tired of life. She missed her old friends and particularly Burghley. She spoke of Essex 'with sighs and almost with tears', and would sit for long periods in silence, 'her mind given wholly to meditation'. Although she would not name her successor (and indeed she had no power to do so effectively) most prudent men about Court, Sir Robert Cecil among them, were in communication with James of Scotland. James himself had moved heaven and earth to get himself acknowledged as heir. All he could get from Elizabeth was a promise that no measure would be permitted to be brought forward in Parliament 'against any title he might pretend to the succession to the English crown'. His title was certainly good, and when, in March 1603, the Queen died in her seventieth year, a messenger rode north towards Edinburgh to give James the news. Essex's fears had been vain. The Infanta had few backers, for not even the English Catholics supported her.

17 Economic and Social History

The rise in prices

For about 150 years before the accession of the Tudors prices in England had been static or nearly so. Moreover, in the following twenty-five years, that is during the reign of Henry VII, they remained stable. Yet from 1510 to about 1620 prices rose rapidly, though at varying speeds, until they stood at about five times their previous height. The variation in the speed of rise is interesting. If we take 100 as the index of prices in 1510, it had risen to 167 by 1521. In the early 1540s it dropped back to 150, then rose to over 200 in the late 1540s, and went on climbing (unsteadily) to about 500 at the end of the century.*

At the time people did not understand why prices had risen, and were inclined to blame it on the selfishness of individuals or classes. Thus the government blamed profiteering middlemen. The rich thought it was due to the greed of the labouring poor, who were always demanding wage increases. Early Protestant preachers put the blame on landlords, whom one stigmatized thus: 'Men without conscience. Men utterly devoid of God's fear. Yea, men that live as though there were no God at all! Men that would have all in their own hands; men that would

*I am indebted to Conrad Russell, *op. cit.*, for much of the information in this section.

leave nothing for others; men that would be alone on the earth; men that be never satisfied. Cormorants; greedy gulls.'

In the middle of the century there was a tendency to blame successive debasements of the coinage, for after 1544, when he found himself short of money for his French and Scottish wars, Henry VIII mixed lead with his silver coins and made £500,000 out of the operation. This played havoc with prices, for in times when coins were judged by their actual silver or gold content, instead of their token value, no one had any confidence in Henry's new shillings and testoons, and this lack of confidence naturally damaged trade. Northumberland, after indulging in a little debasement of his own, tried to put the situation right, but without much success, and it was left to Sir Thomas Gresham, in the first two years of Elizabeth's reign, to call in all the bad coins and reissue coins of a high silver content.*

Neither of these two explanations, however, are today considered by historians to have been the main cause of the Tudor price rise, though the debasement of the coinage is thought to have had some influence. The main objection is that in the 1540s there were similar price rises all over Europe, even in countries where there was no debasement. A popular explanation today is the great increase in minted bullion which occurred in Europe in this century, owing, first, to the development of silver mines in Germany and Bohemia, and, later on, to large imports of American silver by Spain. Mexico was discovered by Cortez in 1519 and Peru by Pizarro in 1532. Great quantities of gold and silver then began to enter Europe, and this flow became a flood when, in 1545, the Spaniards opened up the biggest of the New World silver mines in Bolivia. This explanation thus fits in with the steep price rise which, we have noted, took place in the late 1540s. The difficulty is it does not fit in with the fact that the goods which rose most in price were home-grown foods, particularly the cheaper sorts of grain. If plentiful silver on the Continent had been the main cause, we would expect imported goods, such as wine, swords or silks, to have risen in price the most. But they did not.

Some historians have pointed out that increased government spending could have been a major cause. This theory is supported by the fact that the price rise began about the time when Henry VIII came to the throne and he and Wolsey began to spend the treasure which Henry VII had put aside (and this, be it noted, was before the New World silver began to arrive in Europe). But, although this doubtless had some effect, it can hardly explain the whole matter, as government spending was but a small part of the whole national income.

Another explanation offered is that improved methods of banking (particularly at Antwerp) made credit more readily available. It is

* Sir Thomas Gresham is chiefly remembered as the man who built the Royal Exchange in London and as the author of Gresham's Law—'Bad money drives out good'; in other words, if bad and good money are circulating together, people hoard the good and spend only the bad.

pointed out that modern governments use the restriction of credit as a means of checking inflation and easier credit as a means of inflating the economy. Antwerp bankers developed at this time such devices as bills of exchange, which made it unnecessary for merchants to pay in cash. But, although easier credit probably had some effect, it is doubtful if it explains the whole.

Most historians now think that there were several causes of the price rise, but that the most important of all was the growth of population, for it was subsistence foods like cheap grains, rather than luxuries, which rose fastest in price. This indicates a growth of demand. The total increase in population of England and Wales over the whole sixteenth century is thought to have been between seventy-five and a hundred per cent. We know that there was a land hunger, for entry fines paid to obtain new leases of land rose even more sharply than grain prices. Growth of population then is the explanation most generally accepted today as the main cause of the price rise. What caused the population to grow is something we cannot attempt to explain.

The effects of the price rise on England and Wales were numerous. It accelerated many processes which we think of as marking the end of the Middle Ages—the decline of the feudal aristocracy, the rise of the middle classes, the arrival of capitalism and a pure money economy, the decline of the guilds, the growth of industry. But perhaps the most momentous result of all was the weakening of the Crown. As money decreased in value, the King found it harder and harder to govern without getting grants from Parliament, for much of his income was fixed and could not be increased. Hence he became more dependent on Parliament.

The land and social status

The population of England and Wales in 1500 was about two and a half millions 'having perhaps doubled in the four centuries since Domesday was compiled'.* Nine-tenths of the people earned their living on the land, and those that did not, usually retained some connection with it, townsfolk having their fields around the borough.

London, with its population of perhaps 100,000 mid-century (Peter Ramsey puts it at 200,000 by the end of the century. His figure may be too low) was easily the greatest city. Next to it came Norwich, Bristol, Southampton, Hull etc., all mere country towns with populations of 15,000 or less.

A great deal of corn was needed to feed London. Before 1500 it came mainly from the home counties, but by Elizabeth's reign it was coming also from East Anglia via the port of Lynn or down the river Lea from Hertfordshire, though Kent was still the great provider.

* This quotation is from Sir John Clapham's *A Concise Economic History of Britain* (Cambridge University Press). Clapham was Professor of Economic History at Cambridge and a great authority on his subject. In this chapter I quote from him again and again.

216

Who owned the land in Tudor England? First of all there was the King himself, the greatest landowner of all (*see* Chapter 2). Then there were the great lords, some of them owning the equivalent of half a county. Few of these were descended from the old feudal nobility, though such were the Percys of Northumberland and the Nevilles of Westmorland. More often they were new families. 'Where's Bohun, where's Mowbray, where's Mortimer? Nay, which is more and most of all, where is Plantagenet?' asked Chief Justice Crewe in 1625, and he could as well have asked the question in Elizabeth's reign. The old families had often disappeared in the turmoil of the events and rising gentry had been endowed and ennobled in their places for service to the King. Such were the Stanleys, the Russells, the Cavendishes, the Cecils—names which are still to be found in Debrett's *Peerage* today.*

The turnover of noble families was rapid in the Tudor period, particularly in its first half. Thus between 1485 and 1547 thirty of the fifty-five peerage families died out and were replaced by others. As Peter Ramsey points out, 'The mortality of the peerage under the earlier Tudors was quite as rapid as that during the Wars of the Roses.†

The peerage as a whole was becoming less important, less powerful than it had been in the fifteenth century. Partly this was because times were peaceful and the nobles no longer commanded private armies as in the Wars of the Roses. Was it also because they were becoming poorer (relative to the rising gentry)? The 'rise of the gentry' was a phrase coined by Professor R. H. Tawney. He argued that between 1540 and 1640 'the aristocracy lost ground in the face of rising prices and failed to adjust to the needs of the time. As a class they were too old-fashioned to improve their estates ... and at the same time unwilling to cut their expenses to fit their reduced incomes. Faced with mounting deficits and debts they were forced to sell part of their estates' to the 'more go-ahead owners of medium-sized estates, who applied to land the business-like procedures they had learned in trade or the law. The result was a substantial net swing, both of capital and income, from the aristocracy to the gentry. Thence, it is argued, followed a change in the balance of power. The outcome of the civil war merely set the seal on a change that had already taken place.'‡

This then was Professor Tawney's thesis. It has been attacked and defended in lively controversy ever since he put it forth. Tawney backed up his theory by an analysis (over seven counties) of the number of manors owned by peers in the period 1540–1640. His figures showed a drop in the average number thus owned. But some manors or villages are poor and some are rich. Might not these peers merely have been consolidating their estates by selling off small manors or ones which were difficult to administer and far distant from the main blocs of their estates, and buying large, neighbouring manors instead? The fact is we have

* Notice how often these noble surnames have become Christian names.
† *Tudor Economic Problems*, by Peter Ramsey, Gollancz, 1963, p. 121.
‡ *Ibid.*, p. 122, for this neat summary of Tawney's argument.

not enough evidence to show that the peers were declining economically in the Tudor period.

Next to the nobles as landowners came the gentry. A gentleman was, roughly speaking, someone who owned more land than he could farm himself. Often in England, but not in Wales, he was lord of a manor. This was no longer of course the medieval manor with its service payments, but it was still an economic unit, a village, almost self-sufficing, with the lord living in his great-house, occupying the best pew in the church, farming his demesne land (his home farm) with hired labourers, taking his rents, enclosing from time to time a piece of the waste (the unused land around the village) and buying up the land of peasant proprietors who got into financial difficulties.

Some historians object to the term 'middle class' as applied to the gentry. They point out that the wealthier gentry were richer than the poorer peers, that they mixed socially with members of the peerage, 'intermarried, dined together and cooperated in local politics'.* In theory the title 'gentleman' or its superior 'Esquire' was guarded by the College of Arms, which could forbid people to use it. In practice, however, the attitude of the established gentlemen of the county was what mattered.

It used to be argued that the dissolution of the monasteries created a new class of wealthy gentry out of men who bought up monastery lands cheap. It is now believed that monastery lands were not sold cheap, but at a fair market price. Hence those who bought them had to have substantial capital to do so. 'For the sixteenth century there is not enough evidence to argue convincingly for the general or rapid rise of a middle or gentry class, however this be defined.'†

Three groups of men were certainly 'on the make' and were buying up land with their new-found wealth. The first of these was composed of courtiers, men who sought their fortunes by living at or near court in the hope of picking up favours from the crown. Of course we only hear of the successful ones, such as Sir Walter Raleigh. Many of them must have failed and 'returned disappointed to their country estates'. The second group is composed of merchants, men such as Richard Gresham who bought the abbey of Fountains for £11,000 and had an income from his lands at his death of £800, which brought him up to the level of the poorer peers. Here again there were many failures, rich Staplers and Mercers who fell upon hard times and ended up by leaving the City of London in order to avoid meeting their creditors.

The third group is composed of the lawyers. About forty young men entered the four Inns of Court annually at the beginning of our period and over two hundred at the end. A few, very few, of these became Justices or Serjeants (barristers who had the sole right of pleading civil cases in the Court of Common Pleas) and ended up as wealthy men, leaving substantial estates to their heirs.

But courtiers, merchants and lawyers all needed money to start them

* See Conrad Russell, *op. cit.*, p. 17. I quote from this several times in this chapter.
† See Peter Ramsey, *op. cit.*, p. 127.

218

off in their careers and thus many of them came from the gentry class in the beginning. Did they really then much increase the total number of gentry families? It is hard to say. Perhaps all we can say with certainty is that in Tudor times firm government made the country prosperous and more families rose in wealth and social position than fell. Also the monastery lands did make a difference in the sheer number of substantial landowners. You cannot have a great number (or class) of landowners without plenty of land.

Next to the gentry came the yeomen. They were either freeholders or leaseholders with fairly long leases. The freeholders were entitled to a vote in Parliamentary elections. A yeoman would have servants and perhaps sub-tenants. Beside voting at elections he sat on juries, but 'he would probably not hunt or drink wine or indulge in other expensive habits of gentility'.* Like 'gentleman' 'yeoman' was a title describing a class. Whether you were accepted as being fit to use it depended on your neighbours. Many a man who described himself as a yeoman was described by his neighbours as a mere 'husbandman'.

The yeomen were seen by many writers as the backbone of the nation, men of industry, frugality, patriotism and solid worth. What other country, it was asked, had such a vast body of self-reliant freeholders? It has been estimated that there were about 70,000 yeomen in Tudor England with estates varying from twenty-five acres in good, arable areas to about 600 acres in poor, pastoral districts. The richer yeoman families often intermarried with the gentry.

There were some freeholders, however, in Tudor England who were not reckoned as yeomen, men who owned but twenty or thirty acres.

Tenant farmers were more numerous than freeholders in Tudor England. They were mostly the heirs of the villeins of the Middle Ages, as the yeomen were mostly the heirs of the 'freemen' mentioned in Magna Carta. By the year 1500 labour services had almost entirely disappeared. A few bondmen there still were, 'but English writers, accustomed to boast of English liberty, were getting ashamed of them'. Moreover, the King's courts 'always favoured freedom, as they did in the last recorded case about villeinage in 1618', when the plaintiff was declared to be free.

Tenant farmers were of three kinds—tenants-at-will, customary tenants and copyholders. The first were tenants with no safeguards, who held their land at their lord's pleasure, and who could be turned out or have their rents raised at any time. As prices rose and the landowners found it harder to make ends meet, it was the tenants-at-will who bore the brunt of the 'rack-renting' of which we hear so many complaints.

Customary tenants and copyholders both had the terms of their contracts enrolled in the manorial court roll. They were thus protected by the custom of the manor against rent-rises. The copyholder sometimes actually possessed a copy of the record himself and was thus doubly protected. If his rent was raised, he could sue his lord in one of the king's

*See Conrad Russell, *op. cit.*, p. 16.

219

courts. The customary tenant, early on, sought redress in his lord's manor court, but, by the middle of the century, the king's courts were supporting manorial custom, so that he was as well off as the copyholder.

Copyholders and customary tenants were a minority of tenant farmers, and they tended to decline during the Tudor period. Not all their holdings were held 'of inheritance' and could be handed down automatically from father to son. Some were 'for lives', perhaps the lives of three generations of the tenant's family, after which they came to an end. Moreover, copyholders and customary tenants were naturally unpopular with landlords, and all sorts of pressures were put on them in Elizabeth's reign to get them to alter to a straightforward signed lease (such as putting up the fine which a copyholder's son paid when his father died). By the end of her reign 'leasehold had replaced copyhold as the characteristic contract of the agrarian system'. Perhaps a copyholder would prefer a firm lease to a manorial custom which he was continually driven to defend in the courts. There was certainly a great deal of litigation in Chancery, Requests and the Common Law courts in Tudor times concerning copyholds.

Despite the complaints about rack-renting in this century, there is no evidence that generally rents rose faster than prices. On some estates they did. On many they did not.

The poorer farmer, the 'husbandman', whether leaseholder, freeholder or tenant, might farm only twenty or even ten acres. Beneath him were the landless men, the labourers, who owned nothing except perhaps a little bit of garden round their cottages. This class was certainly increasing in numbers right through the period. Numerous printed pamphlets speak of 'masterless men, rogues and vagabonds' as a problem. One cause of this phenomenon was the growth in population. By English land-law (unlike the old Welsh law) the eldest son inherited. The younger sons thus became landless. Enclosure by the gentry, whether for sheep-farming or arable, was another cause in some localities, for often it led to evictions. The price-rise made it difficult, as we have seen, for landlords to pay their way, and they were inclined to raise rents (where possible) and to take back leaseholds, when they terminated (and Tudor leaseholds were usually short), in order to farm the land themselves.

Lastly, the break-up of feudalism must be considered a cause of the greater number of vagabonds and other landless men. After all, when the feudal system was at its height, everyone had some land, a few strips in the open-field and a few beasts on the common pasture. Now that a free market in land had come about, this was not so. Unprotected by villein-status any more, the weakest of the lower class found themselves pushed out of all landholding.

Historians used to regard the dissolution of the monasteries as a cause of the number of vagabonds in Tudor England. Now that it has been shown that nearly all the monks got jobs or pensions, this cause is usually discounted.

The price-rise naturally made life hard for landless men, for their wages usually lagged behind. This was because the government attempted (often with success) to regulate wages. It was to the advantage of the JPs (themselves landowners) to keep wages down. Between the first and last decades of the sixteenth century day-wages on the land about doubled. As we have seen, in this period the cost of living went up more steeply. Poor men did not live on wheaten bread at the beginning of the century, but, by the end of it, they certainly ate more rough and cheap grain—rye, barley, oats and linseed.* There is, however, one extenuating circumstance (difficult to gauge in its total effect) to this, and that is the spread of wool-manufacture, which gave the agricultural worker's family a way of adding to the family income, for, as we have seen, almost every cottage in Tudor England had its spinning wheel. But, even when this is allowed for, the fact remains that the material well-being of the wage-earner declined in this century.

Yet it must be remembered that there were no instances of famine, such as had haunted earlier centuries, in Tudor times. But memories are long, and famine was prayed against in Cranmer's Litany together with 'plague, pestilence ... battle, murder and sudden death'.

Enclosure

I have already written of the enclosure movement in Chapters 4 and 8. More, however, needs to be said about this important subject. We saw that there were three types of enclosure—enclosure of the waste, of the commons and of arable strips—and that the aim was often sheep-farming, which was profitable in the first half of the century because of the high price of wool. But sheep-farming was by no means the only reason for enclosure. Another, and perhaps a more important one, was increasing population. As more people moved into a village and more houses were built, there came a time when the common pasture could not support the number of animals put on it. To avoid endless squabbles and to make the pasture-land more productive, the villagers might agree (with the lord's consent) to divide it up with fences. 'When enclosure of the fields took place by agreement, it was often accompanied by a re-arrangement of strips so that some consolidation of holdings could be effected'.†

The increasing population of big cities (London particularly) produced a demand for more food, and led to many farmers attempting to improve their production by enclosure. This demand only affected areas adjacent to growing cities or areas which had good water communication with them. It only became a really urgent matter towards the end of the century, when London's population had grown enormously.‡

*See Sir John Clapham, *op. cit.*, p. 211.
† This quotation is from a Historical Association pamphlet entitled *Tudor Enclosures by* Joan Thirsk (1959).   ‡ See Peter Ramsey, *op. cit.*, p. 23.

There were loud outcries against enclosure from writers and preachers of the early sixteenth century. Sir Thomas More in *Utopia* had written:

'Your sheep that were wont to be so meek and tame ... be become so great devourers and so wild that they eat up and swallow down the very men themselves ... and certain Abbots, holy men no doubt, not contenting themselves with their yearly revenues and profits ... leave no ground for tillage, they enclose all into pastures: they throw down houses, they pluck down towns, and leave nothing standing but only the church to be made a sheepcote.'

The modern view is that More and other writers exaggerated. For one thing many counties were already enclosed before Tudor times. Kent and Essex, both of which felt the pull of the London market (so that ambitious farmers had great incentive to enclose) were two of these. Lancashire, Cheshire, Wiltshire and the counties of the south-west were likewise largely enclosed before 1485. 'The reclaimed marshlands of Cambridgeshire, Lincolnshire and the East Riding of Yorkshire' were unsuitable for pasture and we hear no complaints of enclosure there in Tudor times. Likewise, the West Riding, being only suitable for pasture, experienced no change then, while East Anglia was largely enclosed before 1485.

It was the Midlands which were particularly vulnerable to enclosure in this century, and it was from them that nearly all the complaints came. Yet we know that in Nottinghamshire, where there was enclosure trouble in Tudor times, thirty-two per cent of the whole county area (not merely its agricultural area) survived to be enclosed by act of Parliament after 1750.

Professor Beresford nevertheless traced 379 deserted villages dating from this period.* Most of them were small ones in upland areas. The lowland villages, being larger, would present more opposition to eviction.

Enclosure of the open-field usually meant improved arable farming. After all strip culture was wasteful. Time was wasted in moving a plough from one strip to another. The manure was deposited on the common pasture and had to be carted to the arable fields, whereas in enclosed farming a field could be used perhaps for seven years as pasture and then, when well manured, ploughed up for arable for a few years. The fifteenth century, a time of peasant prosperity, saw a good deal of enclosure done for this purpose, when a prosperous tenant would begin 'to buy up strips adjoining his own' and 'put a hedge round the field so created'. Many people regarded this sort of enclosure as good. For instance in 1557 Thomas Tusser, a Suffolk gentleman-farmer wrote his *Hundred Points of Good Husbandry*, which became a best seller. Tusser often wrote in rhyme:

More plenty of mutton and beef,
Corn, butter and cheese of the best,
Where find ye (go search any coast)
Than there, where enclosure is most?

* M. W. Beresford, *The Lost Villages of England*, 1954.

But he saw that enclosure often brought hardship:

The poor at enclosing do grutch,
Because of abuses that fall,
Lest some man should have but too much,
And some again nothing at all.

As Clapham points out, 'If you rearranged fields or commons, the grasping man might come out on top.'

But sixteenth-century enclosure, at any rate in the first half of the century, was often for sheep-farming. (In the second half of the century the price of wool fell and there were fewer complaints.) Also, it was often enclosure of the common land by the lord of the manor. Ket's followers in Norfolk in 1549 complained of 'the overgrazing of the commons by greedy lords, the damage done to crops by the keeping of dovecotes and by rabbits kept in unprotected coney warrens, as well as of rising rents'.

To sum up then—we have no way of telling how much open-field or common pasture was enclosed in this period. We think it was less than the pamphleteers and other writers would have us think, if only because of the amount of open-field that remained in the eighteenth century, but that there must have been a real grievance is obvious from the outcry.

The government was worried because sheep-farming employed fewer sturdy labourers and places like the Isle of Wight might become so depopulated as to be unable to beat off French raids. It passed numerous acts of Parliament and issued proclamations galore. The first of the acts in the Tudor period was passed in 1489 and its wording shows that the problem was not a new one then. In fact there is some evidence to show that enclosures 'were at a peak at the accession of Henry Tudor, if not before, and they may have been on the wane by 1517'.*

Wolsey was an opponent of enclosures and there were proclamations in 1526, 1528 and 1529 ordering the 'casting down of hedges and the opening up of enclosed lands'. Acts were passed in 1534 and 1536 forbidding anyone to keep more than 2400 sheep. The very 'repetition is proof that the efforts of the government were in vain'. Economic forces are usually stronger than laws and of course the local JPs, themselves enclosing landlords, were often loath to enforce the law.

After a time the government became aware of another cause of depopulation of the countryside. This was 'engrossing' or the buying out of a farmer by his neighbour. 'When two or more farms were thrown together, the superfluous farm houses were either reduced to the status of cottages or left to decay. Thus the smaller farmers were deprived of livelihood ... and unemployment ensued.'†

Commissions appointed in 1548 and 1565 were told to enquire into this; so there was obviously a good deal of it going on.

* Peter Ramsey, *op. cit.*
† Joan Thirsk's *Tudor Enclosures*, Historical Association pamphlet, 1959.

The problem of enclosure was less acute in the second half of the century, but then, from about 1580, in the Midlands at least, the tempo increased and enclosure went on faster than ever. Complaints reached the Council from many areas. 'In 1596, after several bad harvests, there were enclosure riots in various districts.' In 1563 Elizabeth's Parliament had passed an act confirming the agrarian legislation of Henry VII and Henry VIII. In 1593 the 'great plenty of grain' led Parliament to repeal this act, but in 1598 'under pressure of renewed high prices, famine and popular outcry against enclosures, there was a reversion to the former policy.*

But by the end of the century popular antagonism to enclosure had somewhat abated. An act of 1597 'explicitly allowed the conversion of arable land to pasture to regain heart ... thus following the advice of the Speaker, who had condemned the old laws against enclosure for 'tye-ing the land once tilled to a perpetual bondage and servitude of being ever tilled"'.

By the mid-seventeenth century enclosure had been accepted as a part of progress and there were no more laws against it.

Farming methods

Throughout the Tudor period there is a steady improvement in farming methods. Pressure of economic circumstances (the price-rise) made it necessary to get more out of the land. The horse was replacing the ox in some areas, not only for the harrow, but also for the plough. But changes came slowly and in some areas came hardly at all. As late as 1750 Devon was said to possess not a single wheeled cart, 'crops and everything else being moved on sledges or on horseback'. The ox as a draught-animal was to survive well into the nineteenth century and even, in Sussex, into the twentieth. Crops were, we think, still being harvested at the end of the seventeenth century 'with a sickle, applied half-way up the straw, precisely as in any medieval manuscript'. Probably in the enclosed areas progress was greater than in the Midlands with its open-field.

The open-field system, however, was never as rigid as the old text-books would have us think. True there was usually a field for winter-corn (wheat, rye or mixed grain), one for spring-corn (barley or oats) and one left fallow. But the spring-corn field usually contained some peas and beans, and vetches might be grown on the fallow field.

Hops came in the late fifteenth century (not, as the rhyme says, with the Reformation) and soon became, as they have remained, a Kentish speciality. Saffron had been known since the fourteenth century, but only became common in the sixteenth, when Walden began to be called Saf-fron Walden. About Pontefract they grew liquorice, as they do today, and made 'Pomfret cakes' flavoured with it. Various districts specialized

*See J. B. Black, *op. cit.*, p. 254.

in hemp and flax (usually grown apart in closes and gardens), in oil-seeds or in the old dye-stuff plants, madder and woad. The potato, supposed to have been introduced by Sir Walter Raleigh, was not grown at all except latterly in a few gardens of the rich. It was certainly not an article of diet for the poor yet. Instead they had peas and beans.

Finally for the poor, as Clapham says, 'there were conies to be trapped, birds to be snared and miscellaneous poachings'. In Wales and Scotland large herds of cattle were raised and driven on the hoof to the London market after fattening for a time on the meadows of the Thames valley or East Anglia. This trade was getting into the hands of capitalist graziers, men who worked on a big scale.

Woollen manufacture

The Tudor period shows a steady though gradual increase in the growth of industry. One reason for this was strong and stable government. Another was the freedom of internal trade. Unlike the Continent with its numerous boundaries of counties and duchies, each restricting the passage of goods, English internal trade was free. Mainly it flowed along the rivers Thames, Trent, Severn etc. Unlike the Seine, where, up to the Revolution, all corn going up or downstream had to be sold at Paris, on these the shires and towns levied no tolls. The reason for this is that English medieval monarchy had been on the whole strong and had not allowed tolls to be taken.

We saw (in the *Introduction*) that in the Middle Ages Britain had been the Australia of Europe, the great exporter of raw wool. We also saw that by 1485 the growth of wool manufacture at home had taken up more and more of this production so that only half the wool was being exported. Throughout the Tudor period this process goes on. Home manufacture takes up more of the market and exports of raw-wool dwindle. With them decline the Merchants of the Staple, who handled the major part of these exports through Calais, so that, when Calais is lost in Mary's reign, it is a much shrunken trade which is hit. The decline of the export of raw wool was largely due to the heavy customs duty levied on it.

Household woollen cloth, home-spun, was made almost everywhere in Tudor England at least in the country districts, as was rough linen cloth. The spinning-wheel was steadily displacing the distaff, on which most medieval spinning had been done. Most cottages had one or the other and the unmarried women of the household, the 'spinsters', earned their keep thereby. Usually each village had one village weaver (or 'webster'). Rough woollen and linen cloths were sold locally, but there were certain areas which specialized in making the better woollen cloths for export. Such was Norfolk where they specialized in worsteds (called after the village of Worstead), a smooth cloth made of fine-spun thread with the fibres combed parallel. By 1564, however, the worsted industry was 'much decayed'. The reason was the rivalry of the 'new drapery',

225

light fabrics of similar type, made in the Netherlands. But then came Alva's persecutions in the Netherlands and many Flemings fled to England. They settled mainly in East Anglia and the government made them welcome and wisely relaxed the apprenticeship rules so that Englishmen could easily learn the new trade. The result was a profitable new industry.

'West of Newbury, over the Wiltshire border,' was another area where woollen manufacture was a main source of wealth. Wiltshire, Gloucestershire and Somerset were all big woollen counties. So was north Dorset (round Shaftesbury and Sherborne) and Oxfordshire (where Witney is still a blanket town). Here were made the broadcloths which the clothiers of Salisbury and the other big towns bought up, enabling them to endow the wonderfully large and well-built churches with which the district still abounds.

Often the clothiers employed the weavers, renting them their looms and paying them a wage for every piece completed—sending round their strings of pack-horses periodically to dump or collect up the goods. But then again, probably more often, the weaver owned his own loom and worked for his customers. But the clothiers usually handled the processes which came after weaving—the fulling, raising, shearing and dyeing, the last three being generally done in a town. Many of the clothiers grew exceedingly rich. For instance Peter Blundell of Devon, when he died a bachelor in 1601 left £40,000 to education and charity.

Further south-west, in west Somerset and Devon, there was a different sort of woollen manufacture. Broadcloths gave way to knitted stockings and to 'lighter and narrower fabrics of worsted or mixed woollen and worsted', such as baize. Exeter and Taunton were big centres for these, Exeter and the district round specializing by 1600 in serge. Abergavenny in Monmouthshire was a stocking town, getting its wool from the flocks of the nearby Welsh hills.

Further north on the Welsh border Shrewsbury was a big market town for Welsh woollens, rough cloth manufactured in the primitive cottages of Wales.

Already the West Riding of Yorkshire was a great woollen area. Here there was an abundance of soft water for washing the wool and the swift-running streams drove the fulling-mills, for, as Clapham points out, 'before 1500 every "clothing" region had its fulling-mills, just as every district whatsoever had its corn mills'. Fulling was a process wherein rough cloth was 'cleaned, thickened and felted in water and some soapy material'. The mills drove hammers which pounded the cloth. After fulling the cloth had to have its nap raised with teazle-heads preparatory to being sheared. This process was also mechanized early in the sixteenth century when the gig-mill, which turned a wheel whose 'rim was set with teazle-heads', was either invented or imported.

Yorkshire concentrated on rough and coarse cloth—'kerseys' as they were called. Leeds was the great market centre, but Halifax and Huddersfield were already beginning to grow as woollen towns.

Cotton had not yet come to Lancashire, for it was only brought into the kingdom in the next century (by the Turkey Merchants).

One may well ask why certain districts had a great woollen industry and others did not. 'A ready supply of raw material was an obvious essential and the west country cloth industry was largely based on Cotswold wool.'* But 'wool could be transported with comparative ease and in point of fact the clothing counties were not identical with the wool-producing ones'. A supply of running water to work the fulling mills was probably a more important reason. (It has already been noted above as existing in Yorkshire.) A fairly numerous rural population was another requisite factor.

The cloth areas suffered terribly when the export trade was interrupted, as it was in 1550–1551 when the Antwerp market became saturated. Towards the end of the century, however, the cloth industry and its markets became more diversified (as the 'new draperies' began to vie with broadcloths and exports went to the Mediterranean as well as to northern Europe) so that the danger became less.†

Much of the best English cloth was exported 'white' to be dyed and finished at Antwerp, Amsterdam or Hamburg (particularly the first). The government disapproved of this and successive statutes in Henry VII's and Henry VIII's reigns made it an offence to ship unfinished cloth below stipulated price-levels. But the merchants 'cheerfully evaded the statutes'.‡ Kent and East Anglia, however, specialized in finished, dyed broadcloths for export, and of course Lincolnshire was famous for 'Lincoln green'. Broadcloths found their customers mainly in Germany and the Netherlands, but the 'lighter and finer kerseys' (chiefly from Berkshire) found their way also to Italy and the Levant. 'Unlike the broadcloths the kerseys were very frequently dyed before export.'

To sum up then, 'English exports in the sixteenth century consisted largely of West Country broadcloths and Berkshire kerseys, and ... the wealth of the great London merchants rested on the sustained efforts of several generations of weavers in some five or six counties.'§

In the reign of Henry VIII 'wool and woollens accounted for four-fifths of the value of English exports'. Overseas trade then was dangerously narrow-based. It was also heavily concentrated in one port, London. This had not always been so. At the end of the fifteenth century other ports, such as Southampton, Bristol and Hull, shared the trade more evenly. But from 1500 onwards London overhauled all its rivals and by the end of Henry VIII's reign was handling eighty-eight per cent of cloth exports. There were various reasons for this. One was the

*See Peter Ramsey, *op. cit.*, p. 85.
† For a fuller account of these changes see the section in this chapter headed 'Overseas trade'.
‡ See Peter Ramsey, *op. cit.*, p. 49.
§ *Ibid.*, p. 50.

nearness of Antwerp. An outstanding economic fact of the Tudor period is the amazing growth of London.

The 'new draperies' introduced, as we have seen, by Flemish refugees in the Norwich and Colchester areas in the 1570s, soon began to spread to the other old-established clothing areas. By the end of the century these lighter cloths (called bays and says) had conquered East Anglia and were appearing in Yorkshire. By the first decade of the next century they were to penetrate Wiltshire itself. They sold well, especially in the new export markets of the Mediterranean, Russia etc.

Industry other than woollens

Iron and ship-building were two major industries in England at the close of the Middle Ages. Iron was smelted with charcoal and the industry was therefore located in the forest areas, such as the Weald of Sussex and the Forest of Dean. Here by Tudor times cannon were made in blast furnaces, as also was pig-iron (to be refined into smith's iron at the forge). Water power had recently come into use to drive the bellows and the tilt-hammers. (We hear of 'great water-hammers' in Ashdown Forest before 1500.) The iron ore was mined locally, but already by Elizabeth's reign, the trees in some areas were being used up (or rather there was a fear they soon would be), and there was a tendency to disperse the industry into other areas where iron-ore, wood and water-power could be found. Hence the first iron-works appears in South Wales in Elizabeth's reign. It was certainly a profitable industry and furnace owners in the Weald in 1573 included the Queen and several earls and barons.

Ships were built in or near all the major ports, particularly where there was forest. Most were of under one hundred tons burden but towards the end of the century there was a demand for more 'great-ships', either to sail the newly-explored oceans or to fish the Newfoundland banks or engage in the growing coastal and Baltic trades.

Coal had long been mined in many places in England and southern Scotland and used locally, especially by smiths to heat their forges. Pits were shallow—open workings or levels usually—and production was small because of limited transport facilities. Only where coal-workings were close to the sea, as at Tyneside or Glamorgan, were they much developed, and here Newcastle led the field, shipping in 1564 33,000 tons coastwise or abroad. A lot of it (perhaps half) went to London where 'sea-cole', as it was called, was used often by the poor (it was regarded as a dirty fuel) in their domestic fires, and also in a few industries such as soap-making. Since the population of London mid-century was about 100,000, obviously wood was still the main domestic fuel, but that was rapidly rising in price, as the forests shrank, and coal was being used more and more.

Brass was a valuable metal in Tudor times. It was used for a number of things, including cannon and the wire, set in boards, for carding wool.

All brass was imported at the beginning of our period, although copper was mined at home on a small scale (but not zinc). Elizabeth's government determined to alter this situation and in 1568 two great companies were chartered, the Society of Mines Royal and the Mineral and Battery Works—'the first industrial companies in British history'. German managers and workmen were brought in to run them, and soon copper was being mined on a fair scale in Cornwall and smelted at Neath in South Wales, where the necessary coal was to be found. Zinc ore was discovered in the Mendips (calamine stone), but 'the projected brass industry grew very slowly'. The Society of Mines Royal also opened up lead mines in Cardiganshire to help in the production of that 'good, flat, English pewter' which had long been manufactured in London both for the home market and for export. (Lead was also of course extensively used in building.)

Coastwise shipping was a big and growing industry. A large fleet of colliers, some of them over 100 tons, carried the Newcastle trade and took Glamorgan coal along the Bristol Channel or across to Ireland. Smaller ships were used in the general coasting trade—carrying corn, malt, timber, glass and other goods. Such ships could use the rivers to reach inland ports like Colchester, Ipswich, Norwich, Exeter and Gloucester.

Three industries which historians have been inclined to neglect because they did not produce for a foreign market are the leather, brewing and building industries. In Northampton (already concerned with boots and shoes) the leather workers were an important group, 'every town of any size had its brewers' and the building industry was quite well organized, its superior workmen, the masons, being already divided up into lodges.*

The Statute of Artificers

One of the great statutes of Elizabeth's reign was passed by her second Parliament in 1563. This was the Statute of Artificers or, as it is also called, the Statute of Apprentices. A depression in the clothing industry after 1560 had caused unemployment, and the price-rise had caused agricultural labourers to demand what were regarded as excessively high wages. Cecil attempted in this act to put these things right and indeed to stabilize the economic structure of society in its lower ranks.

The main provisions of the act were: (1) Qualified craftsmen might be compelled to work at their crafts; men not otherwise employed, between the ages of 12 and 60, could be compelled to work at agriculture. Women between 12 and 60 might be compelled to go into service. (2) The period of apprenticeship in all trades, including agriculture (but excluding the weaving of cloth), was to be fixed at seven years. There was to be a property qualification for apprentices, but (to prevent

* *Ibid.*, p. 83.

apprentices being used as cheap labour) there was to be a limit to the number of apprentices a master could employ. (3) Wages were to be assessed annually by JPs.

One result of the act was to make the seven-year apprentice rule general in industry. It has been argued (by Professor Bindoff) that this was not part of the Crown's original intention, which was merely to deal with the problems of wage-inflation and vagrancy. The government bill was certainly substantially amended in the Commons.

There is nothing very revolutionary about the act. Guilds and companies had long charged premiums to their apprentices, and the act's scale of property qualifications was set so low that only labourers' sons would be excluded. The seven-year period of apprenticeship was already widely established, and the act 'only made a common practice universal'. Most qualified craftsmen would already be working at their crafts anyway.

The act probably strengthened the guild system, but it only affected established crafts, so that new crafts such as mining and metallurgy developed freely outside it.

It is hard to assess how effective the act was. There appear to have been few prosecutions under it in the eighty years before the Civil War. Wage assessments were made annually by JPs up to the Civil War, but shortage of labour on the land probably tempted many employers to exceed the agreed wage. Wage assessments were nothing new, for they had been general in the later Middle Ages.

The act has been attacked by nineteenth-century historians as being restrictive and putting industry in a strait-jacket. However, it may have had some quite liberal results, for instance in making it easier for moderately-wealthy boys to become apprentices in trades where hitherto the premiums had been set too high.*

Guilds

Guilds in the Middle Ages were of two sorts—merchant guilds, of which there was one in each chartered town, and craft guilds, of which there were many (one to each craft). Often the town hall is called the guildhall, that is the hall of the merchant guild, to which all rich traders in the town belonged and which regulated trade in the town.

Some towns had more craft guilds than others. Thus York in the fifteenth century had forty-one, while Norwich had only twenty-six. Southampton had hardly any, because its merchant guild was so strong it 'kept the craftsmen in their place'.

Guilds were fraternities, partly religious, partly social, and partly economic. They charged high entrance fees from which only the relations of guildsmen were exempt. The craft guild exercised supervision over the whole business of production. 'It fixed hours of work, wages and

*I am indebted to Peter Ramsey, *op. cit.*, pp. 150–152, for much of the above.

prices; it punished faulty workmanship; it settled disputes between members and acted as a friendly society; by its maintenance of altar-lights and the performance of a set-piece in the annual pageant, it proclaimed itself to be, under the protection of its proper saint, a separate corporation within the machinery of the parent town.'* Guild ordinances had to be approved by the municipality.

Guilds were at the height of their power between 1350 and 1450. By Tudor times they were on the decline. They had never controlled three of the industries with which we have dealt, iron, ship-building and mining, as these were not located in towns. Weavers' guilds had declined in the Middle Ages when the water-driven fulling-mill took the craft out of the towns into the rural areas. The law-courts in the sixteenth century were against too much economic interference and were inclined to regard the guilds as restrictive—which they were—and not to support them. London had at one time possessed over a hundred guilds and companies. To be a citizen of London you had to be a member of a guild. Yet by 1500 not more than a quarter of the London population were citizens. The fact was that London had grown so much that tradesmen from other towns, 'illegal, unapprenticed men', could easily slip in and set up shop in the suburbs 'out of reach of wardens and search'.†

There is a tendency in the sixteenth century for craft-guilds to amalgamate. Thus in 1511 the Hammerers of Ludlow, besides admitting smiths, ironmongers, pewterers and armourers, included coopers, masons and other tradesmen. The reason for this we do not know. Perhaps it was expense, a single craft being too poor to pay its share of the town pageant. After all in a small town one craft guild might contain only half a dozen men.

Governments of sixteenth-century England disliked the guilds, regarding them as narrow and exclusive. In 1504 an act of Parliament laid down that guild ordinances were not only to be approved by the municipalities, but by the king's justices in their circuits. Then in Edward VI's reign came the confiscation of the religious endowments of the guilds—money left them to hold masses, processions etc. This weakened the guilds still further.

In any case 'new industries grew up either in the country or in towns where guilds were not too powerful, and the future lay with the capitalist entrepreneur operating in a relatively free labour market. There were no guilds in Birmingham or Wolverhampton and the apprenticeship clauses of the 1563 Statute of Artificers were not enforced in Warwickshire or Worcestershire.'‡

*See *The Earlier Tudors* by J. D. Mackie, p. 459.
† But for a fuller account of London and its guilds, see the next section of this chapter.
‡ See Peter Ramsey, *op. cit.*, p. 101.

London in Tudor times consisted mainly of the City, which was still surrounded by a wall on three sides. To the south it was bounded by the river. There was only one bridge, London Bridge, with its narrow arches and its four-storied houses on top. At the eastern end of the wall stood the Tower, which was still a state prison, a treasure house and, at times, a palace. Proceeding westwards one came to the great gates, Aldgate, Bishopsgate, Newgate and Ludgate (Billingsgate was on the river side). Towards the western end of the City stood old St Pauls, a mighty Gothic cathedral, whose middle aisle was 'the market and meeting place of the hucksters, the promenade of the gallants, the labour exchange of the unemployed and the news-room of all London'.* Proceeding westward from St Paul's one passed along Fleet Street 'the main thoroughfare of the City', through Ludgate, to the Strand where stood the great houses of the lords and merchants, Leicester House, Somerset House and Durham House (Raleigh's house, now the site of the Adelphi). Here the streets broadened out and the houses were no longer huddled together, their fronts overhanging, as they were within the City walls. Beyond the Strand one came to St Martin's Church (which really was 'in-the-Fields'), and then to Westminster with its palace of Whitehall, its abbey, its Exchequer buildings and its Hall built in the reign of William II. South of the river, beyond the bridge, lay the borough of Southwark. Here was built, in Elizabeth's reign, Shakespeare's Globe Theatre, for the City merchants disapproved of frivolity and would allow no theatre within the City walls.

'The whole built-up area of the City, Westminster, Southwark and the out-parishes, may in 1485 have had about 50,000 inhabitants, the great majority of them living in the City itself. By 1603 the number had probably quadrupled, possibly quintupled, and a full third of them were living outside the city.'† The great increase in London's population over the Tudor period owes something to the immigration of Flemings and Huguenots, refugees from religious persecution, thousands of whom settled in the London area.

London had no single merchant guild. Instead it had its famous twelve Livery Companies. In the order of precedence established during the sixteenth century (and still surviving today) they were the Mercers, Grocers, Drapers, Fishmongers, Goldsmiths, Skinners, Merchant Taylors, Haberdashers, Salters, Ironmongers, Vintners and Cloth-workers. These companies, of which two, the Merchant Taylors and Clothworkers, were incorporated after 1500, were at the height of their power in the Tudor period. Around them revolved the economic, political and social life of the city.

---

* See Volume 2 of *History of England* by C. E. Carrington and J. H. Jackson, Cambridge University Press, 1936.
† See 'The Livery Companies of Tudor London' by T. F. Reddaway, published in the magazine *History*, October 1966. Much of this section is based upon this article.

All of them had obtained charters from the Crown. This enabled them to hold land, to sue and be sued. They were wealthy guilds of capitalist employers, but they were also friendly societies, interested in almshouses and pensions for the poor and old. Their members did not necessarily practise their trade. A member of the Vintners might be so because his father was one, and might himself set up as a draper or be a lawyer, idler or politician. Those whose fathers did not belong to a company could buy membership (at a great price).

Each Livery Company had its hall. Here was held on its particular saint's day the Company's annual general assembly. Here also was held its wardens' court and lesser general assemblies spread throughout the year. The saint's day general assembly was a very special affair. All the shops and workshops were closed that day and the members of the guild put on their full dress and went in solemn procession to their church to celebrate mass (I am speaking of before the Reformation). Then they returned in procession to their hall and began the business of the day, holding elections, approving new ordinances, reading the guild's rules and finally ending up with a great dinner for the Livery.

Each Livery Company had jurisdiction over its particular trade in London and the suburbs, and its regulations were enforced when the Company Wardens held their court. Here complaints were lodged against those who had broken the guild's ordinances. Perhaps goods had been sold by candlelight so that the buyers could not judge their quality. Perhaps inferior goods had been sold, such as a silver salt weighted with lead. Perhaps apprentices (usually middle-class boys, the younger sons of gentry or sons of burghers or yeomen) had been unfairly treated or had behaved improperly.

The Wardens' Court could have apprentices beaten with rods in the Company's hall, but adults were punished by fines or imprisonment.

The wardens and company officials made regular inspections of the establishments of members of the guild, searching their work and stock.

The twelve Great Companies dominated City politics. The Court of Aldermen of the City was entirely composed of their members. Yet in matters of City government (law and order, supplies of food and water, public health etc.) the City gave the orders and the Companies obeyed. Thus the Companies were ordered to supply the marching watch (which, 'armed and splendidly arrayed', patrolled the city), to maintain supplies of armour and weapons and to provide contingents of men to defend the City, if called upon.

Finally the Companies often received demands from the Crown for loans or taxes, and usually complied, however reluctantly.

Enough has been said to show what an important part the Twelve Companies played in the City of London. The sixteenth century saw the high peak of their splendour and importance. 'Their Halls were richer than they had ever been. Their displays of plate and their feasts were magnificent. ... Their leading men had been knighted and the

233

daughters of those leading men were rich matches for the sons of the nobility. Their property was great and their charities munificent. But they had reached a plateau ...' In the next century they declined and yielded pride of place to the Exchanges and the Bank of England in the commercial life of London.

Overseas trade

It was necessary in these times for merchant vessels on long journeys to sail in fleets. The seas were too full of pirates for single vessels to venture alone. Hence, to encourage the growth of trade, the Crown gave monopolistic trading rights to large companies.

Also the Antwerp trade, although by no means risky, was practically monopolized by the Merchant Adventurers. They exported (what was virtually the only English exports of importance in the first half of the century) undyed woollen cloth. They were a regulated company, that is a sort of trading guild whose members traded with their own capital. To join you had to pay a large entry fee. The Merchant Adventurers were concentrated in London and loud were the protests of Hull and Southampton merchants at their monopolizing the trade. But it suited the government to have some regulation over such an important trade and to deal with one body to apply such regulation. 'A cottage weaver who could not sell his cloth might be unable to buy bread; and a small town clothier in the same situation might have to dismiss his workmen, producing famine and riot. It was therefore the Privy Council's policy to insist that every year when the cloth was brought to Blackwell Hall in London, the merchants should buy it, whether they had any sale for it or not.'*

In the first half of the century then, until the English cloth crisis of 1551, English overseas trade was centred mainly on Antwerp, and its profits went mainly to the Merchant Adventurers. The Adventurers 'shipped their cloth jointly in periodic fleets to the four great annual marts at Antwerp' or to two or three of them. Profits were high. One merchant's accounts (Sir Thomas Gresham's) in Edward VI's reign show a profit of nearly fifteen per cent. About twenty London merchants seem to have monopolized about half the trade.

This was the happy state of affairs until 1551 when the Antwerp market suddenly reached saturation point and the trade collapsed. It was simply a matter of over-production after the boom years of 1542–1550, but the successive debasements of the coinage in England aggravated the situation as did religious persecution in the Netherlands by Charles V. The serious financial situation which ensued with clothiers going bankrupt and weavers out of work showed the folly of 'putting all one's commercial eggs in one basket'.†

One result of this trade collapse, as we saw in Chapter 8, was to make

* See Conrad Russell, *op. cit.*, p. 23.
† See Peter Ramsey, *op. cit.*, p. 68.

234

English merchants look elsewhere for overseas markets, such as Morocco. Here at the western end of the Mediterranean, after Wyndham's voyage of 1551, there developed a small trade in which mainly sugar was imported and mainly cloth exported. An attempt was made to regulate it in 1585 in a company known as the Barbary Company, but this lapsed after a life of only twelve years.

The first English joint-stock company was the Muscovy Company, formed, as we saw in Chapter 8, in Edward VI's reign. Its trade was not substantial. In 1587, 'the peak year of Elizabeth's reign, ten ships brought cargoes of tallow, wax, cordage, flax and hides from St Nicholas'. There was little demand for English cloth in Russia, and foodstuffs and wines were the main exports.

The Levant Company was formed on a joint-stock basis in 1581, taking over some of the East Mediterranean trade which Venice had previously handled. It prospered from the start, exporting grain and fish beside some tin and lead. The Sultan gave the English merchants some trading rights, but they needed a strong convoy system to ward off the attacks of corsairs from Algiers and Tripoli. They established factories at Smyrna and Aleppo and by 1599 had twenty ships in Italian waters alone.

'The second half of the century saw a revival of English trade in the Baltic.'* The Hanseatic League was now on the decline and by 1560 English merchants were handling most of the exports of English cloth to north-east Germany. In 1579 this trade was regulated by the formation of the Eastland Company, which gave the merchants protection against piracy and generally looked after their interests. The Eastland Company prospered reasonably well, but it was the Dutch who captured most of the Baltic trade from the Hansards, and by the end of the century more than eighty per cent of the ships passing through the Danish Sound were Dutch.

In 1591 some Levant Company merchants attempted a voyage to India. It was not a success, but successful Dutch expeditions to the same area tempted them to try again and in 1600 they obtained a charter to found the East India Company.

Thus in the second half of the century English overseas trade had begun to spread to new areas of the globe—to the Mediterranean, the Baltic, the White Sea and India. 'But the importance of these new markets must not be exaggerated.' An analysis of London customs accounts in 1587–1588 show some seventy per cent of the entries to come from ports on the north European coast between Hamburg and Rouen. The old trade routes of the Merchant Adventurers were thus still the main ones for British woollens. What had changed was that English broadcloths no longer monopolized the trade. The 'new draperies', developed around Norwich by Flemish and Walloon refugees from religious persecution, were forming a greater proportion of exports. These cheaper, lighter fabrics were obviously welcome in warm climates, and in James

* *Ibid.*, p. 71.

235

I's reign were to overtake broadcloths as the dominant English exports.

Despite these changes it is hard to be sure whether or not by the end of the century the total of English overseas trade had reached the heights it had attained in the great days of the Merchant Adventurers before the crash of 1551.*

Elizabeth's revenue

'The Tudor monarchy was expensive and, under Henry VIII at least, extravagant. Splendour of the court; building of new palaces; the proper and necessary cost of the navy and of munitions; a more elaborate administrative machinery, no longer run by clerics who were paid in benefices, and an organized diplomacy, all were costly.'† The national finance was still the private finance of the crown. In the Armada year the revenue of the crown came to £392,000. Out of this £148,000 came from Rents and Revenues, the Duchy of Lancaster and the Court of Wards—the ancient landed and feudal income of the crown. Much of the rest was customs, including a sum of £102,000 paid over by the farmers of the customs, merchants who, in return for payment of a lump sum, had the right of collecting certain customs.

The 'extraordinary' revenue consisted mainly of £88,000 from subsidies (money voted especially by Parliament). The subsidy was a tax on land and chattels. It was levied mainly on the rich. Many of these, however, escaped, for, if they had newly acquired their wealth, it probably would not have been taken into the valuation. Bacon said, and he was probably right, that the Englishman was 'the least bitten in the purse' (the least taxed) 'of any nation in Europe'. 'No wonder', says Clapham, 'that great men built splendid houses and lesser men rebuilt strong-timber manors in "brick or hard stone". Even the humblest, hard hit as he was if living by wages, had some reason to remember good Queen Bess; for as nearly as possible he paid no taxes.' Ale and cider were tax free. Except for salt and salt-fish which paid a small poundage, 'hardly anything he ever consumed paid customs'.

Poor relief

We hear much in the literature of Tudor times of 'sturdy beggars', men who terrified villages, wanderers without homes. We have considered, earlier in this chapter, the causes of this phenomenon.

Town councils were the first to try to deal with the problem. London began the licensing of beggars—a thousand of them—in 1517.

The suppression of the monasteries did some harm, but the haphazard charity the monasteries had given had bred beggars as well as relieved them. Confiscation of the religious endowments of the guilds in Edward

* I am indebted to Peter Ramsey, *op. cit.*, for much of the information in this section.
† See Sir John Clapham, *op. cit.*, p. 285.

236

VI's reign possibly did more harm, for the guilds maintained charitable houses in the towns, where they were most needed.

'Rapidly soaring food prices rose far more than the wages of the town artisan who lived on his wages and there is little doubt that his standard of living deteriorated sharply, if not catastrophically' in this century. 'Further removed from the soil, the urban labourer was worse off than his agrarian counterpart in time of harvest failure and acute dearth. It was on this submerged class that the first and harshest impact of the famines of the 1590s fell...'.*

Private charity was the first to try and deal with the problem of urban poverty, providing in many towns almshouses and casual doles for the poor. Next the town councils themselves began to play a part (by about the middle of the century) and finally the government interfered. Thus we find Exeter establishing a bridewell (or workhouse) in 1579 in accordance with the Poor Law Act of 1576.

In London, of course, the problem of poverty was terrible. Many merchants endowed almshouses, and Henry VIII and Edward VI founded the five royal hospitals—St Bartholomew's, St Thomas's, Christ's Hospital, Bridewell and Bedlam.

Early Tudor poor laws were harsh. An act of 1531 ordered the impotent poor to be given a licence to beg by the local JP, but able-bodied vagrants were to be whipped at the cart-tail and then sent back to their parishes. An act of 1536 ordered the support of the impotent poor and the provision of work for able-bodied vagrants. Children found begging were to be taken from their parents and put to service.

All this was very fine, but there were no funds available to do these things, and, although the act empowered church wardens to collect funds, payment was voluntary and therefore mostly not forthcoming.

Finance was indeed the difficulty. JPs were continually being exhorted by the Council 'charitably to persuade and move their neighbours'. In 1563 the JPs were empowered at last to imprison those who refused a poor rate, when they demanded it.

In 1572 came another act. It made a compulsory poor rate binding on all parishes. It instructed 'the unpaid and overworked justices to see to the appointment year by year of parish overseers of the poor—also unpaid'.

In 1576 a further act empowered the justices to spend public money on stocks of raw material (wool and flax usually) to 'set the poor on work'. Every county was to set up a House of Correction for the undesirable poor, a place where they could be made to work.

In the last decade of the century—that unhappy decade with its very high food prices, its long war with Spain and consequent difficulty of selling cloth abroad (at least at Antwerp)—the poor law was codified. 'The best brains of the times' were behind this codification—Burghley and Archbishop Whitgift, Bacon and Coke. An act of 1597 ordered

*See Peter Ramsey, *op. cit.*, p. 109.

overseers to be appointed in every parish. A compulsory rate was to be levied. Children were to be apprenticed to a trade (girls until twenty-one, boys, like other apprentices, until twenty-four). The impotent were to be looked after. Those capable of it were to be set to work and tools and materials provided for them. In a separate act it was stated that those who would not work were to be sent to Houses of Correction, where they would be forced to.

The act of 1597 was an experiment. It was voted for three years. But in 1601 it was renewed in all essentials and became the basis of the British poor law system right up to 1834.

There is evidence to show, however, that Tudor poor law was more impressive on paper than in fact. Careful study of parish accounts for Elizabeth's reign has shown that a poor rate was levied only in times of dire emergency. 'The available evidence suggests that only ten or eleven levies were made annually throughout England in the period 1550–1600 and the sum disbursed in poor relief was a little under £12,000.'* It was a private charity that bore almost the entire burden of poor relief right down to 1660, and 'for a long time the great Elizabethan Poor Law operated only sporadically when famine and distress forced JPs and parish officers to make use of it'. It has been estimated that down to 1660 only seven per cent of the money devoted to poor relief was raised by taxation.

18 Music, Art, Literature and Science

Music

Music played an important part in Renaissance philosophy. 'Before Descartes had reduced the physical universe to a mass of particles in motion, and Newton had postulated the force of gravitation as the arbiter of those particles, rhythm was the principle invoked to explain the creation and movements of the heavenly bodies. Sun, moon and stars whirled round the earth to the music of the spheres, which governed their speeds and motions and prevented their colliding'.†

Here is a poem, written by Sir John Davies in 1596, which shows the underlying belief in the universe as a 'huge choral dance'.

> Dauncing (bright Lady) then began to be,
> When the first seedes whereof the world did spring,
> The Fire, Ayre, Earth, and water did agree,
> By Loves perswasion,—Nature's mighty King,—

---

* *Ibid.*, p. 161.
† See *Music and Poetry of the English Renaissance* by Bruce Pattison, Methuen, 1970—a most helpful book on this subject and one from which I quote frequently in this section.

To leave their first disordered combating;
And in a daunce such measure to observe,
As all the world their motion should preserve.

Since when, they still are carried in a round,
And changing, come one in anothers place;
Yet doe they neither mingle nor confound,
But every one doth keepe the bounded space
Wherein the Daunce doth bid it turn or trace;
This wondrous myracle did Love devise,
For dauncing is Loves proper exercise.

In those days people really did believe that on a bright, starry night
you could hear the ringing of the 'ten translucent and concentric globes
or spheres' which surrounded the earth and whose movements accounted
for the motion of the sun, moon and planets; thus, if music governed
the universe, rhythm must be the necessary thing controlling affairs
of state; or, to put it another way, 'the state could only prosper when
the different interests in it danced to a common tune'.

Gentlemen's and noblemen's sons therefore were taught music as a
necessary introduction to the understanding and conduct of public
affairs. Moreover, personal character was thought, to be improved by
a study of music, which was believed to maintain 'the contradictory parts
of the personality in ordered relationship' and so to stimulate 'to virtuous
action and serene contemplation'.

Here is a passage from Castiglione's *Courtier* (mentioned in Chapter
3):

'For I shall enter in a large sea of the praise of Musicke, and call to
rehearsal how much it hath always been renowned among them of olde
time, and counted a holy matter: and how it hath been the opinion of
most wise Philosophers, that the worlde is made of musicke, and the
heavens in their moving make a melodie, and our soule is framed after
the very same sort and therefore lifteth up it selfe, and (as it were) revi-
veth the vertues and force of it selfe with Musicke ... and I remember
I have understoode that Plato and Aristotle will have a man that is well
brought up, to be also a Musition: and declare with infinite reasons the
force of musicke to bee to very great purpose in us, and for many causes
... ought necessarily to be learned from a man's childhood, not onely
for the superficiall melodie that is heard, but to be sufficient to bring
into us a new habite that is good, and a custome inclining to vertue,
which maketh the minde more apt to the conceiving of felicitie, even
as bodely exercise maketh the bodie more lustie, and not onely hurteth
not civil matters and warrelike affaires, but is a great stay to them.' *

Fortified by such counsels the nobility of the sixteenth century
'devoted itself to music with more fervour than any class at any other

* Translation by Sir Thomas Hoby, Everyman edition.

time in English history. . . . Patronage of composers and performers by the great was regarded as an obligation of gentility'.

Shakespeare in *The Merchant of Venice* makes Lorenzo say:

The man that hath no music in himself,
Nor is not moved with concord of sweet sounds,
Is fit for treasons, strategems and spoils.

No wonder young ladies were all taught to play on the lute or virginals, and 'gallants and dandies affected an interest in music', even if they did not possess it.

The Court set a good example. Henry VII did not stint his Chapel Royal (founded in the early fifteenth century), while Henry VIII, a composer and performer himself, not only 'maintained a large staff of secular musicians in his household', but also 'played the lute well, sang his part at sight, and saw that his children were taught music early'. Elizabeth kept an establishment of sixty to seventy musicians at court.

'The great houses emulated the court.' The Earl of Northumberland in 1512 kept a chapel establishment of ten men and six boys, besides trumpeters and other instrumentalists for secular music. Many other great noblemen did likewise. Often noble households included a musical instructor to teach the young gentlemen pages who came to the household for their education (for it was a common thing for boys of good family to be boarded out in aristocratic houses at a tender age).

Nor was this interest in music confined to the aristocracy. By the second half of the century more and more middle-class families were taking to music, as is shown by the number of madrigal books printed. (Madrigals were Italian in origin, not native to the English, and thus were not sung by the common people.) We have evidence that yeoman and merchant families, towards the end of the century, often held musical evenings in which these intricate part-songs were sung. '''Tis a singing age' comments one of the characters in a play by Fletcher, and we must agree with him.

The Chapel Royal at the beginning of our period 'had become a nursery where English composers developed their technical skill and their creative power'. In the reign of Henry VIII the 'English school was enriched by Flemish influences' and we have a great name in John Taverner (*c.* 1495–1545) who became Master of the Children of Cardinal College in 1526. He is really the last of the old Catholic school of church composers which was broken off by the Reformation.*

Leading figures in the Reformation school of church music were Christopher Tye (1497–1572), who was master of the choirboys at Ely, and Thomas Tallis (1505?–1585), one-time organist at Waltham Abbey and then a Gentleman of the Chapel Royal. They gave church music a new simplicity. Late medieval church music had drowned the words in long runs and ornaments. The Protestants were determined 'that the liturgy

* *The Listener's History of Music* by Percy A. Scholes, Oxford University Press, 1955, gives good accounts of all the chief Tudor composers.

should be heard distinctly'. The 'masses and motets disappeared' and the 'fitting of the music to the words became of supreme importance'. Cranmer in a letter to the King in 1544 declared that 'the song that shall be made for the English service would not be full of notes, but, as near as may be, for every syllable a note, so that it may be sung distinctly and devoutly'. Several of Tye's and Tallis's anthems are still used today.

William Byrd (1543–1623), a pupil of Tallis's, is another great name, probably the greatest among musicians in sixteenth-century England. He was at one time organist at Lincoln; then he moved to the Chapel Royal. Like Tallis he composed some fine church music, but he also took an interest in the secular music which was beginning to arrive from Italy, and in 1588 he published a book of songs which were set, like madrigals, with all parts to be sung by voices. Byrd also wrote some lovely keyboard music for the virginals.

The madrigal was a compromise between the art of the Netherlands and Italian tradition. It blossomed in England at the end of the century. The first English volume to bear the word 'madrigal' on its title page is Thomas Morley's *Madrigalls to Foure Voyces* (1594). Madrigals came late in England, but perhaps the composers were waiting for the poets, like Sidney and Spenser, to adapt themselves to the New Poetry, which also came from Italy. Morley (1577–1602), described by Pattison as 'the first English composer to feel completely at home in the Italian style of the madrigal', composed the music for Shakespeare's lyric, *It Was a Lover and his Lass*.

Another fine composer was John Dowland (1563–1626). His *First Book of Songes or Ayres* was published in 1597. An air was a song for solo voice with an accompaniment which was purely harmonic with no contrapuntal themes. Dowland was lutanist at the Danish court for a time, though he returned to England in 1606.

All these were professional musicians, but the next great song-writer, Thomas Campion (died 1619), was an amateur. He was a physician who had been educated at Cambridge and Gray's Inn and had studied medicine abroad, but he was also a composer and poet of great merit who set his own lyrics to music. Any anthology of the world's great songs today must surely include at least one song by each of Morley, Dowland and Campion.*

While courtiers and gentlemen sang madrigals, the common people sang ballads, which were popular songs, often set to tunes composed by London composers like Dowland.

The dances of the court at this period, pavans and galliards, were slow and stately. Country dances, danced to the tune of a fiddle, were more lively and, towards the end of the century, they too became popular at court. Queen Elizabeth was an enthusiastic dancer. The Spanish ambassador 'sarcastically reported that in the Twelfth Night revels of 1599 "the

* *The Hundred Best Short Songs*, published by Paterson's of Edinburgh, a fine collection, certainly does.

head of the Church of England and Ireland was to be seen in her old age dancing three or four galliards"'. But then, as explained at the beginning of this chapter, dancing was in those times considered much more important and significant than it is today.

To sum up then—there is only a little music of high worth being composed in England in the early part of the century. What there is is church music, chiefly produced under the auspices of the Chapel Royal. But, with the arrival of, first Netherlands, and then Italian influence, there is a great flowering, not only of church but also of secular music, until, at the end of the century, we have the finest school of composers that has ever been seen in England (comparable to the contemporary Italian school, in which Palestrina is the main name). One can easily mention even more names. John Bull (1562–1628), a Gentleman of the Chapel Royal and one-time Professor of Music at Gresham College in the City, has left some fine virginal and organ music. Giles Farnaby (c. 1560–c. 1600), of whose life we know very little, is considered by one authority 'the most attractive keyboard writer of the period'. His works are 'increasingly played'. Thomas Weelkes and John Wilbye (both born about 1574) were both great madrigalists. Truly the English Renaissance had reached its full splendour.

Poetry

English poetry at the beginning of the period 'was at a low ebb; the successors of Chaucer had been ponderous and dull'.* The only two poets of any worth were Alexander Barclay and John Skelton. Both were churchmen. Skelton was educated at Cambridge and was for a time tutor to the young prince who later became Henry VIII. He was employed by the Norfolk family to attack Wolsey in satirical verse and, not surprisingly, ended his days in sanctuary in Westminster Abbey (1529). His lines are slow and ponderous but in recent years there has been a big revival in his popularity. Here are a few lines from his poem on Wolsey:

He is not so high
In his hierarchie,
Of frantic frenesy
And foolish phantasy,
That in the Chamber of Stars
All matters there he mars.
Clapping his rod in the Board,
No man dare speak a word;
For he hath all the saying,
Without any renaying.
He rolleth in his records,

* I am indebted to Professor Mackie's *The Earlier Tudors* for much information in this and the next section.

242

And saith 'How say ye, my lords?
Is not my reason good?...'
He ruleth all the roost
With bragging and with boast ...

Later in the reign of Henry VIII the influence of Italy begins to be felt. It also becomes the fashion (derived from France) for poetry to be considered 'a part of knightly accomplishment'. Two good poets stand out, Sir Thomas Wyatt and Henry Howard, Earl of Surrey (the latter, it will be remembered, was executed in the last year of the reign). Wyatt had been to Italy, where sonnets had first been written (by Petrarch) and where poetry was being written to be sung to the lute, as Greek poetry was sung to the lyre. Wyatt's and Surrey's poetry perhaps contained no deep feeling, but they 'introduced into English verse the personal note and ... restored a sense of music and form which had been absent from it since Chaucer died'. Here is the first verse of one of Wyatt's poems:

My lute awake! Perform the last
Labour that thou and I shall waste,
And end that I have now begun;
For when this song is said and past,
My lute be still for I have done.

Wyatt and Surrey were the first English poets to write sonnets.

In Elizabeth's reign we have a great blossoming of poetry, which begins with Sir Philip Sidney (1554–1586) and Edmund Spenser (1552–1599) and ends with Shakespeare. Sidney might have excelled Spenser had he not been killed on the field of Zutphen before his genius reached its full effulgence. He is the author of perhaps the most beautiful love-poem in the English language, which begins 'My true love hath my heart and I have his'. Spenser lived to complete his masterpiece, *The Faerie Queene*, which has been described as 'the only poem in the language that a lover of poetry can sincerely wish longer'. Both Sidney and Spenser were influenced by the New Poetry which had spread from Italy to France. Sidney visited Paris in 1572 and probably met Ronsard, a poet who followed the new Greek-inspired Renaissance trend. Spenser was much inspired by the Italian poets, Ariosto and Tasso, who were his contemporaries. *The Faerie Queene* is an allegory, in which knights go forth to do battle with the moral evils of the world, each knight possessing the particular virtue needed to overcome his adversary. It is a poet's protest against the squalor and meanness of ordinary life. E. de Selincourt wrote of Spenser, 'He recreated English prosody, giving back to our verse the fluidity and the grace that it had lost since the days of Chaucer, and extending the range of its achievement.' * Spenser's influence on the English poets of the next three centuries is thought to have been very great, and it has been said of him, 'The true memorial to

* See the Introduction to *Spenser's Poetical Works*, Oxford University Press.

243

Spenser is to be read in the work of his successors.' Though English by birth, Spenser spent most of his working life in Ireland, where he held various government posts, and something of the beauty and the sadness of that country invests his later poems.

Finally, at the end of the century we have Michael Drayton (1563–1631) and Shakespeare himself (1564–1616). The latter is not only the greatest dramatist the modern world has known, but also the greatest sonneteer in English literature (unless you insist on Milton as greater).

Drama

Unlike poetry, drama had no Chaucer to set a standard for it. All that came down from the Middle Ages were miracle plays and pageants. In cities, such as York or Lincoln, the various craft guilds would take wagons round the streets at festivals, such as Christmas, and act little episodes or parables from the Bible on them. Thus the York miracle plays (recently revived) include one on the parable of the sheep and the goats (*Matt.* 25, vv. 31–46), vividly enacted with the devils rushing on at the end to take the people who, when 'I was an hungered ... gave me no meat', to hell. These miracle plays certainly inc'ıded some very vigorous prose and blank verse, but they were only short ـketches, lasting perhaps ten to fifteen minutes.

In Henry VIII's reign there was a great deal of pageantry, but really very little that could be called drama. Sir Thomas More's household contained a group, including More himself, which had a taste for acting 'interludes', which were little more than dramatic dialogues.

In drama, as in poetry and music, inspiration came from Italy and from the classical tradition. At Oxford and Cambridge and the Inns of Court play-acting, inspired by classical authors such as Seneca, became popular after the middle of the century. Also enlightened schoolmasters like Richard Mulcaster, first headmaster of Merchant Taylors, saw the educational opportunities of drama in teaching Latin, and got their pupils to act classical plays. Nicholas Udall, Headmaster of Eton, actually wrote the first English comedy constructed on a classical model—*Ralph Roister Doister*. Then in 1560 Cambridge produced 'a roaring farce', *Gammer Gurton's Needle*.

After 1575 two streams may be detected. First Elizabeth's Court grew very fond of drama and we have the plays of John Lyly. Second, and more important, outside the Court companies of players were formed under the patronage of various noblemen, and public theatres came to be built. The first of these was the *Theatre* in Shoreditch (1576), but the hostility of the City (to such lewd goings-on) led soon to the founding on the South Bank of the *Rose*, the *Swan* and finally the *Globe* (1598). 'Conditions were ripening for the outburst of genuine dramatic writing. The theatres, public and players existed; noble and even royal patronage

244

smiled on the play; the example of ancient Romans and modern Italians had transformed the interlude.' *

Thomas Kyd (1558–1595?) was the first of the great school of dramatists which now arose. His *Spanish Tragedy* (1586) is a 'drama of the horrific type', full of corpses. Kyd was soon outclassed by Christopher Marlowe (1564–1593), who added to drama something which Kyd had not possessed, magnificent blank verse. His four great plays are *Tamburlaine the Great*, *Doctor Faustus*, the *Jew of Malta* and *Edward II*. Soon after the last was written (1592) Marlowe was killed in a tavern brawl, aged only twenty-nine. Marlowe's plays have a grandeur and singleness of purpose which make it possible he might have equalled Shakespeare himself, had he lived.

All the English dramatists before Shakespeare were university men, as indeed were the poets and other writers of this period. But Shakespeare (1564–1616) came from 'the despised actor community'. He started with some rather mediocre plays, *Love's Labour's Lost*, *The Comedy of Errors*, *Two Gentlemen of Verona*, and the three parts of *Henry VI*, but between 1592 and the end of the century he wrote most of his historical plays, *King John*, *Richard II*, *Richard III*, *Henry IV* and *Henry V* and the great romantic comedies, *The Merchant of Venice*, *Much Ado About Nothing*, *As You Like It*, *Twelfth Night*, *The Merry Wives of Windsor* and *The Taming of the Shrew*, besides *Midsummer Night's Dream* and *Romeo and Juliet*. The great tragedies were to come later, in the reign of James I.

Shakespeare was only one of a whole school of dramatists which includes, besides Marlowe, Ben Jonson, Thomas Dekker, John Webster, Francis Beaumont and John Fletcher. He overtops them all, but, if he had not lived, they would have represented a formidable dramatic school on their own, comparable perhaps with the best periods of French or Russian drama.

Prose

In prose there is little to report in the first half of the sixteenth century in the secular field. More's *Utopia* (1516) is outstanding, but it was written in Latin and published abroad. The Bible translators, however, particularly William Tyndale, wrote magnificent prose, and they were soon followed by Thomas Cranmer and his Prayer Book. More's *Utopia* and his *Historie of Kyng Richarde the Thirde* appeared in 1557 in English, both in a fine prose style. In the second half of the century we have William Camden, the antiquarian, who travelled all round England describing it patiently county by county and borough by borough. His *Britannia* was published in 1586 in Latin, but soon afterwards appeared in English. Camden was a schoolmaster and clergyman. His dates were 1551–1623, and in James I's reign he was to publish his *Annals* of Elizabeth's reign, probably the finest historical work produced in England up to that time.

* G. R. Elton, *op. cit.*, p. 451.

In 1589 Hakluyt's *Voyages and Discoveries* appeared, to be greatly enlarged ten years later (*see* Chapter 14). Like Camden's *Britannia*, Hakluyt's work is a painstaking collection of facts, but both are written in attractive styles and are still read today. Next we have Hooker's *Ecclesiastical Polity* (already discussed in Chapter 16). The first five volumes appeared in the author's lifetime (he died in 1600). Here is an example of his clear and surprisingly modern style (a passage by the way which it behoves many of us to take to heart today):

'He that goeth about to persuade a multitude that they are not so well governed as they ought to be shall never want attentive and favourable hearers, because they know the manifold defects whereunto every kind of regiment is subject; but the secret lets and difficulties, which in public proceedings are innumerable and inevitable, they have not ordinarily the judgment to consider.'

Do we not hear in this passage the authentic forerunner of Burke himself?

Francis Bacon belongs really to the Stuart period rather than the Tudor, but his *Essays* were published in 1597 and are usually taken as models of English style with their short, crisp sentences, compactness of expression and use of simple, Anglo-Saxon words.

History

The Renaissance brought about a great change in the writing of history. Medieval historical works were merely chronicles, like that of Matthew Paris, a monk of St Albans, who wrote in the time of King John, or Froissart, the French chronicler, who wrote about the Hundred Years' War. These authors often gave eye-witness accounts, but they made little attempt to check their sources or to arrange their material in topics (foreign policy, finance etc.), or to develop any critical comment. In other words not very much thought went into their chronicles. Yet the ancient Greeks had produced great historians, like Herodotus and Thucydides, both of whom wrote history as thought-provoking as anyone could desire, while ancient Rome had produced Livy and Tacitus. Naturally the Renaissance meant a renewed study of the works of these classical historians. It also meant a great deal of research into documents, and it was not long before the Italians were discovering that many medieval manuscripts were forgeries. The most notable forgery discovered was the famous Donation of Constantine, whereby the first Christian Roman Emperor, on his retirement to his new capital on the Bosporus, was supposed to have left Rome, Italy and the West to Pope Sylvester and his successors in perpetuity. This was proved a forgery by fifteenth-century Italian humanists. Soon historians were arising in Italy who were able to write histories with a really critical approach. One such was the great Machiavelli.

The first man to write the new sort of history in England was an Italian called Polydore Vergil 'who came to England as a sub-collector of papal revenue in 1502, became a naturalized Englishman ... and, except for occasional visits to Italy, remained in his adopted country until the year 1551', when he retired to end his days in Italy. Since Polydore, at the time of his arrival, was already a writer of some repute, Henry VII asked him to write a history of England. He set to work with great energy and his *Anglica Historia* appeared in 1534 (in Latin of course). It was received 'with a storm of obloquy', for Polydore tore to ribbons some of the cherished myths of English history, especially those fostered by Geoffrey of Monmouth, whose *Historia Regum Britanniae*, written in the twelfth century, had been a wonderful mixture of truth and legend with King Arthur much in evidence.

It was a hundred years before 'this heretical assailant of the antiquity of Britain', as Professor Mackie calls Polydore, found a defender, but chroniclers like Edward Hall and Raphael Holinshed (who published their works in 1548 and 1578 respectively) made use of his work. We must wait, however, until early Stuart times before the first real works of history appear from the pens of Englishmen. These are Sir Walter Raleigh's *History of the World* (1614), Camden's *Annales Regnante Elizabetha* (1617) and Sir Francis Bacon's *Henry VII* (1622).

Shakespeare used Holinshed's Chronicles as the basis of most of his historical plays, which is why, though they are very good in their understanding of human nature, they are wrong in many of their facts.

Architecture

Tudor church architecture was still Gothic-inspired. It still had fan-vaulting and pointed arches, though the latter had become rather flat. The style is known as 'late-perpendicular'. Windows were large and their stone mullions ran straight most of the way up, unlike the intricate curved stone of the old 'decorated' style. A good example is the abbey church at Bath which was erected in the reign of Henry VII. Another is King Henry VII's chapel at Westminster, in which, Professor Mackie thinks, 'English architecture reached its supreme height'. Then the roof of King's College Chapel, Cambridge, with its elaborate fan-vaulting, was built in Henry VII's reign, though the chapel was begun by Henry VI. All this was done by English craftsmen (except some of the glass work which was probably Flemish), to whom the flattened Gothic arch no doubt offered a challenge in technique, being more difficult to build than the old, sharp-pointed arch.

For the recumbent statues in Henry VII's chapel an Italian sculptor, Pietro Torregiano, was called in.

It was a great time for towers. The central tower of Canterbury Cathedral was built in Henry VII's reign; so was the tower of Fountains Abbey in Yorkshire. Numerous church towers were built, while Magdalene tower at Oxford was begun in Henry VIII's reign.

Now that monasteries were out of favour, much charitable money was allotted to the building and endowing of colleges at Oxford and

Cambridge. At Oxford we have Brasenose, Corpus Christi and Cardinal College (which was founded by Wolsey and later renamed Christ Church), while Cambridge gained Jesus, Christ's, St John's (even today sometimes called Lady Margaret's after its founder, Henry VII's mother), Magdalene and Trinity. The gatehouses of John's and Trinity with their battlements and corner turrets are typical of Tudor domestic architecture. In the second half of the century there is a decrease of both university and church building, no doubt because of the Reformation. Nevertheless Oxford gained Jesus College and Cambridge Emmanuel.

In domestic architecture the style reflects the fact that the age was a safe one, because of good, strong government. Hence moats, defensive walls, draw-bridges and so on are out. The manor house replaces the castle, as it had already begun to do in the fifteenth century. Battlements survive as ornament. Windows are square, larger than before, and with numerous mullions and small panes of glass. In the bigger houses a lofty hall is an essential, but it is now graced often by great bay windows. (Sometimes, as the century progresses, the hall is divided into two or three stories by the insertion of floors.) Kitchen, buttery and pantry are close to the hall at one end, and at the other there are the living rooms (including usually a long gallery) and bed rooms, arranged in two or three stories, the whole often grouped round a courtyard of which the hall forms one side. Somewhere there is always a chapel, besides a dairy and brew-house, for 'almost all the food, drink and delicacies of the land-lord's family came off the estate'. As the century progressed and the need for fortifying a house was completely forgotten, 'it became usual to adopt an open courtyard with three sides only, or to adopt the E-shaped form'.

The construction of these manor houses varied according to the local materials available. In Gloucestershire, Yorkshire and Derbyshire, stone was used, but in most parts of the country timber-framed houses were normal, often with brick filling between. Sometimes, particularly in the east of England, where timber was in short supply, brick only was used, but to build in brick alone was still a new and difficult art.

Chimney stacks were inclined to be ornate, especially when made of brick. Professor Black sums up the style thus: 'high-pitched gables, wreathed chimneys, mullioned and transomed windows with leaded lights, heraldic devices over the doorways, oak-panelled rooms and central hall with open timbered roof'.

In the cities, where space was valuable, timber-framed houses usually had their upper stories overhanging the street, so that you could almost shake hands from the top storey with your neighbour across the way. In the country too the upper stories of a timber-framed house were usually corbelled out in this way. Tudor manor houses which still survive include Chastleton House and Broughton Castle in Oxfordshire, Dodd-ington Hall (Lincolnshire), Braemore House (Hampshire), Hardwick Hall (Derbyshire), Moreton Old Hall (Cheshire), Compton Wynyates (Warwickshire), Parham Park (Sussex), Sutton Place and Loseley Park

(Surrey), Montacute (Somerset) and Hoghton Tower (Lancashire), beside many others. Fine examples of Tudor town houses are still to be seen in Bristol, Glastonbury, Salisbury, Norwich and several other towns. There is a good one in Hereford which dates from early Stuart times.

One curious thing about Tudor manor houses is that they are seldom sited on a southern slope, it being a belief of the time that the south wind was unhealthy. Windows are for the same reason usually grouped on the north and east sides.

After the dissolution of the monasteries many abbeys were converted into manor houses. Typical is Buckland Abbey in Devon, which was converted to a dwelling house by Sir Richard Grenville. He 'swept away the domestic buildings of the abbey and built himself a mansion inside the church itself'. Later he sold the house, which then came into the hands of his great rival, Sir Francis Drake.

We should not leave the subject of Tudor domestic architecture without mentioning Hampton Court. It was built for Wolsey and was a vast palace made of brick. Wren later added a splendid wing, but the west-front, the base-court and the clock court with the great hall on one side of it, are today as Wolsey built them. With its 'fine hall, its courts, its high-pitched gables, its bay-windows and its gracious chimneys' Hampton Court is a good example of the Tudor style.

Was there then no Italian Renaissance building in England in this century? The answer to this question is, 'In general, no.' Some of the later manor houses, like Kirby Hall in Northants and Wollaton Hall near Nottingham, have been described as having a 'Gothic frame-work with a classical overlay', but on the whole the classical or 'italianate' style which was all the rage abroad in the sixteenth century was not fully received into England until Stuart times. The exceptions were Somerset House, built by the Protector, in the Strand, and Gresham's Royal Exchange in the City, built between 1566 and 1570 by a Flemish architect, using Flemish and German craftsmen. Both these were italianate in style, and the latter, with its marble floors, was intended to be an imitation of the great Bourse at Antwerp.

Common houses and the cottages of the poor 'were still of timber or half-timber with clay and rubble between the wooden uprights and cross-beams. William Harrison, the parson, writing in 1577 of the improvements which he had seen in his lifetime, noted that chimneys had become general even in cottages, whereas 'in the village where I remain', old men recalled that in their young days under the two Kings Harry "there were not above two or three chimneys, if so many, in uplandish towns [villages], the religious houses and manor places of their lords always excepted, but each one made his fire against a reredoss in the hall where he dined and dressed his meat."' * No doubt the increasing use of bricks made it easier to build chimneys.

* Quoted by G. M. Trevelyan in his *English Social History*.

Furniture

Furniture in Tudor times was on the whole rough and simple. Tables, benches, chairs and cupboards were usually made of oak (at least the ones that have come down to us were), and were often carved. Beds were something of a rarity, for the poor slept on straw palliasses, but the well-to-do often possessed large four-poster beds heavily carved in oak (and often, incidentally, mentioned in wills). Here is William Harrison describing in 1577 the great improvement in comfort which he has seen in his own lifetime:

'Our fathers yea and we ourselves have lien full oft upon straw pallets, covered only with a sheet, under coverlets made of dagswain or hop harlots and a good round log under their heads instead of a bolster. If it were so that our fathers or the good man of the house had a mattress or flockbed and thereto a sack of chaff to rest his head upon, he thought himself to be as well lodged as the lord of the town [village], that peradventure lay seldom in a bed of down or whole feathers. Pillows were thought meet only for women in childbed.'

Harrison also records during his own lifetime a change of 'treen [wooden] platters into pewter, and of wooden spoons into silver or tin'. Forks, which were known in Italy, had not yet been introduced into England.

Painting

It was a very fine age for portraiture (as also was the latter half of the fifteenth century), but as yet most of the artists who worked in England were foreigners, usually Italians, Germans or Flemings. Henry VII and Henry VIII both employed Flemish portrait painters. No doubt Henry VIII would have liked to secure the services of great Italians like Leonardo da Vinci, who graced the court of his rival, Francis, at Amboise, but he certainly obtained the next best thing when in 1536 Hans Holbein of Augsburg came to work at his court. Holbein had already worked in England for Sir Thomas More and painted many fine portraits of various important English personages. But in the seven years he worked at court before his death of the plague in 1543, he painted and drew the great series of portraits of the King, queens and courtiers 'which have made the age real to us'. He is one of the very great portrait painters of all time, and we certainly cannot match him anywhere in the world today. Some people think his portraits a little flat, but somehow he managed to make every face interesting and brought out the character of his sitter. I do not think any portrait artist, working in England, has since equalled him (with the possible exception of Van Dyck), and certainly Elizabeth's reign brought no one of equal power. For Holbein founded no school of portraiture in England. The portrait painters of Edward's, Mary's and Elizabeth's reigns were mostly Netherlanders or Italians. It was only the miniaturists of the second half of the century,

Nicholas Hilliard and Isaac Oliver, who developed a real English tradition, combining skill in portraiture with the vivid colouring, particularly blues and golds, of medieval illuminated manuscripts.

Education

Both Oxford and Cambridge were flourishing, as the new colleges already mentioned prove. But of the two it was Cambridge which more readily accepted the new ideas of the Renaissance. This was partly because Erasmus had taught at Cambridge and partly because the friars, who of course hated Greek and all the new-fangled learning, were stronger at Oxford. Thus, when Bishop Fox, Henry VII's minister, who had already founded Corpus Christi College, established a lectureship in Greek at Oxford, the 'Trojans', as they were called, opposed it. Wolsey, however, intervened and founded a readership in Greek and, later, six professorships to give public lectures in the new humanist fashion. It was after all Oxford which produced William Tyndale to whom we owe so much of our Bible.

It was, however, Cambridge which produced most of the great men of Tudor England, especially in the second half of the period. Cranmer was a Cambridge man. So was Gardiner. Bishops Ridley and Latimer both came from Cambridge.* So did Roger Ascham, Elizabeth's tutor, John Dee, the geographer, Walsingham and William Cecil (and indeed all the chief Elizabethan statesmen except Raleigh who went to Oxford, but never completed his time there). The poet, Edmund Spenser, was a Cambridge man.

Subjects taught at the universities were theology, civil law, the philosophy of Plato and Aristotle, medicine 'as expounded by Galen or Hippocrates', mathematics (including arithmetic, geometry and astronomy), dialectic, rhetoric, Greek and Hebrew. The teaching was done in Latin.

What of schools? Eton, Winchester and Westminster were already in existence at the beginning of our period. St Paul's, as we saw in Chapter 3, was founded by Colet in 1509—the first school to teach Greek. In 1552 we have Shrewsbury (useful for the sons of rich Welsh and Border squires) and in 1553 Christ's Hospital, founded for poor children of the area. Between 1559 and 1590 Repton, Rugby, Uppingham, Harrow and Merchant Taylors were founded. Some of these were endowed with money taken from the dissolution of the chantries or other old charities; some were endowed by local landowners or merchants. Occasionally, Parliament made a grant to found a school or improve an old foundation. Meanwhile up and down the country almost every corporate town had its grammar school, long since founded by some cathedral, monastery, chantry or guild, or perhaps by some wealthy fifteenth-century merchant, acting on his own. In these usually a master and an usher taught

---

* Hence Macaulay's remark that 'Cambridge had the honour of educating those celebrated Protestant bishops whom Oxford had the honour of burning'.

251

a few bright boys the rudiments of Latin. Usually these were the sons of yeomen, small gentry or burgesses. Shakespeare himself went to Stratford Grammar School, where he is supposed to have learned 'small Latin and less Greek'. We must assume that, like Winston Churchill, he was largely self-educated.

The greatest educationist of the age was, I suppose, Roger Ascham (1515–1568). The foremost Greek scholar of his day, this gentle schoolmaster was tutor to two queens (Lady Jane Grey and Elizabeth). Two years after his death his book, *The Scholemaster*, was published. It abounds in sound common sense and is still useful and instructive, probably much more so than much of the advice which our modern educationists produce.

After St Paul's had set the example, a few schools took up the teaching of Greek—Eton, Harrow, Westminster, Merchant Taylors and Shrewsbury among them. But Latin remained the basic subject taught. That progressive schoolmaster, Richard Mulcaster of Merchant Taylors, 'grounded his pupils in Hebrew, Greek and Latin; he trained them daily in music, both vocal and instrumental, and was a convinced advocate of the study of the mother tongue and of the educational value of acting. He presented plays yearly before the court, in which his boys were the actors, and "by that means taught, them good behaviour and audacity".' *

Lawyers were not trained in the universities, but in the four Inns of Court in London. This was because the common law was a living thing, continually changing, not static. At the Inns of Court 'besides taking part in mock trials and hearing discourses, he attended the great courts in Westminster Hall and saw how things were done'. After having served his time at his Inn, the student became a barrister, and, sixteen years after entering his Inn, he stood a chance of being selected by the Lord Chancellor as a *serjeant-at-law*. This was an expensive affair as he had to give a feast and make various presentations, but he now had the right of pleading in Common Pleas and of becoming perhaps 'one of the half-dozen justices who presided in each of the two great courts'—Common Pleas and King's Bench.

The Tudor period was a litigious one for the gentry. Land titles were less clearly defined than they are today and nearly all the gentry were concerned in a law-suit some time in their lives. Hence the sons of gentry very often finished off their education in an Inn of Court, sometimes having already attended Oxford or Cambridge.

Science

Science was one branch of human achievement in which the English played little part in Tudor times. It was a Polish astronomer, Copernicus, who in 1543 produced the theory that the planets moved round the sun,

* See the Introduction to *Spenser's Poetical Works*, Oxford University Press.

thus destroying or at least undermining Ptolemy's explanation of the universe as earth-centred, which had held the field for over fourteen hundred years. A few leading English thinkers, such as Dr John Dee, became enthusiastic Copernicans, but the average Elizabethan remained a believer in the Ptolemaic theory. Both Shakespeare and Hooker, it is apparent from their writings, believed in the old theory.

Most people likewise believed in astrology—that the stars affect the lives of men and that the sign of Zodiac under which you are born determines your nature and fate. Sir Walter Raleigh argued that there must be some meaning for mankind in the elaborate pattern of the stars in the heavens; why else was it put there? By the end of the century, however, belief in astrology was declining. Did not Shakespeare make Cassius say,

> The fault, dear Brutus, is not in our stars,
> But in ourselves, that we are underlings. ?

And in *King Lear* Edmund says,

> 'When we are sick in fortune,—often the surfeit of our own behaviour,—we make guilty of our disasters the sun, the moon and the stars: as if we were villains by necessity'.

As for that other bastard science, alchemy, here also there is a decline. But as late as 1564 Dr Dee was appointed the royal adviser in mystic secrets, including alchemy. Doubtless some alchemists practised with honest intent; 'but the great majority were sharks who preyed on the credulity and greed of an acquisitive age'. At the end of the century dramatists began to poke fun at alchemists, the greatest exposer of their deceits being Ben Jonson's play *The Alchemist* (1610).

In medicine, as in astronomy, great things were being done on the Continent, but the English played little part. For centuries the theories of the second-century Greek physician, Galen, had held the field. Now he was being steadily undermined. At Padua Vesalius, a Belgian professor, began the dissection of human subjects in the 1530s (it was frowned on by the Church) and created a new school of anatomical research. Soon Galen's theories, like Ptolemy's in astronomy, were toppling. Henry VIII gave a charter to the College of Physicians (1518) and one to the Company of Barber-Surgeons (1540), and he established professorships of medicine at both Oxford and Cambridge in 1547, but, despite these encouragements, Britain lagged behind, and in Elizabeth's reign those who wanted to study medicine preferred to go abroad to Padua, Montpellier, Basle, Heidelberg or Leyden. As late as 1577 the surgeon of St Bartholomew's Hospital published a treatise on anatomy using a fourteenth-century manuscript and making no mention of Vesalius!

The sale or purchase of drugs was still in the hands of apothecaries, whom nobody supervised. Shakespeare's description of the one from whom Romeo obtained his poison, is not reassuring. Many of them were probably little better than charlatans. Most mothers and grandmothers had their own herbal remedies which were handed down from mother to daughter.

APPENDIX A
Were the Tudors despots?

Much has been written in this book on the vexed question of the Tudor Constitution,* but perhaps it would be helpful to try and make a few things clearer. One has to ask oneself, where did power reside? How much resided with the King, how much with the House of Commons, how much with the great feudal lords, how much with the bishops, how much with great officials like the Lord Treasurer and the Lord Chancellor, how much with the judges? The answers to these questions are not easy and of course they vary from time to time as the century proceeds on its way. The greatest variation is caused by the personality of the monarch. Henry VIII was probably the strongest, Edward VI, being a minor, the weakest. Elizabeth was a good deal stronger than Mary.

We stated in Chapter 7 (p. 102) that the 'old idea of the "Tudor despotism" has now been rejected by historians'. This old idea was much favoured by John Richard Green, whose *Short History of the English People*, published in 1874, was the book upon which our late Victorian forefathers were reared. Green's theme was that 'at the close of the Wars of the Roses these older checks' on the power of the Crown (he meant the Church, the barons and the middle class) 'no longer served as restraints upon the action of the Crown. The baronage had fallen more and more into decay. The Church lingered helpless and perplexed, till it was struck down by Thomas Cromwell. The traders and the smaller proprietors sank into political inactivity. On the other hand the Crown, which only fifty years before had been the sport of every faction, towered into solitary greatness.'† Green called the chapter in which this passage occurred 'The New Monarchy'. His ideas held the field for a long time, but in the last twenty or thirty years historians (Professor G. R. Elton prominent among them) have torn them to shreds. These historians have pointed out that, far from being despots, the Tudors were recognized by their people as being under the law. They might only make laws of which the judges would take notice 'in Parliament'. They could only make important decisions 'in Council'. Far from being despots, they shared their power with an upper and an upper-middle class and had therefore to tread warily.

Besides, this school of historians point out, the Tudors could not have

---

* See the Introduction, sections on 'Law' and 'Parliament'; Chapter 2, sections on 'Henry's finance', 'The Kings Council', 'Conciliar jurisdiction' and 'Parliament and the Church'; Chapter 7, sections on 'Cromwell's achievement' and 'Administrative reforms'; Chapter 16, section on 'Elizabeth's Parliaments'.
† *A Short History of the English People* by J. R. Green, Macmillan.

been despots because they had 'no standing army, no adequate revenue, no effective administrative machinery, no reliable system of communication'—all things essential to a government which wishes to force its will on a nation. Therefore, it was argued, Tudor government could have survived only if it was based on the goodwill of the people.

In 1967 something of a reaction to these views set in with the publication of a famous pamphlet by Professor Joel Hurstfield, entitled *Was there a Tudor Despotism after all?**

Professor Hurstfield's theme is that there existed 'an enormous gap between the constitution and the political reality'. He points out that the Tudors could 'break by force every movement of political and religious dissent', they could and did muzzle the press (for everything printed had to be censored by the Church or by the Privy Council), they evolved a powerful machine which pumped out propaganda through press and pulpit and through proclamations read out in the market place, they controlled foreign policy as well as religious doctrine and practice, and they had ministers responsible to the Crown alone. All these things the Tudors did. It is true they had no standing army; yet they successfully quelled all rebellions against themselves, sometimes (as in 1549) hiring foreign mercenaries to do so.

Surely we must admit, despite these arguments, that the Tudors were not despots even 'in the political reality'. Numerous cases occur in which they were thwarted of their will by their own people. In 1489 the people of Yorkshire murdered the King's official, the Earl of Northumberland, when he was trying to collect a tax. A Parliamentary grant in 1497 led to a rebellion in Cornwall. Henry VIII had to abandon his war with France in 1524 because not enough money could be raised. He had to abandon his new war in 1525 because of the failure of the Amicable Grant. Then we have the rebellions in the time of Somerset which led to a change of government. We have Mary failing to get her husband crowned king, failing to pass bills restoring monastery lands (indeed she never dared even to introduce one), failing to get the money she needed for her war with France. We have Elizabeth bending to Parliament's wishes on more than one occasion—on the matter of the Church Settlement at the beginning of her reign, on the question of monopolies at the end, on the question of freedom of speech, when the Puritan 'choir' was in full voice.

There is ample evidence that Parliament could successfully oppose the sovereign. What of the Council? Here it is more difficult to be certain, because Council meetings took place in secret and we have not got the evidence from private diaries which throw so much light on later Tudor parliaments. Tudor sovereigns of course selected their own councillors and could at any time dismiss them. But this does not mean they could disregard them or treat them as mere servants. After all government would have broken down altogether if the great officials of state had de-

---

* Transactions of the Royal Historical Society, 1967.

cided not to co-operate. The navy could not function unless the Lord Admiral gave the orders. Revenue could not be collected without the help of the Lord Treasurer (who was head of the Exchequer), the Chancellor of the Duchy of Lancaster and the Treasurer of the King's Chamber. The judges and JPs could not be given orders except through the Lord Chancellor.

Mary would have liked to have declared war on France in the autumn of 1556, when Philip first requested it. When Philip returned to England in the spring of 1557, she desired it even more. But the Privy Council opposed the idea, and even when she threatened to dismiss most of the councillors, it remained adamant. Only in June 1557, after a French-sponsored raid on Scarborough, did it give way. In fact Mary was often opposed by Gardiner and other members of her Council. Wolsey at the height of his power dared to declare war on Spain in 1528 without consulting King or Council (and such was Henry's faith in Wolsey's skill in diplomacy that, when he was told, he let the declaration stand, despite the protests of other councillors);* but this declaration of war was only a diplomatic move, as we have seen, and fighting was not intended.

Elizabeth had eighteen men in her Privy Council in the spring of 1559. Ten of them had been privy councillors to Mary. She soon added others including Henry Cary, her cousin, a good soldier, whom she created Baron Hunsdon, and Sir Francis Knollys, a noted Puritan and husband of Henry Cary's sister. Her councillors often had opposing ideas about religion, but they regarded themselves more as civil servants than as politicians. Cecil, as Principal Secretary, was the only one daily concerned with foreign affairs. Most of the others had departmental duties. She seldom met her whole Privy Council in full and formal session—only indeed at moments of crisis. Usually she had the final say herself, and her foreign policy was hers rather than her Secretary's. Whether she could have overruled her whole Council if it was united against her is doubtful, but the situation never occurred, as far as we know.

If the sovereign thus found it difficult to act without the agreement of the Council, it is nevertheless true he could strike down any one councillor as he wished. Both Wolsey and Cromwell were dismissed by Henry VIII when their positions seemed unassailable.

Why, one wonders, did the legend of Tudor despotism ever grow in the minds of historians? It was surely because of the extraordinary power wielded against individuals by Henry VIII. Wolsey's and Cromwell's dismissals have already been noted. No less startling was the way he got rid of the Duke of Buckingham in 1521. Buckingham, the son of the great duke who rebelled against Richard III was High Constable of England, 'a nobleman in the grand manner . . . a great Welsh Marcher lord (the last of his kind) whose possessions straddled much of England, a magnate who rode with a large retinue',† who owned twelve castles and who was descended from Edward III. His mother, Catherine Woodville, had

* See R. B. Wernham, *op. cit.*, pp. 118 and 230.
† J. J. Scarisbrick, *op. cit.*, p. 121.

been a sister of Edward IV's queen, his wife was a Percy, his son had married a Pole, his daughters had married respectively the Earl of Surrey, the Earl of Westmorland and Lord Bergavenny. Such a man might well have seemed impregnable in his position. Yet he was arraigned before a panel of his peers in Westminster Hall and found guilty of treason. Doubtless the jury, which included the dukes of Norfolk and Suffolk, acted in fear and for favour of the King.

Yet, when religious passions ran high after Wyatt's rebellion, a London jury acquitted Sir Nicholas Throckmorton of complicity in the rebellion 'in defiance of the evidence and to the cheers of the spectators'. But it was, as Professor Wernham points out, an 'almost unheard-of occurrence' for the accused to be acquitted in a Tudor treason trial.

Buckingham had of course been an enemy of Wolsey. The other duke who was struck down by Henry, the Duke of Norfolk, had survived both Wolsey's enmity and Cromwell's. In fact he had ousted both of them. In the end he was attainted by Parliament. Certainly, if the king wanted to get rid of a man, he could usually manage it, but that does not mean he could have turned against a whole number of powerful aristocrats and overwhelmed them. He needed the help of the rest to overthrow the one he was proposing to eliminate. The great feudal aristocrats were still rich and powerful, though the invention of gunpowder had made their castles no longer impregnable and the acts against retaining passed by Henry VII could be invoked against them if their retinues grew too long. It is noticeable that there was nearly always a Howard or a Herbert in the Privy Council right through the century, just as there was always a Portman or a Luttrell on the bench of JPs in Somerset, for it would have been difficult to govern Somerset without the co-operation of these two families.*

Yes, the great magnates still retained a great deal of power. We noticed in Chapter 1 (section on 'Rebellion') that Henry VII was lucky at the beginning of his reign to have to deal with a weakened aristocracy, owing to attainders, confiscation of property and minorities. In the reign of Elizabeth there was only one rebellion of the old nobility (that of 1569) and that was a half-hearted one. It seemed to be the House of Commons which chiefly opposed the Queen. But this is misleading. Many members of the Commons were sons and brothers of lords. Since the bishops and privy councillors, if they all voted together, could almost command a majority in the Lords, a back-bench lord who wanted to voice a protest often did it through his brother or son in the Commons. Thus the Puritan Earl of Huntingdon might protest through his brother, Sir Francis Hastings, in the Commons more effectively than if he spoke himself in the Upper House. The Lords' influence over the composition of the Commons lasted all through the sixteenth century, for many an MP owed his seat to the influence of a lord and this might carry obligations.†

We should be cautious in attributing too much power to the Eliza-

* See Conrad Russell, *op. cit.*, p. 42.
† *Ibid.*, pp. 41 and 220.

bethan House of Commons. Remember it could not construct policy. It could only obstruct.

Let the wise Sir Thomas More have the last word on the question of the king's power. 'Master Cromwell', he once said, 'you are now entered into the service of a most noble, wise and liberal prince. If you will follow my poor advice, you shall, in your counsel-giving unto his Grace, ever tell him what he ought to do but never what he is able to do. ... For if a lion knew his own strength, hard were it for any man to rule him.'

Luther was more outspoken. 'Junker Heintz will be God', he said, 'and does whatever he lusts.'

Before our period Richard III overthrew one baronial rebellion (Buckingham's) and succumbed to another one, which received foreign aid. It was to be nearly forty years after the death of the last Tudor that the monarchy was again overthrown, and this time the rebellion was not of the great feudal lords, but of a Parliamentary opposition in which the merchants played a large part. In the century and a half which intervenes between these two events the comparatively strong and stable government of the Tudors gave institutions like Parliament and the Privy Council a chance to grow and develop, to gain traditions and administrative procedures.

The breach with Rome gave Tudor sovereigns control over the bishops, whom, as Supreme Governor of the Church, they could both appoint and dismiss (or suspend), but this in turn brought new dangers from abroad and, as the threat of foreign invasion by Catholic powers grew, the government's dependence on Parliament increased, as it was continually in need of money. Parliaments were rare in Henry VII's reign and under Wolsey. From the time of the Reformation Parliament onwards they were more frequent and increasingly hard to handle. Elizabeth needed to be vigilant in her management of the Commons 'if government measures were to be passed and the royal initiative preserved'.*

A contemporary French jurist, Jean Bodin, attempted to discover where sovereignty lay in Elizabethan England and he did not find it easy. Men still read the works of Sir John Fortescue, the fifteenth-century judge, and rejoiced in the powers of the Common Law; but the prerogative courts, Star Chamber, High Commission and the Court of Wards and Liveries, were flourishing, though as yet, except by a few unfortunates like the Puritan, John Penry, they were regarded as aids to quick justice rather than the engines of tyranny they became under the Stuarts.

There were frequent treason trials in Elizabeth's reign and martial law was used to punish the followers of the Northern Earls in 1569. But Elizabeth never had the bloody reputation of her father or her half-sister, Mary. 'I was never horse-leech for blood', she once wrote. She was

---

* The quotation is from *Elizabeth I* by B. W. Beckingsale, Batsford, 1963, p. 71, a book which gives a valuable summary of the Queen's powers (pp. 142–143).

careful to show respect for the Common Law and, unlike James I, never dismissed a judge for an unwelcome ruling. With her common sense and her genius for compromise she worked hard at the task of governing and on the whole the English people were happy to be ruled by her. Her death, however, left a terrible gap and we are bound to agree with Sir Thomas Wentworth in the next century when he declared the monarchy was 'the keystone of the arch of government'. But this does not mean it was the whole of the arch.

APPENDIX B
The Fall of Empson and Dudley

At the accession of Henry VIII, in accordance with Henry VII's will, 'persons with claims of debts and injuries were invited to apply for remedy'.*

As a result the Council was overwhelmed with claims for the redress of injustices. 'To still the outcry Empson and Dudley were placed in the Tower.' Also, a Great Council was summoned, the first since 1496, and, a month later, commissions of *oyer* and *terminer* were sent round the country to inquire into crimes and disorder and (significantly) into breaches of Magna Carta and other statutes of the realm. As a result of these commissions several lords had their recognizances, imposed by Henry VII, cancelled. It appears probable that the sending out of these commissions was initiated by the Great Council, and that what had in fact taken place was a revival of aristocratic power, led by the Duke of Buckingham, the Earl of Surrey and other great magnates. The King was, after all, only eighteen, and could hardly be expected to keep the baronage in check as his father had done. This baronial revival lasted only a few years, but long enough to get rid of Empson and Dudley, who were put to death in 1510 'on trumped-up charges of treason'.

* See R. L. Storey, *op. cit.*, p. 208.

Select Bibliography

The Earlier Tudors, 1485–1558 by J. D. Mackie, Oxford University Press, 1952

The Reign of Elizabeth by J. B. Black, 2nd edition, Oxford University Press, 1959

England under the Tudors by G. R. Elton, 2nd edition, Methuen, 1974

Tudor and Stuart Britain by Roger Lockyer, Longman, 1964

Before the Armada, the Growth of English Foreign Policy 1485–1588 by R. B. Wernham, Cape, 1966

The Crisis of Parliaments, English History 1509–1660 by Conrad Russell, Oxford University Press, 1971

Henry VII by S. B. Chrimes, Eyre Methuen, 1972

Henry VIII by J. J. Scarisbrick, Eyre Methuen, 1968

Henry VIII by A. F. Pollard, Longmans, 1905

The Reign of Henry VII by R. L. Storey, Blandford, 1968

The Tudor Age by James A. Williamson, 2nd edition, Longmans, 1957

Queen Elizabeth I by J. E. Neale, Cape, 1934

Elizabeth I and her Parliaments, 1559–1581 by J. E. Neale, Cape, 1953

Elizabeth I and her Parliaments, 1584–1601 by J. E. Neale, Cape, 1957

The Tudor Revolution in Government by G. R. Elton, Cambridge University Press, 1953

Tudor England by S. T. Bindoff, Pelican, 1950

Elizabeth I and the Unity of England by Joel Hurstfield, English Universities Press, 1960

Thomas Cromwell and the English Reformation by A. G. Dickens, English Universities Press, 1959

The Defeat of the Spanish Armada by G. Mattingly, Cape, 1959

Tudor Economic Problems by Peter Ramsey, Gollancz, 1963

Tudor Rebellions by Anthony Fletcher, Longmans, 1968

The Tudors by Christopher Morris, Batsford, 1955

The Reformation by Owen Chadwick, Pelican, 1964

A History of Scotland by J. D. Mackie, Pelican, 1964

A History of Ireland by Edmund Curtis, 6th edition, Methuen, 1950

Papists and Puritans under Elizabeth I by Patrick McGrath, Blandford, 1967

The Religious Orders in England, Volume 3 by Dom David Knowles, Cambridge, 1959

Elizabeth I by B. W. Beckingsale, Batsford, 1963

The Essential Erasmus by John P. Dolan, New English Library, 1964

Renaissance and Reformation by V. H. H. Green, Edward Arnold, 1952

A History of Europe, Volume 1 by H. A. L. Fisher, Eyre & Spottiswoode, 1935; Fontana Library

A History of Europe 1494–1610 by A. J. Grant, Methuen, 1931

Lectures on Modern History by Lord Acton, Macmillan, 1906

The English Reformation by A. G. Dickens, Batsford, 1964

Yorkist and Early Tudor Government, 1461–1509 by B. P. Wolffe, Historical Association pamphlet, 1966

Tudor Enclosures by Joan Thirsk, Historical Association pamphlet, 1959

Was there a Tudor Despotism after all? by Joel Hurstfield, Transactions of the Royal Historical Society, 1967

Politics and the Nation 1450–1660 by D. M. Loades, Fontana/Collins, 1974

The Elizabethan Renaissance by A. L. Rowse, Vol. I, *The Life of the Society*, Vol. II, *The Cultural Achievement*, Macmillan, 1971 and 1972.

Shakespeare the Man by A. L. Rowse, Macmillan, 1973.

Time Chart

Domestic Events	Events Abroad	
1461 Battle of Towton		
Edward IV gains throne		
1464 Woodville marriage		
1470 Edward temporarily deposed		
by Warwick		
1471 Edward IV regains throne		
1483 Death of Edward IV	Death of Louis XI	1483
Richard III obtains throne	Charles VIII succeeds to	
	French throne	
1485 Henry VII invades		
Battle of Bosworth		
1486 Henry VII marries Elizabeth		
of York		
1487 Lambert Simnel's invasion		
Battle of Stoke		
	Murder of James III of Scotland	1488
	Death of Duke of Brittany	
	Treaties with Brittany and	1489
	Maximilian	
	Treaty of Medina del Campo	
1491 Perkin Warbeck appears at Cork	Anne of Brittany marries	1491
	Charles VIII	
1492 Kildare deprived of post	Treaty of Etaples	1492
as Deputy	Columbus discovers West Indies	
1493 Trade broken off with Netherlands		
1494 Poynings to Ireland	Charles VIII invades Italy	1494
1495 De Facto Act		
Warbeck lands troops at Deal		
Execution of Sir William Stanley		
1496 Kildare reappointed as Deputy	*Magnus Intercursus* signed	1496
1497 Cornish rebellion	Treaty of Ayton with Scotland	1497
	Death of Charles VIII	1498
	Louis XII succeeds	
1499 Warbeck and Warwick executed		
1500 Death of John Morton, Lord		
Chancellor		
1501 Marriage of Arthur and		
Catherine of Aragon		
Edmund, Earl of Suffolk flees to		
Netherlands		
1502 Death of Arthur	Marriage treaty with Scotland	1502
1503 Death of Elizabeth of York	Death of Pope Alexander VI	1503
Marriage of Margaret and		
James IV of Scotland		
1504 Statute of Liveries and	Death of Isabella of Castile	1504
Maintenance		
	Treaty of Blois	1505
1506 Treaty of Windsor	Death of Philip of Burgundy	1506
	Treaty of Calais with Maximilian	1507

1509	Death of Henry VII		
	Henry VIII succeeds		
		Holy League formed	1511
1512	Expedition to Bayonne		
1513	Expedition to Calais	Battle of the Spurs	1513
	Battle of Flodden	Death of Pope Julius II	
	Death of Garret More	Leo X Pope	
		Peace treaty with France	1514
		Death of Louis XII	
1515	Wolsey Lord Chancellor and	Francis I renews treaty with	1515
	Cardinal	England	
	Wolsey dismisses Parliament	Battle of Marignano	
1516	Mary Tudor born	Death of Ferdinand of Aragon	1516
		Treaty of Noyon	
		Luther's ninety-five theses	1517
1518	Wolsey papal legate		
	Treaty of London		
		Death of Maximilian	1519
1520	Field of Cloth of Gold	Charles elected Emperor	
1521	Execution of Buckingham	Zwingli makes his protest	1521
		Treaty of Bruges	
		Death of Pope Leo X	
		Emperor conquers Milan	1521-2
1522	Earl of Surrey invades France		
	Albany returns to Scotland		
	Wolsey levies Forced Loan		
1523	Duke of Suffolk advances on Paris	Death of Pope Adrian VI	1523
	Wolsey calls Parliament	Clement VII Pope	
1525	Henry sends embassy to Spain	Battle of Pavia	1525
	Henry Fitzroy made Duke of	Tyndale's translation of Bible	
	Richmond	Charles breaks off marriage	
	Peace with France	treaty with England	
		Charles marries Isabella	1526
		of Portugal	
		Treaty of Madrid between	
		Charles and Francis	
		League of Cognac formed	
1527	Henry begins to press for 'divorce'	Sack of Rome	1527
1528	Wolsey declares war on Spain	Pope sets up court to try	1528
		Henry's marriage	
1529	Wolsey dismissed as Chancellor	French defeated again in Italy	1529
	Reformation Parliament meets	Treaty of Cambrai	
1530	Death of Wolsey		
1531	Thomas Cromwell in Council	Death of Zwingli	1531
1532	The Submission of the Clergy		
	First Act of Annates		
	Death of Warham		
1533	Henry secretly marries Anne	Pope draws up bull	1533
	Cranmer appointed Archbishop	excommunicating Henry	
	Act of Appeals		
	Act of Annates confirmed by		
	letters patent		
	Birth of Elizabeth		
	Kildare arrested		

Domestic Events	Events Abroad	
1534 Second Act of Annates Act of First Fruit and Tenths Act of Supremacy Cromwell Principal Secretary Statute of Treasons Rebellion of Silken Thomas in Ireland	Death of Pope Clement VII Paul III Pope	1534
1535 More and Fisher executed Cromwell appointed Vicar-General	Death of Francesco Sforza Bull of excommunication against Henry by Paul III	1535
1536 Death of Catherine of Aragon Act dissolving lesser monasteries Execution of Anne Boleyn Henry marries Jane Seymour Pilgrimage of Grace Death of Duke of Richmond Ten Articles accepted by Convocation	Francis I invades Savoy Death of Erasmus	1536
1537 Silken Thomas and five other Geraldines executed		
1538 Cromwell's Injunctions against shrines Execution of several Yorkists Matthews' Bible in every church	Paul III promulgates his bull of excommunication Charles and Francis make truce Turks threatening Hungary	1538
1539 Act of Six Articles Statute of Proclamations Act dissolving greater monasteries		
1540 Anne of Cleves marriage Cromwell arrested and executed		
1540 Henry marries Catherine Howard	Society of Jesus established Calvin settles in Geneva	1540 1541
1542 Execution of Catherine Howard Battle of Solway Moss		
1543 Henry marries Catherine Parr War declared on France	French send force to Scotland	1543
1544 Hertford's expedition to Scotland	Capture of Boulogne Peace of Crépy between Charles and Francis	1544
1545 Francis attempts invasion of England		
1546 Peace with France	Death of Luther Council of Trent opens	1546
1547 Death of Henry VIII	Death of Francis I Battle of Pinkie Battle of Mühlberg	1547
1548 Gardiner to the Tower	Mary Stuart sent to France	1548
1549 First Prayer Book Rebellions in Cornwall and Norfolk Arrest of Somerset Warwick in power		
1550 Peace with France		
	Slump in Antwerp woollen market	1551

1552	Execution of Somerset	Henry II captures Metz	1552
	Second Prayer Book		
1553	Death of Edward VI	Chancellor and Willoughby's	1553
	Mary obtains throne	voyage	
	Act of Uniformity repealed		
	Mary marries Philip by proxy		
1554	Wyatt's rebellion		
	Reginald Pole arrives		
	Heresy laws reenacted		
1555	Burnings begin		
	Philip leaves England		
		Charles V abdicates	1556
		Philip II King of Spain	
		Ferdinand I Emperor	
1557	England at war with France	Battle of St Quentin	1557
1558	Death of Mary	Loss of Calais	1558
	Elizabeth succeeds to throne		
1559	Acts of Supremacy and	Treaty of Câteau-Cambrésis	1559
	Uniformity	Death of Pope Paul IV	
	Fleet and army sent to Scotland	Death of Henry II	
		Treaty of Edinburgh	1560
		Death of Francis II	
1561	Mary Stuart returns to Scotland		
1562	Expedition to Le Havre	Hawkins' first slaving voyage	1562
		Civil war breaks out in France	
1563	Elizabeth's second Parliament		
	Convocation draws up		
	Thirty-nine Articles		
	Statute of Artificers		
		Death of Calvin	1564
		Mary marries Lord Darnley	1565
		Murder of Riccio	
1566	Parker's Advertisements	Birth of James	1566
	Second Parliament recalled	Calvinist Fury in the Netherlands	
		Alva arrives in the Netherlands	1567
1568	De Spes arrives as ambassador	Fight at San Juan de Ulloa	1568
	Mary arrives in England	College founded at Douai	
	Seizure of Genoese bullion		
	Trade broken off with		
	Netherlands		
1569	Rising of Northern Earls		
		Assassination of Murray	1570
		Pius V issues bull	
		excommunicating Elizabeth	
1571	Elizabeth's third Parliament	Battle of Lepanto	1571
	Thirty-nine Articles accepted		
	by Queen		
	Ridolfi Plot		
1572	Norfolk executed	Treaty of Blois	1572
	Burghley Lord Treasurer	Sea Beggars capture Brill	
1572–3	Drake's raid on Panama	Massacre of St Bartholomew	
1573	Restoration of Netherlands	Alva leaves Netherlands	1573
	trade		
	Walsingham Principal Secretary		

Domestic Events	Events Abroad	
1574 First seminarists arrive	Death of Charles IX	1574
	Henry III King of France	
1575 Death of Archbishop Parker		
Grindal Archbishop		
1576–8 Frobisher's voyages	Death of Requesens	1576
	The Spanish Fury	
1577 Grindal suspended	Don John arrives in Netherlands	1577
1577–80 Drake's voyage round the		
world		
	Death of Don John. Parma	1578
	takes over	
1579 Desmond rebellion in Munster	Fitzgerald's attempt to	1579
Eastland Company founded	invade Ireland	
	English Jesuit College set	
	up in Rome	
1580 High Commission Court set up	Throne of Portugal vacant	1580
First Jesuit mission arrives		
1581 Levant Company founded	Morton executed in Scotland	1581
1583 Death of Archbishop Grindal		
Whitgift Archbishop of		
Canterbury		
1584 Throckmorton Plot	Death of Anjou (Alençon)	1584
Mendoza expelled	Assassination of William	
	of Orange	
1585 First Virginia settlement	War of the Three Henries	1585
Leicester to the Netherlands	break out	
Drake despatched to West		
Indies		
1585–7 John Davis's voyages		
1586 Treaty of Berwick		
Babington Plot		
1587 Execution of Mary Queen of Scots		
Drake attacks Cadiz		
1588 Spanish Armada		
Death of Earl of Leicester		
1589 Drake's expedition to Portugal	Assassination of Henry III	1589
Hakluyt's *Voyages* published		
1590 Death of Walsingham	Henry IV defeats Catholic	1590
	League at Ivry	
1591 British force sent to Brittany		
	Death of Duke of Parma	1592
1593 Hooker's *Ecclesiastical Polity*	Henry IV becomes Catholic	1593
published		
1594 Rebellion of Hugh O'Neill		
1595 Death of Hawkins		
1596 Death of Drake		
Robert Cecil Secretary of State		
Essex and Howard attack		
Cadiz		
1597 Death of Peter Wentworth		
Essex's abortive raid on the		
Azores		

Domestic Events	Events Abroad
1598 Globe theatre opened	Peace of Vervins
Death of Lord Burghley	Death of Philip II
1599 Essex sent to Ireland	
1600 Mountjoy to Ireland	
East India Company founded	
1601 Execution of Essex	
Battle of Kinsale	
Monopolies debate	
Poor Law	
1603 Death of Elizabeth	

Index

Adrian VI, 68
Advertisements, Parker's, 166
Albany, duke of, 63, 64, 67, 69
Alchemy, 253
Alençon, duke of (later duke of Anjou), 163, 164, 173–4
Allen, Cardinal, 134, 170, 209
Alva, duke of, 132; in the Netherlands, 154–5, 160–4
Amicable Grant, 59, 69, 256
Anjou, duke of, see 'Henry III'
Annates, first act of, 83, 85
Annates, second act of, 85
Anne, duchess of Brittany, 23, 24
Anne of Cleves, 99, 100
Anti-clericalism, 77–9
Antonio, Don, 197
Antwerp, 9, 11, 12, 25, 91, 108, 119, 123, 154–6, 161, 173, 176, 215, 234
Appeals, act of, 84, 101
Architecture, 247–9
Aristotle, 43, 239, 251
Armada, the, 192–6
Arran, earl of, 175
Art, 250–1
Arthur, Prince, 20, 21, 23, 26, 34, 36, 49, 95
Artificers, statute of, 229–30
Arundel, earl of, 157–8
Ascham, Roger, 141, 251–2
Aske, Robert, 89–91
Association, Bond of, 191
Astrology, 253
Attainder, acts of, 3, 5, 25, 26, 29, 39, 73, 100–1, 105, 107, 258
Augmentations, Court of, 89, 93, 103
Ayton, treaty of, 35

Babington, Anthony, 192

Bacon, Sir Francis, 19, 21, 26, 31, 34, 38; his essays, 246
Bacon, Nicholas, 165
Barnes, Robert, 75–6, 91, 101, 144
Barrow, Henry, 170, 210
Beaton, David, 98
Beaufort, Margaret, 8, 20
Bergavenny, Lord, 42
Berwick, treaty of, 175
Bilney, Thomas, 75, 91, 144
Bishops' Book, 92
Blois, treaties of, 38, 160, 161, 163
Boleyn, Anne, 72, 83–4, 86–7, 140
Bonner, Bishop of London, 116, 121, 126, 144
Bordeaux, 12, 56
Bosworth, battle of, 9, 18, 19, 20, 22, 25, 28, 32
Bothwell, earl of, 150–1
Boulogne, 24, 106, 114–15, 120, 187
Bourbon, duke of, 68, 69
Bray, Reginald, 20, 34
Brill, descent on, 161–2
Brittany, 8, 23, 24, 56, 198
Browne, Robert, 170, 210
Bruges, treaty of, 67
Bucer, Martin, 110, 116, 135
Buckingham, Henry, duke of, 6, 22
Buckingham, Thomas, duke of, 68, 257–8, 260
Bull, John, 242
Bullinger, Henry, 110, 116, 166
Burghley, William Cecil, Lord, 141, 161, 164, 168, 180, 181, 192, 200; and the Puritans, 168, 169; and the navy, 188; his death, 200

Burgundy, duchy of, see 'Netherlands'
Byrd, William, 241

Cabot, John, 31, 123, 176
Cabot, Sebastian, 31, 123–4, 177
Cadiz, raids on, 193, 199
Calais, 24, 25, 56, 67, 68, 105, 133, 145, 147, 194, 225
Calvin, John, 110–14
Calvinism, 164–6, 168–70, 210
Cambrai, treaty of, 71, 73
Cambridge, university of, 16, 53, 60, 75, 94, 116, 167, 169–70, 244, 248, 251
Camden, William, 245
Campeggio, Cardinal, 65, 72
Campion, Edmund, 171
Campion, Thomas, 241
Caraffa, see 'Paul IV'
Carracks, 186, 188
Cartwright, Dr Thomas, 167, 210
Casket Letters, 151–2
Câteau-Cambrésis, treaty of, 143, 145, 153
Catherine of Aragon, 24, 26, 36, 39, 55, 67, 72–3; death of, 86
Catherine Howard, 100, 101, 104
Catherine de Medici, 147, 148, 162, 163
Catherine Parr, 105, 107, 108, 114, 142
Cavendish, Thomas, 184
Cecil, Sir Robert, 208, 211, 214
Chamber, King's, 32, 103
Chancellor, Richard, 124
Chancery, Court of, 58, 220
Chantries, 107, 115, 121
Chapel Royal, 240–1
Charles the Bold, 22, 23
Charles V, Emperor, 38, 64; elected emperor, 65; and the treaty of Bruges, 67; and Wolsey, 66–72; and the 'Divorce', 72–3; 79, 84, 86, 97, 98; his alliance with Henry VIII, 105, 124; and Mary Tudor, 127, 129;

abdicates, 132; and the Council of Trent, 137
Charles VIII, 21, 23, 24, 26, 36
Charles IX, 147, 160, 162, 163
Charles, archduke of Austria, 158
Charterhouse, the London, 88
Church, 14, 15, 16; Henry VII's relations with, 40; and Wolsey, 60–2; its unpopularity, 77–9; Elizabeth's settlement of, 142–5; in the 1590s, 209–11
Clarence, George, duke of, 5, 7, 22, 98, 129
Classical movement, 168–9
Clement VII, 61, 68–9, 70–1; and the 'Divorce', 72, 73, 79, 80, 83, 85; his death, 134
Cloth of Gold, Field of, 67
Coal mining, 228
Cognac, League of, 70, 71
Colet, John, 49–50
Coligny, 160, 161, 162
Colonisation, 182–5
Commons, House of, 13, 14, 20, 40, 258, 259
Congregation, Lords of the, 146
Contarini, Cardinal, 135
Convocation, 61, 79, 81, 83, 90, 91–2, 100, 143, 144, 166
Cooke, Sir Anthony, 165
Copernicus, 252
Copyholders, 219–20
Cornwall, rebellion of (1497), 25, 26, 31, 42
Cornwall, rebellion of (1549), 116
Council of the North, 33, 91, 158–9
Council of Wales, 33, 95, 212
Council, King's; under Henry VII, 28, 33, 34, 35; Privy, 103; its powers, 256–7
Council Learned in the Law, 32, 34, 35
Counter-Reformation, 108, 134–9, 153
Courtenay, Edward, 126–8
Courts, conciliar, 34–5

270

Covenant, the, 146
Coverdale, Miles, 75, 92, 107, 121
Craigmillar Castle, 150
Cranmer, Thomas, 79–80, 83–4, 87, 89, 91, 104, 107, 116, 121, 126; his First Prayer Book, 116; his Second Prayer Book, 122; his death, 130, 131; his prose, 131, 245
Cromwell, Thomas, 59, 81; his origins, 82; and the breach with Rome, 82–6; and the dissolution of the monasteries, 87–9, 93–4; and the Union with Wales, 95–6; and Ireland, 96–7; and the Catholic powers, 97–9; and the Act of Proclamations, 99; his fall and execution, 100, 101; his achievement, 101–2; his administrative forms, 102–4

Dacre, 18, 158, 159
Darcy, Lord, 90
Darnley, Lord, 149–51
Davis, John, 178, 185
Debasement of the coinage, 108, 119, 123, 215, 234
Dee, Dr John, 177, 251, 253
De Facto Act, 26
Desmond, earl of, 27, 202
'Divorce', the, 72–3
Douai College, 170, 172
Doughty, Thomas, 181
Dowland, John, 241
Drake, Sir Francis, 157, 176, 180–82, 190; raids Cadiz, 193; and the Armada, 194; and the attack on Lisbon, 197; his death, 199
Drama, 244–5
Drayton, Michael, 244
Dudley, Edmund, 32, 35, 55, 260
Dudley, Guildford, 125, 128
Dues, feudal, 32
Dunstable, 84

East India Company, 184, 235

Eastland Company, 235
Edinburgh, treaty of, 146, 147
Education, 251–2
Edward IV, 3, 5, 8, 12, 19, 20, 21, 22, 23, 27, 30, 33, 34, 42, 185
Edward V, 6
Edward VI, 114–19; and Northumberland, 120–3; his death, 124–5
Edward, prince of Wales, 5, 7, 8
Edward, earl of Warwick, 5
Eleanor (sister of Charles V), 39
Elizabeth of York, 8, 20, 21, 36, 55
Elizabeth Woodville, 3, 6
Elizabeth 1, 107, 128, 139; her character, 140–1; and the religious settlement, 142–5; and Scotland, 145–6, 174–5; and Mary Queen of Scots, 148–52; and the Netherlands, 152–5, 161, 173–4; excommunicated, 159–60; to marry Anjou, 160–1; and the Puritans, 164–70; and the war with Spain, 189–200; and Ireland, 201–3; and Parliament, 203–9; and Essex, 211–13; her death, 214
Elizabeth of Valois, 145
Embracery, 11
Empson, Richard, 32, 35, 55, 260
Enclosures, 58, 90, 117, 221–4
Erasmus, 49, 50–4, 60, 65, 135
Essex, earl of, 198, 199–200; in Ireland, 202–3; his conspiracy and death, 211–13
Etaples, treaty of, 24, 26, 31, 35
Exchequer, 32, 103
Exiles, Marian, 142–3, 165
Exploration, 124, 176–85

Farming methods, 224–5
Farnaby, Giles, 242
Ferdinand, king of Aragon, 23, 26, 36–7, 39, 56, 64, 139
Ferrars, bishop, 130
Field, John, 168

Finance, government; Henry VII's, 31–3; Wolsey's, 59–60; in Henry VIII's last years, 108; under Mary, 134; in the Spanish war, 190; Elizabeth's, 236

First Fruits and Tenths, act of, 85

First Fruits and Tenths, court of, 103

Fisher, bishop, 78, 79, 81, 85–6

Fitch, Ralph, 179

Fitzgerald, 171

Flodden, battle of, 56, 63

Flushing, 161, 176, 194

Fortescue, Sir John, 13, 259

Forty-two articles, 122

Fox, Richard, 20, 251

Foxe, John, 131, 134

Francis I, 47; and Wolsey, 63–72; and Cromwell, 97–8; attempts invasion of England, 106; his death, 114

Francis II, 114–15, 141, 145, 147

Frobisher, Martin, 176, 177, 198

Furniture, 250

Gardiner, bishop of Winchester, 54, 77, 79, 81, 101, 104, 107–8, 116, 120, 126; as Lord Chancellor, 126–30; his death, 130, 132

General Surveyors, court of, 103

Gentry, 11, 218

Gigs, Margaret, 88

Gilbert, Sir Humphrey, 161, 176, 177, 182

Granville, Cardinal de, 153, 155

Gravelines, battle of, 194

Greenwich, treaty of, 70

Gregory XIII, 162, 171, 173

Grenville, Sir Richard, 176, 177, 184, 197, 202

Gresham, Sir Thomas, 123, 134, 215, 234

Grey, earl, 6

Grey, Lady Jane, 57, 125–6, 128

Grindal, Archbishop, 165–9

Gueux, 154, 161

Guilds, 17, 216, 230, 231

Guise, Francis, duke of, 133, 141, 145, 147

Guise, Henry, duke of, 162, 175

Hakluyt, Richard, 185, 246

Hales, John, 117

Hall, Edward, 247

Hanseatic League, 18, 30, 123, 130, 156, 235

Hawkins, John, 156–7, 176, 179–80, 188, 196, 199

Hawkins, William, 176

Henry of Guise, 162, 175

Henry of Navarre (Henry IV), 162, 175, 189, 198, 200

Henry II, 114–15; declares war on England, 120; 124, 125, 132, 141; his death, 145

Henry III (formerly duke of Anjou), 160, 164, 192, 198

Henry IV (Bolingbroke), 1, 15, 17

Henry V, 1, 8, 15

Henry VI, 1, 5, 7, 8, 10, 13

Henry VII, 7, 10; his birth and exile, 8; invades, 9; traditional picture of him, 19–20; establishes his position, 20; his personality, 20–1; his foreign policy, 23–4, 35–9; and Warbeck's rebellion, 24–6; and Ireland, 25, 26–9; and trade, 26, 30–1; his finance, 31–3; and Parliament, 31, 39–40; and law and order, 40–2; and the navy, 186

Henry VIII, 36, 47; a Renaissance prince, 54, 55; his foreign policy, 55–7, 62–72; and the 'Divorce', 72–3; his character, 76–7; and the breach with Rome, 82–6; gets rid of Anne Boleyn, 86–7; dissolves the monasteries, 87–9, 93–4; and Ireland, 29, 96–7; and the Catholic powers, 97–9; and Anne of Cleves, 99–100;

and the fall of Cromwell, 100–1; his last years, 104–6; his will, 107; his achievement, 108; and the navy, 56, 106, 186–7
High Commission Court, 169, 170, 259
History, 48, 246–7
Holbein, Hans, 99, 250
Holinshed, Raphael, 247
Holy League (1495), 26, 36
Holy League (1511), 55–6
Hooker, Richard, 210–11, 246
Hooper, bishop, 121, 126, 130
Houghton, John, 88
Howard, Lord, of Effingham, 188, 193–4, 199–200
Huguenots, 146, 147, 160, 162–4, 232
Humanism, 43–7
Hus, John, 15, 75, 136

Immigration, 226, 228, 232
Inns of Court, 13, 180, 218, 244, 252
Inquisition, 135–6, 180
Institutes of the Christian Religion, 110–12, 165
Intercursus Magnus, 26, 36, 38
Intercursus Malus, 38
Ireland: under Henry VII, 22, 25, 26–9; and Cromwell, 96–7; its conquest by Elizabeth, 201–3
Iron manufacture, 228
Isabella, queen of Castile, 23, 36, 139
Italy, 12, 16, 24, 26, 35, 36, 42, 43–7, 70, 243
Ivry, battle of, 198

James III, 21, 63
James IV, 25, 26, 35–6, 56, 63, 149
James V, 63, 69, 98, 105, 115
James VI, 151, 174, 175, 192, 214
Jesuits, 97, 138, 170, 172, 201
Jesus, Society of, 137–9

Jewel, bishop, 144, 165, 166
Joanna of Castile, 38
John, Don, of Austria, 173
Julius II, 55, 65, 72, 74
Julius III, 129
Justices of the Peace, 40–1, 58, 221, 223, 230, 237, 257
Justin of Nassau, 195, 196

Ket, Robert, 118, 120
Kildare, Gerald Fitzgerald, 8th earl of, 25, 28, 29, 96
Kildare, Gerald Fitzgerald, 9th earl of, 96
Kinsale, battle of, 203
Kitchen, bishop, 143
Knox, John, 106, 113, 114, 121–2, 126, 131, 142, 146, 148, 151, 165
Kyd, Thomas, 245

La Marck, 155, 161
La Rochelle, 163, 164
Latimer, Hugh, 75, 89, 91, 98, 107, 116, 117, 126, 130
Law, 13; under Henry VII, 34, 40–2; under Wolsey, 58; and lawyers, 252; and Elizabeth, 259, 260
Lee, Rowland, 95
Lefèvre, 110
Le Havre, 106, 147–8, 187
Leicester, Robert Dudley, earl of, 147, 149, 158, 161, 165, 168, 173, 176, 180, 181, 190–1, 196, 211
Leith, 105, 146
Lennox, earl of, 149, 151, 159, 174
Leo X, 57, 61, 63, 67–8
Lepanto, battle of, 161, 173, 178
Lethington, Lord, 150
Levant Company, 178–9, 235
Lincoln, John de la Pole, earl of, 22, 23, 28
Liveries, 10, 11, 19, 41
Livery Companies, 12, 232–4

Lollards, 15, 16, 74
London, 6, 11, 12, 16, 18, 22, 26, 126, 128, 166, 196, 216, 222, 227, 228, 232–4
London, treaty of, 65, 67, 72
Lorraine, cardinal of, 141, 145
Louis XI, 21, 23
Louis XII, 36, 56, 63, 65
Louis of Nassau, 154
Loyola, Ignatius, 137, 138
Luther, Martin, 66, 74–6, 109–10
Lyly, John, 244

Machiavelli, 47–8, 246
Madrid, treaty of, 69
Maintenance, 11, 19, 41
Margaret of Anjou, 5
Margaret of Burgundy, 5, 22, 23, 25
Margaret of Parma, 153, 154
Margaret of Savoy, 23, 36, 38
Margaret Tudor, 35, 63, 69, 107, 141, 149
Margaret of Valois, 162
Marignano, battle of, 63, 65
Marillac, 101, 187
Marlowe, Christopher, 245
Martyr, Peter (Vermigli), 116, 165
Mary of Burgundy, 23
Mary of Guise, 105, 141, 145, 146
Mary, Queen of Scots, 105, 114–15, 141, 145; returns to Scotland, 148; and the murder of Darnley, 150–1; in England, 151–2, 157–60; her end, 192
Mary Tudor (daughter of Henry VII), 38, 57, 63, 107
Mary Tudor, queen, 65, 67–9, 85, 126; succeeds to the throne, 126–7; her marriage, 127–8; and Wyatt's rebellion, 127–8; reconciles England to Rome, 129–30; her last years, 131–3; her achievements, 133, 134
Maurice of Nassau, 198, 199, 201

Maximilian, emperor, 21, 23, 25, 26, 36, 38, 63, 65
Medicine, 251, 253
Medina del Campo, treaty of, 23, 24, 26, 36
Medina Sidonia, duke of, 193–6
Mendoza, 175
Merchant Adventurers, 12, 25, 91, 123, 130, 155–7, 234
Mildred, Lady Burghley, 165, 167, 168
Militia, 189
Monasteries, 15, 78; dissolution of, 87–9, 93–4
Monopolies, 208, 256
More, Sir Thomas, 7, 49–50, 54, 59, 65, 77, 81, 83, 85, 222, 259; his trial and execution, 86
Morley, Thomas, 241
Morton, archbishop, 18, 20, 33, 40
Morton, earl of, 159, 164, 174, 175
Mountjoy, Lord, 50, 203, 213
Mühlberg, battle of, 116
Mulcaster, Richard, 244, 252
Murray, earl of, 149–52, 159
Muscovy Company, 124, 178, 235
Music, 21, 238–42

Navigation acts, 30
Navy, 25, 55, 56, 94, 106, 185–9
Netherlands, the, 9, 12, 22, 23, 25, 38, 132; unrest in, 153–5; revolt of, 161, 163, 173–4; stoppage of trade routes with, 25, 30, 157, 163; war in, 176, 190, 198
Nobility (as landowners), 217
Norfolk, Thomas, second duke of, see 'Surrey'
Norfolk, Thomas, third duke of, 73, 77, 90, 96, 100, 101, 105, 107, 126, 128, 258
Norfolk, Thomas, fourth duke of, 157–60; arrested and executed, 160

Norfolk, rebellion in, 117–18
Norreys, Sir John, 197–8
North of England, 18, 89
Northern Earls, rebellion of, 157–9, 258, 259
Northumberland, John Dudley, duke of; as Lord Lisle, 105; quells rebellion, 118; as ruler of England, 120–1; his religious policy, 121–2; method of keeping in power, 122–3; encourages exploration, 123–4; his French alliance, 124; and the Jane Grey plan, 125–6; execution, 126; and the navy, 187
Northumberland, Thomas Percy, earl of, 158
Noyon, treaty of, 64–5

Ormonde, earl of, 27, 201
Oxenham, John, 180
Oxford, university of, 16, 57, 94, 116, 133, 244, 248, 251
Oxford, earl of, 8, 20, 42

Paget, Lord, 128
Parker, Matthew, archbishop, 144, 166, 167
Parliament, 13, 14; under Henry VII, 39; the Reformation Parliament, 79, 82–5; Cromwell and, 102; Mary and, 127–30; and the Puritans, 169; Elizabeth and, 203–9; its power, 259
Parma, Alexander Farnese, duke of, 174, 176, 194–5, 198
Parsons, Robert, 171, 209
Paston Letters, 1, 11
Paul III, 86, 97, 98; his reforms, 135–6
Paul IV (Caraffa), 132; as Pope, 135–6; his death, 136
Paulet, Sir Amyas, 191
Pavia, battle of, 69
Philip of Burgundy, 23, 38
Philip II, king of Spain, 127, 128; as Mary's husband, 128–32;

140–2, 144; marries Elizabeth of Valois, 145; and the Netherlands, 153–5; and Portugal, 174; prepares invasion, 191–2; and the Armada, 193; and the war with England, 192–200; his death, 200
Pilgrimage of Grace, 18, 89–91
Pinkie, battle of, 115
Pius IV, 144
Pius V, 159
Plato, 16, 45–6, 239, 251
Poetry, 242–4
Pole, Reginald, 91, 98; as archbishop, 131, 132; his death, 133; 134
Poor relief, 236–8
Population, 216
Portugal, 12, 174, 197
Poynings, Sir Edward, 20, 28
Poynings' laws, 28–9
Press, printing, 49, 104, 169, 256
Prices, rise of, 214–16
Printing, invention of, 49
Proclamations, act of, 99
Prophesyings, 168
Prose, 245–6
Puritanism, 164–70, 205–7

Raleigh, Sir Walter, 176, 182–4, 199–200, 211, 247
Ratisbon, Colloquy of, 135
Recusancy laws, 158, 172
Renaissance, 43–54
Renard, Simon, 126–7, 129
Requesens, Luis de, 164, 170, 173
Requests, court of, 35, 119, 220
Retainers, 10, 11, 19, 41, 42
Riccio, David, 149–50
Richard III, 6, 7, 8, 9, 19, 20, 22, 26, 28, 32, 35, 259
Richard, duke of York, 3
Richard, duke of York and Norfolk, 6, 7
Richmond, duke of, 70
Ridley, bishop, 121, 126, 130
Ridolfi, Roberti di, 158–9

Rivers, earl, 6
Robsart, Amy, 147
Rogers, John, 92, 130
Rome, sack of, 70
Rouen, treaty of, 64
Russell, John, earl of Bedford, 117–18
Ruthven, raid of, 175

St Bartholomew's Day Massacre, 162–3
St Germain, treaty of, 160
St Quentin, battle of, 132
Salisbury, countess of, 98, 129
San Juan de Ulloa, 157, 179–80
Santa Cruz, marquis of, 191–2
Schmalkaldic League, 97
Schools, 16, 251–2
Science, 252–4
Scotland, 7, 21, 25, 35; and Wolsey, 63; war against, 105; Somerset and, 114–15; Warwick and, 121; Elizabeth and, 145–6, 164, 174–5
Seymour, Jane, 86, 87, 97, 108
Shakespeare, William, 5, 7, 45, 232, 240–1, 243–5, 247,
Shaxton, Nicholas, 91, 98
Sidney, Sir Philip, 191, 241, 243
Simnel, Lambert, 22–3, 28, 35
Six Articles, act of, 54, 98, 107, 115, 128
Skelton, John, 242
Socrates, 45–6
Solway Moss, battle of, 105
Somerset, Edward Seymour, duke of; as Lord Hertford, 105; and Scotland, 114–15; his religious policy, 115–16; his fall, 116–19; his character, 118–19; his execution, 123
Spanish Fury, 173
Spenser, Edmund, 202, 241, 243–4
Spes, Guerau de, 157–8, 160
Spurs, battle of the, 56
Stanley, Lord, 8, 9
276

Stanley, Sir William, 9, 25
Staplers, 12, 218, 225
Star Chamber, 19, 34–5, 58, 259
Stoke, battle of, 22, 28, 31
Strasbourg, 110, 113
Strickland, William, 167, 205
Stuart, Esmé, earl of Lennox, 174–5
Submission of the Clergy, 83
Succession, act of, 85
Suffolk, Edmund de la Pole, earl of, 38
Suffolk, Charles Brandon, duke of, 57, 68, 73, 77
Suffolk, Frances, duchess of, 125
Suffolk, Henry Grey, duke of, 128
Supremacy, act of (1534), 85, 102
Supremacy, act of (1559), 142–3
Surrey, Thomas Howard, earl of (later second duke of Norfolk), 22, 25–6, 33, 56, 260
Surrey, Henry Howard, earl of, 107, 243
Sussex, earl of, 159

Tallis, Thomas, 240–1
Taverner, John, 240
Tenant farmers, 219–20
Ten Articles, 54, 92
Thirty-Nine Articles, 144, 169, 210
Three Henrys, war of the, 176
Throckmorton, Francis, 175
Tournai, 56–7, 65
Towns, 12
Trade, 11, 26; under Henry VII, 26, 30; 119, 123–4, 234–6
Travers, William, 210
Treason, statute of, 85, 100, 115
Trent, council of, 136–7
Tribunal, special, to deal with corruption, 35, 41
Trinity house, 186
Tudor, Edmund, 8
Tudor, Jasper, 8, 20, 34
Tudor, Owen, 8

Tunstall, bishop of Durham, 121, 126, 144
Tye, Christopher, 240–1
Tyndale, William, 75–6, 80, 91, 245
Tyrconnel, Hugh O'Donnell, earl of, 202–3
Tyrone, Hugh O'Neill, earl of, 201–3

Udall, Nicholas, 244
Uniformity, acts of; Edward VI's, 116, 122; Elizabeth's, 142–3
Union, act of, 95–6, 204
Universities, 16, 45, 49

Vagabondage, 220, 237
Valor Ecclesiasticus, 88
Vere, Sir Francis, 198, 201
Vergil, Polydore, 20, 21, 246–7
Vervins, treaty of, 200
Vesalius, 253
Vestiaran controversy, 166
Villeinage, 10, 219
Virginia, 184

Wales, 9, 13, 17, 33; and the Act of Union, 95–6, 204; and Essex, 211–12
Walsingham, Sir Francis, 161, 164, 173, 175, 181, 191–2, 211
Warbeck, Perkin, 24–6, 28, 30, 35
Wardrobe, 103
Wards, court of, 103–4, 236, 259
Warham, William, archbishop, 57, 61, 81, 83
Wars of the Roses, 1, 10, 11, 13, 17, 20, 21, 28, 255
Warwick, earl of (the 'King-maker'), 3, 5, 22, 185
Warwick, Edward, earl of, 22, 26
Warwick, John Dudley, earl of, *see* 'Northumberland'

Wentworth, Peter, 205–7
Westmoreland, Charles Neville, earl of, 158–9
White, John, 184
Whitgift, John, archbishop, 167, 169, 210, 237
William of Nassau, 161
William of Orange, 154, 161, 173, 176
Willoughby, Sir Hugh, 124
Willoughby, Lord, 198
Wiltshire, earl of, 77
Winchester, marquess of, 134
Windsor, treaty of, 38
Winter, Sir William, 188
Wishart, George, 106
Wittenberg, 74, 139
Wolsey, Thomas, 57; his climb to power, 57–8; and the law, 58; and finance, 59–60; and the Church, 60–2; and foreign policy, 62–72; and the 'Divorce', 72–3; his fall, 73, 76
Woodville, Elizabeth, 3, 6
Wool trade, 9, 30, 38, 119, 157, 163, 227, 234, 235
Woollen cloth industry, 9, 18, 119, 123, 221, 225–8
Wyatt, Sir Thomas, 127–8, 141
Wycliffe, John, 15, 74
Wyndham, Thomas, 124, 178, 235

Ximénez, Cardinal, 53, 139–40

Yellow Ford, battle of, 202
Yeomen, 219–20
York, conference of, 152

Zürich, 92, 109–10, 121, 131, 143, 165
Zwingli, Ulrich, 109, 110